The Political Theory of the Delhi Sultanate

The Political Theory of the Delhi Sultanate

(Including a translation of Ziauddin Barani's *Fatawa-i Jahandari*, Circa, 1358-59 A.D.)

Mohammad Habib
Afsar Umar Salim Khan

AAKAR

The Political Theory of the Delhi Sultanate
Mohammad Habib and Afsar Umar Salim Khan

First Published 1961
First Aakar Edition 2020
Reprinted 2021

ISBN 978-93-5002-612-0

Published by
AAKAR BOOKS
28 E Pocket IV, Mayur Vihar Phase I
Delhi 110 091 India
aakarbooks@gmail.com

Laser Typeset at
Sakshi Computers, Delhi

Printed at
Sapra Brothers, Noida.

IN MEMORIAM

Dr. Ziauddin Ahmad, M.A., Ph.D., D.Sc.
Vice-Chancellor, Aligarh Muslim University, Aligarh

Contents

Foreword by Khaliq Ahmad Nizami ix

Introduction by Mohammad Habib 3

Translation of *Fatawa-I Jahandari* by Afsar Begum

Preface of Ziauddin Barani 27

Advice I The Personal Safety of the King 27

Advice II On the Effects of the Good Faith of the King 29

Advice III On the Blessings of Consultation and Advice 38

Advice IV On Correct Determination; Difference Between Correct Determination and Tyranny and Despotism 45

Advice V On the King's Justice 48

Advice VI On the Grading of Officers and Notables 52

Advice VII On the Army 56

Advice VIII I. On Intelligence Officers 70

II. The Pious Caliphate Was an Interlude in World History—Mankind Returns to its Old Ways 75

Advice IX I. Price Control 77

II. Contradictions Between the Principles of Islam and the Institution of Kingship 83

Advice X On the King's Time 86

Advice XI On the Establishment of Truth at the Centre 90

1. The Doctrine of Contradiction: The Unity of Opposites is Impossible, for Neither of the Two Opposed Forces Can Totally Annihilate its Opposite 90

	2. Barani Pleads for an All-Out Struggle Against Hinduism	94
	3. Barani Admits that Muslim Kings in India are Tolerant: (a) Hindus are Prosperous; (b) Sinful Professions are Permitted to the Musalmans; and (c) Philosophers are Allowed to Teach	97
	4. Barani Advocates that Education be Prohibited to the Lower Orders, for Education Will Make Them Efficient and Capable	99
Advice XII	On the Administration of Justice	105
	I. The Ruler's Innate Sense of Justice	105
	II. Special and Universal Equality	106
	III. Hearing of Complaints by the King	109
Advice XIII	The King's Mercy and Punishments	110
Advice XIV	On State-Laws (Zawabit)	124
Advice XV	On the King's High Resolve	135
Advice XVI	On the Diseases of the Kingdom	142
Advice XVII	On the Advisability of Forsaking Severe Exactions	151
Advice XVIII	On the Contradictory Qualities of the King	156
Advice XIX	On the Noble Birth of the Supporters of the King	166
Advice XX	That No One Should Have Ascendancy Over the King	174
Advice XXI	On the High Born and the Low Born	175
Advice XXII	On the Advantage of the King's Protecting Old Families	181
Advice XXIII	Meannesses Which Do Not Assimilate with Kingship	195
Advice XXIV	The Basis of All Advice—That the Salvation of the King Depends Upon the Supplication That Fills His Heart	201
	Ziauddin Barani's Epilogue	204

Life and Thought of Ziauddin Barani by Mohammad Habib

Chapter I	Introduction	233
Chapter II	Literary Works	240
Chapter III	Ziauddin Barani: Family and Early Life	259
Chapter IV	State Laws	265
Chapter V	The Governing Class	**279**
Chapter VI	Ziauddin Barani: Youth and Age	294
Chapter VII	Theory of Kingship	322
Appendix		331

Foreword

It is my pleasant duty as the Editor of *Medieval India Quarterly*, in which the present work first appeared, to introduce it to the public.

It is obvious that there will be a number of conflicting political theories in every country and in every age. Unfortunately the only book on political theory that survives to us from the period of the Delhi Sultanate is the *Fatawa-i Jahandari* of the famous historian, Ziauddin Barani. It gives us the ideas of a particular thinker and the view point of a particular group. But that alone is not enough.

The political theory of the Sultanate period should start with the *Jahandari*. But the theories of that book should be critically examined, first, with reference to the life of the author, so that his personal prejudices may be eliminated, and, secondly, with reference to the political facts of the period, so that the veracity of its statements and the soundness of its judgments may be tested.

This is what the present book aspires to do.

The translation of the *Fatawa-i Jahandari* was made by Dr. Afsar Begum (Mrs. Afsar Salim Khan) under the guidance of Dr. Peter Hardy of the London School of Oriental and African Studies. On returning to Aligarh she revised her translation, but the form in which her translation was now put, made most of her old footnotes useless. Dr. Afsar Begum, who was appointed to the University of Peshawar, left the revised typescript of her translation with Prof. Habib along with some footnotes in her handwriting. The remaining footnotes, which are mostly of a critical character, were prepared by Professor Habib with the help of Miss Anees Jahan, M.A. (Lecturer in History, Maharani Laxmibai College, Bhopal) who collected all the material, checked the references and faired the manuscript of the notes for the typist.

At this stage, Professor Habib, who was writing and destroying several pages, demanded that it was my duty as the Editor of *Medieval India Quarterly* to advise him on how to proceed. I suggested that he should write a short Introduction which would, along with the footnotes, make the translation of the *Fatawa-i Jahandari* intelligible, and that he should add after the *Jahandari* a dissertation on the life and the ideas of Ziauddin Barani, so that a theory of the Sultanate period may be evolved by a critique of the *Jahandari* and the other works of the period.

For the students of the Delhi Sultanate, the *Fatawa-i Jahandari* is a valuable discovery. It gives us an idea of the political climate of the middle ages—the ideals and aspirations of the governing class and the activities of the pressure groups. Besides, it supplies the key to the understanding of the *Tarikh-i-Firoz Shahi*. Indeed it will take a permanent place in India's historical literature.

Khaliq Ahmad Nizami

The Fatawa-i Jahandari

by

Ziauddin Barani

Introduction

The *Fatawa-i Jahandari* of Khwaja Ziauddin Barani is at present the only known Indo-Persian work, exclusively devoted to political theory, which has survived to us from the Sultanate period. Its translation into English by Dr. Afsar Begum (Mrs. Afsar Salim Khan) should be welcomed by all students of Indian history. The Persian text is being edited by Miss Kishwar Rashid, M.A., Research Assistant of the M.U. History Department.

A detailed introduction to the *Fatawa-i Jahandari*—or rather to the political theory of the Sultanate period—is being prepared by me and may be printed one day. But for a proper comprehension of the translation of the *Jahandari*, the following points are submitted for the kind consideration of the reader:

I: The *Fatawa-i Jahandari* is really the continuation of the author's famous *Tarikh-i Firoz Shahi.* It strives to put into the form of a coherent system of political philosophy the basic ideas which Barani has already expressed in his earlier work.

II: This fact enables, us to define the character of the *Fatawa-i Jahandari.* It gives us the political theory, and defines the political objectives, of the second most important political pressure-group of the period—the group of 'free-born' or 'noble' officers, as distinguished from the 'slave-officers'. Barani condemns the latter group as *zar-kharida* (cash-purchased), but they had, on the whole, a predominant, though not an exclusive, control of the machinery of the state. These were the only two pressure-groups who were interested, in the running of the government as a whole. There were many other pressure-groups—the Hindu mercantile classes, the Hindu landed aristocracy, the Muslim mystics, the *ulama,* the army officers and soldiers, the city working-classes, etc.—but they were concerned only with the preservation of their own particular interests, economic and cultural, and had no theory of government.

Barani belonged to a family the noble origin of which could not be questioned and he was brought up to believe that aristocratic birth was the primary fact for the social order. But the failure of his class and personal frustrations had embittered his feelings. He was given no post in the government of Alauddin Khalji; he was a courtier of Mohammad bin Tughluq for twenty-seven years, but after the accession of Firoz Shah, when Barani, was in his seventieth lunar year, charges were brought against him and he was interned at Bhatner. His life was spared but his property seems to have been confiscated, for he spent the rest of his life, some eight or nine years in dire poverty. He describes himself as old, bent, white-haired, half-blind, friendless and unable to borrow any money; and this frail, helpless man wrote two of the greatest books of the Sultanate period with a three-fold object—approval of Sultan Firoz Tughluq and his officers, attainment of paradise, and the instruction of noble-born readers in generations to come. He failed in the first object, but he may have succeeded in the second; the fact that the *Jahandari* is being edited and translated (and that the *Firoz Shahi*, first edited by Sir Syed Ahmad Khan, is being re-edited by Professor S.A. Rashid) almost exactly six hundred years after Barani's death proves that Barani has at least succeeded in the last object.

The *Tarikh-i Firoz Shahi* records our author's persistent protests against the political power of the low-born from the period of the forty slave-officers (*chahalgani*) who obtained control of the Delhi empire after the death of Shamsuddin Iltutmish to the men of humble birth whom Mohammad bin Tughluq appointed to high positions on account of their 'efficiency' and 'loyalty'. When he wrote the *Jahandari,* our author's belief in the principle of birth had risen to the height of a religion. "The merits and demerits of men," he tells us, "have been apportioned at the beginning of time and allotted to their souls. The acts and deeds of men are due to Divine commandments; whenever Almighty God instils goodness or wickedness, virtue or vice, in a man, He also endows him with the faculty of giving expression to that goodness or wickedness, virtue or vice...This aptitude for arts, fine and coarse, is hereditary...And as excellences have been put into those who have adopted the nobler professions, they alone are capable of virtue...They are, consequently, said to be noble, free-born, virtuous, religious, of high genealogy and pure birth...These groups alone are worthy of offices and posts in the government of the king...The promotion of the low and the low-born brings no advantage in this world, for it is impudent to act against the wisdom of Creation...Do not be captivated by the cleverness and the agility of the low-born and the mean, for their excellences are imitative and not real excellences" (Advice XXI).

III: The basic feature of the *Fatawa-i Jahandari* is, therefore, its class character. Barani interprets both religion and politics in terms of aristocratic privileges. He wants free-born or noble Muslims to be divided into grades and sub-grades, and they are to have the monopoly of all offices and pensions. And since education makes low-born Muslims efficient and capable, so that they are able to challenge and surpass their betters, Barani insists that the state should prevent Muslim boys of the lower orders from obtaining education, and anyone who ventures to teach them should be punished and exiled from his city. For Barani the shopkeepers and all classes below them are low-born. Barani's hatred of shopkeepers *is* intense. May be, they refused to supply him commodities on credit.

And this theory of aristocratic privileges is pushed into religious life and the affairs of the next world, in opposition to, all authoritative Quranic commentaries and the whole religious literature of Islam. The famous Quranic verse—"Indeed, the pious amongst you are most honoured by Allah"—is interpreted as follows, *Piety is the privilege of good birth.* Consequently, if a man is pious, there must have been some element of aristocracy among his ancestors; but if his low birth is proved, then his piety is a mere pretence. It would be a scandal if the sons of butchers, weavers and shopkeepers have more honour in the eyes of Allah than the sons of *khans, maliks* and *amirs.* Similarly, Barani's king is the highest of saints (*qutb*) and partakes of the status of the prophets, while the king's well-born counsellors can discern those secrets which God has hidden in His Preserved Tablets (*Lauh-i Mahfuz*). Another expression of the same attitude is Barani's condemnation of those who have accepted Islam through personal 'free-choice'; Islam, like good wine, must have matured in the muscles and tendons of a man's ancestors; to be spiritually effective, Islam must be hereditary.

IV: "Though I speak with the tongues of men and of angels and have not charity, I have become as sounding brass or a tinkling cymbal (*Corinthians*)." Barani certainly does not speak with the tongue of angels. He confesses that when he was interned at Bhatner after the death of Mohammad bin Tughluq, his enemies attributed "a thousand kinds of poisonous words" to him before Firoz Tughluq. They may have been correct. Barani as a writer is too fond of abusive phrases, many of which are only intelligible when translated literally from Persian into plain Hindi. But while in the *Firoz Shahi* there is some literary flavour about his abuses, in the *Jahandari* they are merely coarse. Also the Lord in His mercy had denied to Barani the virtues of charity, tolerance and forgiveness. He hated intensely and considered his hatred a virtue. Among the Muslims his hatred was directed against philosophers, scientists, heretics, all low-born Muslims and particularly against such of them as had attained to high office. He may have hated the slave-aristocracy with equal venom, but on that matter he had to speak indirectly and with restraint. He hated all non-Muslims and particularly the Hindus, and in order to justify "an all-out war against Hinduism" which the kings refused to undertake, he even misrepresented the doctrines of Imam Shafi'i. Our author, we should remember, had been "driven to madness by the polo-sticks of the hatred of his enemies"; so unable to abuse those who had injured him personally he found a spiritual consolation in, cursing those who had done him no harm.

V: The form of the *Fatawa-i Jahandari* is curious. The only available copy of the book is the manuscript in the Commonwealth Library from which the present translation has been made. In the first page of this manuscript "Zia-i Barani" declares himself to be the author. Then some pages are missing and we are left to guess what Barani might have said. As we read on we discover that Sultan Mahmud is the hero of the book, but curiously enough we find three persons speaking one after another—Sultan Mahmud, a contemporary of Sultan Mahmud and Barani himself—and it is difficult to say where the speech of one of them ends and the speech of the other begins. Also Mahmud is sometimes spoken of as living and at other times as dead. The third person is probably Maulana Qaffal, a Shafi'ite doctor who (according to Ibn-i-Khallikan) converted Mahmud to the Shafi'i creed at Merv. A bogus book, the *Tarikh-i Mahmudi,* had been written by someone in the name of Maulana Qaffal, and in the *preface* to his *Tarikh-i Barmaki,* Barani refers to the fact that he had been reading this work of Qaffal. It probably inspired Barani with the idea of giving this peculiar form to his book. Of the Sultan Mahmud of history, Barani knew little or nothing; in fact his ignorance is appalling. But Mahmud has to bear the whole burden of Barani's philosophy, though he would have repudiated it from A to Z. Writing in this curious form was permitted by contemporary literary tradition, and Barani seems to have preferred this form partly in order to obtain for his doctrines such credit as the legendary figure of Mahmud could give but primarily in order to escape criticism and persecution. After all, no one could blame him for what Mahmud and Qaffal had said. The contradictions about Mahmud, which we find throughout the book, I am inclined to attribute to Barani's failing memory. In the closing paragraphs of the work—which Afsar has called 'Barani's Epilogue'—our author again begins to speak in the first person about his frustrated life and his hopes of favour for his book from the great officers of the future. The form of the *Jahandari* inevitably precluded Barani from referring to any events or persons after Sultan Mahmud; his reference to Sultan Sanjar is probably due to ignorance or oversight. The *Jahandari* does not refer to any Sultan of Delhi by name, though in many passages he seems to have them in mind.

VI: That Barani was a surpassing recorder of contemporary events is proved for all time by the excellence of tlie *Tarikh-i Firoz Shahi.* He was a good Arabic scholar and knew the main events of the period of the Prophet and the Pious Caliphate. Regarding the rest of Islamic history he knew very little and what he knew was all wrong. In the *Preface* to his *Tarikh-i Firoz Shahi,* Barani refers to some bogus books and also to the works of the following well known authors—Tabari, Utbi, Baihaqi, Firdausi and Minhajus Siraj. An examination of the *Fatawa-i Jahandari* will prove that Barani had either never read the works of these authors in the original or else had completely forgotten them. The former alternative is more probable. Similarly, the books referred to in the *Jahandari* were either cheap and worthless fabrications, which have not survived to our days, or else existed only in the imagination of our author.

This question requires a careful consideration. There have survived to us from the Sultanate period many books on mysticism (*tasawwuf*) which were certainly not written by the saints and scholars to whom they were attributed. A visitor, for example, told Shaikh Nizamuddin Aulia that he had read in Awadh a book written by the Shaikh. "But I have written no book," the Shaikh replied, "and no Shaikh of my (Chistiah) *silsilah* has written any book." Nevertheless books in prose and verse were even then being fabricated in the names of all the great Chishti saints and their leading disciples. Shaikh Nasiruddin Chiragh protested against this bogus literature but it continued to grow. Nobody knew where it came from and no one could be held responsible for it. This literature, a part of which I have examined carefully, has two very distinctive features. *First,* the level of scholarship is very low. The authors are unacquainted with well known historical facts; they know very little about mystic principles; and they keep manufacturing miracles which contradict 'history-time' and coining names of books which could never have existed. *Secondly,* all this literature is quite purposeless; even any mischievous intent cannot be attributed to the authors. Their only purpose was to write something—anything—in the names of the great and widely respected saints or their disciples.

There is no alternative but to conclude that this mystic literature was fabricated because there was a widespread and uncritical demand for it. If a man needed a book during the Sultanate period, he had to employ a *katib* to write it for him. But the booksellers kept ready for immediate delivery books of which they could push the sales. Now the great saints of the Chishti *silsilah* had written no books; nevertheless the public insistently demanded books written by them. It is safe to assume that enterprising booksellers got literary hacks to prepare without much trouble the bogus books the public was prepared to buy on account of its faith in the saints to whom they were attributed. There was no question of copyright; after the first bookseller produced some copies of a book prepared by him, other booksellers were welcome to make any profit they could by having it copied and sold. Shaikh Nasiruddin Chiragh, as has been pointed out, protested against this sort of literature in the reign of Firoz Shah on the ground that it was stupid and not authentic. Critical scholars of later days, like Shaikh Abdul Haq in the time of Akbar, refused to consider it as authoritative. But it was, nevertheless, copied and recopied and sold; public respect for the saints to whom it was attributed assured its survival. Finally, time gave it a sort of sanctity. Fabricated mystic books of smaller size have had a large sale in India during the last two generations both in the original Persian and in Urdu translations. Manuscripts of the larger fabricated works are easy to find in private collections and public libraries. It would not be safe to say that even now additions to this sort of fabricated literature have stopped.

Similar bogus literature appeared in the field of history also during the Sultanate period. The public wanted books written *by* great kings like Jamshed, who never existed, or on great kings like Sanjar, whom it wanted to be praised. So the booksellers produced a *Testament* (*Wasaya-i*) of Jamshed and a biography of Sanjar written by his supposed secretary, Muin Asam. This sort of literature seems to have been fairly voluminous. But it did not have the same good fortune, because it had not the same sanctity, as the fabricated literature on mysticism. When it was proved that a work on history was a pure fabrication, no one was concerned about its preservation; so most of this fabricated historical literature seems to have vanished. Now it was, unfortunately, on the basis of his acquaintance with this bogus, fabricated literature that Barani claimed the status of a historian. The *Historical Illustrations* in the *Jahandari* are a sufficient proof of this. Barani's ignorance of history is appalling even with reference to the basic authorities available in the Delhi of his days, and his ignorance of geography is even more so.

But the difficulties under which Barani worked should not be forgotten. After his dismissal in 1351 AD that is, from the age of sixty-eight solar years onwards, Barani wrote at least seven books—the *Sana-i Mohammedi* (or *Na't-i Mohammadi*); *Salat-i Kabir*; *Inayat Nama-i Ilahi*; *Ma-asir Sadaat*; *Tarikh-i Firoz Shahi*; *Hasrat Nama*; and the *Fatawa-i Jahandari*. He could write from memory; he could translate; he could write a book of his own on the basis of the work of another author; or he could put in logical order (as in the *Jahandari*) the ideas that had been developing in his mind for a long time. But it was not within his means to undertake any investigation or research.

VII: No writer on political theory can ignore world history. And Barani had imagined a world history in consonance with the basic postulate of his political philosophy—the devolution of all offices of the state according to the principle of hereditary right. "In the regime of the Kisras of Iran (Ajam) from Kaimurs (son of Adam) to Khusrau Parvez (the last of the great pre-Muslim emperors)," he tells us in his *Firoz Shahi*, "the office of the king went to the king's son; the office of *malik* to the *malik*'s son and nobility was confined to the free-born." Similar statements will also be found in the *Jahandari*. All facts not in consonance with this simple postulate are just ignored.

VIII: Barani's attitude towards the Hindus deserves a careful examination.

British rule in various parts of India lasted only from three to seven generations. And the chief feature of British rule was that a foreign race, determined to remain foreign and sharply distinguished from the natives in colour and features and definitely raised above them by its cultural, administrative, scientific and industrial capacity, controlled both the political and the economic system of the country; British rule in India was, further, backed by the irresistible military and economic resources of a great white empire which dominated the globe. Now writers during the British period naturally visualised the so-called 'Muslim rule,' of which they only studied the wars and kings, in terms of the 'British rule' of which they had first-hand knowledge. This is unfortunate. It is true that Muslim kings, mostly of foreign extraction, sat on Indian thrones for some six or seven centuries. But they could only do so because their enthronement was not the enthronement of 'Muslim rule'; had it been otherwise, they could not have lasted for a single generation. The Muslims were a minority in the land with no foreign contacts and no foreign support; they consisted of all classes and groups from the richest to the poorest; and there was nothing in their favour except the tendency to equality in their social system and their freedom from caste. The working classes of the two communities had the same tools, possessed about the same average skill, sold their products in the same markets at the same prices, wore the same clothes somewhat differently cut and sewn, and lived in houses made of the same material but somewhat differently designed. And since the mass of the Muslims belonged to the lower middle class and the working classes, it is an error to visualise 'the Muslims' as a governing race.

Now a careful examination of the *Jahandari*, specially Advices IX and XI, will show that while the Muslim upper classes had a predominant influence over the administrative machine, the economic system of the country was entirely in the hands of the upper class Hindus. They were bankers, transport-merchants, market-merchants; and the machinery of credit, which controlled a greater quantity of commodities than the coins in actual circulation, was entirely in the hands of Hindu bankers. Whoever may govern the land, this Hindu aristocratic banking and commercial monopoly was unbreakable.

"On the matter of the Hindus", Afsar Begum correctly remarks, "Barani was mentally unsound." But what drove him to madness was the fact that in the empire of Delhi no privileges whatsoever were given to a Muslim as such. He had to find his livelihood in an economic system dominated by the Hindu groups. And the Muslim kings, as Barani laments, were in no mood to challenge a system without which their governments could not have functioned.

IX: Barani's solid contributions to political theory should not be ignored. His greatest contribution is his analysis of the institution of monarchy with reference to Islamic religion and social needs. He frankly declares monarchy to be anti-Islamic. The principles and traditions of monarchy violate the injunctions of the Quran, the precepts of the Prophet and the traditions of the Pious Caliphate. But it was justified by the needs of the age, for without it the social order would have perished. Barani in his heart, however, longed for an 'institutionalised monarchy.' He wanted the king to select his counsellors with care and to be guided by their advice. And his basic precept is: "No opinion for kings." The duties of the king with reference to almost every institution are surveyed by the *Jahandari* in detail.

X: The *Fatawa-i Jahandari* also enables us to understand the real character of the empire of Delhi. It was not a theocratic state in any sense of the word. Its basis was not the *shari'at* of Islam but the *zawabit* or state-laws made by the king. "A *zabita* or state-law in the technique of administration," Barani declares, "is a rule of action which a king imposes as an obligatory duty upon himself for realising the welfare of the state and from which he absolutely never deviates." (Advice XIV). It is obvious that such legislation would tend to favour the ruling dynasty and the upper class Muslim (or rather Turkish) cliques, who had a monopoly of the highest military and administrative posts. Its foundation was, nevertheless, non-religious and secular. It was not based on any religious texts or their interpretations by the *ulama,* but upon the opinion of the king (or the king and his advisers) as to what was acceptable for his kingdom and his people. Barani leaves us in no doubt that in cases of conflict the state-laws overrode the *shari'at.* But in order to comprehend the matter properly, we must first examine the character of the *shari'at* (about which Barani is silent) and then survey the field of conflict.

The basis of the *shari'at* or the law of Islam are the Quran and the Prophet's traditions (i.e. what the Prophet did and what he said). But since the Quran and the traditions did not provide solutions for all the problems that arose in a society that was becoming increasingly complex, the great legists who built up the *sahri'at* of Islam had recourse to two great canons—*first, qiyas* or the extension of a principle laid down by the Quran and the traditions to similar cases; *secondly, istihsan* or the public welfare. Reason and experience were, of course, necessary for the understanding and interpretation of the scriptures, but the Muslim legists (*faqih*), unlike the Roman jurisconsults, were not prepared to acknowledge that reason (*aql*), unsupported by the scriptures, could be the foundation of any *shari'at-law.* They preferred to be silent about problems concerning which the principles of the scriptures, even when extended by *qiyas* and *istihsan,* could give no guidance. We should not try to find in the *shari'at* what was never put in there.

During the first five centuries of Islam the principles of the *shari'at* were an acute topic of controversy. But a century before Barani all controversies were brought to an end. Where agreement was possible, agreement had been attained; but where agreement had proved impossible, disagreement was accepted as a settled fact, and the *qazi* in deciding with a case (and a Muslim in directing his own footsteps) could follow any recognised doctor of law. The textbooks of the *shari'at* simplified the matter by noting down the opinions of the great legists under their names in matters on which *ijma* (consensus of opinion) had been impossible. The great *Hidayah* was a comprehensive treatise on the subject and plenty of textbooks based upon it appeared in various parts of the Muslim world.

Now the chapters of any book on the *shari'at* or *fiqh* are easily divisible into two groups—those which deal with *'ibadat* or religious devotions and those which deal with *mu'amilat* or human affairs. All *shari'at* books insisted on laying down laws about religious devotions, but on this matter Muslim religious consciousness refused to accept them as authoritative. They were formal, mechanistic, and by ignoring the spiritual element in life, they reduced religion to the performance of meaningless routine duties. But devotions are a matter between man and his God; the state is not entitled to interfere. The chief laws that concern us here are the laws of crime, civil laws and public laws.

In the *shari'at* of Islam, as in Roman law the law of crime has remained undeveloped. Muslim legists, on the whole, were very reluctant to base any law of crime on the traditions of the Prophet; consequently they had to confine themselves to the discussion of those crimes (*hudud*) for which the Quran has prescribed a punishment. Other offences, however grave, were not crimes for the *shari'at* and the silence of the *shari'at* left all of them to the law of the state.

There was no difference of opinion on the question that the Quranic punishments were too severe and there was a universal desire to 'avoid' them. And they were avoided on two pretexts. First, in accordance; with the precept referred to by Barani—'Avoid punishments on the ground of doubts'—the laws of evidence in the *shari'at* were made so severe that proof of such crimes was in practice impossible unless they had been committed at a public place. Four witnesses were required to prove every crime and the slightest difference in their statements caused the case for the prosecution to fail. Secondly, the definition of Quranic crimes was restricted within the narrowest possible limits.

A brief survey of the Quranic *hudud* (punishments) will give us some idea of the exact position.

(i) *Theft:* The Quranic punishment for 'theft' is severance of the hand. But it was ruled that if a person took wrongful possession of movable property to which he had any sort of claim, his crime would not amount to theft (*sirqah*). Thus misappropriation by a partner in business was not theft; also stealing from the public treasury was not theft because all Muslims were partners in the public treasury. Similarly, it was ruled that stealing of eatables was not theft, nor stealing adjuncts to eatables, like wood and charcoal. Thus the whole field—both as to evidence and punishment—was left to state-law. And the state punished according to the degree of guilt, and tried to reduce punishments as far as possible. The chief object was to prevent the recurrence of the crime. But there was no hesitation, when the situation demanded, in inflicting a severe punishment not permitted by the Quran; highway robbery, for example, was punished with death. You came across thieves in Delhi—thieves who had been punished. But none of them had severed hands,

(ii) *Murder:* The Quran, it is believed, leaves to the heirs of the murdered man the choice between demanding the death of the murderer and accepting a money composition from him. Such a principle (as a Gujarat king of the fifteenth century remarked) would mean a licence for the rich to kill the poor. So it was ruled that the king was the heir of all murdered men and that he was in no need of a money composition. But it was, nevertheless, within his power to be content with a punishment short of the death penalty. So a distinction was made between various types of killing and appropriate punishments were prescribed for each. But the king could permit the heirs of the murdered man to accept a money composition; if that arrangement better served the ends of justice.

(iii) *Adultery and Fornication:* The *Kanz,* a very useful summary of the *Hidayah,* declares as follows: "If the adulterers are married persons, they are to be stoned to death in an open plain and the stoning should be begun by the witnesses; but if they have been punished on their own confessions, then the Imam should throw the first stones...The man should be stoned while standing, but a pit should be dug and the woman put into it up to her breasts before she is stoned...If the fornicators are unmarried then one hundred strokes of the whip are prescribed for free persons and fifty strokes for slaves. The whips should have no knots or thorns and the strokes should be of average strength, not very severe and not vert light. The man should be deprived of his (upper) garments and thrashed while standing; the strokes should fall upon the different parts of his body, except the head, the face and the sex-parts. According to Imam Abu Yusuf he should also be thrashed on the head, but according to Imam Shafi'i, he should only be thrashed on the back. The woman should be thrashed while sitting; she should not be deprived of her (upper) garments, but her cloak and other coverings are to be removed...For persons who make false accusations concerning adultery, the punishment is eighty strokes of the whip for free persons and forty for slaves."

There was no desire to have these severe laws enforced—not even among the advocates of the *shari'at*. Barani in his *Firoz Shahi* quotes the opinion of a great theologian, Syed Nuruddin Mubarak Ghaznavi, who flourished during the reign of Shamsuddin Iltutmish to the effect that the profession of the prostitutes should be permitted, otherwise the rascals who go to them will attack the sanctity of Muslim homes. This represents the average opinion of the medieval *ulama*. Adultery was not a cognisable offence; the fact was hard to prove and the rules of *shari'at* procedure were entirely in favour of the accused. We hear of no stoning of adulterers in Delhi, though Alauddin Khalji says that in such cases he caused the man to be castrated and the woman to be put to death. Though people differed in opinion as to what the state should do, dancing-girls, prostitutes, brothels, taverns and gambling-dens were all permitted under conditions prescribed by state-laws.

(iv) *Apostasy:* The punishment for apostasy, according to *shari'at* books, in case of men is death, and in case of women it is imprisonment for life. But the definition of 'apostasy' was never clarified. On the one hand, there was a desire to treat as apostates all Muslims who deviated from the orthodox path, the extreme case being the Ismailies. On the other hand, there was a general conviction that no inquiries should be made into the inner thoughts of men. Punishments for apostasy were rare (except with reference to heretic Muslim sects) and the matter in all cases came within the sphere of state-laws.

To sum up: The whole sphere of criminal law had, by means of the arguments and legal procedures, which have been briefly indicated, brought within the jurisdiction of the state. It was claimed that the Prophet himself had tried to 'avoid' the *hudud*.

The great merit of the *shari'at* is its civil law, which was the best in the medieval world. The Quran does not give us many laws, but the traditions of the Prophet, both directly and by extension through the principle of *qiyas*, were considered valid 'in the sphere of civil laws. Add to this, there was the principle of *rawayat*—knowledge of how things were done in the days of the Prophet and the Pious Caliphs. The intelligence of the great Muslim jurists had also added many principles to civil laws, which had been their primary concern. It was expected that the king and his *zawabit* would not interfere with the private rights of citizens as defined by the *shari'at*. But even here there were at least three exceptions. First, it was acknowledged that *shari'at-law* could be overridden by custom or *urf*. Thus the rights of inheritance, which the Quran gives to all Muslim women, have often been denied to them by custom. In a conflict between *shari'at* and local custom the state could intervene. Secondly, where the *shari'at* was silent, the state-law had to fill the gap. Thus the Samenid kings (so the *Zainul Akhbar* of Gardizi tells us) finding that the *shari'at* was silent about canals and water-rights, had a law-book compiled on the subject. Lastly, where private rights came into conflict with public law, the matter came within the jurisdiction of the state. The best examples of this in India were rights relating to land. That the cultivator was entitled to the produce of his toil was a moral right which no one questioned. But the extent to which he was to be taxed, the method of levying the tax and the position of the intermediaries, whether hereditary revenue-collectors or government officers, were questions for state-law to decide. The fact that medieval states did not interfere with the laws of *inheritance and marriage* of *any* community has created the wholly wrong impression that the state was dominated by the *shari'at*.

The Quran has only one principle of public law—the decision of matters by common consultation. Are the political traditions of the Prophet and the Pious Caliphs binding on the monarchical state? Barani's two reasons for answering this question in the negative will not, perhaps, commend themselves to most thoughtful Muslims. The Prophet, he says, was guided by Divine revelation and the Pious Caliphs were inspired by the personal influence of the Prophet. How can we, to whom this good fortune is denied, follow in the footsteps of the Pious Caliphs? Also the times are bad. "Such Islam and such Muslims are not left that one can govern them like Abu Bakr or 'Umar,'" (Advice VIII). This argument, if correct, would overthrow the validity of the whole

Muslim creed. The traditions of the Prophet are binding because the Prophet, though inspired by God, was a human being. In any case the Quran is very clear and definite: "There is for you in the Prophet of Allah a good example"—an example which has to be followed and not ignored. An extension of Barani's argument from politics to other spheres would threaten the whole structure of Islam.

Still though Barani's reasons for it are not correct, his basic precept is valid. There was a contradiction in the position of the second Caliph; he governed several countries but was responsible to the people of Medina alone. In the time of the Third and the Fourth Caliphs this contradiction caused great difficulties. When Hazrat Ali left Medina for Iraq, the city-state of the Prophet came to an end. Many traditions of the republic of Medina were by their nature inapplicable to the mammoth empires of the *Omayyads* and the *Abbasides*. The democracy of the Medinite republic, which centred round the Prophet's mosque in a small city where everybody knew everybody else, was gone and would never return. Democracy may appear in a new form, but it could not be revived in the form of a city-state; that form Islam had transcended for all time. The change had been a progress and not a fall. If the principles of Islam were of value to mankind, then we should not regret the price that had to be paid for their expansion. Barani's opinion that the only political traditions by which Muslims could live were those of the Sasanian monarchy were shared by all his contemporaries. It was, nevertheless, erroneous. In the four centuries preceding Barani, the thinkers of Iran had 'reconstructed' the history of her Sasanid and pre-Sasanid rulers for the guidance of their kings but without any reference to historical authorities. The legendary Iran of Barani was the creation of the Iranian Renaissance. It had never existed.

If the transition from the city-state to the territorial state made the continuation of the traditions of the Pious Caliphate impossible, it was also difficult to follow the traditions of early Islam in other matters—land-revenue, import duties salaries of officers and soldiers, etc.—owing to differences in geographical environment production-systems, character of fruits and crops, social traditions and the like between the Arab and the non-Arab world.

Barani is certainly correct in thinking that neither the *shari'at* nor the known traditions of the Pious Caliphate gave to Muslim society the laws on which the administrative structure of the extensive monarchical empires of the middle ages could be based. Such empires required state-laws based upon the personal authority of the king, but made after consultation with his council. Barani advises the king to follow old laws, in case they have worked well and are suited to the circumstances of the day. But this is a changing world and new circumstances require new laws. These new laws should be made with care. Barani tells us in detail how he wanted the king's council to work. The members were to be carefully selected; they were to be of equal status and acquainted with all the secrets of the state. They were to have the fullest freedom of expression and no one was to be in danger of his life or his post. The king was to withhold his opinion to the end; in fact his primary duty was to allow the council to arrive at a unanimous opinion (*tawafuq-i ara*). This unanimity, subject to certain conditions. (e.g. when the council had been swayed by its passions), Barani considered to be a guarantee of correctness. Legislation was a continuous process and Barani wanted the council, and not the king, to be responsible for the continuity of state policy. He warns all kings against self-will.

Obviously a state resting on laws so made is a royal state, a governing-class state. But it is in no sense a theocratic state. Its foundation are experience and secular reason. The king in such a state is 'sovereign' in the sense that term has been defined by Hobbes and Austin. He strives to secure obedience to the laws he has made as well as the laws he has adopted from his predecessors by his awards and punishments. He is a human superior and acknowledges no other human superior. He is obeyed by the 'bulk' of the subjects, but if driven to despair his subjects have always in their hands the power of overthrowing him.

XI: Barani expounds with emphasis the theory of contradiction, as it was taught by the formal logic of his day on the basis of the precept: 'the unity of opposites is impossible.' Some aspects of its application deserve to be noted. According to Barani all contradictory forces are eternal; one of them may, for a time, overpower another but no force can completely eliminate its opposite. In terms of human life he concludes that "it is impossible for all kingdoms of the world to be united into one state or for all false creeds to be overthrown." (Advice XI). This would mean the end of our human hopes owing to an eternal war of kings and creeds. Our belief today lies in the hope that all contradictions disappear in a higher unity—that 'thesis' and 'anti-thesis' lead to a higher 'synthesis'. And we hold that there are principles according to which states can be federated into a peaceful world-union and religions made to live and work side by side in peaceful cooperation.

Barani's application of the principle of contradiction to monarchy is unfortunate. After condemning monarchy as un-Islamic and sending kings to hell-fire, he goes to the opposite extreme and makes the king a partner in 'the contradictory qualities of God' and declares him to be God's 'deputy' and 'agent'. No educated contemporaries of Barani would have seriously agreed with this assertion. The attributes of God seem to be contradictory but they are only contradictory *for us*; their contradiction is phenomenal, not real. The unity of the Supreme Being transcends all contradictions. Similarly, contradictions in human beings, whether kings or plain citizens, should not be a matter of pride. All contradictions are frustrations and all frustrations are unfortunate. The perfection of the state—and of the king in so far as the attributes of the state are expressed in him—lies not in the contradictory manifestations of its power but in the ultimate unity of its purpose. Barani's fundamental error lies in his conception of God as a bundle of contradictory attributes; his other errors follow as an inevitable consequence.

Lastly, Barani's theory that the rights of the governing class are based upon the divinely ordained principle of birth leads to insuperable difficulties within the Muslim period. The old pagan aristocracy of noble birth had been overthrown by the expansion of Islam and no new aristocracy could take its place. No one cared to inquire into the paternity of the rulers and no distinction between a legitimate king and a usurper was in practice possible. Rival cliques, consisting mostly of low-born adventurers, competed for power, and every clique that captured the government treated the group it had overthrown with ruthless ferocity. "By every means that comes to their hands they overthrow and reduce to poverty and distress many families, classes and tribes of the preceding king merely for the preservation and protection of their lives... Some they spare; others, they kill; some they imprison, others they exile; and some they deprive of their properties". (Advice XXII). Barani had seen enough of this himself. He tries to find a solution by describing the humane treatment meted out to the Simjuris by Sultan Mahmud. But he also realises that unless the members of a fallen governing class are deprived of their lives, there will be persistent rebellions which make the new government impossible. Barani has really no solution for this constant struggle between the governing classes. It was not possible in the political circumstances of the period to confine the throne permanently to a particular dynasty; and though Barani praised this principle with reference to pre-Muslim states, he did not recommend it as a remedy for the misfortune of India's governing classes. The Mughal empire was still far off.

It is quite in harmony with his mode of thinking that Barani is drawn to contemplate a non-religious, non-Islamic society-the Qara Khitais of Qadr Khan—which has no prophets and no revealed books and which, while guided by experience, tradition and reason, is not cursed with the equality of the Muslim creed. His approval of such a society is unreserved, for it has a permanent governing class and a permanent royal dynasty. No one should accuse Barani of any religious prejudices beyond the pale of Islam.

Barani's repeated discussions of price control should be studied along with his account of Alauddin Khalji's System. One of his basic demands—that the power of the state should crush the monopolists who fixed market-prices by their exclusive control of transport and credit and indulged in regrating and cornering—has been already discussed. His second basic demand is for 'social security' through the permanent fixation of wages and prices in an economic order in which everyone is assured of the reward of his labour on the principle of production-cost (*nirkh-i baraward*).

XII: The highest element of Muslim religious life is found in its *tasawwuf* or mysticism. And at no time in Indian history has Muslim mysticism found a higher expression both in literature and in life than during the two generations represented by Ziauddin Barani and his father. The dominating mystic teachers of the period were Shaikh Fariduddin Ganj-i Shakar, Shaikh Nizamuddin Aulia and Shaikh Nasirududdin Chiragh, while Qazi Hamid Nagauri, a friend of Shaikh Fariduddin, must be considered as one of the profoundest Muslim mystic writers of all time. The works of Hamid Nagauri are hard to find, but the teachings of the three great Shaikhs mentioned above have been preserved for us in the *Fawaidul Fuwad* of Amir Hasan Sijzi, the *Siyarul Aulia* of Amir Khurd and the *Khairul Majalis* of Hamid Qalandar. Amir Khusrau and Amir Hasan Sijzi were disciples of Shaikh Nizamuddin Aulia and mystic poets of standing. But though Barani was a disciple of Shaikh Nizamuddin Aulia and claimed to be an intimate friend of Amir Khusrau and Amir Hasan, the teachings of the great Shaikh and the mystic literature of the day had not touched even the periphery of his soul. His conception of Islam is formal, mechanistic and of the earth, earthy. He is a complete stranger to the spiritual elements of Muslim life and must not be considered a representative of contemporary Muslim religion and culture.

XIII: It must be mentioned to Barani's credit that, within the very narrow limits mentioned above, he was singularly humane. He protested vehemently against torture. He was horrified by the custom, which had became common in his day, of ruthlessly punishing the innocent women and children of political offenders. He relates with disgust the large-scale murders perpetrated in his day in order to establish the prestige of the government through a reign of terror. Since the *shari'at* was silent on the question of political punishments, Barani undertook to discover some principles for regulating them on the basis of secular reason and humanity. Most readers will be inclined to agree with his conclusions. The punishments for theological offences, which he needlessly demands, had no reference to the India of his day, when all communities respected all religious leaders.

XIV: Barani wrote the *Fatawa-i Jahandari* in his extreme old age; it is probably his last work and his powers were visibly failing. But all his faculties had not decayed to the same extent. His capacity for thinking had certainly not suffered; in his own mind his thoughts had the same clarity as eight years before. But his capacity of expression had declined and there is a great fall from the literary level of the *Firoz Shahi*. Other weaknesses also appear. Our author forgets what he has written and is tiresome in his repetitions. He also again and again contradicts himself about historical facts; this also is probably due to his failing memory. The manuscript is full of lacunae, but owing to Barani's habit of repeating himself again and again, nothing of value has been lost.

Dr. Afsar Begum, when going to the Peshawar University, left her typescript with me. I have confined myself to correcting typing errors; some footnotes which I have added are indicated by my initial in square brackets: Afsar's original work (translation and notes) was prepared by her for her Ph.D. thesis at the London School of Oriental Studies under the supervision of Professor C.H. Phillips, Dr. Peter Hardy and Professor Dr. Miss Lambton. Inevitably it was literal and not particularly readable for all the defects, repetitions and lacunae of the original Persian text were brought scientifically into the English translation. So in view of the peculiar character of the Persian original, I advised Afsar to re-prepare the whole translation keeping the following objects in mind:—(a) Barani's long Historical Illustrations, unless relevant to his main theme, were to be drastically summarised; (b) all repetitions were to be ignored; (c) abuses which Barani repeats were to be translated only once or twice, but it was to be indicated clearly that such abuses were habitual; (d) Barani's confused arguments were to be put in as logical form as was possible by a mere rearrangement of sentences; (e) elimination of unnecessary adjectives, so far as possible; (f) where Barani's discussion was long and tiresome, it was to be summarised within square brackets; (g) and, finally, the translation was to be made as readable as possible and, while remaining sternly faithful to the original, an attempt was to be made to give to the translation 'the strength' which Barani would have certainly given to the original had he written it eight or ten years earlier. The book is divided into 24 chapters called *Nasihats* (Advices); where an Advice covers more than one topic, it has been subdivided into sections in the English *translation with a separate heading in square brackets.*

The *Fatawa-i Jahandari* is the most thought-challenging work of the Sultanate period and Afsar's translation seeks to do justice to Barani's thoughts.

It remains to thank a few friends on behalf of my ex-pupil and myself. Professor S.A. Rashid and Maulana Abrar Faruqi helped Afsar in the interpretation of the Persian text by sending her a revised copy of it from here and also such other material as she required. Dr. Hardy who has spent so much time in studying the *Fatawa-i Jahandari* with Afsar will (I hope) approve the present form of the translation. To Mr. Khaliq Nizami I am (among many other things) grateful for his 'five minutes instructions' about the lines on which the present Introduction has been written, though he is in no way responsible for the opinions I have expressed. All intellectual workers at Aligarh owe to Shri Syed Bashiruddin, our Librarian, and his staff a debt of gratitude which it is difficult to express in words; to me personally this association of some thirty-five years with 'Bashiruddin and the Library' has been one of the happiest inspirations at Aligarh.

Mohammad Habib

The Fatawa-i Jahandari

ENGLISH TRANSLATION

by

Afsar Begum

The Fatawa-i Jahandari

(Principles of Government)

by

the Well-Wisher of the Sultan's Court

ZIA-I BARANI

Gratitude and praises are due to the Creator, who has adorned religion-protecting sultans and strong rulers with the virtue of justice and has made the people of the world obedient to their commands and the permanent devotees of their administrations, and who has caused the earth to be inhabited through his affection while order has also been established.

And offerings of purity to the great soul of the Leader (*Khwaja*) of the created world, the Prophet Mohammad Mustafa[1], who is the guide of the guides of angels and men! Praises on him and peace—and on all who believe!

And peace be on his companions; Abu Bakr, Umar, Usman, and Ali bin Abu Talib and on Hasan and Husain!

And blessings of God on these four Caliphs, who on becoming the successors of the Prophet, brought the world under the shadow of the banner of Islam!

So says the well-wisher of the Sultan's Court[2], Zia-i Barani after the study of books...[3]

Advice I

[The Personal Safety of the King]

[So many pages are missing from the beginning of this Advice that it is impossible to be sure about its subject-matter, but the surviving paragraphs refer to the personal safety of kings.]

Whenever before embarking on his political enterprises, a king throws himself under the protection of God and His Word, God keeps him safe and secure from the instigations of Satan and from the consequences of defective designs and faulty plans.[4]

[But kings, in addition to praying to God, must also take the practical steps necessary for their personal protection.]

A wise king does not consider himself secure from the deceptions and conspiracies of wicked men. All wise kings, ancient and modern, have therefore, kept themselves surrounded effectively with guards and watchmen in order to be safe from rebels and assassins, who, overpowered by their passions or by their envious and wicked nature, are reckless of all consequences. For having been made dumb and blind by their passions, these people are often prepared to throw themselves into fire and to face fearlessly the risk that their heads will be cut off like herbs and radishes. Extensive experience has proved that no fear of ultimate consequences comes to the minds of these ill-starred wretches, when they are overpowered by their wicked passions. It also often happens that owing to some reasons these people have a personal resentment against the king and are constantly thirsting for revenge; so in order to quench their wrath and to satisfy their desire for vengeance, they keep seeking for an opportunity of overpowering him.

[This Advice is illustrated by a somewhat detailed account of the Saffarid brothers, Yaqub bin Lais, who died in 878 A.D., and his brother, Amr (878–903), and a description of Amr's struggle with Amir Ismail Samani. This account, if Barani is to be believed, is based on an extinct book, the *Tarikh-i Samanian* (*History of the Samanid Dynasty*, 837–999). It is full of errors.[5] Our author, for example, makes the wholly inaccurate statement that Yaqub bin Lais was captured by the Caliph's army and died in prison 'in the worst conditions'. Barani's object in referring to the Saffarids is not clarified here, but he returns to this topic in Advice XXI and leaves us in no doubt about his reason for hating the Saffarid brothers. Yaqub bin Lais started his career as a copper-smith (*saffar*) though Barani and some other authors say that he was a carpenter. Yaqub was not ashamed of his origin and often referred to it with pride. The Saffarid dynasty is the first royal family of working-class origin in the history of Islam; it was of purely Iranian origin and it had more power and independence than any preceding dynasty in Iran. Barani hated the two brothers on account of their low birth. Add to this, they challenged the aristocracy and the existing social order. "The sympathy of the historians from whom we derive our information on the struggle between the Samanids and the Saffarids", says Barthold (*Turkestan,* pp. 225–226), "is unquestionably on the side of the first. The Samanids, by their origin, in contrast to these military despots, who rose from the ranks of the people, were the natural continuators of the work begun by the Taharids, and the natural protectors of law and order, in the maintenance of which the higher classes of society were mainly interested. From the expressions of Tabari it is evident that the wealthy and the *dihqans* (feudal magnates), whatever may have been their relations with Ismail, proved faithful adherents to him in his struggle with Amr."]

Advice II

On the Effects of the Good Faith of the King

Sultan Mahmud has said: O, Sons of Mahmud![6] You are to know for certain that the success and failure of the political and administrative affairs of a Muslim king depend upon his good and bad religious faith. If there is firmness in the faith of the king, and he believes for certain that what the prophets have brought to mankind through the revealed books is correct and true and that there can be no doubt about the matter, then this is the basic principle of correct religion and the designation of 'true faith' is given to it. Owing to the blessings of the king's faith and his firmness in it, his political designs are achieved and the wishes of the people of his kingdom are also granted by God.

If the king's faith in the religion of the Prophet is firm and unshakable, then there is no harm if he is not excessively given to his religious devotions and cannot fulfil the supererogatory duties prescribed with reference to fasting and prayers. Similarly if there is no fault or defect in the religious beliefs of the king, the enjoyments and pleasures in which he indulges as a human being are forgiven to him out of consideration for his firm faith. On the ground that he protects and promotes the Muslim religion, the sins due to his human nature are erased from the record of his life. Is it not strange that in spite of his failures in supererogatory devotions and his sinful life, a king should be ranked among the *abdals*,[7] and if he is pure-minded and given to religious devotions, he should be the *qutb*[8] of the world?

The test of the king's faith is that he keeps the inhabitants of his kingdom on the path of Religious Law (*Shari'at*)[9]. Even if he is involved in personal sins owing to his (physical) desires, yet through the dignity and power of his kingship he maintains the authority of the orders of the Shari'at in such a way, and so firmly enforces all its commands and prohibitions, that no one can openly practise anything against the Law in his country. The dignity of a Faith-protecting king is beyond all description. For it is owing to his protection and promotion of the Faith that the Musalmans can apply themselves to their devotions with peace of mind, that the orders of the *Shari'at* of the Prophet become current in the provinces, that the correct creed becomes dominant over other creeds, that the chastity and the lives of the Musalmans and of the mass of the *zimmis* (non-Muslims) are protected and secure, and the customs of the Islamic Faith are elevated to the dome of the sky. The rewards for these achievements, which are beyond calculation and computation, are put to the credit of the Faith-protecting king, who is the cause of these good deeds, virtues and devotions. If he personally fails in his supererogatory devotions and even in the prescribed fastings and prayers, and his mind is contaminated with human sinfulness, nevertheless, owing to his protection of the Faith, all his sins are forgiven. Compared with all the virtues and devotions, which his justice, kindness, power and prestige make possible for the people of God, what do the sins of his single soul matter?

[The kings of Islam should not allow Satan to put the following idea into their minds. "As we are passing our lives in pleasures and enjoyments, organising receptions and parties and spending the money of the Treasury on our personal vanities, and in most of our expenditure for maintaining the prestige and power of kingships we are acting against the traditions (*sunnah*)[10] of the Prophet, how can we compel the people to refrain from what the *Shari'at* has prohibited by severe punishments or insist on their doing what is virtuous?"]

The policy of the state is distinct from the personal life of the king; it would, of course, be appropriate for kings to set the example of obeying the laws they impose on others; but the fact that they are themselves falling into sinfulness is irrelevant to the functioning of their governments.

The religious scholars of old days have explained clearly and in detail the tests for the virtuous faith and firm religious convictions of kings.

One of these tests is that in their capitals and their cities, in their provinces and their towns, they appoint harsh-tempered censors of morals (*muhtasibs*)[11] and honest judicial officers (*amir-i dads*)[12] and strengthen their authority in various ways, so that these officers can establish the dignity of 'ordering the good and prohibiting the evil' among the Musalmans and can by their severe punishments embitter the lives of all open, persistent and public sinners. These officers should keep harassing all persons who make sin into an art and a profession. Tavern-keepers, harlots and gamblers should be prohibited from making a public display of their sins. If prohibitions, stern orders, insults and humiliations cannot restrain them, if in spite of their claim to be Musalmans and true believers, they do not openly and publicly give up their shameless and dirty sins, and if respect for the Faith and fear of the king's orders are unable to dissuade them, then the rich among them should be punished with deprivation of property and the poor by imprisonment and other punishments. Tavern-keepers should be sent out of the capital[13] (Delhi), so that they may live in a corner; if they are Musalmans, they should be treated ruthlessly. It should be so arranged that no Musalman takes up the profession of a tavern-keeper. All male prostitutes (*mukhannas*) should be prevented by severe kicks from adorning themselves like women and wailing like women and from practising their other sins; they should be treated with harshness and cruelty so that they may leave the City (Delhi), and go to the countryside and obtain their livelihood there by agriculture or other lawful occupations. These groups have made dirty sins their professions and the open practice of their professions in the Capital of Islam (Delhi) is against the dignity of the Faith. Public immorality should be prohibited in all cities and these sinful groups should be told to leave them and hide in nooks and corners in the countryside. The construction and public use of music-halls (*tarababad*) should not be permitted in cities; if such places have been constructed, they should by stern measures be pulled down, brick by brick.

In short, they should not permit the open profession or display of anything prohibited by the *shari'at,* but if persons accustomed to these sins indulge in them secretly and in privacy, no severe inquiries into them should be usually made. If anything prohibited by the *shari'at* is seen by the *muhtasibs* or *amir-i dads* or comes to the notice of the public, it should be totally suppressed. Nevertheless, what is private and secret should not be revealed and published.

The novelties (*bid'ats*)[14], which are injurious to the traditions (*sunnah*) should be suppressed so far as possible; the suppression of novelties, wherever they are seen, should be considered a duty. The Musalmans should be insistently asked, *mohalla* (city-quarter) by *mohalla,* street by street, and house by house, to observe the five basic duties of Islam—i.e. the recitation of the Oath of Affirmation (*Kalema*) saying the five obligatory (*farz*) prayers, fasting during the month of Ramazan (*ruza*), giving the obligatory charity (*zakat*) and the pilgrimage to Mecca (*haj*). People who are irregular about their obligatory prayers should be warned by various means, and people who ignore their prayers altogether should be compelled to say their prayers by stern measures. The rich should be asked to give obligatory charity (*zakat*) to the poor and no excuses from them should be heard. And as to those reckless people, who either eat or drink openly or commit dirty sins in public during the fasting month of Ramazan, regardless of the respect due to the Faith and with no fear of the king's orders, they should be arrested and brought bound to the king's court, so that the king may, in his discretion, with his firm judgment and as a warning to the public, punish them with long imprisonment, exile to distant places, or the shedding of blood. The molesters of the correct faith and of the *shari'at* of the Prophet (should be controlled) for the sake of elevating the True Word, for creating respect for the observance of religious rites and for ensuring the grandeur of Islam. The Musalmans should be brought to the highway of the Islamic faith and the non-Muslims within the dominion of those who believe in one God.

The real aim of true Muslim kings in their battles and wars should be the desire for martyrdom, and they should find a longing for it in their hearts. From the view-point of bravery, they should seek to overpower the enemy, but from the view-point of the Faith, they should desire the path of martyrdom.

[Barani then proceeds to state that Sultan Mahmud adhered to the principles he has laid down. Barani's statements in the following paragraphs have nothing to do with the actual policy of Sultan Mahmud of history, but they are excellent illustrations of his own fanatical attitude.]

No other sciences were allowed to be publicly taught in the kingdom of Sultan Mahmud except Quranic commentary (*tafsir*), the traditions of the Prophet (*hadis*) and law (*fiph*), divested of all false interpretations. In short, apart from the sciences which are based on the affirmations, 'God has said' and 'the Prophet has said', all other sciences were banned.

When Sultan Mahmud conquered Khawarazm, he heard that the Mu'tazilite creed was current there and that many men of learning were Mu'tazilites[15]. He ordered these Mu'tazilite scholars to be exiled from Khwarazm; if anyone after the promulgation of this order followed the Mu'tazilite creed or even took its name, he was to be sent bound to Ghaznin. By the God who has rescued Sultan Mahmud in every difficulty, if Ibn-i-Sina (Avicenna), who is the reviver of the philosophy of Greece and the leader of all philosophers in Muslim countries, had fallen into the hands of Sultan Mahmud, he would have ordered Ibn-i-Sina to be cut to pieces and his flesh given to kites[16]. Twelve years have elapsed since Ibn-i-Sina has absconded from Khwarazm.

At the time when Mahmud went to Gujarat to overthrow the idol of Manat (Somnath), he heard there that there was a group called Sewra[17]. They seduced the wives of grocers and led people into the false faith of agnosticism (*dahriyat*[18]). Mahmud ordered them all to be put to death.

(Sultan Mahmud, so Barani affirms, took with himself two unfulfilled desires to the grave. *First,* he wanted to capture Baghdad, which was full of erring sects, false religions and false dogmas, so that he may put to death the teachers of erroneous doctrines, philosophers, agnostics and all opponents of the *shari'at.* This statement is not historically correct; also Baghdad at the time of Sultan Mahmud had ceased to be the centre of heresy. *Secondly,* he wanted to invade India again for the complete liquidation of Hinduism. "If Mahmud", our author tells us, "with the power, prestige, soldiers, servants and equipment he possessed, had attacked India once more, he would have put to the sword all

Brahmans, who maintain the commandments of *Kufr* and the traditions of *shirk* in that wide and extensive land. He would have put two hundred thousand or three hundred thousand Hindu leaders to death and would not have replaced his Hindu-slaying sword back in its scabbard till the whole territory of India had accepted Islam and recited 'the Oath of Affirmation' (There is no god but Allah and Mohammad is His Prophet). For Mahmud belonged to the Shafi'i creed and according to Imam Shafi'i the order about Hindus is—Either Death or Islam". There is no point in translating and re-translating Barani's fanatical words. On the matter of the Hindus, Barani was mentally unsound. However, he has put his fanatical case as strongly as he could in Advice XI but with the frank confession that (a) Indo-Muslim kings do not follow the policy he desires and (b) that the Hindus are prosperous. Imam Shafi'i's doctrines about the relations of Muslims and non-Muslims were entirely the opposite of what Barani says; he believed in freedom of peaceful religious preaching, which was established by the Prophet's Treaty of Hudaibia with the Meccans. The matter is discussed in an endnote to Advice XI).

[This Advice is illustrated with the account of a meeting between the Caliph Harun-ar Rashid and the well-known mystic, Fuzail Ayaz[19]. Barani with his stupendous ignorance puts the meeting in Medina, whereas if it took place at all, it must have been at Mecca where Fuzail was living. He claims that he has taken the account from the *Tarikh-i Khulafa-i Abbasiah* (*History of the Abbasid Caliphs*) of Imam Asma'i[20]. But his having had access to the works of that author is very doubtful.]

Notes on Muhtasibs, Amir Dads, the Mu'tazilas and Ibn-i Sena

6. *Muhtasib.* Barani often refers to the *muhtasibs* and their duties. The functions of the *muhtasibs* and their Department (*Diwan-i Ihtisab*) as it functioned during the later days of the Abbasid Caliphate is discussed by Mawardi in his *Ahkamus Sultaniyah* (Urdu translation, pp. 376-405). Only a broad indication of these functions can be attempted here. The *muhtasib* could not enter any person's house; the Quran definitely forbids entrance into any house without permission. He could not consider any matter which required judicial investigation and the balancing of evidence; all

such cases went to the qazi's court, to which the *muhtasib* was subordinate. Concerning public nuisances, the morality of the streets and similar matters, the *muhtasib's* authority was confined to things proved—e.g. he could prevent a Muslim widow from marrying before the time of her *iddat* (four months and ten days after the death of her husband) and he could prohibit a person not properly qualified from issuing *fatwas*. All the multifarious affairs of municipal life—prohibition of open drinking, preventing shopkeepers from blocking the streets, provision of drinking water, supervision of weights, measures and wages, prevention of cruelty to slaves and animals, etc. came within his jurisdiction. But generally his duties were of a purely moral and persuasive type; thus if widows, who wanted husbands, appealed to him, he could only draw the attention of their guardians to the matter. Mawardi admits that in his days the Department of the *Muhtasibs* had lost its prestige. "Since the Sultans have begun appointing ordinary people to be *muhtasibs*, the office has become a source of corrupt livelihood (p. 404)." For an account of the *muhtasibs* in English based primarily on *Mawardi*, see Levy, *Sociology of Islam* (Vol. I, pp. 367-373) [H]

6. *Amir-i Dad.* Barani and other Indian writers of the middle ages often refer to the *amir-i dad* (officer for justice), the chief of whom was *Amir-i Dad-bek-i Hazrat* (the Central *Amir-i Dad*). The *amir-i dad*, a secular officer with the force of the state at his disposal, was superior to the *qazi* and took charge of those cases in which the *qazi* was helpless, such as crimes of government officers against each other and against the members of the public. The legal procedure of the middle ages did not permit an appeal from a *qazi*'s judgment to another *qazi*, but appeals could be made from the judgment of a *qazi* to the state, and such appeals would go to the *amir-i dad*. The functions of the *amir-i dads* of India seem to have been similar to those of the *Diwan-i Mazalim* of the Abbaside Caliphate. But all officers were bound to perform their duties according to their individual and specific appointment orders, and these orders often varied according to local conditions. [H]

9. *Mu'tazila.* "The Mu'tazila", says Dr. H.S. Hyberg (*Encyclopaedia of Islam*, Vol. II, p. 787) "is the name of the great theological school which created the speculative dogmatics of Islam." It is said to have been founded by Wasil bin Ata and Amar bin Ubaid, whose working life coincided with the Caliphate of Hisham and

his Umayyad successors (723-748 A.D.). The Mu'tazila flourished under the great Abbasides, specially under the Caliph Mamun. The Mu'tazilas said many wise things and raised many painful controversies. But as a living school they did not survive the great Abbasides.

Tradition is probably correct in stating that Abul Hasan Ashari (873–935 A.D.) succeeded in reviving orthodoxy and killing the Mu'tazila school. But in the centuries to come orthodox theologians kept repeating the postulates of the *Mu'tazila* in order to make a show of refuting them. The *Mu'tazila* school had completely disappeared by the time of Sultan Mahmud. Barani in his ignorance confuses the *mu'tazilas* with the leading philosophers and scientists, who had collected at Khawarazm. A fairly detailed account of the Mu'tazila doctrines and of their refutations will be found in the *Kitabul Millal-i wan Nahl* of Shahrastani, (1074–1153 A.D.) (Persian translation, pp. 4–108). According to Shahrastani, only a few *mu'tazilas* were left in his time in the lands of western Islam. [H]

10. *Ibn-i Sena* (*Avicenna*). Barani has a very vague idea of what really happened and is reckless in his dates. Shaikh Bu Ali, son of Abdullah, son of Sena, the greatest of Muslim physicians, was born in the village of Akhshiya in the territory of Bokhara in 980 A.D. His father was a revenue officer of the Samanid kingdom. His career as a student was remarkable. He did not sleep at night and he studied all day; if he was perplexed about a problem, he went and prayed in a mosque till a solution was found; if he felt weak owing to overwork, he drank wine as a tonic. "All historians agree that at the age of eighteen Shaikh bu Ali Sena had completed his study of all rational and traditional sciences and surpassed all contemporary scholars". But the Samanid kingdom was declining and Bu Ali Sena migrated to Khwarazm at the age of twenty-two. Here he was welcomed by the Khwarazm Shah, Ali bin Mamun bin Mohammad. Four other leading scientists—Abu Raihan al Beruni, Abu Sahl Mashi, Abu Nasar and Abul Khair Khammal—were also at the Khwarzmian court. Sultan Mahmud sent Abul Fazl Mikal to the Khwarazm Shah with an order that the scientists were to be sent to Ghaznin, but the Khwarazm Shah informed the scientists about Mahmud's message before granting an audience to Mikal. Al Beruni and Abul Khair preferred to

be sent to Ghaznin, but Ibn-i Sena and Abu Sahl decided to run away. Abu Sahl died of 'heat and thirst' in the Qara Qum desert, but Ibn-i Sena managed to reach Jurjan and sought protection with its cultured ruler, Qabus bin Washmgir. Meanwhile, Sultan Mahmud had ordered the circulation of the portraits of Ibn-i Sena on 'wood and paper' with the order that he be arrested and sent to Ghaznin wherever found. One of these portraits was in due course sent to Qabus Washmgir. Ibn-i Sena saw that the political fortunes of his host were on the decline and proceeded further west. The rest of his life, cataclysmic in its vicissitudes, was spent in the service of the Dailami rulers. We are told that at one time his house was plundered by the irate soldiers who also wanted to kill him. But during the period he was a wazir, he enjoyed his life to the full. After sunset he gave lessons to students and leading scholars who came to study with him from distant places; after they had dispersed, he called for his dinner, musicians and wines. When Sultan Mahmud and his son Masud marched on Iraq in 1029 A.D., Ibn-i Sena was the wazir of Alauddoulah; both king and wazir fled from fear of Mahmud to Naishapur. But Mahmud retired owing to the first signs of the galloping consumption of which he was destined to die and his son, Masud, preparing for the inevitable war of succession, left Isfahan to Alauddoulah. The great scientist survived Sultan Mahmud by seven years. When Alauddoulah started for Hamadan, he took the Shaikh with him. On the way the Shaikh's complaint of cholic increased, and on reaching Hamadan he realised that his recovery was impossible. He refrained from taking any more medicines, repented of his past sins, distributed his property among the poor and set free his slaves. For three days he read the Quran and then died on a Friday of Ramazan, 1037 A.D. (See the *Habibus Siyar* of Khondamir, Persian text, Vol. II, pp. 160–162, Tehran edition).

The greatest of the Shaikh's works are the *Kitabush Shifa* and *Al Qanun fit Tibb.* Though at present revered primarily as a physician Ali Sena's works cover the whole field of medieval learning. "He was for centuries and still is in parts of the Muslim East considered the prince of all learning, *al Shaikh, Al Rais*. In logic and epistemology he closely follows Al-Farabi. His physics, on the whole, is based on the Aristotelian tradition." (*Encyclopaedia of Islam,* Vol. III, pp. 419–420). [H]

Advice III

On the Blessings of Consultation and Advice

Sultan Mahmud says: O sons of Mahmud! You should know that the prophets of God are the best and the greatest of all created beings and that our Prophet Mohammad is the greatest of them all. And even to our Prophet, in spite of his perfect wisdom and the continuity of Divine revelation, God gave the order: "And consult them in your affairs".[21] How then can kings, who receive no Divine inspiration and whose judgment is vitiated by their passions, succeed in administering the affairs of their governments without consulting their experienced officers and sincere well-wishers? The highest objects of man's passions are self-will and domination; this is specially the case with kings, whose souls, owing to their excessive passions, become equal in power to a thousand mad elephants. But if the king subdues this madness of his soul, refrains from being self-willed, and decides the affairs of the kingdom in consultation with his advisers, the kindness of God will shine on his forehead and all his state enterprises will end in success. It has been known to all wise men, ancient and modern, that eradicating the evils of the kingdom—suppressing disturbances, undertaking great enterprises, making state-laws (*zawabit*) and discerning the ultimate consequences of state-policies—is not possible without the advice of wise and experienced men, who are the well-wishers of the government and the chosen people of the kingdom.

[Barani then proceeds to give a long and tiresome list of the duties of government and says that consultation about them is necessary].

Mahmud has read in the *Wasaya-i Jamshedi* (*Testament of Jamshed*), which Jamshed[22] wrote for his descendants: O descendants of Kaimurs[23], who attain to kingship! You are to know that prophethood was given to our grand-uncle, Shis, son of Adam, and his descendants, while kingship was given to our ancestor, Kaimurs and his descendants. Almighty God has, therefore, guided Shis and his descendants by Divine inspiration, and, consequently, there are no faults whatsoever in their words or acts. But to us, who are the descendants of Kaimurs and bear the kingly office, God has given the sword of government, and for the guidance of our hearts, He has given us accomplished ministers, so that we may, through our policy and the blows of our sword keep the world inhabited, prosperous and orderly. Great errors and defects are caused in the judgments of kings owing to the instigations of Satan and the incitements of their own passions. If kings merely give orders according to any ideas that come to their minds, they are sure to commit great errors. For this reason kings have resorted to consulting wise men (*hakims*); if some erroneous idea comes into their minds or into the minds of some of their advisers, it will not come into the minds of others, for there is seldom a unanimity of opinion in an error... Moreover, the mistakes and errors of kings are not like those of other men, for owing to the errors of kings a whole world is turned upside down... [Further, the king owing to his high position will be inclined to assume that he cannot make a mistake.] Consequently, wise men have said: "No opinion for kings." [A king should have no opinion of his own, but should be guided by his advisers].

O sons of Mahmud! You are to know that wise men have often prescribed (the following) tests for the correct judgment of kings and ministers. *First,* the counsellors should consider the good of both the parties; i.e. the good of the king as well as the good of the subjects. *Second,* the counsellors should consider the possibility of both the failure and the success of an enterprise; they should not have their attention fixed upon one alternative only. *Third,* the success of the enterprise undertaken should not injure the religion of the king and his subjects. *Fourth,* the policy adopted should lead to ultimate benefit and not merely to temporary advantages that end in final ruin. *Fifth,* success should bring good reputation and not bad reputation. *Sixth,* enemies should be turned into friends and not friends into enemies. *Seventh,* the public should be inclined to the undertaking decided upon and desire its success; it should not excite public resentment or ire. *Eighth,* the decision adopted should appear wrong to fools, idiots and persons with incorrect ideas, who in their pride will consider it to be erroneous. *Ninth,* it should lead to ease and comfort and not become the cause of endless difficulties and trials. *Tenth,* it should win the approval of all men of perfect wisdom, and there should be no difference of opinion about it. The *eleventh* test of a correct judgment is that the contemplation and execution of it is opposed to men's passions.

Asaf Barkhia, who was the wazir of the prophet Solomon and also the son of his aunt, has said concerning the dignity and prestige of good counsel: "Good counsel is a great blessing from God on His creatures." Its significance lies in the fact that everything which is going to happen is written in the Preserved Tablet (*Lauh-i Mahfuz*)[24] and that knowledge of it comes by way of inspiration to the mind of the good counsellor. Unless a man has been created for eternal bliss, his heart will not be inspired (by God) with that correct judgment, which leads to religious and secular welfare. And what greater good fortune can there be for the counsellors than this. By the light of their vision and their discerning judgments they see what is engraved about the unknown future in the Preserved Tablet, they can give reasons about what they have seen, and with their inner discernment they can discover beforehand what Destiny has ordered. Is not this a portion from the stations (*muqam*)[25] of the prophets?

The sons of Mahmud ought to know that from among the chosen men of God two persons have been kings of the inhabited world; *first,* Solomon and *secondly,* Alexander[26]. Solomon was a prophet for certain; there have been differences of opinion about Alexander, but there can be no doubt that he was at least one of the saints. For both of them rulership was a means for the elevation of their own spiritual status and securing the welfare of their subjects. The greatest blessing, which God vouchsafed to them, next to prophethood and saintship respectively, were ministers of perfect intelligence. Thus, Asaf was the wazir of Solomon and Aristotle was the wazir of Alexander. The judgments of these two wazirs were correct and without errors; consequently nothing except what was good and beneficial became current in the two kingdoms. The reigns of these two kings, therefore, have become a wonder in the ancient as well as the modern history of mankind. And apart from attaining to spiritual bliss, both wazirs became models for ancient as well as modern ministers, and their virtues and achievements will remain engraved in the hearts of men till the Day of Judgment. Further, the great reputation of Ardsher Babakan[27] and Nausherwan,[28] though they turned aside from the true Faith, spread both among friends and enemies. It has been written in the histories of Arabia and Iran that the memory of the glories of their kingdoms, which were due to the wise counsels of Abr Sam and Buzurchemehr, will survive among mankind.

[What Barani says in the next two paragraphs can be more conveniently put into plain English. If an incorrect decision, which has now to be defined as a decision not based on consultation, leads to success, then this sort of success is the miracle of the sinner (*istidraj*); persistence in such behaviour is sure to lead to ruin in this world and the next. An error is an error even if it succeeds. Conversely, if a correct decision arrived at after consultation is unsuccessful, its failure must be attributed to the will of God.]

[Mahmud advises his sons to find wise wazirs.] There is not, and cannot be, a greater source of pride and glory for a king than a wise wazir, who is inspired with correct judgment. *Without a wise wazir kingship is vain;* and the ancients have said that a king without a wise wazir is like a palace without foundations and like bread without salt. If the wazir is wise, the folly of the king does not lead to the ruin and the destruction of the kingdom; for example, many kings have ascended their hereditary thrones during their childhood and their wazirs have looked after the affairs of the state. But if the opinion of the wazir is defective, there can be no doubt about the ruin and destruction of the kingdom. Lastly, no one is entitled to the post of wazir unless the nobles and commons of the kingdom are unanimous in their opinion about his wisdom.

It is written in the book, *Ma-asir-i 'Umari* (*Traditions of Caliph 'Umar*) that Umar often declared from the pulpit: "How am I to thank Allah for the fact that he has made me ruler over the kingdom of the Prophet and so many great Companions of the Prophet (every one of whom is like the prophets of Israel, for on their hearts owing to their association with the Prophet, correct inspiration descends) have become my advisers in the affairs of the Caliphate. The Lord has enabled me to settle the affairs of the religion and the kingdom of the Prophet with their advice. And He has made them kind and affectionate towards me, so that they do not hide from me any ideas that come into their minds concerning the affairs of state."

The wazirs of ancient days have prescribed some tests for the good counsellor. *First,* fear of God. If the counsellor has plenty of obstinacy and no fear of God, he will never be inspired with that correct judgment, which leads to good ultimate results. *Second,* knowledge of ancient kings. The counsellor should have knowledge of the circumstances of ancient kings and the policies through which they escaped calamities; if he does not possess this knowledge, his judgment will be defective. *Third,* practical knowledge of state affairs acquired as a confidential officer; such experience leads to maturity of judgment. *Fourth,* perfection of intelligence; a man of perfect intelligence discovers how to realise his aims with a little reflection. *Fifth,* perfect judgment in discerning character. If a person is not capable of correctly estimating the qualities of men, he will make blunders in the allotment of duties in government enterprises. *Sixth,* lack of greed. If the counsellor happens to be greedy and avaricious, his mind will not be inspired with correct judgment on account of his greed. *Seventh,* the counsellor ought to be stout-hearted and firm of mind; correct judgment does not come to the hearts of the weak-willed and the lazy-minded; nor does it inspire the faint-hearted. *Eighth,* the counsellor should have self-respect and the virtue of forgiveness; correct judgment cannot be expected from the hasty and the ferocious. *Ninth,* an inevitable condition for every counsellor is his sincere loyalty to the king, for this is the basis of all other virtues, especially in the hearts of the wise.

Buzurchemehr has said: Policy and judgment are terms used with reference to kings and wazirs, whose decisions appertain to the carrying out of state enterprises and to great affairs. The decisions of private persons, who consult their friends about their personal affairs, which are their exclusive concern, should not be called policies. In the same way the descendants of the Prophet and of kings are referred to as *A-al* (dynasty), but not the descendants of ordinary people....

Great kings have observed many conditions about consultations and have been very cautious in the matter. Consequently, the opinion of their counsellors has seldom erred.

The *first* condition of consultation is the frank expression of opinions by the counsellors—that is, in the Royal Consultative Council (*Majlis-i Rai*)[30] all counsellors should, without any fear, be able to say whatever comes to their minds about the execution of state enterprises, to give reasons and arguments for their opinions and to discuss frankly with each other. Ultimately, when all their minds are in agreement and no objection remains, they should apply themselves to the execution of their policy.

This, in the technique of consultation, is known as "agreement of opinions" (*tawafuq-i ara*). No reliance can be placed upon any decision arrived at unless there is unanimous agreement.

Second, the counsellors ought to be permanent; and they should be nearly equal to each other in their experience, in their loyalty and in their status before the king. If one counsellor is perfect in intelligence and the others are defective, one high in status and the others insignificant, there will be a danger of incongruity (*shutur-gurbah*) in the decisions arrived at.

Third, all counsellors should be acquainted with the secrets of the state and none of them should be unworthy of being taken into confidence. If a counsellor has no information concerning the secrets of the state, he will not be able to arrive at a correct decision, just as a physician cannot prescribe proper remedies unless he knows the real symptoms and diseases of the patient.

Fourth, the counsellors, in addition to having been chosen by the king and being near to him, ought to have perfect security for their lives and their posts, so that they may not resort to flattery in the Royal Consultative Council. They should be able to express their real opinions, with the lid taken off, and they should be convinced that this free speech will lead to the increased recognition of their loyalty. They should have no reason to be afraid of the ill-temper of the king, for so long as fear of the king tortures their breasts, sincere advice will not come from their hearts to their tongues.

Fifth, the king should (to begin with) keep his opinions secret from the Consultative Council. He should, first, acquaint himself with the opinions of his counsellors, hear the views they have to express and wait for the decision they arrive at. If the king expresses his opinion in the Council at the beginning, the counsellors will find it necessary, willingly or unwillingly, to praise his decision and to suppress their own views. No one will have the courage to oppose the decision of the king or to give any reasons against it. This fact has been proved by experience.

Sixth, the discussions of state affairs should be undertaken at the purest time (*safi tarin waqt*); in particular, the discussions should be held before eating and drinking. Many kings have kept fasts during the days of consultations and have asked their counsellors to fast also. In the hope that correct decision may come to the hearts of the kings and their advisers, they have made pilgrimages to the graves of saints; they have also asked for Divine assistance by the distribution of charities and have wept and prayed to God. They have not considered these consultations a useless formality but the very essence of all government business. And lastly, persons who do not know what proper decisions mean and who are not aware of the fact that the minds of the officers receive inspiration from God about what is good and evil, have not been allowed to come near the Consultative Council.

Seventh, if the agreement of the opinions of the counsellors is not against their passions (*hawa*) and dangers arise in the execution of their decision, then this unanimity of opinion should be carefully reconsidered. It should be borne in mind that any decision, which is in consonance with the passions and action according to which is pleasing to the mind, is not likely to be free from defects. The understanding of this subtlety about consultations is beyond the apprehension of the greedy victims of desire; only far-sighted wazirs can comprehend it. All errors into which kings have fallen have been due to the fact that their decisions have been in consonance with their passions and have, therefore, appeared to them to be good and pleasing. But as the decisions which they considered to be good were really erroneous, and they had failed to discern the merits and demerits of their counsellors, they ended by throwing their kingdoms to the winds by following injudicious and wrong decisions. It is possible to give lengthy explanations about the aforesaid condition, but at this place for the sake of brevity I have only written so much... [The next two paragraphs have been rendered useless owing to the lacunae, but the surviving sentences show that they were only repetitive. The Advice is brought to an end by some paragraphs in praise of Sultan Mahmud.]

[As the first Illustration to this Advice, Barani refers to the Caliph Umar's well-known policy of consulting the senior Companions in all government affairs. He also refers to a particular incident on the basis of the *Tarikh-i Mukhtasar* of Waqidi[31]. When Abu Ubaidah Saqafi, who had been sent with an army against the Persians was defeated and slain, the Caliph was so pained by the misfortune that he decided to lead the campaign against the Persians in person. But the senior Companions prevailed upon him to allow them to discuss the matter and it was decided to put Sa'd bin Wiqas in charge[32]. Sa'd defeated the Persians at the famous battle of Qadsiya (November 635 AD) and captured Madain, the capital of Persia].

[The second Illustration is of the opposite type. During the struggle with Mua'wiya, the Caliph Ali decided to move from Medina to Kufa. Some senior Companions—among whom Barani enumerates Sa'd bin Wiqas, Abdullah bin Umar, Usama bin Zaid Mughaira Shubah and Abu Ayyub Ansari[33]—protested against the Caliph Ali's going to Mecca, but he did not abide by their advice.]

Advice IV

On Correct Determination; Difference Between Correct Determination and Tyranny and Despotism

Correct determination is the robe of kingship and the garb of royalty, and in the technical language of religious kings, correct determination is very different from tyranny and despotism, though they may appear to be similar.

The rulers, who before our time have kept the world in security and order through their justice and kindness, have said that correct determination (*azm-i durust*) is a necessary condition of government. If a king shows correct determination in the enterprises of government, and permits no weakness or disorder in the management of affairs, his political designs will be realised sooner and with greater ease. Further, his prestige will be established more firmly in the hearts of his enemies and friends; faith in his firmness of will, which is the pillar of state-affairs, will be engraved more effectively on the minds of those who are far and near; the fear his rivals have of him will not decrease; and the subjects will have confidence that, if the king has undertaken an enterprise, he will not withdraw his hands from it till it has been accomplished. This public confidence in the king's firmness of will is very useful to the administration. If, on the other hand, the king obtains a reputation for weakness of will, and his vacillation and inconstancy in the prosecution of affairs become visible to the people, then his well-wishers will lose their confidence in the permanence of his favours, his enemies will have no fear of him, the *ra'iyyat* will have no assurance about the proper execution of his orders and prohibitions, the public will have no respect for his words and deeds, and he will have no prestige left among his equals. The Persian word, *azm*, means 'turning one's face to any action', and *azm* and *qasd* are equivalent terms. If a man turns his face towards any action, he is said to have 'determined' or 'resolved' upon it. Now 'determination' (*azm*) or 'resolution' (*qasd*) may be for good or evil, for welfare or disruption, for religious affairs or worldly affairs; and the result of it may be beneficial or harmful. Also the resolution may appertain to things possible or impossible, to difficult enterprises or easy matters; it may bring prosperity or ruin, good reputation or bad reputation, profit or loss. In other words, 'will' in the abstract has no moral character; but when in actual operation, it may be good or bad.

Now kings have visualised their 'determination' as follows. Anything they resolve upon, persist in and do not give up, is for them 'the determination of kings'; that is, when kings have determined upon a thing, there is not and cannot be any turning aside from it—just as there can be no turning aside of the verdict of Destiny. And Satan has laughed at their beards and moustaches and put this idea into their dark minds: "You are the gods of this earth; there should be no turning aside from your determination, for if your determination can be changed, then people will not worship you as gods."

Now every resolve (*qasd*) of kings should be considered 'correct determination' if its object is well-being, welfare, virtue, good reputation, or if it is a means to beneficial ends, provided, of course, that the king's object is within the bounds of the possible. Persistence in such a resolve has been a source of pride for them. On the other hand, the terms 'despotism' (*satihash*) and 'tyranny' (*istibdad*) have been applied to all royal determinations when their object has been mischievous and evil, or if they have been impossible of attainment or have actually led to ruin, public hatred, distress and misfortune. To turn aside from such tyrannical and despotic determinations, it has been correctly written and said, is the basis of the religious character of kings, and the great men of the religion and the state have not considered it a weakness of will. If, however, a king of Islam, owing to his fearlessness, has shown persistence in his defective and evil determinations and has followed in the footsteps of tyrants and Kisras[34], the religious scholars and wise men of Islam have called it 'despotism' and 'tyranny' and not 'correct determination'.

It is the duty of kings, before they have made up their minds about an enterprise or policy and published it among the people, to reflect carefully on the likelihood of its success and failure as well as its effect on their own position, on the religion and the state, and on the army and the people. They should, in confidential meetings with their counsellors, discuss all aspects of the enterprise—its beginning and its termination, its incidental effects, its ease and its difficulties and the alternative results of persistence and retreat. With the eyes of insight—and not with the eyes of terror and rulership, which are always blind to ultimate consequences—they should find out whether their enterprises for good objects are possible and realisable; they should also ensure that wise men do not consider them impossible or shudder at their being accomplished. With reference to an enterprise thus undertaken, the kings should publish their determination, persist in it and try to realise their aims and objects as soon as possible. If all their treasures have to be spent on the enterprise, they should spend them, so that they may have applied the principle of the 'determination of kings' at the proper occasion....

The kings of Islam in determining upon enterprises and managing their affairs should look to the 'determinations' and 'resolutions' of the Prophet and the Pious Caliphs. They should also consider the principle of 'cancelling' (*nasikh*) and 'cancelled' (*mansukh*) in the verses of the Quran and the traditions of the Prophet[35]. We have to reflect that even in the sphere of the *shari'at,* which it would be infidelity to attribute to anyone except God, orders have been cancelled—the original orders have been abrogated and people have been asked to obey new orders. The object of royal consultations is the welfare of the religion and the state. Thus Almighty God says in the Quran: "We do not cancel a verse or cause it to be forgotten (but) bring one better than it or one like it."[36] A king will not be condemned for weakness of will if he gives up his enterprise and resolution for the sake of the public good and does not owing to the false doctrine of 'royal determination' behave like a despot and a tyrant. On the other hand, if he makes his passions his guides in his enterprises, while the prestige and power of kingship in turn strengthen his passions, and he undertakes enterprises which lead to his fall and the fall of his people, he will have overthrown himself and his people with his own hands. And of what use then will the doctrine of 'the determination of kings' be to him in this world or the next?

Nevertheless if the king begins an enterprise for his own welfare and the good of his people and wisdom and experience have no doubt about its advisability, and then his resolve slackens and he gives up the enterprise, he will, no doubt, obtain a reputation for weakness of will. No one will have any further confidence in his enterprises, and his prestige will be injured, for his orders will in future sit lightly on the hearts of the people.

The following Illustrations are given for this Advice.

(1) The Caliph Abu Bakr's very wise and statesmanlike decision not to make any compromise with 'apostates' is referred to on the basis of the *Tarikh* (*History*) of Imam Waqidi[37].

(2) The determination which the Caliph Mutasim showed in conquering Umriyya from the Byzantines is approved; the incident is quoted on the authority of the *Tarikh-i-Khulafa-i Abbasi* (History of the Abbasid Caliphs)[38].

(3) Mahmud's persistence in marching on Somnath in spite of a large fall of hail-stones[39].

(4) The insolent behaviour of Khusrau Parvez[40], king of Iran, towards the Arabian Prophet. The Iranian king brushed aside the advice of his wazir, who wanted him to leave the Prophet alone, and passed an order for the Prophet's arrest, which it was found impossible to execute. But before matters could go further, Khusrau Parvez was killed by his own son.

(5) The order of Yazid, son of the Caliph Mu'awiyah, issued against the advice of his counsellors, ordering his officers at Medina to exact the oath of allegiance to himself from Imam Husain son of Hazrat Ali, Abdullah bin Umar and Abdullah bin Abbas.

Advice V

On the King's Justice

Sultan Mahmud advises: O Sons of Mahmud! You should know that from the time of Adam to our own days, the select as well as the common people of all communities, ancient and modern, are united in the opinion that justice is a necessary condition of religion and that religion is a necessary condition of justice. For it is not possible for the sons of Adam to live without having dealings with each other; and in these mutual dealings a person may be strong or weak, good or bad, Muslim or non-Muslim, wise or foolish, learned or illiterate, citizen or villager, resident or traveller, deceptive or straightforward, ruler or subject, minor or grown-up.

Now justice is the balance in which the actions of people, good or bad, are weighed. The distinction between righteous and wrongful claims is clarified by justice. Justice exposes cruelty, oppression, forceful misappropriation and plunder. Consequently, there can be no stability in the affairs of men without justice. No religion, which is founded on Divine Commandments (*ahkam*), can do without justice. Both ancient and modem thinkers have said, 'Religion and justice are twins.' For justice breaks the strong arm of the tyrannical, the oppressive and the mighty—of misappropriators, plunderers, rebels, traitors, the people of incest (*ibahatis*)[41] and disbelievers in the Day of Judgment and Accounts—in order to protect the money, property, women and children of the weak, the obedient, the helpless, the young, the submissive and the friendless. Justice prevents tyranny and oppression through the mandates of religion. If there was no justice and equity on the earth, there would be complete community of women and property (*ibahat*); the distinction between one man's property and another's would vanish; no time or place would be free from disorder, and no son of Adam would be able to drink his cup of water in his corner in peace or to stretch his legs and sleep on his bed in security for a single night; and, finally, the world would cease to be prosperous owing to immense tumults and disorders.

A ruler with force and authority is needed to enforce justice among the people. For if all the wise men of the earth try to govern a village, or even a household, through mere policy or precepts of wisdom without judges endowed with power, they will not succeed. Justice is the basis of the social organisation and the civil order, and it is administered by the strong ruler among the people. The real justification for the supremacy[1] of kings and of their power and dignity is the need for enforcing justice. Through their royal power and prestige the kings can prevent the strong from having recourse to oppression in their dealings with the people; the seventy-two communities[42] can then attain contentment of heart and everyone can devote himself to his art, profession and means of livelihood, and the world can become inhabited and prosperous. If there is no justice, no one will be able to help or rescue another and no one will be able to obtain any profit from his work. Finally, if the affairs of men are not organised at the 'centre', there will be no stability in works of Faith or the commandments of Islam and recompense and punishments will not bear their fruits.

Further, the object of the creation of mankind was the worship of God. As Almighty God has said in the Quran—"We have not created men or jins except that they may worship Us."[43] (Barani here refers to a doctrine, which he explains in detail later, that the virtues inculcated by Islam are directly opposed to those qualities which a king has to develop in himself if he is to perform his functions properly. These qualities are akin to Divine attributes. Consequently kings claim Divine attributes for themselves and the proper place for such claimants, in Barani's opinion, is 'darkness within darkness'). Now if some worldly-minded scholars of Islam (*ulama-i dunya*)[44] consider it permissible for Muslim kings to claim Divine attributes, the reason for it is that the king can come to the rescue of the helpless and enforce the claims of the oppressed. Owing to the king's power and authority the enforcement of justice attains to excellence, no rebel or traitor is allowed to oppress the weak and the helpless, the molestors of the Faith and the *shari'at* are overthrown and disgraced, the royal orders are enforced on the seventy-two communities, and by the just orders of the king the glory of Islam is raised; and thus owing to the consequences of the commands of religion the world is put into order and kept in order.

Since all virtues, devotions and acts of beneficence and kindness only become possible owing to the enforcement of justice, the holy Prophet has said: "The justice of one moment is better than the devotions of seventy years." This sort of exaggeration has not been used concerning any other act of religion. Further, as only the justice of the king has made all good acts possible, there is put down to the credit of the king a Divine reward, which is equal in quantity to the total reward earned by the people through their virtuous deeds, and this reward is not subject to any misfortune or cataclysm.

The divine Plato (*Aflatun-i Ilahi*)[45] has declared: Kings do not realise the value of their authority, which is a great blessing. They merely use their position and the power it brings to them for the satisfaction of worldly desires and for the attainment of those pleasures and enjoyment of life, in which they are on a par with wild animals and beasts. But when the power of kingship is used for the satisfaction of desires, the kings are so overcome by their passions that they cannot distinguish between the blessings and the wrath of God. And owing to their unbridled passions and excessive power, they just do what they like. Yet public justice is a necessary condition of kingship and the supreme command; and if the quality of justice is innate in kings and predominant in their actions, no virtues, except the virtues of the prophets, can be higher than the virtues of kings.

The great men of religion and the state from ancient as well as modern communities have said: Man has not, in any matter which appertains to human affairs, been ordered to go to extremes or excesses. A long time has passed since they propounded the precept—In all actions moderation is best[46]. The duty of moderation in all actions is also approved by the *shari'at* and reason. Nevertheless, it is necessary for the king to go to extremes in the enforcement of justice. If justice is not an innate virtue in the king and if all his other virtues are not inspired by the desire for justice and equity, the effect of his justice will not become visible in the behaviour of his sons, relations, companions, slaves, supporters, followers, friends, qazis and government officers, who are his partners and co-sharers in the work of the state; and till all the officers of the king are not just and equitable, the ordinary people will also have no regard for justice in their dealings with each other... A king is just only if no injustice is left in his country and all oppressors have been overthrown. If a single person behaves tyrannically in the country and his tyranny continues in spite of the king's knowledge of it, then the king is not just and impartial, The sign of the enforcement of justice by the king and his officers is that calamities and misfortunes seldom befall the realm and the favours of Heaven constantly descend upon it...

Injustice is excused to the king in the matter of expenditure. The money the king takes from the Public Treasury for himself and his supporters is necessary, for kingship cannot be maintained unless the king and his officers live with dignity and prestige. Nevertheless, in every expense that he incurs the king should consider whether it is necessary; and while maintaining his supporters (from the Public Treasury) he should not forget the answer he will have to give for it on the Day of Judgment. If the king does not keep these considerations in view, and seeks only to please himself by spending money recklessly on himself and his followers, his position will be one of great spiritual danger. He must know for certain that while others spend the public treasures on their pleasures and enjoyments, he will be unable to answer (for this wastage of public money) on the Day of Judgment[47].

But as to the king's gifts to the leaders of the Saiyyeds, religious scholars, *shaikhs*[48], men of virtue or wisdom or skill, persons of merit, travellers, the helpless and the needy his grants to schools and mystic houses (*khanqahs*)[49] and his expenditures on all occasions where charity is recommended—the more there is of all this, the greater will be the king's success in this world and his rewards in the next. In such matters there can be no question of excessive expenditure or lack of thrift. The precept that there can be no over-expenditure in good works is based on this principle.

[With reference to this Advice the following Illustrations are given. (1) Some leaders of non-Muslim groups as well as big feudal magnates protested to Abu Ubaidah Jarrah,[50] the Governor of Syria, against the poverty in which the Caliph Umar was living. Abu Ubaidah sent them to Medina along with the seven thousand camel-loads of spoils he had collected. They saw the Caliph distribute the spoils in three days outside Medina and return empty-handed to his house. (2) Barani quotes the *Tarikh-i-Abbasi* as stating that on one occasion the Caliph Mamun was so generous in the award of Id-gifts that the hoarded treasures of the Caliphate were distributed away and the government had for a time to be run on loans. (3) The Caliph Mamun had appointed his son, Abdullah, to succeed him. But one day he overheard a conversation between Abdullah and his servant, which convinced him that Abdullah was remarkably stingy. He thereupon called an assembly (*mahzar*) cancelled his nomination of Abdullah and appointed his brother, Mutasim, to succeed him.]

Advice VI

On the Grading of Officers and Notables

Sultan Mahmud has said: Sons of Mahmud and Kings of the earth! You are to know clearly that the basic duties of the king are divisible into two broad heads: *First*, the discharge of his obligations towards the generality of his subjects through affection, kindness, generosity and good treatment, *secondly*, the discharge of his obligations towards the notables (*khawas*) of the kingdom.

The claims of the notables are of various kinds—e.g. relationship to the Prophet through the Prophet's daughter (*sayadat*), learning, piety, descent from noble citizens, and other merits such as courage, experience, technical skill and excellence of manners (*adab*). It is the duty of the king's government to confer rewards in recognition of every merit. In the same way as the king bestows gifts and awards to his supporters (of various grades) out of regard for their loyalty to himself, he should also create ranks and grades of the notables of his kingdom (who are not in government service) on the basis of their merit and pay them according to their estimated claims.

The holy Prophet has said: 'Give to every true claimant his due.' A king of perfect wisdom deals with the common people as well as the notables—his sons, brothers, associates, loyal officers, servants of the court and the select men of the kingdom—after putting them into defined ranks and grades. If he does so, there will be no confusion (*shutur gurbah*) in his gifts and presents and in the dignity and status of his officers; his arrangements will not be thrown into confusion; rightful claimants will not go unrewarded; love for him will grow in the hearts of his subjects; and in consequence of all this, his administration will become firm.

Ardshir Babakan, whose words and deeds were regarded as precedents by the Kisras of Iran in the affairs of government, has said: He alone can be considered a righteous king who in his dealings with the people has regard for their ranks and grades, so that all his subjects become his loyal well-wishers. Then if a calamity befalls the king, all his subjects in their hearts consider themselves his partners and co-sufferers; they try to help him and until the mind of the king is not at ease, his subjects also find no peace or rest in their hearts. This good fortune is not possible unless the king creates general ranks and grades of notables, and gives a portion of that dignity and power, which God has bestowed on him, to every notable according to his birth and merits; for God has made the whole world dependent on his doorsteps and his gate is an altar (*qibla*) for the realisation of the necessities of the people.

But as to the adventurer, who collects a large number of people on his side, caring for no right or merit in them except their loyalty to himself, he is to be called a usurper and not a king. Such a usurper rules the country through the power of his followers; he strikes, takes, seizes and bestows, and thus every day he is able to show more favours to his supporters. He increases their prestige and dignity, thinking that the permanence of his kingdom is due to them, and strives for their prosperity without paying any regard to their real defects and merits. The eyes of such an adventurer are turned away from God Almighty; he is all the time exclusively devoted to his helpers and supporters; and, finally, matters come to such a pass that he turns all low, mean, base, defective and worthless men, who are of bad and low origin, into the pillars of his state, provided only that he discerns in them sincere loyalty towards himself along with substantial power and prestige. No doubt thousands and thousands of such usurpers have arisen on this earth from every class that can be imagined; they have ruled for a little while with the support of a body of partisans and have then taken themselves and their followers to Hell. At the same time they have also left this earth in such a way that neither their names nor any traces of them have remained in the conversations or the hearts of the people. But all rulers, whose eyes have been wholly fixed on God Almighty, have created general grades and ranks of merit based on good birth, piety, nobility, wisdom, skill and morality; they have discharged their obligations to every merit through the resources of their governments and to the full extent of their power; and in the discharge of their obligations they have looked at everyone with the same eye. Their memory will remain till the Day of Judgment among the people of God, and this fact is a sufficient proof of their salvation and dignity in the next world.

O sons of Mahmud! You ought to know that concerning all officers of the court from the gate-keeper upwards, whose posts have been created by the wise men of the past, the design has been to define the grade and status of every royal servant, so that, in accordance with their worth and their loyalty, the claims of all officers may be kept in view by the king's court. (Barani then recurs to his favourite obsession. The noble born men in the king's court will bring him honour, but if he favours low-born men, they will disgrace him in both the worlds.)

If the king does not reward merit in accordance with permanent orders for fixing ranks and grades, many things disapproved by reason and religion will have to be tolerated:

First, the elevation of the unworthy and the disgrace of those eternally worthy will lead to despotism in government policy, and this will bring about religious and secular ruin.

Second, if the base-born are honoured and given precedence over the nobles and the free-born, the low-born will often be appointed to government offices and the well-born will have to serve and obey them. It will then become necessary for the king to be despotic and tyrannical.

Third, in promoting the low-born and degrading the well-born the king, so to say, bears witness to his own base origin.

Fourth, the helpers and supporters of the king—his wazirs, governors, judges, officers and army-commanders—should be persons of merit and should not be involved in any baseness. And this object is not attained without creating ranks and grades of merit and without exposing baseness and worthlessness. Therefore, the publication of ranks and grades of notables is obligatory for the king. (It is implied that if there are no grades, no promotion or demotion will be possible.)

Men of experience have said that the merits, which entitle a man to honour and dignity at the king's court, are of two kinds:

First, there is 'absolute merit', which has to be tested by the touchstone of reason and the mirror of experience, for many base men have the appearance of the meritorious. Publishing ranks and grades of persons, who are endowed with 'absolute merit', is useful to the king in issuing the orders of government; thereby the man of merit obtains his reward and becomes aware of his estimated rights. Further, the public display of those merits, which have been attained by personal efforts, becomes a means for elevating the low character of others. On the other hand, persons involved in vices are rid of their false expectations. So there is a great advantage in publishing the grades of every merit (after careful examination). And with reference to every merit, if we reflect upon it, there will be a low, a medium and a high degree—e.g. in birth, in genealogy, in learning, in wisdom and excellence of good behaviour, in fine arts and in varieties of skills. These qualities and virtues indicate 'absolute merit' and in accordance with the degree of their merit—low, medium and high—the notables are entitled to recognition at the king's court.

The *second* kind of merit is 'relative to the king'. When God makes a man the ruler (*amir*) of a country, he gives him honour and dignity above everyone else and makes the inhabitants of the land dependent upon him. The high position of the king brings dignity to his sons, brothers, relatives, well-wishers, partisans, courtiers and slaves. Merit of this kind cannot be called absolute but there can be no doubt about its being 'relative'. For example, good birth is an absolute merit, but relationship to the king is a greater merit than good birth. Thus the legality of power bears its fruits, and the aforementioned groups, as a matter of necessity, become co-sharers and partners of the king in affairs of state. Relationship to the king becomes the basis of their rights, and these merits, though they are relative, becomes superior to other merits, which are 'absolute'.

But controversy is about this. If those who have the merit of being the king's relatives are base, mean and low-born, how can they have a right to offices of the state and positions of dignity? Much has been said about the matter. That all or most possessors of merits should be of low or mean birth is exceptional; and there can be no law about exceptions. And some great men have also said, *"The possession of state-power makes men of mean qualities into possessors of merit."* Nevertheless, the publication of the ranks and grades of merit is one of the obligatory duties of kings, *and the basic principle of all such distinctions is the fact of birth.*

(Two Illustrations are offered for this Advice. (1) Claiming the authority of the *Tarikh-i Ma-asir-i Sahabah* (*History of the Good Deeds of the Companions*), Barani explains how the Caliph Umar divided the Musalmans into classes and grades[51]. (2) The *Tarikh-i Abbasiah* (*History of the Abbasides*) of Iman Sualibi, Barani would have us believe, says that the Caliph Mamun also fixed the ranks of all notables among the servants of the Caliphate and of the (leading) inhabitants of Baghdad.

Advice VII

On the Army

Sultan Mahmud has said: O sons of Mahmud! You ought to know that without a large, powerful and magnificent army and the proper management of its affairs, it has not been possible for any ruler or king, ancient or modern, to attain to any of the following objects: Preserving the kingship; directing the administration; establishing the prestige of his conquests to the hearts of the people and bringing the world under his control; crushing rebels and adventurers and subduing the refractory and the disobedient, suppressing the contentions of rivals and the opposition of equals and the hostility of the powerful; overthrowing the enemies of the religion and the state of the Prophet; uprooting molestors of the Muslim *shari'at* and establishing the glory of the True Creed over false religions; making the orders of the *shari'at* current among the seventy-two communities; conquering countries and provinces from the infidels with the blows of the sword and obtaining booty beyond reckoning for the victors and holy warriors and for those rightfully entitled to it among the Musalmans; and closing all avenues to the enemies of the country and the molestors of the government.

Kal-Khusrau[52], who was the ruler of the whole inhabited world, propounded the precept: 'Kingship is the army and the army is kingship'. Kingship is maintained by two pillars—the first pillar is administration and the second pillar is conquest. Both pillars are supported by the army. For if there is no army, or if the army is small, demoralised and disorderly, neither good administration nor conquests will be possible. Therefore great kings have said that the heart of the ruler should be always devoted to the army, for only then will the affairs of the army be properly managed. If the king is negligent about the army, he will be destroying both the army and the kingdom with his own hands. Also, if the king's heart is devoted exclusively to the collection of treasures, the affairs of the army will not be properly managed; no treasures will be collected and even what the king possesses will be soon lost. But if the king's attention is concentrated on the army, then it will be organised and equipped properly; and owing to the strength of the army he will collect more wealth than can be accommodated in any treasury. This fact has been obvious to wise men for years and it has also been proved by experience.

The historians of Iran have written that they asked Jamshed: 'What is the basis of kingship?' Jamshed replied: 'Plenty of soldiers and excess of justice and kindness.' Three times they put the same question to Jamshed and every time he gave the same reply. Then they asked him: 'What is your reason for giving precedence to a large number of soldiers over justice and beneficence?' Jamshed replied: 'If the world is not kept in subjection by the army, if the disobedience of traitors is not turned into obedience, and if through the strength and the power of the army law and order are not maintained, neither the enforcement of justice nor royal beneficence will be possible.'

Alexander asked Aristotle: "On what things does the large size and the proper organisation of the army, which is the basis of kingship, depend?"

Aristotle replied: "An army becomes large and stable through four things. *First,* the affairs of the army should have the exclusive and whole-hearted attention of the king; under no circumstances must he fail to attend to them and he ought to know for certain that his existence is dependent upon the existence of the army.

"*Second,* the army becomes large and well-organised by the bold expenditure of enormous treasures. Unless money is spent recklessly, the army will not become large and well-organised.

"*Third,* the officers should be affectionate and kind to their soldiers and they should possess the virtues which have been specified by wise men. The king comes into contact with the army only occasionally but the officers have to live and deal with their men day and night. If their qualities of leadership are defective, the army will not be properly maintained.

"*Fourth,* the cause of the large size and strength of the army is the excellence of the *Central Ariz* (*Ariz-Asl*), also called Minister of War (*Ariz-i Mumalik*[53]) to whose judgment and care all the general, and detailed affairs of the army are assigned. The *Central Ariz* should possess the king's confidence to the same extent as the wazir and in loyalty to the king he should reach the extreme limit. He should be unsurpassed in trustworthiness, efficiency, honesty, affection of heart, truthfulness, noble birth, dignity correctness of faith and the fulfilment of promises. The greater the loyalty and the orthodox virtues (*ausaf-i sunniah*) of the *Ariz,* the greater will be the size and the strength of the army he can control. Further, when a *Central Ariz* with perfect judgment and all *possible* virtues is appointed, these qualities will also be found in all the army officers. Such an *Ariz* will not assign the charge of the army to base-born idiots, mischief makers, liars and crooks; he will only appoint to the higher army commands officers who are of good character, good behaviour, experienced and trustworthy. Even if a military enterprise is great and difficult, it will succeed according to the king's wishes—and no fear about its success will be entertained by discerning men—if the army from top to bottom has been put in the charge of good, wise and kindly officers.

When Alexander heard Aristotle's reply, he asked him again: "What should be the extent of the king's devotion to the affairs of the army?" Aristotle replied: "The king's devotion to the affairs of the army should be such that he may desire to give away his own horses and arms to every horseman to enable him to enlist in the army as a *murattab* (fully-equipped cavalier). If he sees or hears of any defect in the army, he is unable to sleep to his satisfaction, to have any peace of mind or to devote his attention to anything else until, by whatever means that are available, he has removed that defect."

Alexander next asked for an elucidation of the qualities that are necessary for the army-officer (*sar-lashakar*). "There are", Aristotle replied, "ten qualities that are necessary for the army officer; *First,* fear of God; if there is no fear of God in him, he ought not to be assigned the command of even ten horsemen. And if they ignore this postulate of wisdom and experience and appoint an officer who has no fear of God, they will see from him what they will see. *Second,* loyalty to the king; if a person is not loyal to the king, a post in the army, which is the pillar of kingship, should not be assigned to him. *Third,* balance of mind; if the officer has not a balanced mind, the fact of so many persons being obedient to his orders will put wrong ideas into his head and this will be injurious both to him and to his subordinates. *Fourth,* nobility of birth; if the officer is not of good birth, the soldiers will not be secure from him and he will not be capable of any enterprise in support of the religion or the state. *Fifth,* faithfulness; the officer should be so faithful that he may not try to sit on a new branch every time. *Sixth,* experience of war; if the officer has no experience of war, he will not be able to keep himself and his men in security. *Seventh,* the officer should belong to a good tribe and have followers from it; if so, he will be worthy of confidence and the soldiers will have respect for him, while at the same time his tribe and his followers will be a surety for his good behaviour. *Eighth,* the officer ought to be courageous and clever and expert in affairs. *Ninth,* he ought to be generous, so that he may not be willing to see his soldiers hungry and naked; the permanent stability of the army cannot be left to miserly people. *Tenth,* truthfulness of speech and purity of mind, so that the soldiers have trust in his words and deeds, and he does not, in the presence of absence of any man, look at his women or children, whenever an officer has the aforementioned qualities, everyone under his command will be satisfied and secure."

(On the basis of a book, *Ma-asirul Wuzara,* Barani declares once more that all disorders arise because low-born men are appointed to high posts.)

(Barani returns to the topic of the *Central Ariz* and makes Ardsher Babakan declare as follows:)

The *Ariz* should be kinder to the soldiers than a mother and a father; and he should throw a veil over the crimes of his men. He should punish and put right the soldiers in the same way as a kind father punishes an undutiful son; he should not resort to extreme cruelties and punishments, and in every penalty that he inflicts he should keep the door of reconciliation open. He should be able to discriminate (between offences) so that loyal and brave officers are not deprived of their dignity for every small fault. He should be content to punish wrong-doers and criminals, who have been impelled by their passions, by depriving them of their prestige, administering a few lashes and handing them to the military police (*sahmal hashman*) for being kept in confinement. He should from time to time keep the king informed of the crimes and defects of the army and, so far as possible, he should prevent the king from inflicting death-penalties and severe and harsh punishments on the army personnel. He should not make the king the enemy of the army, or the army the enemy of the king. He should consider the misfortunes of the soldiers to be his own misfortunes; he should be saddened at the sorrows and delighted at the joys of his men; and he should find his peace of mind, comfort and ease in providing properly for them. In all affairs and in all conditions, the *Ariz* should deal with the army in such a way that its confidence in him does not decrease; his awe and dignity should be inscribed in the hearts of the men, and owing to their excessive confidence in him, the troopers should deem themselves to be his tribesmen (*khail*), followers, slaves and servants. To deal according to the above-mentioned principles with so many thousands and thousands of men of different tempers and variegated characters needs the genius of a Buzurchmehr or an Asaf.

The rulers of the past have been extremely careful about the collection and preservation of their forces; and in this matter, which is the most important enterprise of the state, they have ignored no principle suggested by wisdom and experience. Only thus have they been able to collect four hundred thousand or five hundred thousand selected warriors, whom they have kept armed and fully-equipped. Owing to the strength of their army, they have prosecuted world-conquests and brought countries and realms within their sway. They achieved great enterprises for the sake of the religion and the state, and owing to their good deeds their names will survive to the Day of Judgment. It is the duty of rulers to follow the precepts of such great kings and not the advice of people who have no knowledge of the affairs of government and who cannot properly administer a town or even a village. Such persons may be experts in all branches of learning, such as law, literature, eloquence, grammar and poetry, but their acquaintance with those branches of knowledge which are needed for the affairs of government and conquests is meagre and, in fact, quite useless.

[The following five regulations are attributed to the Caliph Harun-ar Rashid on the authority of the *Tarikh-i Khulafa-i Abbasi* (*History of the Abbasid Caliphs*)].

First Regulation—An account of the enlistment of soldiers in the army should be brought to the king's knowledge year after year, and it should be made clear before the king's throne as to who has been enlisted and the place from where he has come.

Second Regulation—The king should know correctly the amount of salary which, in years of plenty and scarcity, is needed to provide equipment for the soldiers and to set their minds at ease about the needs of their families.

Third Regulation—It is necessary after examination to prepare a record of the horses and arms of the men twice a year. The soldiers should be examined by persons concerning whom there can be no suspicion of misappropriation or falsehood so that there may be no tumult at the time of postings or during battles. This review (*arz*) should be at such times and places that it can be finished at one stretch.[54] The order of review should be for all.

Fourth Regulation—The veterans (*ghazis*) and holy warriors (*mujahids*) should be tested in the art of horsemanship, so that other people, who have nothing to do with the art of war and belong to groups of artisans or other professions, do not find a place among them. The enrolment of amateurs among veterans throws the work of the army into disorder.

Fifth Regulation—To secure the increase and stability of the army, the officers ought to be select and distinguished men, well-born, brave and virtuous.

Mahmud has had to strive for twelve years to collect and organise 30,000 horsemen from among his slaves. Of these 30,000 slave-horsemen, 15,000 are Hindus and 15,000 are from the countries of China and Khita.[55] Perhaps if all the old and young among their families are counted, they would amount to more than a hundred thousand souls. He has found both advantages and disadvantages in collecting an army of slaves.

First, owing to a large number of slaves the king looks powerful and dignified. If a king has plenty of military equipment and a large number of elephants, his power and greatness are proclaimed and his enemies, both far and near, are terrified; a large body of slave-soldiers creates the same impression. The king seems to be of great value in the eyes of men owing to his numerous and well-equipped slaves.

Second, in order to maintain their peculiar distinction and to establish their superiority in courage and loyalty over the king's ordinary servants, the slaves enter into battles and fort-sieges before the rest of the army; and they strive with their hearts and souls for the success of every enterprise. They hurl themselves like balls into running waters and flaming fires. Then it becomes necessary for the whole army to take the same path as they have done. The value of the slaves (as a shock-battalion) is obvious.

Third, the pride and arrogance of the army-officers decreases at the sight of their organisation.[66] When the slaves are numerous, no community or group from fear of them can think of over-powering the government; they know that the slaves are a hostile organisation, and that they will not befriend or follow anyone not from their own group. This too is not a small advantage.

The disadvantages of collecting slaves and keeping them together are these. Most of the slaves are reckless and shameless.

Fear of God and the characteristics of hereditary Islam, which are mixed with the fluids and tendons of the Musalmans, cannot be implanted in the minds of Hindu slaves even during the many years they grow up from childhood to maturity among the Musalmans. As to the Mongols, even if favours are shown to them for years, no thoughts came to their minds apart from plans for domination, revolt and beastliness.[57] Mahmud has been constantly harassed by anxieties owing to these slaves dwelling together in large numbers. They are of one group and one mind and there can be no permanent security against their revolt. Slave-revolt is a great menace and causes anxiety and dread. Also it is a long time since wise men have framed the proverb: it is difficult to put out a household fire.

The sons of Mahmud and kings of Islam ought to know the following principles of managing the army:

First, if a man is only worthy of being a commander of one hundred, and if with the utmost effort and with the help of others he can just manage to keep one hundred men in proper order, then one thousand or two thousand men should not be put in his charge. Rulers, who insist on holding experience and reason in contempt, should wash their hands of the hope of being able to manage horsemen whom they have assigned to the charge of worthless officers; and they should consider the resulting disorder and distress as due to their own acts. Conversely, if a man is capable of commanding one thousand or two thousand soldiers and can keep them well-equipped and disciplined, and his loyalty to the king has also been proved and confirmed, then he should not be given charge of one hundred or fifty men only, for this will break his heart and the disappointment of army-officers is not desirable. When a man does not get the rewards of his merit and sees the unworthy in high office, it is certain that his loyalty will suffer and he will always be discontented.

Second, if fifty thousand horsemen are sufficient for the kingdom, the king should not be content with fifty thousand only; he should keep permanently and well-equipped at least half as many more. Thus, while these fifty thousand soldiers remain in their places, the king will not (owing to the extra men he has enlisted) be helpless in a sudden and unforeseen contingency. Inexperienced and unreliable horsemen are not only useless but dangerous in a crisis; and they should not be enlisted at such a time.

(The king should consider everyone his enemy, even if he happens to be his brother or son, who suggests a reduction: of the army or a reduction of the expenditure on the army.)

You should twice every year personally examine the work of the Ministry of War (*Diwan-i Hashm*). Inquire into the actual number of soldiers present, and if on these occasions more persons than are on the rolls do not pass before you in the review, you should consider that the affairs of the army are not being properly managed. For this is a world of change and disturbances; what disappears at one place reappears at another place and even increases there.[58] Had it not been so, this world would not have been stable. You should, consequently, make the organisation of your army very firm. Give an order that they should be always busy in enlisting men for the army; even if a few men are enlisted, the officers of the review should not be idle about the matter and the door of enlistment should not be closed. You are to know that if by any means it becomes clear to the muster-masters, army-officers and governors of your territories that you are not particularly anxious about the increase of your army or that your desire to save money prohibits it, then the army will not increase; and even the army you have will not remain stable but will diminish day by day.

Third, the army should never be left idle. It should be kept employed in collecting the revenue, guarding the frontiers, cutting forests, building forts and hunting. This is specially necessary on account of those officers who are ambitious for leadership or from whom disturbances are to be feared. If the heart of the king is at ease about the affairs of his own kingdom and its political condition is satisfactory, he should give preference to conquests above other enterprises, and along with his stouthearted and trusted officers, he should undertake campaigns and holy wars. The master of no imaginable art or profession can keep himself in proper form without constantly practising it; similarly, if the army is not employed in its own profession, other desires will stir in its heart and other ambitions will take possession of its mind.

Keeping the army at rest is also not without its advantages. But it has its fixed limits. There should not be so much rest for the army as to cause disturbances or stir up meaningless ambitions in its mind. But after the army has been appointed to an enterprise, it is sufficient to keep it at test till the marching begins.

(This Advice is illustrated by an account of Mazdak, the Communist,[59] who obtained influence over the Iranian emperor, Qubad, father of the famous Naushirwan. Barani says his account is based on the *Tarikh-i Akasira*; it is in any case different from the account in Firdausi's *Shah Nama.* It serves, however to explain Barani's idea of *ibahat*—'community of women and property'—to which he so often refers. Mazdak having obtained influence over Qubad, induced him to decrease his army by one-third every year; after the reductions of the first two years, practically no army was left. Qubad was, consequently, helpless, and Mazdak could start preaching his own creed. "The bastard Mazdak then disclosed the creed of incest (*ibahat*) and preached his false religion of atheism (*ilhad*) among the people. He ordered a general proclamation to be made in the bazaars and among the assemblies of the people... There is no distinction in property rights, cash, goods, women, children, slaves and slave-girls among the sons of Adam; all are the common inheritance of mankind. Sons in their inheritance are partners with their fathers; the property and goods of this world are common to all. Brothers and sisters are not forbidden to each other. In the time of Adam, brothers took their sisters in marriage; the order now is as it was at the beginning of the world." But Mazdak's power was shortlived. Qubad died broken-hearted and Naushirwan after ascending the throne suppressed Mazdak and his followers.)

Notes on the Kara-Khitais and Mazdak, the Communist

(4) The *Kara-Khitais,* Barani repeatedly makes the mistake of putting the Kara-Khitais (or Khitais) as contemporaries of Sultan Mahmud, though a reference even to the *Tabaqat-i Nasiri* would have told him that the Kara-Khitais did not come within the vision of Muslim kings till over a century after Mahmud. Most Muslim historians are confused about the origin of the Kara-Khitais, but the matter is clarified by Dr. Bretschnieder on the basis of Chinese records: "At the beginning of the tenth century the chief of the Khitain, named Ye be Apaoki, having subdued all the Khitain

tribes, made himself master of a greater part of Mongolia and in 916 proclaimed himself emperor with the (Chinese) name of Tai tsu, 916–927. The son of this conqueror, Tai-tsung, 927–947, conquered a part of northern China, and gave his dynasty the title of Liao. This Khitain or Liao empire subsisted for two centuries in Manchuria and Mongolia. It is well-known that the name of Kathay, applied by Muslim authors and by medieval European travellers to China or rather Northern China, originated from the word Khitain... A few years before the overthrow of the Liao dynasty, a prince of the imperial family escaped westwards, gathered an army and conquered eastern and western Turkestan, and Khuwarazm became a tributary to him. His empire became known as Kara-Khitai in western Asia, and subsisted for nearly a century. Its rulers caused great trouble in the Mohammadan countries. It was destroyed by Changiz Khan." (*Medieval Researches from Eastern Asiatic Sources*, pp. 208–209). The *Tabaqat-i Nasiri* (p. 327) gives the names of the rulers of the Khitai dynasty, including a queen regnant, but the Chinese original names have lost all meaning after erroneous transliterations and the errors of the copyists. The Kara-Khitai kingdom was founded more than a century after Sultan Mahmud and no author of the time of Mahmud has referred to the Kara-Khitais. They had vanished more than a century and a quarter before the *Fatawa-i Jahandari* was written.

There were no Chinese slaves at the court of Sultan Mahmud; there was a contingent of Hindus but they were not slaves. [H]

8. *Mazdak.* Barani is incorrect in stating that Mazdak was overthrown by Nausherwan. All writers are agreed that the Sasanian emperor, Qubad (487–531 A.D.) was deposed and imprisoned and his brother placed on the throne; but he succeeded in regaining both his freedom and his throne and overthrew Mazdak during his second reign. Qubad was not the nonentity Barani thinks, for he fought bravely against the Romans in the west and the White Huns in the east. "At his death, notwithstanding the failure of his last campaign, the prestige and power of Iran were very high, and he left behind him an army trained to fight both White Huns and Romans, a splendid body of seasoned veterans." (Sykes, *Persia*, Vol. I, pp. 441–448).

For the orthodox fanatics of eastern Islam, Mazdak has been the typical 'communist' and the legend of his bad character and bad faith has grown with time. Only three stages in the growth of 'the Mazdak legend' can be noted here.

The *Shah Namah* of Firdausi (932–1021 A.D.) gives Mazdak a good certificate for personality, character and capacity. No wicked deeds, magic or trickery are attributed by Firdausi to Mazdak or his followers but only the claim of 'reforming the creed of Zoroaster', which, according to them, had degenerated. *First,* during a famine Muzdak, with the permission of Qubad, directed the starving poor to help themselves to the granaries of the rich and the granaries of the state. *Secondly,* he advanced the following postulate: "There are five things that deflect even wise men from the right path—poverty (*niaz*), envy (*rashk*), hatred (*khashm*), revengefulness (*kin*) and sex-impulses (*a-az*). If you can rid yourself of these five demonic passions, the path of the Lord will be clear to you. The cause of these five evils are (exclusive) wives and private property, which have destroyed 'true religion' in the world. If (exclusive) wives and private property did not exist as obstacles between men, there would be no danger to the true creed. Consequently, these two obstacles between men in society should be removed so that the evil passions of men may disappear." Now Plato had said almost exactly the same thing in his *Republic* and Mazdak may have got his basic idea from the greatest of Greek thinkers. But as a practical postulate such a principle could not be accepted by the landlords and the Iranian priesthood. The reactionary heir-apparent, Nausherwan, collected the leading priests together and Mazdak was defeated in a grand debate because he was unable to answer two questions, which no one can answer if 'the postulates of bourgeois society' are assumed to be correct—*first,* if there is no private property, how can the higher classes of society be maintained; *second,* if there is a community of women, how will descent of sons from fathers be traced? Qubad was won over by the reactionary priests and he handed Mazdak and his followers to Nausherwan for punishment. Firdausi puts the followers of Mazdak at about one hundred thousand. Of these some three thousand were selected for the extreme penalty. They were buried head downwards in a garden—'the garden of Mazdak'—with their legs rising out of the ground like small trees. Mazdak was called to see the punishment meted out to his followers. He was then hung, head downwards, from a high gibbet and killed by arrow-shots. "If you have intelligence," concludes Firdausi, "You will not follow the path of Mazdak." Mazdak had challenged the vested interests and lost, but Firdausi does not blacken his character.

Nizamul Mulk Tusi (1018–1092), the famous wazir of Malik Shah Seljuqi, collected the misrepresentations that had grown in the course of a century in his well-known *Siyasat Namah* and added to them something of his own. Nizamul Mulk was a bitter enemy of the Ismailis and the Carmathians and he declared that they were a pre-Muslim sect—'the sect of Mazdak'—continued into Islam. The great minister had scant regard for historic truths and proceeded unhesitatingly to blacken Muzdak's character and misrepresent his teachings. Muzdak now ceases to be a Platonist and is painted to us as an astrologer and a man of tricks and guiles. It is not possible to take note of all the stories, often conflicting with each other, which have been manufactured about Mazdak. But as to Mazdak's teachings, Nizamul Mulk says: "Mazdak declared, property is a common gift to all men for they are the creatures of God and the sons of Adam. Why should they be in want? Let them share each other's property so that they may all be equal and no one may be poor or destitute'... He next said, 'Your women are like your property; you should consider your women as belonging to others also, so that the door for the fulfilment of desires may be opened to all mankind and everyone may satisfy his sex-passions and longings for pleasure'. Men were drawn to Mazdak's religion owing to this community of women and children, specially the common people. Mazdak established such customs as the following. If a man invited twenty guests to his house, he would offer them bread, meat, wine, fruits and music; ultimately, everyone of the guests would cohabit with his wife and they did not consider anything wrong in this. Similarly, if a man went to a woman, he would leave his hat at the door of the house; another man, who wanted to go in, would see the hat and wait till the first man had come out." (Schefer's text, pp. 168–169)

Now it will be seen that the Mazdak of the *Siyasat-Namah* is the very reverse of the Mazdak of Firdausi. The Mazdak of Firdausi wants to establish a new and truly religious society in which the growth of the five evil passions, which degrade the mind of man, is to be prevented by the community of women and property; also his argument (like Plato's) is fundamentally academic; it appeals to reason against tradition. At a time, like ours, when Plato's

Republic is so well known, it should not be necessary to emphasise the fact that the 'community of women', whether practicable or not, would mean not a laxity but a more stringent control of sex-relations. The *Siyasat Namah,* on the other hand, accuses Mazdak of advocating the immediate satisfaction of those very passions which Mazdak had condemned in the present, unreformed social order.

Mirkhond (died 1498 A.D.) in his *Rauzatus Sofa* places still more crimes at Mazdak's door and blackens his religious dogmas also. "The creed of this wicked man was as follows. All property and women were to be held in common, and he considered cohabitation with nearly related women (with whom religion and tradition have prohibited marriage) to be an act of virtue. He said that men should content themselves with eating the products of plant-life (*nabatat*), eggs, milk, cheese and the like, and forbade the killing of animals and the eating of animal flesh and fat. Mazdak wore woollen clothes and took to religious devotions; owing to this poor men, rascals, and loafers joined his followers and their number increased... Low-born people captured the women of the rich through his support and a lot of property was plundered. During this period the parentage of children could not be known and no one could trust in the continued possession of his property and belongings." (p. 258).

"That Mazdak," says Professor Bernard Lewis, "introduced communism of property may be taken as certain; that he introduced communism of women is questionable". The link between Mazdak and the Ismailis is provided, according to the *Siyasat Namah,* by Khurramah, the widow of Mazdak, who founded the sect of the 'Khurram-diniya' of which Abu Muslim and Sindbad the Guebre were adherents. The identification of this movement with Shiasim, which was made for purely opportunistic reasons, is expressed in the phrase, 'Mazdak is a Shia.' (*The Origin of Ismailism*, pp. 96–97).

The original Mazdak, the Mazdak of the *Shah Namah,* only resorted to the distribution of property—in fact only to the distribution of hoarded grain in a time of scarcity—as a measure of famine relief; he also raised the question of the 'community of women and property' as a principle of social reform. But there was no question of trickery, deceit and even of practical implementation. The ease with which the Arabs knocked down the Sasanid empire proves that the Persian aristocracy of the day was rotten to the core. Mazdak tried to achieve by an internal revolution what was in fact achieved by an external conquest—a limitation of the exploitation of the feudal and the priestly classes, which had become unendurable, and the emancipation of women to the extent of giving them at least some human rights, e.g. the right of inheritance, the right of owning property and some say in their marriages.

Nizamul Mulk was a great wazir; still he had no time for historical investigations and the *Siyasat Namah* is full of historical errors. But he was a great Sunni and an unquestionable exponent of the prevalent popular fanaticism, by which he lived and for which he died. We are bound to accept his statement that the orthodox Sunnis of his day really believed the Ismailies of their own generation as well as the Sasanid Mazdakites to be 'fraternities of incest'. But in both cases the charge was quite baseless and untrue. [H]

Advice VIII

I. On Intelligence Officers

[This Advice begins with a paragraph on gold and silver. "Many persons have been created with a greater inclination for gold and silver than for their own lives." Next, all the defects of the social order are laid at the door of the philosophers. "The disorders and sins which appear on this earth are due to those who do not believe that God has a knowledge of the whole world as well as its details, or else they have doubts about His knowledge and do not believe for certain that He knows and sees." Obviously, the author had not decided the subject-matter of the Advice when he began to write; it will also be observed that the *Jahandari* has no Advice on taxation or finance in general. Probably Barani's first intention was to devote this Advice to taxation but he seems to have changed his plan while writing. The case for the appointment of intelligence officers has been made out by Barani at too great length and with excessive repetitions, and I have felt myself justified in summarising some paragraphs and eliminating others. A very important topic—Barani's favourite theme that the government of men, such as they are, cannot be managed according to Islamic principles—is discussed as a part of the Illustration, though it has no relevance to this Advice. I have, therefore, considered myself justified in dividing this Advice into two unrelated Sections.]

When God raises a man to the dignity of kingship and assigns the affairs of the people to his discretion and judgment, it is his duty to deal with the people in a way that may be conducive to the benefit of the religion and the state, and also to the welfare of the people. But this will not be possible if the king is ignorant of the good and bad actions of men. In particular, if persons near the king as well as his army-commanders, officers, judges, governors, courtiers, revenue-collectors and accountants discover that the king is ignorant of their good and bad acts, they will not tremble and be afraid of him in their dealings with the people. Moreover, if the king is unaware of the condition of the people, he will not be able to devise means for their prosperity. Lastly, when tomorrow, on the Day of Judgment in which we believe and to which we testify, they ask the king about the condition of everyone of his subjects, how will he be able to give any answer if he knows nothing? And if the king says: 'I do not know and could not know,' this answer will not be accepted. A king should only rule over so much territory that he can keep himself acquainted with its affairs.

It is, consequently, a duty and obligation of kings to appoint intelligence officers (*barids*)[60].

[Barani next tries to prove that the Quranic injunction: 'Do not investigate into sins'—*wa la ta jassasu isman*[61]—does not apply to kings as they are responsible to God for all the good and bad actions of their subjects, Their position before God with reference to their subjects will be the same as that of the head of a family with reference to its members.]

And now that so many generations and ages have passed since that era of piety and virtue—the period of the Prophet and the Pious Caliphate—and dishonesty, sinfulness, impiety, deceit, cheating, cruelty, injustice, jealousy and envy have permeated most minds and new things have arisen and become customary in the religion and the state, while the traditions of the Prophet have been replaced by novelties an account of which would fill up libraries, the rulers cannot perform their duties properly without appointing honest intelligence officers, truthful spies and reliable auditors. If they do not do so, the work of the world will be thrown into disorder and tumults will arise.

The office of a ruler is a position of great dignity on this earth and, consequently, his sons, brothers, near relations and favourites tend to become intoxicated and blind. But if they are convinced of the king's firmness and know for certain that reports of all their good and bad actions are going to reach him, they will be aroused from their intoxication. Not only will this do them good, but the king also, on his part, will not have to punish the members of his own family owing to their evil deeds and to turn his supporters into his enemies. It is also a great advantage to the subjects if the ruler is well-informed, while his ignorance is injurious to both parties.

Another object of religious kings in the appointment of intelligence officers has been this. If any rebellion arises in the capital or the provinces or rebels come from outside (the country), information about the numbers, strength and unity of the rebels will be brought to the king and the ways and methods of the mischievous will be discovered before they can act. If information about a (planned) rebellion reaches the king in time through his intelligence officers and spies, he can suppress the movement in such a way that it does not become necessary for him to smear his hands with the blood of Musalmans after they have actually taken up arms in revolt. For in the infliction of the death-penalty, thrashing and other punishments, a distinction should be observed between what has been designed and what has been done; there should be one punishment (*hukm*) for consulting and conspiring about rebellion and another punishment for giving effect to treasonable designs by deeds. Also if conspirators know that no conspiracies can remain hidden from the king, they will often get frightened and refrain from holding their conspiratorial meetings; though evil intentions may be in their hearts, they will not express them and they will not venture to join together and rebel. If the king is well-informed, it will be of advantage both to him and to his subjects......

[Barani asserts that even the Caliph Umar in spite of the virtuous age in which he lived had to appoint intelligence officers and spies].

Religious kings have had the following good and virtuous intentions in the appointment of intelligence officers, spies and auditors:

First, when it becomes clear to the *qazis,* governors, officers and revenue-collectors, both far and near, that their good and bad actions are going to be brought to light, they will not oppress and tyrannise over the *ra'iyyat,* demand bribes, accept presents or accede to recommendations. They will not depart from righteousness in order to engage in sinfulness and wrong-doing and they will always be fearful and trembling about their own fate. Owing to this awareness on their part, they will remain safe from the consequences of substantive as well as technical punishments. *Second,* when the subjects are convinced that the good and bad deeds of the select as well as the common people will be reported to the king and that office-holders have been appointed for this purpose, they will behave properly; they will neither rebel, nor seek to overpower each other, nor oppress the weak. *Third,* if revenue-collectors and accountants know that their actions will be brought to the notice of the king, they will not steal or misappropriate and will thus remain secure from the punishments of the king and escape humiliation and disgrace. *Lastly,* if the king's sons, brothers, relations and high officers know that all matters are being reported to the king, they will not, on account of their high position, step beyond the bounds of justice in dealing either with their own people or strangers, or slaves and servants (Reference is then made to the system of *barids* established by Alexander, the great, and Sultan Mahmud.)

Religious kings have observed many conditions concerning the appointment of intelligence officers. The most necessary conditions, of course, are the intelligence officer's qualifications. He should be truthful in speech, truthful in writing, reliable, well-born, worthy of confidence, careful of his dignity and residence and infrequent in meeting and associating with people so that his object, which is obtaining correct information for the king's business, may be attained. For the king on getting correct information can take action which is conducive both to his own welfare and the welfare of the people.

But if the intelligence officer is a thief, a man without rectitude, low-born, mean, a frequenter of every place and a caller at every door, corrupt, greedy, covetous and reckless, the king's efforts for the welfare of the people will be misdirected. For the dishonest and low-born intelligence officer, who is a master of intrigues and wire-pulling, invents many lies which look like the truth, and owing to his testifying to false information, affairs are thrown into disorder. Injuries are inflicted where benefits should have been rendered; the man worthy of punishment is favoured while the man worthy of favours is punished. The dishonest intelligence officer, owing to his greed, avarice and bad character, which are the consequences of his innate nature and low-birth, keeps the people of God, both day and night, in the grip of fear. He frightens one man into giving him a horse, from another he expects a slave-girl, while from a third he demands gold. He makes the sale of lies the basis of his livelihood and resorts to enmity, revenge, anger and retaliation. For some time, in order to establish his reputation, he writes a few reports that are absolutely correct and discharges efficiently the duties of his office. But after obtaining a reputation for honesty, these lying, low-born, mean and Godless intelligence officers plunder the houses of men, exact money from people in diverse ways and injure and oppress them under various pretexts. They make the king the enemy of his people and the people enemies of the king. The appointment of such persons leads to the overthrow of the people of God and not to their prosperity. Therefore kings, prior to the appointment of intelligence officers, auditors and spies, should inquire about their birth. The majority of the officers they appoint should be men of good character, free-born and truthful in words and actions. Such persons will not have turned their backs on the desires of this world, but neither in their desire for worldly office will they have turned away their faces from God.

[The rest of what Barani says on this topic may be summarised as follows. The Pious Caliphs and the Companions took up worldly offices in the pursuit of religion. "This work has finished with them." Men of true religious merit will not accept government posts in these days for "their meritorious qualities do not allow these praiseworthy men to come near the affairs of the world or to accept government posts."[62] So the king has to do the best he can "for if absolute merit is demanded, government posts will remain unfilled." Still, estimated relatively, the king will find more virtue and reputation for virtue in some men, while virtue is seldom seen in others and the rest have a reputation for wickedness.]

[Barani here adds a story about Sultan Mahmud. He asked his wazir, Hasan Maimandi,[63] to select two hundred persons for appointment as intelligence officers and added a stern clause about punishments in case of misbehaviour. When these people were brought before his throne, he was informed that one hundred and thirty had consented to serve and seventy had requested to be excused. Mahmud thereupon appointed the seventy who had refused to serve and commanded the appointment-orders of the others to be torn up. Barani admits that such a trick, though excellent, can only be played once.]

[This Advice is illustrated by an incident for which Barani claims the authority of the *Tarikh-i Khulafai Abbasi* (*History of the Abbasid Caliphs*). The Caliph Mamun-ar Rashid, while still at Merv, took to religious life and started giving lessons to pupils in the Prophet's traditions. He cast aside the customs of royalty and dismissing all intelligence officers and *amirs,* assigned governorship of provinces to scholars, pious men, recluses and mystics. The wazir, Fazl bin Sahl,[64] in mild, smooth open, indirect and diversified language drew Mamun's attention to the consequences of what he was doing. Mamun would not hear, but when there were rebellions on all sides, Mamun cast aside his religious ways and his wazir put the affairs of the Caliphate in order.]

II. The Pious Caliphate Was an Interlude in World History—Mankind Returns to its Old Ways

[The following words, which he puts in the mouth of Fazl bin Sahl, are really the essence of Barani's own theory about the necessity and sinfulness of kingship.]

"The governance of men is not possible without the dominance and prestige of royalty. No one has been able to govern the people in any other way. It was entirely due to their nearness to the Prophet's time, and may be considered as one of his miracles, that just for one generation the Pious Caliphs were able to exercise the powers of government and keep the world in proper order in spite of their religious life and their poverty. Consequently, from the days of Adam to the end of the world, they have considered the generation of the Pious Caliphate a wonder for all times. The

Pious Caliphs in all matters, great or small, followed the traditions of the Prophet. But if later kings follow the Prophet's traditions, they will not be able to keep their kingship for a single day.

"Nevertheless, three of the four Pious Caliphs, who from fear of deviating from the *sunnah* of the Prophet did not adopt any of the laws and customs of secular kings ended by sacrificing themselves for the Prophet's traditions; Umar, Usman and Ali were martyred by reckless devotees. It has not been possible for any ruler of Islam in the past, apart from the Pious Caliphs, to carry on the administration of a country while living according to the Prophet's traditions of poverty; nor is such a thing conceivable in the future. For the world is full of demonic men, who have the characteristics of lions, carnivorous animals and beasts of prey. Command and control over them cannot be established without the terror and power of dominating kings. Moreover, the helpers and supporters of the Pious Caliphs were the noble Companions of the Prophet, who owing to the light of the Faith and their great devotion sacrificed their lives, wealth, wives, children, property and goods in the path of the Lord. As they had associated with the Prophet and witnessed the Divine inspiration, their love for God and his Prophet was so great that the whole world was not in their eyes worth the cheapest of coins. So in order to secure the supremacy of the True Word, they threw themselves into burning fire and did not sleep during the nights owing to their longing for martyrdom. All the Immigrants (*Muhajir*) and Helpers (*Ansar*) were men of miracles and religious vision. So it was possible for the Pious Caliphs, owing to the help of the Companions, to govern like kings while they lived like poor people.

"Now that the Caliphate has come to the Commander of the Faithful (Mamun), two hundred years have passed since that period, and firm faith in the correct creed is left only in a limited number of individuals; the appearance and character of Islam have greatly changed; the world has come back again into the hands of the followers of custom and they all seek the good of this world only. *Before the advent of the Prophet, the valour and courage of the sons of Adam was for the objects of this world only, and the same is the case now.* The supreme command and the *masnad* of the Caliphate cannot be established or become firm without the terror, prestige and power of kingship and without adopting those royal traditions and policies of (secular) kings, which subdue the disobedient and reduce the rebellious and the strong-necked to impotence. Government, conquests and kingship are incompatible with a life of religious poverty. Unless the prestige and power of the monarchy are maintained; men will begin to suppress each other lawlessly, the obedient will become disobedient, the dignity of the supreme command will vanish and the execution of government orders will become impossible. Without exercising the terroristic power of the Kisras and resorting to the pomp and magnificence of Jamshed, it is not possible to subdue the seventy-two communities and make them obedient to orders.

"Such Islam and such Musalmans are not left that one can govern them after the manner of Abu Bakr and Umar."

Advice IX

I. Price Control

Sultan Mahmud has said: O Sons of Mahmud and kings of Islam! You should know for certain that all the policies and enterprises of the state are interdependent. For example, just as the army cannot become stable without payments from the Treasury, similarly it cannot be stabilised without the low price of commodities. And just as the cheapness of commodities is necessary for the proper organisation of the army, in the same way without the cheap price of the means of livelihood there can be no prosperity, splendour and stability among the people. The gate and the court of the king are the object (*qibla*) of the people, but unless they provide what mankind needs, regard for the prestige and greatness of royal authority will not grow in the hearts of persons far and near. The generality of the select as well as the common people are of one opinion about this. If owing to the high price of the necessities of life the inhabitants and the *raiyyat* of the country are driven to distress and all or most of them are faced with disaster and ruin, they will forsake their beloved homeland along with their old houses and turn their faces to the country where the means of livelihood are cheap and easily available.

Consequently, on the basis of the preceding postulates it is obligatory for kings to strive hard, and to put in their full endeavour, for the reduction of the price of the requisites of the army, such as horses and arms, as well as the price of corn and cloth which affect the livelihood of the select as well as the common people. They should understand that the stability of their kingdom depends upon the stability of the army and the people; and that the stability of the army and the people depends upon the low price of the means of livelihood. During a famine, which is a calamity from the sky, there is a terrible decline in food-production because no rain falls. This the hand of the ruler cannot rectify. In the days of famine a king's efforts are perforce limited to the remission or reduction of the tribute (*khiraj*) and the poll-tax (*jizya*) and the granting of such help as he can from the Treasury; his efforts cannot reduce famine-prices and he is therefore excused. But during the period of plentiful vegetation, when rainfall comes as a blessing, and crops, fruits, cultivated fields and gardens grow in luxurious abundances the transport merchants (*saudagar-i karawani*) and market-merchants (*saudagar-i bazari*); nevertheless, adopt the practice of selling at high prices, and owing to the great profits which result from high prices, all men of wealth take to business and regrating (*ihtikar*); it is then the primary duty of the kings to try to control prices by whatever means they can and to strive hard for their reduction. They should not permit persons, who have developed a bad character and have made selling at high prices the source of their livelihood, to resort to their own devices in the transactions of buying and selling.[65]

The king should settle before his own throne the prices of all things according to the principle of production-cost (*nirkh-i baraward*)[66]. Intelligence officers and honest and harsh-tempered judges should control the transactions of buying and selling; and they should make excessive inquiries and investigation about them. The low price of grain, cloth and other commodities should not be considered an easy or trifling matter in the affairs of administration. All kings should consider the low price of the means of the people's livelihood to be the basis of their good management of the country and of their administration of justice. They should order the *gumashtas* (agents) of the *mandis* (grain markets) and the *shuhnas* and *kotwals* (market-officers and police superintendents) of the cities not to permit regrating in the capital under any circumstances; they should confiscate and sell the corn of the regraters, for the Holy Prophet has done so. The man who regrates, and takes to regrating as his profession, has made himself an obstacle to the people's livelihood and has limited the blessings of plenty upon them. If he does not refrain from regrating in spite of government orders, he should be punished with confiscation of property and exile as a warning and a lesson to others.

The officers (*ra'ises*) of the markets should be directed to keep the shopkeepers in subjection and not to leave the fixation of prices to them; they should strive hard in fixing prices (as ordered by the government) and in inquiring into the transactions of buying and selling. In this great enterprise, the success and failure of which affects both the select and the commons, they should not be guilty of any slackness or be tempted to work for their own advantage. They should not consider the question of prices a matter of detail. It is their duty to come to the help of those buyers or sellers, who happen to be ignorant, young, village-born, helpless and weak. They should enforce justice in the market-transactions of buying and selling, and they should punish cheats, swindlers, makers of false promises and vendors of false goods in humiliating ways. They should not, deceived by their pretences of submission and helplessness, allow shopkeepers, grocers (*baqqals*), artisans and other shameless people to sit in their shops in order to tyrannise over the helpless, the shy, the young and the ignorant; or to resort to strange ways of business-dealing, knavery, rough-handling, impudence and shamelessness; or to give their own glass-beads the name of diamonds in order to sell them at the price of diamonds, and to declare the diamonds of the sellers to be mere stones so that they may purchase them at the price of stones.

If a king, in spite of his power to enforce his orders, allows such mishandling of the helpless, the poor, the infirm, the distressed, the young and the ignorant by knaves, rogues, shopkeepers, shameless and Godless people, if he does not order the necessary inquiries and investigations to be made and does not enforce uniform justice in the dealings of the seventy-two communities, then he cannot be considered 'the shadow of God' or a legitimate ruler.

The king should also know that every arrangement (*naqsh*) in the matter of buying and selling and price-fixation which he makes for his capital will also appear in all his provinces. The officers and *raiyyat* of his country will accept it and follow it[67].

O sons of Mahmud! You should know that in the cheapness of the requisites of the army and the necessities of the people's livelihood there are many religious and worldly advantages conducive to the well-being of both the king and the subjects:

[*First advantage:* The army becomes stable and strong. *Second advantage:* The king's capital, owing to the large number of select men who come and settle there—the skilled and trained men of every art and craft—becomes a world-capital. *Third advantage:* The king's enemies on seeing the strength of his army and the prosperity of his subjects do not harbour any design of overpowering his country.] *Fourth advantage:* The low prices of the necessities of the people's livelihood bring to the king a good reputation which lives in the memory of the people for years and generations. Also anger and jealousy disappear from among the people and are replaced by mutual affection. Blessings, peace and goodwill appear on every side. *Conversely:* Though owing to high prices and regrating a limited number of houses belonging to the dishonest are filled, yet thousands and thousands of houses belonging to the purchasers are reduced to poverty and distress and the enmity of regraters and commodity-sellers grows in the heart of the public along with the desire for revenge. *Fifth advantage:* Cheap prices are advantageous to the king's Treasury, which is also the *Baitul Mal* of all Musalmans. If corn and commodities are dear, plenty of money has to be spent in the work of government and this depletes the Treasury. Under these conditions the position of the ruler and the subjects is reversed. Normally, the Treasury is filled with money given by the *ra'iyyat,* but when corn and commodities are dear, the money of the Treasury goes to the houses of the *ra'iyyat*. There are then no limits or bounds to government expenditure, for even in one royal establishment (*karkhana*) fodder has to be provided for several thousand horses. The injury caused by high prices directly affects the capital, and from the capital it spreads over the whole country. *Sixth advantage:* This advantage also appertains both to the king and the *ra'iyyat.* The supreme object of kingship is the enforcement of justice and equity. But whenever in the capital of the kingdom, which ought to be the fountain of justice and equity there is open and public injustice in the transactions of buying and selling and the king does not order matters to be reformed; when the houses of regraters and commodity-sellers are filled with the people's money without any labour or trouble on their part while the houses of others, who have obtained what they have with the sweat of their brows, are emptied without any natural calamity or misfortune, and everyday their distress and poverty increase, and the king, whose function is to enforce justice, does not discharge his duty by fixing prices and by warning and punishing regraters and commodity-sellers—then the administration of the king falls into disorder, he is held responsible and punishable before God, and everything is attributed to his negligence. *Seventh advantage:* One of the purposes of Divine wisdom in the establishment of the institution of kingship has been that it should discharge the obligation—"Take from the rich amongst you and give it to your poor." The poor cannot by force establish their rights to a claim on the property of the rich. The regraters and commodity-sellers are none but the rich; and the regraters in the course of their business take from the poor and the destitute whatever source of livelihood they have, and openly under the pretence of sale they take everything from them to their own homes. Thus the Divine purpose is flouted. There can be in cheap prices no higher benefit than this—that one of the purposes of Divine wisdom is manifested among the select and the commons. *Eighth advantage:* Regrating and selling at high prices are social sins; they do not belong to the category of sins against the self as their harm affects others[68]. But by the orders and the efforts of the king, they can be suppressed. The Divine reward for rendering this service is not concealed from the wise.

Ninth advantage: This also includes the prosperity of the ruler and the ruled. Regrating is the profession of the Hindus, Magians (*Gabrs*), infidels and polytheists of the country[69]. The man who calls himself a Musalman and yet adopts regrating as his profession and deprives the people of God of their livelihood by his cleverness, is ignorant of the Muslim Faith and has not been influenced by it. In consequence of regrating, wealth goes from the houses of Musalmans, whose honour is in harmony with the commands of God and his Prophet, to the houses of Hindus and Magians, whose property, wives and children can, according to some Muslim sects, be considered the legitimate spoils of war[70]. Thus persons, whose humiliation and degradation is a duty demanded by the Faith are respected and honoured owing to the wealth obtained by regrating from the Musalmans, while Musalmans, who are honoured and favoured by God, become low and contemptible owing to their poverty and lack of means. If the king strives in the matter of cheap prices, those honoured by God will gain still greater honour in society and those whom

God has condemned will become even more destitute and helpless. This is a great benefit in the matter of administration. *Tenth advantage:* Owing to the cheap price of grain and the means of livelihood, every group, class, caste and community among the *ra'iyyat* of the country devotes itself to its own craft, work, art and profession. And one of the chief factors of stability in the affairs of government is that everyone confines himself to his own proper work as owing to this the administrative arrangements of the country improve. But whenever plenty of profit is seen in regrating and selling at high prices, and not much profit remains in other professions, people discard their own profession by an instinct of nature. Soldiers take to agriculture; cultivators, seeing plenty of profit in it, take to trade; regrators, owing to the influence of their wealth, extend their hands to high posts; shopkeepers try to become officers; men of noble birth become merchants; and transport-merchants desire to become government officers (*amirs*) and commanders of the army. Consequently, affairs do not remain stable. But no disorders or chaos appears among the *ra'iyyat* of the country as a result of cheap prices.

Those who have no knowledge and experience of the real nature of administration and conquests say that kings should not strive for price-control and price-fixation *for low prices are contingent upon plenty*[71] and the holy Prophet has said, 'God is forgiving'. Such a contention, on the face of it, seems correct. But this is a changing world, and owing to the rotations of the variegated sky, the sons of Adam are by nature born to different ways and manners in every epoch and generation. In these later generations, which come nearer to the Day of Judgment and recede farther from the good days of the Prophet and his Companions, excess of merit has been transformed into excess of meanness, love of the material world has overpowered the hearts of all except those about whom God has willed otherwise, and Satan and the lower passions have obtained control over the generality of mankind. So in spite of continuous rain and plenitude of fruits and good harvests, the greed and temptation for the high price of corn and cloth overcomes these people owing to their excessive sinfulness. They do not give up regrating and selling at high prices and are not afraid either of God or the king. The rich sell corn and cloth at whatever price they like to the poor. And owing to their cleverness in regrating and selling at high prices, they will by no means permit the ruler, who has been appointed for the public welfare, to make inquiries or investigations, or to control prices and fix rates, or to enforce justice in the transactions of buying and selling among the people by warnings and punishments, or to use his power to protect his people from injustice. What will be the ruler's answer for all this on the Day of Judgment and how will his excuses for his negligence be accepted?

II. Contradictions Between the Principles of Islam and the Institution of Kingship

Let it be known for certain to the sons of Mahmud and, in fact, to all kings of the earth that Mahmud has taken good care to understand that true religion consists in following in the footsteps of the Prophet, Mohammad son of Abdullah Quraishi. Consequently, he who follows the Prophet's guidance and leadership in his mode of life and livelihood, and in his words and actions, is said to be religious and has the benefit and good fortune of religion. But royal government on the contrary can only be carried on by following the policies of Khusrau Parvez and the great emperors of Iran. And whoever follows their policies and precedents and adopts their mode and manner of life will be able to attain kingship and government; the people will be obedient to him and his orders will be executed in this world.

Now, between the traditions (sunnah) of the Prophet Mohammad, and his mode of life and living, and the customs of the Iranian Emperors, and their mode of life and living, there is a complete contradiction and total opposition.

When in the generation of the Companions of the Prophet, the countries of Iran and Syria were conquered, Abu Bakr, Umar, Usman and Ali became *kings,* rulers and supreme governors; and owing to the perfection of their religion, they risked their lives and did not waver even by a needle-point from the Prophet's mode of life and living, his traditions of piety and poverty and his principles of dealing with the people. They did not adopt the policies and traditions of the Iranian Emperors, which are necessary for government and kingship; and as a miracle of the Prophet, they alone have been able, among all early and later generations, to combine poverty (*darweshi*) with kingship (*jamshedi*). They governed the world while wearing tattered clothes, poor and starving. Nevertheless Umar, Usman and Ali were martyred by reckless devotees.

After them, the Caliphs and kings of Islam were faced with two irreconcilable alternatives, both necessary for the religion and the state. If they followed the traditions of the Prophet and his mode of life, kingship and government would be impossible for them. On the other hand, if in their customs of sitting, standing, eating, dressing and in their general mode of life they followed the policy of the Iranian Emperors, which breaks the headstrong, subdues rebels and is necessary for the execution of state-orders, it would be necessary to violate the traditions of the Prophet, which are the foundation and the basis of the Faith.

A careful reflection upon the character of the kings and those near them leaves us in no doubt that *prophethood is the perfection of religion and that kingship is the perfection of worldly good fortune. These two perfections are opposed and contradictory to each other, and their combination is not within the bounds of possibility.*

For submission to God (*bandagi*) is the necessary condition of religion and the necessary conditions of submission are humility, supplication, helplessness, poverty, self-abasement, self-abnegation, poverty and tears. On the other hand, the requisites of kingship, which is the perfection of worldly good fortune, are power, pride, singularity or status, luxurious living, self-glorification, disregard of others, grandeur and prestige. The qualities enumerated here are among the attributes of God. And since kingship is the deputyship (*niyabat*) and vice-regency (*khilafat*) of God, it is not possible to be a king by adhering to the virtues of submission.

Consequently, it became necessary for the rulers of Islam to follow the policy of the Iranian Emperors in order to ensure the greatness of the True Word, the supremacy of the Muslim religion, the power of Truth, the suppression and overthrowal of the opponents and enemies of the Faith, the execution of the orders of religion and the maintenanee of their own authority. They have adopted the policy of unbelievers in God (the Iranian Emperors) for establishing their own power so that they may use their authority and strength for the protection and promotion of the Faith, for ensuring the greatness of the True Word by constant holy wars (*jihad*) intended to overthrow idolatry and polytheism and for raising the prestige of Islam by killing and slaughtering the enemies of the Faith.

Nevertheless Islam totally forbids and prohibits the inequities committed by the Iranian Emperors.

But just as the eating of carrion, though prohibited, is yet permitted in times of dire need, similarly the customs and traditions of the pagan Emperors of Iran—the crown and the throne, singularity of status, pride, aloofness, rules about sitting down and getting up in the king's court, high palaces, court ceremonials, asking people to prostrate themselves before the king, collecting treasures, misappropriating properties, wearing gold ornaments and jewels and silk clothes and making other people wear them, putting people to death on grounds of state-policy, keeping large *harems*, spending recklessly without any right and seizing countries without any claim of *inheritance—should from the view-point of truth and the correct Faith, be considered like the eating of carrion in times of dire need. It is the duty of religious kings to be afraid and regretful of such actions, which are a danger to religion, to ask for Divine forgiveness during the nights with weeping and lamentations, to know for certain that all the customs and ways of kingship are violations of the traditions of the Prophet and that in this violation they and their followers and their servants are involved.* [Barani refers to the fact that the Prophet did not eat meat by cutting it with a knife because this was the custom of the Iranian Emperors.]

So, O sons of Mahmud: Know well that *kingship is not possible without following the traditions of the Emperors of Iran, and it is known to all religious scholars that these traditions are opposed to the traditions of the Prophet and to his mode of life and living.*

[*No king who adopts these traditions should, therefore, consider himself a Musalman or entertain any rational hopes of salvation unless he uses his power for certain objectives which Barani enumerates as follows:* protecting the Islamic faith; elevating the True Word; enforcing the prohibitions and orders of religion; overthrowing idolatry and polytheism; suppressing novelties and the introducers of novelties; uprooting the molestors of the *shariat*; making the seventy-two communities submissive to the *shariat*; not permitting, except from necessity, that any idolator, polytheist or introducer of novelties be honoured in the country; rescuing the oppressed and enforcing justice.]

It should also be evident to the kings of Islam that, while it is possible for a few persons in the whole kingdom to tremble at the three orders—'Allah has commanded', 'the Prophet has commanded' and 'Religious scholars have commanded'—the mass of the people tremble only from fear of the Sultan, his terror and his power, and his blood-shedding sword. The Caliph Umar, son of Khattab, has said: "Those who fear the sultan are more numerous than those who fear the Quran." For fear of the Quran is the result of true Faith, and true Faith in these later days is rare like red sulphur. Consequently, if the king by his terror and power does not enforce justice and truthfulness in the affairs of the seventy-two communities; his power and authority will be considered frivolous.

[The Illustrations for this Advice are as follows: (1) The *Tarikh-i Ma-asir-i Sahabah* is quoted as an authority for the price-control established by the Caliph Umar, who had stationed fifty thousand troops round Medina. And then the following sensible remark is added: "Cheap prices are from God, but they are dependent upon the justice, the good management and the efforts of kings. God is the creator of milk and rice but putting them in the pot and cooking them is the work of man." (2) Next, the measures taken by the wazirs of the pre-Muslim emperors of Iran for the *stocking* of grain and ensuring the plentiful supply of horses are described, but no authority for these statements is given.]

Advice X

On the King's Time

[This Advice only repeats what Barani has said elsewhere. There are also some commonplace remarks that will come to the mind of anyone who cares to reflect on the matter. The following paragraph should suffice.]

The essence of the king's recognition of his great blessing is that he realises the value of time and does not waste his time, which is more precious than the time of any other man. He should devote himself to affairs of government and administration in such a way that it may bring him nearness to God, and owing to this the ladder of Divine approval may come into his hands. After the performance of the necessary religious duties, he should devote himself only to administrative affairs and consider himself dedicated to public service. He should not throw away his precious life in the pursuit of pleasures. But properly attending to public business is not possible unless the king strictly allocates his time, both day and night, and assigns a period to every business and during that allotted period he does not leave that specific business to attend to some other work. So as far as possible, he should attend exclusively to government business and not waste his precious life in frivolities, amours and useless things.

[Two Illustrations are given for this Advice. (1) On the authority of the *Tarikh-i Ma-asir-i Sahabah* (*History of the Good Deeds of the Companions*) of Imam Mohammad Ishaq[72], it is stated that the Companion, Abu Hazifa, gave the following account of the daily life of the Caliph Umar to the Byzantine emperor.]

"In the early hours of the morning the Caliph leads the Companions in their *fajr* prayer in the Prophet's mosque and recites a long chapter from the Quran in a way that arouses both the hope and the fear of God in the minds of his listeners. He then reads the Quran and recites his prayer-formulae (*aurad*) till sunrise, which is the time for the two genuflections of his Ishraq-prayer.

"By then the people have collected together. The Caliph takes his seat facing them with his back towards the arch of the mosque. He summons the Companions, and they take their seats in accordance with the precedence they had before he became Caliph. Then with the advice and counsel of the great Companions the transaction of business begins (in the following order):

"The Caliph reads the reports of events that come to him from all the lands of Islam and the petitions (*arz dasht*) of the provincial governors. To those who are nearly equal to him in status, the Caliph writes with his own hand and his orders begin with the words: "From Abdullah, the Caliph of the Faithful and the servant of the Musalmans." Usman son of Affan, who is the son-in-law of the Prophet, replies to all other persons on behalf of the Caliph.

"The Caliph then inquires about the money, if any, which has been received on account of tribute, poll-tax (*jizya*) and spoils of war. He often sends this money to the houses of the Companions, but precedence is given to the family of the Prophet and to the Prophet's relations among the Bani Hashim. After this the Caliph attends to the legal disputes between the people of Medina which have been brought before him. He makes detailed inquiries and investigations about the facts of every case and passes judgments in accordance with the law of God and the Prophet. If the facts of a case have not been clearly proved, he keeps it pending for further inquiries.

[He then attends to the treasury and the army.]

"He gives pay-orders on the treasury to those entitled to them. Inquiries are made about the condition of horses and camels and orders are sent to the treasury about their fodder and other requirements. If a province needs military assistance, the Caliph equips and sends the forces needed. The heads of the tribes and the army-commanders are asked about the condition of the army, which the Caliph has settled around Medina, and appropriate orders are issued.

"If a complaint about the misdeeds of any man are brought to the Caliph, the accused is summoned immediately if he happens to be in Medina; and the Caliph (after careful investigations) metes out to the criminal, even if he happens to be the Caliph's own son or brother, a punishment that is a warning to others. If the accused is not in Medina, the Caliph tries to console the injured party and sends a severe-tempered messenger to summon the accused. The Caliph then inquires about persons deserving assistance and about the relations of those soldiers, who have been sent with the army. He sees to it personally that whatever it needs is sent to every tribe. He has also asked the Companions to be constantly inquiring about deserving persons and to bring them to his notice.

"At midday the people disperse.

"If the Caliph is not fasting, he goes to his house, eats dry bread from his personal income and has a short nap. After that he returns to the mosque and says his afternoon (*zuhr*) prayer at the earliest time with composure and calmness. But if he is fasting, he does not go to his house; he puts a brick under his head, lies down on a sack-cloth in a comer of the mosque and sleeps for a while. The Caliph has one or two camels sacrificed and cooked every day. Occasionally at the time of the early *zuhr* prayer he has food laid before him and invites travellers, poor and destitute men to partake of it. He himself places the food before them and washes their hands at the beginning and the end of the meal.

"After the afternoon prayer the Caliph again attends to public business. Most punishments for the violation of God's laws (*hududallah*)[73] and *shariat*-laws are inflicted at this time. Occasionally after finishing his afternoon prayer the Caliph takes his whip in hand and walks down on foot to the market. Fear and terror of him have permeated the people and the shop-keepers tremble. He has warned all merchants against selling at high prices, deception, fraud, regrating and shameless practices. If there is evidence of such crimes anywhere, punishment is meted out to the wrong-doer in accordance with the orders of the *shari'at*. If any case of regrating comes to his knowledge, he orders the regrated commodity to be confiscated and sold, and the proceeds to be used for purchasing fodder for the horses and camels of the army. If commodities are sold at high prices or there is shameless deception in buying and selling, he punishes the shopkeepers severely and whips them with his own hand.

"Near the time of the evening (*maghrib*) prayer, hot and perspiring, the Caliph returns to the mosque, makes his ablutions before the door and leads the congregation at the prayer. After the obligatory evening prayer, he says his supererogatory (*awwabin*) prayer, with twenty genuflections. Then once again he sits with his back towards the arch of the mosque while the Companions take their seats round him. For a third part of the night they keep talking about the Prophet—his good deeds, virtues, gracious behaviour and his campaigns (*ghazwas*), in which they took part. The Caliph and the Companions weep at their separation from the Prophet and their heart-blood flows out of their eyes. They are in the habit of making repeated pilgrimages to the Prophet's tomb, and at the time of these pilgrimages, owing to their longing for the Prophet, their souls come near to leaving their bodies.

"The Caliph recites the night (*isha*) prayer with the congregation. Then he goes to his house and attends to the wants of his family. But if there is no work for him in his own house and no member of the Prophet's family has asked him to do anything he takes his whip in his hand, picks up two or three of his closest friends from their houses, and for half a quarter or one quarter (*pas*) of the night they wander about Medina like patrols. During this patrolling he enquires about the condition of orphans and widows, and about the sick, the helpless and the oppressed. If he finds anyone in need he fixes the amount of assistance to be given to him on the spot and directs the money to be sent to him from the treasury next morning. The Caliph has been nurtured in the company of the Prophet and the light of the Prophet's virtues has shone upon him."

[The second Illustration refers to Arzu Shah, a king of Khorasan. He was so headstrong and ill-advised that he collected his forces and marched against an enemy at the end of the summer when the rainy season (*birshikal*[74]) was near. But the enemy was clever and would not come out of his capital to fight Arzu. Soon afterwards the rainy season (*birshikal*) set in; it rained continuously, and every little stream became a river. Arzu's soldiers ran away from his camp and he was captured by the enemy.]

Advice XI

On the Establishment of Truth at the Centre

[1. *The Doctrine of Contradiction: The Unity of Opposites is Impossible, for Neither of the Two Opposed Forces Can Totally Annihilate its Opposite.*]

Sultan Mahmud says: O sons of Mahmud and kings of Islam! You should know that since the activities of the king are not merely confined to the satisfaction of his physical desires but also, in the affairs of government, he lays claim to partnership in the attributes of God, his salvation and spiritual progress are not possible unless he makes arrangements by which 'Truth is established at the Centre', and the status and honour of the religion of the Prophet are increased through the strength of his government.

You should know that the establishment of truth at the centre does not mean that falsehood (*batil*) totally disappears and that truth alone remains in the world. For Almighty God has said: "Of every thing We have created pairs[75]"—that is all things have been created in (opposed) pairs, and that after one thing has been created another thing opposite to it has been brought into existence. Opposed to truth they have created falsehood and opposed to peace they have created disorder. In the mysteries (*runniz*) of good, evil has been created; opposed to devotion to God there is sinfulness and opposed to obedience there is disobedience. Similarly, day and night, light and darkness, sky and earth, religion and irreligion, theism and polytheism have been created in opposed pairs and as reflections of each other.

The object of the above postulate is this. The establishment of truth at the centre does not mean that falsehood is totally overthrown. For if all prophets and Muslim kings collect together and try to liquidate and eliminate 'falsehood', which includes infidelity, disorder, sin and wickedness, from this world so that only 'truth', which means Islam, peace, obedience and virtue, may prevail, they most certainly will not be able to do this. For it is not within the realm of possibility that there should be only goodness on this earth and no evil; only peace and no disorder; only Islam and theism and no infidelity and polytheism. For truth becomes manifest owing to the existence of falsehood, good owing to the existence of evil, Islam owing to the existence of infidelity, and theism owing to the existence of polytheism. So it comes to be known that this is truth and this is falsehood; that this is good and this is evil; that this is Islam and this is *kufr*; that this is theism and this is polytheism. All things are distinguishable owing to their opposites.

Further, if in 'falsehood', which denotes wickedness, infidelity, polytheism, disorder and sin, there had not been a wisdom which we do not comprehend, God would not have created it. Also Hell, which the people of falsehood will fill up, would not have been created; for Almighty God has said: "We will fill Hell with jinns and men all together."[76]

It is beyond the imagination of men that the following should be totally eliminated and disappear from the world-infidelity, polytheism, wickedness, mischief, falsehood, depravity, lying, uttering of false coins, drunkenness, adultery, sodomy, anger, victimisation of innocent persons, injustice, cruelty, lawless overpowering of others, misappropriation, rebellion, disorder, trespassing the limits of justice, enmity, revolt, disobedience, dishonesty, cheating, fraud, misrepresentation, violation of the rights of parents, disloyalty, false accusations, framing of false charges, evil-speaking, slander, calumny, impiety, jealousy, ill-will, lack of self-respect, shamelessness, treachery, theft, sedition, highway robbery, usury, regrating, ingratitutde, non-recognition of rights, adulteration of commodities, and commission of unlawful and disapproved acts; or that infidels, polytheists and men of bad religion, bad faith and bad dogmas, introducers of innovations and molestors of the Prophet's *Shari'at* along with rebels and mischief-makers should be totally uprooted; or that all kingdoms should be united into one state and all false creeds overthrown.

The complete overthrowal of evil is not possible either through the guidance and preachings of the prophets or through the prestige, power and terror of Muslim kings.

For man in his real nature has been made of contrary qualities; he has been created with merits and meannesses. And in the original Record the Pen of Divine command has written at the beginning of Time apportioning to men Islam or infidelity, virtue or wickedness, guidance or error, obedience or sinfulness. Consequently, the total elimination of sins and evils is among things impossible and beyond achievement; it simply cannot be realised.

So the real meaning of 'truth being established at the centre is that truth shall overpower falsehood and falsehood shall not overpower truth, so that the honour of truth and the greatness of Islam may be vindicated through, the humiliation and disgrace of polytheism and infidelity.

Now whenever the king with pious intentions and resolute courage and all necessary arrangements strives to the utmost—along with all his supporters and followers and with all the terror, power and prestige of his government, realising that the fundamental purpose of his religion and his state is the glory of the Prophet's creed—the following objects are attained: The habit of obeying commands for the good and prohibitions of the evil appears in the capital and the provinces, and as a consequence of it the traditions of Islam are elevated from time to time; virtue and rectitude increase and charity and obedience manifest themselves with the beat of drums; sins and impieties, wickedness and wrong-doings sink low and remain in hiding and secrecy; justice and kindness are widespread and oppression and cruelty become seemingly non-existent and take to flight; the sciences of the orthodox (*sunnat wa jama'at*) appear sweet to the hearts of men and their minds are repelled by novelties (*bid 'ats*), knowledge of novelties and books on novelties; religious people and protectors of religion attain to distinction and high positions, while men of bad intentions, bad dogmas, bad religions, introducers of novelties and enemies of the Faith become contemptible, destitute, worthless and of no account; the good acts of religion become current and disbelievers in the *shari'at* are disgraced; things disapproved and prohibited by religion seem as if they had never existed; love of God and the Prophet is strengthened in the hearts of the Muslim community and love of this world, which is a source of trouble in the path of truth and the cause of inclination towards wickedness and evil, is lessened in all breasts; the longing for the next world is increased in the hearts of men and there is disgust at worldly desires and inclination to repentance from them; the virtues of man's nature overpower its evil tendencies; truth becomes graceful and adorned and the truthful are honoured while liars are disgraced and dishonoured; *saiyyids,* religious scholars, *shaikhs,* pious people, ascetics, devotees, recluses and virtuous men attain to eminence, honour and distinction in the minds and hearts of men, while the ignorant, the mischievous, the dishonest, the shameless and those slack in their prayers become contemptible, valueless and of no account; purity of intention appears in holy wars and holy campaigns and the desire for martyrdom illuminates the hearts of holy warriors and victors; truthfulness and rectitude laugh while dishonesty and deception weep; the good and the just attain to offices of the state and religion while the tyrannical and the evil-minded are either suppressed or, by a change of character, they become just and good; the rich and the wealthy discharge the obligations imposed upon them by God and take to bestowing gifts and charities and establishing beneficent foundations; the poor and the needy, instead of being allowed to perish, are rescued from hunger and nakedness; the means for honest and lawful livelihood become plentiful and abundant, while means of livelihood, which have been prohibited, disapproved or considered doubtful, grow less and hide themselves in quiet corners, being ashamed of justifying themselves by false interpretations and cheating; deception and hypocrisy lead to disgrace; good deeds and acts of beneficence are honoured while evil and wrongful acts go underground and vanish; justice appears in the transactions of buying and selling, and selling at high prices and regrating disappear owing to the efforts of the brokers (*dallals*); shopkeepers do not resort to deception and cheating and come to consider corrupt sales and purchases a great sin for they can neither cheat the ignorant nor adulterate their commodities under various false pretences; both buyers and sellers obey the orders of the brokers (*dallals*) and judicial officers, while the brokers, on their part, follow the path of equity; practising professions of sin and wickedness appears to people as wicked as infidelity (*kufr*) and their suppression is considered necessary; the obedient and the submissive spread their legs on their beds without anxiety and sleep in peace while the rebellious and the headstrong tremble day and night from fear of the king's sword; universal peace and security prevail and contentions and strifes disappear from the hearts of men; the strong do not overpower the weak and the hand of tyranny is broken; rebelliousness does not appear in men's minds and the door of disorder is closed; the bands of highway robbers are cut off owing to their crimes; God-fearing and honest officers are promoted while cheats and swindlers are dismissed and become destitute; trustworthy officers are distinguished and dishonest officers are disgraced; free-born persons and persons of noble birth are appointed to offices and the low and the mean are ignored; hypocrisy, jealousy, evil-speaking and ill-will are erased from men's minds and are replaced by goodwill and sincerity; mosques, schools, mystic houses (*khallqahs*) and charitable kitchens (*ziafat-khallas*)[77] are full; sons become obedient to their fathers and mothers and the rights of patrons are repaid with love; truthfulness appears in the conversations of men, proper behaviour among slave-girls and loyalty among slaves; the poor and the needy get what is enough for them, widows and orphans do not suffer from want, travellers do not go to sleep hungry, and waifs and strays are given money to return home; gratitude for the blessings of God becomes current in the conversations of the select as well as the common people while ingratitude is diminished; contracts can be firmly relied upon and promises are fulfilled; the thought of rebellion does not come into minds of the people; the laws of the *shari'at* and the punishments of kings make all things that are inequitable, forbidden, disapproved or prohibited bitter to the minds of men; and, finally, regard for religion prevents the open profession of sins and wickedness.

Truth is established at the centre when the above-mentioned objects have been attained.

[2. *Barani pleads for an all-out Struggle against Hinduism*]

The Muslim king will not be able to establish the honour of theism (*tauhid*) and the supremacy of Islam unless he strives with all his courage to overthrow infidelity and to slaughter its leaders (*imams*), who in India are the Brahmans. He should make a firm resolve to overpower, capture, enslave and degrade the infidels. All the strength and power of the king and of the holy warriors of Islam should be concentrated in holy campaigns and holy wars; and they should risk themselves in the enterprise so that the true Faith may uproot the false creeds, and then it will look as if these false creeds had never existed because they have been deprived of all their glamour. On the other hand, if the Muslim king, in spite of the power and position which God has given him, is merely content to take the poll-tax (*jizya*) and tribute (*khiraj*) from the Hindus and preserves both infidels and infidelity and refuses to risk his power in attempting to overthrow them, what differences will there be in this respect between the kings of Islam and the Rais of the infidels? For the Rais of the infidels also exact the poll-tax (*jizya*) and the tribute (*khiraj*) from the Hindus, who belong to their own false creed, and fill their treasuries with money so obtained; in fact, they collect a hundred times more taxes.[78]

Further, if the kings of Islam, despite their royal power and prestige, are content to preserve infidels and infidelity in return for the tribute and the poll-tax, how can effect be given in this world to the following tradition of the Prophet: "I have been ordered to fight all people until they affirm 'There is no God but Allah'; but when they affirm this, their lives and properties are protected from me, subject to the law of Islam (as between Muslims)."

The Divine object in sending one hundred and twenty-four thousand prophets has been to overthrow infidels and infidelity and this has also been the object of early and later Muslim kings. But the succession of prophets has come to an end with our holy Prophet and the liquidation of infidelity through the preachings of prophets is no longer possible. Consequently, the overthrowal of infidelity and the disgrace of infidels and polytheists is now only possible if the king, after all necessary arrangements, concentrates his courage and his high resolve on this one object in order to win the approval of God and the Prophet by establishing the supremacy of the true Faith. But if the king is content merely to take the poll-tax and, the tribute from the Hindus, who are worshippers of Idols, and cow-dung, and the Hindus are able with peace of mind to preserve the customs of infidelity, then, of course, infidelity will not be liquidated, truth will not be established at the centre and the True Word will not be honoured. [A paragraph which repeats the same idea in about the same words has been omitted from here.]

It is *possible,* nevertheless, that kings through their determined efforts may first put their governments in order and then with their high resolve risk their power, dignity and prestige so that the true religion defeats and prevails over the false creeds the traditions of Islam are elevated, and what has been designed by Providence comes to pass by the establishment of truth at the centre. But it is necessary for kings to understand what the establishment of truth at the centre means, so that they may devote their lives to striving for it, deeming it to be the main objective for the attainment of which they should be prepared to risk themselves and their supporters. The kings in reward for their efforts in this enterprise, which has been the object of prophets, caliphs, saints and truthful men (*siddiqan*) as well as of the earlier and later kings of the Muslim community, will obtain in this world praises for their good deeds which will last till the Day of Judgment and in the next world they will have the status of prophets, truthful men, saints and of those near to God (*muqarribin*) and a share of that Divinely promised blessing "which the ear has not heard of and the eye has not seen." Also by that increase of spiritual rewards that is due to kings, such rulers will be blessed in Paradise by a variety of good things, while love for them will survive in the hearts of the people of this earth and their good deeds will be recounted generation after generation. The religious perfection of, the Muslim kings lies in this—*they should risk themselves as well as their power and authority and strive day and night to establish truth at the centre.* The sons of Mahmud and kings of Islam ought to know that in the *Sunni* faith the establishment of truth at the centre is both excellent knowledge and excellent action. This is the highest of all good works with the exception of the mission of the prophets.

Sons of Mahmud and kings of Islam! You should with all your royal determination apply yourself to uprooting and disgracing infidels, polytheists and men of bad dogmas and bad religions, if you wish that you may not have to be ashamed before God and his Prophet and that in your record of life—concerning what you have said and done, the clothes you have worn and the food you have eaten—they may write good instead of evil.

You should consider the enemies of God and His Faith to be your enemies and you should risk your power and authority in overthrowing them, so that you may win the approval of God and the Prophet Mohammad and of all prophets and saints. You should not content yourself merely with levying the poll-tax and the tribute from the infidels and you should not allow infidelity to be preserved in spite of your royal power and authority. You should strive day and night for the degradation of infidelity so that (on the Day of Judgment) you may be raised (from your graves) among the prophets and be blessed with the sight of God for all eternity and "may find a seat among the truthful near the Powerful King (God)".

The majority of religious scholars and wise men of early (Islamic) as well as later times have been sure that if Muslim kings strive with all their might and power and the power of all their supporters on this path, the following objects will be attained: The true Faith will gain a proper ascendancy over the false creeds; the True Word will be honoured; the traditions of infidelity and polytheism will be weakened; Musalmans will be favoured and honoured; infidels and men of bad faith will be faced with destitution and disgrace; the orders of the unlawful state and the opposed creeds will be erased; the laws of the *shari'at* will be enforced on the seventy-two communities; and the enemies of God and the Prophet will be condemned, banished, repudiated and terrorised.

[3. *Barani admits that Muslim Kings in India are Tolerant:* (*a*) *Hindus are Prosperous;* (*b*) *Sinful Professions are permitted to the Musalmans; and* (*c*) *Philosophers are allowed to Teach.*]

But as a matter of fact truth cannot be established at the centre, the elevation of the True Word is not possible and the true Faith does not overpower the false creeds because the kings of Islam, in spite of the power and prestige that Islam has obtained on this earth and in spite of their seven centuries of hereditary Muslim faith permit that in their capital (Delhi) and in the cities of the Musalmans the customs of infidelity are openly practised, idols are publicly worshipped *and the traditions of infidelity are adhered to with greater insistence than before.* Openly and without fear, the infidels continue the teaching of the principles of their false creed; they also adorn their idols and celebrate their rejoicings during their festivals with the beat of drums and *dhols* and with singing and dancing. By merely paying a few *tankas* and the poll-tax (*jizya*) they are able to continue the traditions of infidelity by giving lessons in the books of their false faith and enforcing the orders of these books. How (under these conditions) can the traditions of Islam be elevated or the orders for enforcing the good and prohibiting the evil be made effective?

But the desire for overthrowing infidels and knocking down idolators and polytheists does not fill the hearts of the Muslim kings (of India). On the other hand, out of consideration for the fact that infidels and polytheists are payers of tribute and protected persons (*zimmis*), these infidels are honoured, distinguished, favoured and made eminent; the kings bestow drums, banners, ornaments, cloaks of brocade and caparisoned horses upon them, and appoint them to governorships, high posts and offices. And in their Capital (Delhi), owing to the status of which the status of all other Muslim cities is raised, Muslim king's not only allow but are pleased with the fact that infidels, polytheists, idol-worshippers and cow-dung (*sargin*) worshippers build houses like palaces, wear clothes of brocade and ride Arab horses caparisoned with gold and silver ornaments. They are equipped with a hundred thousand sources of strength. They live in delights and comforts. They take Musalmans into their service and make them run before their horses; the poor Muslamans beg of them at their doors; and in the capital of Islam, owing to which the edifice of Islam is elevated, they are called *rais* (great rulers) *ranas* (minor rulers), *thakurs* (warriors), *sahas* (bankers), *mehtas* (clerks) and *pandits* (priests).

How under these conditions can the Faith prevail over the false creeds or truth be established at the centre?

Further, if the desire to protect the Faith and to enforce the orders of the Prophet's *shari'at* does not catch hold of the skirts of the kings of Islam, they will allow the Musalmans to take to dirty and sinful trades and professions, to keep taverns, brothels and gambling houses in every bazaar and lane and to organise splendid music parties. But the kings are content to levy taxes on these groups, and as a result sinners and organisers of public immortalities are busy with their work without fear or apprehension in every lane, bazaar, and city-quarter. How can the principle of 'ordering the good and prohibiting the evil', which is the essence of the Muslim faith and an obligatory duty of all Muslim kings, be construed to permit such things? And how (if such things are permitted) can the prestige of Islam increase and truth become firm at the centre?

Further, if the kings like and approve it, philosophers and all other people of bad faith, who are opponents of the correct religion and enemies of the Prophet, will teach their books openly. They give to the sciences of the Greeks, which are the enemies of the traditional commands of early and later prophets, the name of rational knowledge (*ilm-i ma'qulat*) and to the sciences of the *shari'at* they give the name of traditional knowledge (*ilm-i manqulat*). They consider that the world is eternal and proclaim it to be such. "They do not consider God to have a cognition of details. They are disbelievers in the Day of Judgment and in the rising up of men (from their graves), in Account-taking (on Judgment Day) and in Heaven and Hell, though belief in these things is the basis of the Faith and has been asserted in three hundred and sixty revealed books of the prophets. They not only teach (their doctrines) but also write rationalistic books in denial of these things. Now if such people are allowed to live with honour and dignity in the capital of the king and to promulgate their doctrines and to show their preference for the rationalistic over the traditional, how can the correct Faith be made to prevail over the false creeds, or the traditions of Islam elevated, or truth established at the centre, or the prestige of ordering the good and prohibiting the unlawful established?

[*4. Barani advocates that Education be Prohibited to the Lower Orders, for Education will make them Efficient and Capable.*]

[Barani illustrates this Advice by making the following statement on the authority of the *Ma-asirul Khulafa* (*Good Deeds of the Caliphs*). Nothing stated here is historically correct, but it expresses Barani's own ideology. During the war of succession between the two sons of the Caliph Harun-ar Rashid—Mohammad Amin and Mamun, the administration of Baghdad became lax and in consequence of it two great evils appeared. *First,* sin and wickedness became public; music halls (*tarabadads*) were started; tavern-keeping, gambling and whore-mongering became prosperous professions.

Secondly, philosophers appeared on the scene. Many philosophers came to Baghdad in the guise of religious scholars and established themselves in the city. They openly gave lessons to the Muslamans in the mosques on their wrong doctrines and false dogmas. They published books of their false faith and misled students by putting it firmly into their minds that nothing is possible unless it can be proved by the canons of reason. The non-worldly religious scholars, such as Imam Ahmad Hambal, Imam Yahya Ma-in, Abdullah Mubarak and other pious and religious men were unable to see prohibited things rampant in the city of Baghdad[79]... They took to secluded lives, closed their doors to the coming and going of people, gave up attending the congregational prayers of Friday and the two Ids, and ceased to associate with their fellowmen.]

[When Mamun came to Baghdad after his brother had been defeated, he summoned an assembly (*mahzar*) and wrote out an order (*manshur*) with his own hand. Barani gives the text of this order, which is a pure fabrication. This alleged order defined in detail the awards to be given and the punishments to be meted out to every group. It is unnecessary to go into the details of an order that could not have existed, but the following paragraph from it is of particular interest as revealing Barani's attitude to the Muslim working-class.]

"Teachers of every kind are to be sternly ordered not to thrust precious stones down the throats of dogs or to put collars of gold round the necks of pigs and bears—that is, to the mean, the ignoble and the worthless, to shopkeepers and to the low-born they are to teach nothing more than the rules about prayer, fasting, religious charity and the Haj pilgrimage along with some chapters of the Quran and some doctrines of the Faith, without which their religion cannot be correct and valid prayers are not possible. But they are to be taught nothing else; lest it bring honour to their mean souls. They are not to be taught reading and writing, for plenty of disorders arise owing to the skill of the low-born in knowledge. The disorder into which all affairs of the religion and the state are thrown is due to the acts and words of the low-born, who have become skilled. For, on account of their skill; they become governors (*wali*) revenue-collectors (*amils*), auditors (*mutasarrif*), officers (*farman-deh*) and rulers (*farman-rawa*). If teachers are disobedient, and it is discovered at the time or investigation that they have imparted knowledge or taught letters or writing to the low-born, inevitably the punishment for their disobedience will be meted out to them."

Notes on Imam Shafi'i and Mamun Rashid

4: *Imam Shafi'i's Doctrine with reference to Non-Muslims.* Though the Quran not only implies but affirms that prophets have been sent to all peoples from time to time, and tradition fixes the number of such prophets at 124,000, Muslim legists have nevertheless drawn a distinction between (a) the 'People of the Book', or followers of revealed books referred to in the Quran and (b) other non-Muslims. Now Barani's bright idea is that while Imam Abu Hanifa has permitted peace with those non-Muslims, who have no revealed books referred to in the Quran, on the payment of the *jizya,* other religious leaders have prescribed eternal war with them. Thus in the *Tarikh-i Firoz Shahi* (p. 291) he puts the following statement in the mouth of Qazi Mugheesuddin of Bayana: "Apart from Imam-i-Azam Abu Hanifa, to whose sect we belong, there is no decision (*rawayat*) in favour of the followers of other religions. According to other religious scholars, the order about the Hindus is—'Either Islam or the Sword'!"

Now the real reference is to Imam Shafi'i, whose teachings on the matter Barani grossly misrepresents, Islam even then covered but a small part of the globe and it was obvious that if the Muslamans took up the sword against all polytheists, the latter would do the same and no one could foresee the result of such a far-flung and unending conflict.

But what principles did Imam Shafi'i really lay down? The original works of Imam Shafi'i—his *Ikhtilafatul Hadis* (*Variation in the Prophet's Saying*) and *Risalas* (treatises)—were printed in Egypt after the First World War. They may have been hard to find in the India of Barani's days. But the works of the famous Shafi'i traditionist and theological writer, Abu Bakr Ahmad Baihaqi, (died 1067 A.D.) were then available in India. In his *Ahkamul Quran,* a re-edition of a work of the Shafi'i scholar, Mohammad bin Idris, who died in 203 A.H. (printed Cairo, 1952), Baihaqi states:

1. "Shafi'i has said: God has ordered: Fight against those who do not believe in Allah and the Day of Judgment and who do not

forbid what Allah and His Prophet have forbidden and who do not join the true faith from among the people of the book till they give the *jizya* with their hands and they are subdued (p. 51)'...and (in this matter) the Arab and non-Arabs are to be treated equally." (p. 53)

2. "But the duty of fighting the worshippers of idols from among the polytheists (*mushriks*) is this: Fight them, *if you have power over them* (*iz qudira alaihim*) till they accept Islam and it is not permitted to you by the Quran and the Sunnah of the Prophet to accept *jizya* from them." (p. 53)

Now the essence of such a postulate is the conditional clause—"if *you have power over them*"—and if this clause is omitted, the whole meaning of Imam Shafii's postulate is changed. He was not advising the Musalmans to perish in a hopeless struggle. Also living in the heart of what was once pagan Arabia, the Imam could not fail to realise that while Islam could liquidate Arab idolatry, it would have to make permanent terms with the Jews and the Christians. This is the basis of the practical distinction between 'the people of the book' and the 'idol-worshippers', Imam Shafi'i is silent about the Hindus but he distinctly says: "The Prophet of Allah has permitted the acceptance of *jizya* from the Magians" (*Ahkamul Quran*, Vol. II, p. 53). And from the view-point of the medieval Muslim legists, the Hindus and the Magians (Zoroastrians) stood in exactly the same category. But this is not all.

3. "Imam Shafi'i says: 'War has been made obligatory against non-Muslims who are not people of the book till they accept Islam and against the people of the book till they pay the *jizya*. But the Quran also states, 'Allah does not impose upon any person a duty beyond his power' (*Sura II*, verse 276). Consequently, only that is a duty of the Musalmans which is within their power; and if they are helpless about a matter, then they are not in duty bound to do what is beyond their power. So there is no punishment for the Musalmans if they refrain from fighting a group of polytheists and make peace with them.' (p. 62)" ..."And Imam Shafi'i continues: 'The Prophet of God made peace with the people of Mecca at Hudaibia; it was a peace between them for ten years, and during this journey the revelation came to him, 'We have granted to you a clear victory so that God may forgive you (*Sura XLVIII*, verse 1-2).'" (*Ahkamul Quran*, p. 62).

"And Imam Shafi'i says, 'Ibn-i Shahab has said, 'There was no greater victory for Islam than the treaty of Hudaibia'; and Shahab added, 'People joined Islam and became true believers.'" (*Ahkamul Quran*, pp. 62–63)

The fanaticism of Barani, it will be seen, finds no support in the teachings of Imam *Shafi'i.* It has to be added that, according to Professor Abdul Ghani Abdal Khaliq, the learned Egyptian editor of Baihaqi's *Ahkamul Quran,* the statements attributed by Baihaqi to Imam Shafi'i are to be found in the Imam's *Ikhtilafatul Hadis* in exactly the same words. The attitude of fanaticism adopted by Barani in Advice XI is not supported by any school of Muslim legists. The ideal of Imam Shafi'i, as he clearly states is the opportunity of peaceful preaching secured to the Musalmans by the Treaty of Hudaibiah.

5. **The 'Orthodoxy' of the Caliph Mamun Rashid:** It is impossible to point out all the mistakes with reference to facts that Barani makes in the course of his Illustration to this Advice. (a) It *is* true that there was both rebellion and disorder in Baghdad till Mamun entered the capital in August 819 A.D. But there is nothing to justify the picture of the dominance of philosophy and sin which Barani tries to paint. (b) With his usual recklessness and cheap theological fanaticism, he confuses the Mu'tazilas (the followers of Wasil bin 'Ata) with the philosophers, who were the followers of Aristotle and the Greek thinkers. Only the Mu'tazilas had some public influence at Baghdad then; the philosophers did not count, (c) Imam Ahmad Hambal (780–855 A.D.), the founder of the *fourth* Sunni school and Imam Yahya Ma-in (who may have died in 848 A.D.) were close friends. Ibn-i Khallikan would have us believe that they were both pupils of Imam Shafi'i (See *Ibn-i Khallikan,* Vol. I, p. 44 for Imam Ahmad bin Hambal and Vol. IV, pp. 24-26 for Imam Yahya Ma-in). In any case Imam Hambal, like most Muslim thinkers of the highest type, considered the service of government to be sinful and he would not eat food at the house of his own son, because his son had been in government service as *qazi* for a year. Further, he was an opponent of the Mu'tazilites, and because he would not subscribe to their doctrine that 'the Quran was created (*makhluq*),' he was put into chains by Mamun's orders and only Mamun's death in 833 A.D. saved him from further persecution. (d) The name of the mystic, Shaikh Abdullah Mubarak, is needlessly brought into the affair; he had died some

twenty years before this event (*Tazkiratul Auliya* No. 15, *Kashful Mahjub*, p. 76).

But Barani's ignorance of history is perhaps best displayed by his attempt to paint Mamun Rashid as an orthodox ruler of the type he approved. Nothing could be further from real facts. Mamun was a great patron of the Mu'tazilites, the heretic group of *theologians* whom Barani detested. "In some matters indeed the liberality of Al-Mamun was sufficiently wide. Thus a few years previously he had abolished the ban imposed by his predecessors on the favourable mention of Mu'awiya or any of the Umayyad Companions, and even to Christians liberty of discussion on the comparative claims of the Gospel and Islam was allowed. But the Persian predilection which he all the time entertained inclined him at last zealously to canvass the doctrines of the liberal-minded, if freethinking, Mu'tazilas... In the end he avowed his conversion to certain tenets opposed to the orthodox faith. Amongst these he held Freedom of the Will in place of Predestination; and that the Quran, though inspired, was 'created' in place of the hitherto undisputed tenet that it is 'uncreate and eternal'... The Quran itself was explained allegorically, and the difficulties besetting the orthodox, such as offended reason or cramped the growth of society, easily evaded." (Muir, *Caliphate*, pp. 506–507).

And Dr. Letterstien says: "Mamun's rationalistic tendencies made him join the Mu'tazilites... While he persecuted the orthodox and catechised them severely about the soundness of their belief in the Mu'tazila, he treated the Alids with the greatest consideration. In his reign poetry and learning reached their golden age... The Caliph also took a special interest in philosophy and the exact sciences." (*Ency. Isl.* Vol. III, p. 222).

The whole matter has been discussed in detail by the late Maulana Shibli in his *Al-Mamun* and there can be no controversy about it. The great Caliph was a Mu'tazilite and a sworn opponent of that group of orthodoxy, which was to rule in future under Abul Hasan Ashari (873-935) and which was found to be one of its cheapest and most superficial exponents in Ziauddin Barani. The alleged *Manshur* or order of Mamun quoted by Barani has to be dismissed as a pure fabrication. [H]

Advice XII

On the Administration of Justice

[I. The Ruler's Innate Sense of Justice.]

[The beginning of this Advice is missing in the manuscript but it appears from the surviving part that its subject-matter was the administration of justice.]

[Barani declares that according to wise men (*hakims*) a ruler endowed with an innate sense of justice (*'adl-i jibilli*) is distinguished by the following twenty qualities:—]

(1) Kinship with the oppressed, desire to protect the weak, hatred of the unjust and enmity of the oppressors is written in his heart.

(2) He has no feeling of retaliation or revenge, even when he is giving judgment against his own enemies.

(3) He is incapable of making compromises or tolerating wrongs or exceeding proper limits where justice is concerned.

(4) His heart trembles lest the innocent be punished.

(5) No one can influence him where the administration of justice is concerned.

(6) He cares neither for the *criticism* nor the approval of men when he is passing judicial judgments.

(7) No consideration of any harm to himself or to his government can prevent him from enforcing justice.

(8) He is incapable of self-deception and does not make his principle flexible.

(9) Though stern in enforcing the just claims of others, yet he prefers to be forgiving where he is personally concerned.

(10) He finds no peace in his heart till he has exacted the claims of the weak from the strong.

(11) He avoids putting himself under the obligations of others from fear that these obligations may influence his mind (as a judge).

(12) Though he seeks justice, yet his heart is kind and affectionate.

(13) His just anger is for the sake of God only and no animal passions of hostility are excited in him.

(14) In his heart he hates his power as the supreme commander because it entails the obligation of passing orders against the honour and the blood of Musalmans.

(15) His mind instinctively rejects deceptions, lies, false excuses and trickeries, for the touchstone of intelligence for distinguishing the false from the true is present in his breast.

(16) He desires that all cases appertaining to his subjects should be decided by him personally.

(17) Love for such a ruler is inscribed in the hearts of his subjects, and even if injuries are caused by his orders, his subjects do not hate him on that account.

(18) His heart beats restlessly if he hears of any case of injustice or wrong in east or west.

(19) His mind is always absorbed in thoughts of overthrowing the unjust and enforcing justice.

(20) When dealing with peaceful men, he is guided by the precept that "punishment should be based on evidence", but when dealing with oppressors, sinners and criminals, who are by their nature inclined to wrong-doing, he does not allow doubts (about their guilt) to sway his mind.

[II. *Special and Universal Equality*]

[By 'special equality' is meant the equality of all litigants before the ruler, because justice is no respector of persons. By 'universal equality' is meant the equality of the ruler and the ruled. Some irrelevant and repetitive sentences have not been translated.]

According to early and later kings, justice means putting all litigants on a par and enforcing equality between them. But early religious scholars of the correct Faith have divided equality from the view-point of the rulers into two kinds. One kind they have named 'special equality' (*masawat-i khas*) and the other 'universal equality' (*masawat-i 'am*). The latter also implies the equality of the ruler (with his subjects).

'Special equality', which is confined to the equality of the litigants only, is known in this technical sense all over the world. It means that the caliph, king, *qazi,* governor, ruler, officer—in fact, anyone who for any reason has the power of decision in his hands—enforces equality between the accuser and the accused.

He treats them equally during the trial with reference to their speeches and actions, and (the privilege of) sitting and standing before him) and does not give preference to either party for any cause. At the time of giving and enforcing his judgments, he has no regard for the strong or the rich, or for the government and its officers. No consideration for the dignity, merit, honour, status or greatness of either party prevents him from meting out impartial justice. In the enforcement of justice he looks with the same eye at relations and strangers, the distinguished and the, ignoble, the employed and the unemployed, officers and citizens, rich and poor, nobles and commons, supporters and opponents, friends and foes. He accepts no gifts, bribes, presents or souvenirs, valuable or cheap, from either party. In the enforcement of justice be has no regard either for the policy of the state or for his love for his father, mother, brothers and sons; and no fear, either about the decline of his own power or the opposition and the enmity of the people, crosses his mind. He has no regard for any bonds or ties; he flatters no one and considers no recommendations. Justice means keeping in regard the above-mentioned principles; a person who acts in opposition to them cannot be called just. The reward for one hour (*sa'at*) of justice, which is based on the conditions mentioned above, is higher and greater than seventy years of devotions. A ruler who has been created (by God) with the virtue of justice—i.e. who has been born just from his mother's womb and justice has been made the companion of his soul from the beginning of time—will be able to bear the burden of enforcing such justice for a while, and his spiritual reward can neither be computed nor calculated. But a ruler, who has not been created with the virtue of innate justice, will not be able to adhere to the above-mentioned conditions.

The *second* kind of justice implies 'universal equality'. It is a consequence of the perfection of piety and an exclusive feature of the four Pious Caliphs of the Prophet's Faith. It has ended with Abu Bakr, Umar-i Khattab, Usman and Ali Murtaza, But the radiance of 'universal equality' has also shone on the reign of 'Umar bin Abdul Aziz'[80]. It is like this. The Caliph, who wields the powers of a Jamshed or a Khusrau over realms subordinate to his orders, not only discharges the obligations of 'special equality' between litigants but lives in the same way as the *faqirs* and the poor people of the community. In spite of his great authority and status he prefers a life of poverty. He passes his days in indebtedness, in distress and in lack of material means; his food and dress is the same as of the poorest people. He does not take from the Public Treasury more than he requires for the minimum needs of his life and he eats and dresses in the same way as his slaves. And this achievement, which appears to be the harmonisation of two opposites—kingship and poverty—has been considered a miracle of the Prophet and a wonderful achievement of the Pious Caliphs.

The Sons of Mahmud ought to know that God maintains the earth and the heavens (*samawat*) through justice. From the time of Adam till today the prosperity of the earth has been maintained through the justice of men of equity. The enforcement of the canons of every religion, whether false or true, has only been possible on the principles of justice. Even (ancient) rulers, who blackened their faces by claims to divinity, maintained the 'forms' (*surat*) of justice according to the religion, creed, customs and ways of their time.

[Barani illustrates this Advice by referring to the Caliph Umar and Naushirwan, emperor of Iran. The regulations attributed by Barani to Naushirwan have not been translated.]

Scholars of history have written that Umar-i Khattab, the second Caliph of Islam, and Naushirwan, the Just, emperor of Iran, have been remarkable for their justice. The wise men of Arabia and Iran are agreed that after discharging the obligations of 'special equality', Umar also did justice to the principle of 'universal equality'. Naushirwan, the Just, strove hard for special equality, but he had no share or portion of 'universal equality'. Now 'special equality' is a necessary condition of 'universal equality', but 'universal equality' is not a necessary condition of 'special equality'. The leaders of Arabia and Iran have stated that 'Umar-i Khattab did whatever Naushirwan did, but Naushirwan was unable to do what Umar did; for devotion, piety, renunciation of the world and self-sacrifice are pre-conditions of 'universal equality'.

All scholars of history are agreed that during the time of his Caliphate Umar Khattab had seventy-seven patches on his torn cloak. It often happened that, in spite of the grandeur and dignity of his supreme command, he obtained the means for the maintenance of his family by manual labour; he often obtained his daily livelihood by making bricks. Though the chief parts of the inhabited globe were subordinate to his authority, he passed his days in poverty and starvation; and in the manner and mode of his livelihood he was like the *faqirs* and poor people of the community. The Companions used to say to each other. "The poorest house in Medina is the house of Umar, the Commander of the Faithful." It was owing to the principle of universal equality that on his journey to Jerusalem (*Baitul Muqaddas*) he took turns in riding and walking with his slave; one day he rode while the slave held the camel's bridle, while on the second day the slave rode while Umar held the bridle and walked on foot. He had no other camel but this, though he was marching to Syria with seventy thousand Arabs. He sent to the Companions and the leaders of the tribes all the delicious dishes, varieties of luxuries and all kinds of fruits, which the feudal lords (*marzuban*) of Iran and the *zamindars* of Iraq brought to him in large quantities; he neither stretched his own blessed hand towards these things nor would permit his sons to do so. He used to live with his sons in the courtyards of the Juma mosques inside the cities and would not take up his residence in anyone's house.

As to what Umar-i Khattab did for special equality—how he fulfilled its conditions superlatively and beyond the possibility of further attainment and how he paid no regard to any relationship, cause or consideration—all this is too well known to need description. He had no hesitation in passing a just judgment on his own son, and his paternal affection did not prevent him from enforcing the punishment prescribed by the *shari'at*. Wise men will comprehend that such an equitable man, who is born perfectly just and allows his son to die under the lashes prescribed by the *shari'at*, will not allow any relationship to catch hold of his hands or to restrain him in enforcing the orders of the *shari'at*.

[*III. Hearing of Complaints by the King*]

[It is obvious from the whole line of Barani's argument that 'universal equality' is beyond the attainment of Muslim kings. But they should strive for 'special equality' and in particular they should be personally accessible to the victims of oppression[81].]

O Sons of Mahmud and kings of Islam! It is your duty to give up your pleasures hunting and riding for one day every week.

And on that day you should hold your public court (*bar-i 'am*) in a plain, sit on some elevated ground and receive the petitions of the oppressed with your own hands. The dignity of your kingship, the sensitiveness of your minds and your pride in your prestige and power should not prevent you from performing such a duty, for it makes amends for your sins as a king. It is your duty to examine the criminal. If it is clear to you that it is his first offence and that it has been due to error and negligence, then compel him with humiliation and disgrace to pay the claims of the injured man and after that forgive him on condition of repentance. But if repeated crimes have been proved against him and you see that criminality is ingrained in his nature, then compel him to pay the claims of the injured man with compensations in addition to it and drive him out of your country. You should know well that tyranny cannot be removed from the kingdom till tyrants are uprooted. You should organise (for this task) a group of persons from among your officers in whom the desire for religion has overpowered the desire for this world, so that through their orders (for enforcing justice) you may attain good reputation in this world and salvation in the next. This is the essence of all precepts; if kings recognise the value of this precept, they will not fail in their religions or secular enterprises.

[Barani again returns to one of his favourite themes and asks kings to suppress *dishonest shopkeepers*.]

Advice XIII

The King's Mercy and Punishments

[1. *The Need of Moderation and Discrimination*.]

[It has been necessary to omit the translation of some paragraphs in this Advice as they repeat the same ideas in almost the same words. Also some paragraphs have been transposed to put the author's arguments in proper sequence.]

Sultan Mahmud says: O Sons of Mahmud! You should know that the forgiving, overlooking, disregarding and veiling of faults is one of the duties and obligations of kingship. There will be no permanence for the king or the state if the king is so severe that he neither forgives the crimes of his *ra'iyyat*, nor overlooks the shortcomings of his officers nor shuts his eyes to negligences and defaults, till matters come to such a pass that no one among his subjects entertains any further hopes from him and a fierce hatred is excited against him among his own helpers and supporters. On the other hand, if the king does not subject the rebellious, the cruel, the mischievous—thieves, insolent persons, misappropriators, usurpers, the reckless, the shameless, the heedless and the designers of wickedness—to punishments, chastisements, penalties, bonds and chains, some men will eat up others and no one's wealth, property, wife and children will be safe. The king should, therefore, know the appropriate occasions for both forgiveness and punishment.....

Moreover kings should understand that the correct meaning of the term *siyasat* is 'putting right the affairs of the world'. Now various kinds of policies are needed so that the world is put right, the people are permanently settled on the path of equity and justice, truth is established at the centre, the hearts of the select and the commons are pacified, and the king becomes secure from the people and the people from the king. One kind of policy consists in benevolence, affection, favours, gifts, rewards, bounties and kindnesses; by this policy many people of the kingdom become prosperous and are put right. In the technique of royal administration this policy is also known as *siyasat*. Another variety of *siyasat* consists in insulting, disgracing, dismissing, showing lack of regard and confiscating property; by this policy also a group of people are put right and a large number of persons are warned. Another variety of *siyasat* consists in the infliction of kicks, blows with sticks and warnings; such severities are necessary for putting many people right while others are properly frightened and learn a lesson. Another variety of *siyasat* consists of bonds, chains, imprisonment and confinement, which the policy of the state may necessitate for a particular group; it keeps the would-be revenue offender on the straight path, terrorises others and is conducive to the good order of the kingdom. Another variety of *siyasat* is exile, and exiles are of different kinds. Some persons, as a matter of policy, the kings exile from their capital to a part of their kingdom and assign to them villages and pensions in accordance with their status. Others they exile for a fixed period, removing them from their positions (near the throne) and sending them to some place, far or near. A few are also exiled to distant lands. These three kinds of exiles are political punishments (for officers). But unless the *shari'at* has permitted, kings should not put Musalmans to death for every little fault. So long as imprisonment, bonds, chains and exile are effective deterrents, the lives of Musalmans should not be taken and their blood should not be shed.

The great men of the religion and the state of the Prophet have said: Every king who understands well the meaning of the Quranic verse—"God is the forgiver of sins, the acceptor of repentance and strict in His punishments[82]"—will also be able to discern the appropriate occasions for forgiveness and punishment. Efficient administration and good order will appear during his reign, and owing to the policy of his government he will attain to salvation.

Religious scholars have also said: Whenever the king behaves towards the people in accordance with the above-mentioned Quranic verse, he obtains happiness from his kingdom during his life-time and after his death his name remains on this earth. The Quran has also said: "If God punished men according to what they deserve, no living creature would be left on the back of the earth.[83]" God forgives and pardons and does not punish. The Prophet has said: "The best of the sons of Adam, whether they have committed wrongs or not, are those who pray for God's forgiveness."

And great kings who feared God have said: Kingship cannot be properly established without forgiveness and punishments. He alone can be called a farsighted king, who knows well the correct occasions for forgiveness and punishment and who at the time of issuing his orders and enforcing his commands has a proper regard for the *stability* of state-affairs. If a man can be put right by kindness and favours and they treat him with *severity* and harshness, then this is not *siyasat* or 'putting right' but disorder and demoralisation. Similarly, if in order to set right the affairs of the state, it is necessary to put a man in bonds or to exile him or put him to death, but they assign him a province or an office near the throne and shower favours on him then by such *siyasat* they will ruin the edifice of the state. Also if kings wish to inflict punishments before the affairs of the state have been stabilised, or insist on treating minor faults in great enterprises as crimes, or persist in exacting their minute claims before the select and the commons have become accustomed to the execution of their penal orders—then by such severities they will only throw the affairs of the state into disorder. If for some reason the king has been cruel to a person near to him, the injured man's resentment should be removed from his heart through gracious royal favours. The king should live with the helpers and supporters of his kingdom in such a way that his prestige is not lessened while they also are not dishonoured. This is a conclusive proof of the king's perfect intelligence, but it is a difficult, very difficult, task.

[2. *The King's Recognition of Rights.*]

Ancient kings have said: A necessary virtue of kingship is the recognition of rights. If a king does not recognise the rights of people, no trace of his kingdom will remain and he will not attain salvation in the next world. The distinctive features of a king who recognises rights have been often described. The foundation of the king's recognition (of the rights of men) is his obedience to the commands of God; that he is guilty of errors, negligence or sins is another matter, but he should not be insolent towards God and the Prophet in religious or secular affairs.

(1) With reference to his brothers, wife, children, old friends and old well-wishers, the king's recognition of rights means that on becoming the king he deals with them in all the affairs of life, subject of course to the maintenance of his own royal dignity, a thousand times better than he did before; he discharges the obligations of everyone of them in accordance with his royal means, but not so excessively that he is unable to answer for his actions on the Day of Judgment.

(2) A king's recognition of rights with reference to the helpers and supporters of his kingdom—the high and chosen officers of the court and the sincere well-wishers of the state—means that, in addition to the mutual security between them and the king, the king also veils and overlooks their faults and does not disgrace them for every little cause, and that if others also wish to attain their favoured positions, this will not be possible.

(3) The king's recognition of rights with respect to old servants and slaves means that he keeps them honoured and respectable; nevertheless, he should not raise them to high offices except on grounds of personal merit, for this will lead to their ruin and to the ruin of the kingdom. The affairs of state cannot be stabilised through excessive favours without reason. Favours and gifts

should be given in accordance with the honour that is due and in proportion to services rendered. Failure to recognise past services leads to bad reputation and lack of trust; but excessive favours to the unworthy lead to oppression, deviation from the right path, paucity in recognising the rights of the deserving, and to defects of policy.

(4) The king's recognition of rights with respect to the select men of the kingdom, who are adorned with orthodox virtues but have no claims of personal services on him, means that he should create honour and respect for them among the people at his gate and his court in accordance with their merits; and that he should make them the sincere well-wishers of his state by his favours and personal contacts.

(5) The king's recognition of rights with respect to his *ra'iyyat* means that he forgives their sins, accepts their repentance, refrains from minute inquiries and fault-findings (concerning them) and does not inflict upon them impositions beyond their power of endurance. He should look upon them with the eyes of affection and make the generality of his subjects his well-wishers through excessive justice and equity. Whenever the king obtains a reputation for recognising the rights of the people and for keeping his promises, the affairs of his state are stabilised and his subjects and his soldiers become his supporters and well-wishers.

[3. *Some Problems of Punishment*.]

[The passages on this subject have got mixed in the manuscript, but put into logical sequence they deal with the following topics:—(1) The king should not interfere with *shari'at* punishments. (2) The death-penalty for political offences should only be inflicted in extreme cases. (3) The Quran and the traditions are silent about the punishment of political offenders and the great legists of Islam have merely said that kings are responsible before God and man for the political punishments they inflict. A king should, therefore, be able 'to discern those occasions of inescapable necessity' when alone he is justified in inflicting the death penalty. Barani pleads for the principle that no more punishments should be inflicted than are absolutely necessary for the welfare of the state. (4) Theological punishments which are quite unrelated to Indian society and traditions. (5) Punishments for insulating the king.

(6) Offences against the Public Treasury. (7) Conditions under which the king should permit people to intercede with him.]

1. All kings should know that they have no authority to increase or decrease the penalties, punishments and compensations that have been prescribed for the Muslim community by the *shari'at.* In fact, the king's duty of protecting the Faith demands that he should appoint honest officers for the enforcement of the *shari'at* and support them so effectively that the orders of the *shari'at* are executed without any false interpretations or trickeries. These officers should have no respect for persons nor should they pay regard to anyone's prestige or status; also they should not go beyond the obvious meaning of the legal rulings (*rawayat*) that have come down to us from religious-scholars. They should not resort to dissimulations or strained interpretations; and they should bring before the king matters in which *shari'at* laws cannot be enforced.

2. During the phenomenal kingship of a few days the *sunnah* (traditions) of God should be followed[84]. There are various kinds of created men in this world and the king ought to deal with every group, community and class according to its traditions, business, profession and habits. He should treat the virtuous and the obedient with affection and the submissive with kindness. He should overlook the faults of his well-wishers, ignore their shortcomings and draw a veil over their inefficiencies; he should also forgive their minor misdemeanours, minute faults and their sins against their own souls. But he should mete out appropriate punishments to the rebellious, the headstrong and the mischievous, and also to political offenders, conspirators, rebels, rascals and shameless persons. In every punishment due regard should be paid to its limits; and so far as possible restraint should be exercised in the taking of men's lives for 'man is the building of God'. Efforts should be made that the limits of the *shiari'at* are not overstepped in the matter of compensations, penalties and punishments.

Indeed, kings in inflicting the death penalty have not acted according to the precepts of any religious scholar.

Now concerning the classes and groups mentioned above, if the object of putting them right (*siyasat*) cannot be attained by lesser punishments, then after great hesitation and reluctance the death penalty has been permitted. To the generality of the people *siyasat* means 'putting to death'. There are various opinions about the death penalty. The killing of man is prohibited in all religions, and the killing of a Musalman, except in accordance with the laws of the *shari'at,* is extremely dangerous, though at the time of inflicting the death penalty it may seem easy[85]. Further, in all cases of punishments, consideration of the circumstances is necessary. Refraining from inflicting the death penalty, to the utmost extent possible, has been a prominent feature of the policy of religious Muslim kings.

3. But the real distress and difficulties that face a religious king pertain to the penalties and capital punishments which are demanded by his political policy. No clear precept has come down to us about the question of political punishments from the religious scholars of the four (*Sunni*) sects; all that is found is the statement that kings are responsible for the political punishments they inflict. Now there can be no greater embarrassment for the kings of Islam in their worldly affairs than that they should have to turn their backs on what God and the Prophet have commanded, and without the permission of the *shari'at* and on their own responsibility shed the blood of a Musalman, which God has forbidden—that for the kingdom of a few days they should make themselves responsible before the Divine Throne for the killing of Musalmans and deem the preservation of their individual persons, the glory of their royal affairs and their own honour and greatness to be identical with the peace and prosperity of the peoples of the world.

The first kind of death punishment mentioned above is known as the *shari'at* death penalty (*qasas-i shar'i*) and the second as political death penalty (*siyasat-i mulki*). According to Sultan Mahmud all the pleasures of this world do not outweigh the responsibility for the political death penalty, and one drop of the blood of a believer in God, which is shed unjustly, is not worth all the pomp and glory of kingship.

The sons of Mahmud should know that political punishments for which religious scholars have considered kings to be responsible, and the limits of which have not been fixed, are of various kinds.

One kind of punishment concerns conspiracies against the king. A small or a large number of persons conspire to rebel against the king, but he discovers the conspiracy before they can resort to open rebellion and their intentions and plans are revealed and conclusively proved. Now such conspirators, whether ten, twenty or more in number, are (in practice) put to death by the king, regardless of the fact that they are Musalmans and had not yet been guilty of any overt rebellion, in order to set right the affairs of state, to warn other conspirators and to ensure his own welfare and the welfare of his dependents. The judgment of the king demands the death of such persons and their repentance is not accepted. Religious scholars have no clear verdict about persons who have merely conspired to rebel; they have only said summarily that 'political affairs have been assigned to the responsibility of kings'. *Now the shari'at only permits the infliction of the death penalty when a man has wrongfully killed another or has appostatised from Islam or has committed adultery with a married woman, and there is no verse of the Quran nor any tradition of the Prophet nor any clear precept from any recognised religious scholar for the infliction of the death penalty for merely conspiring and joining to rebel.* The king puts conspirators to death in order to warn and admonish others and to maintain his own power and the power of his supporters. Nevertheless, such death punishments, though they may appear conducive to the prosperity of the king and his government and serve as a warning to others, are extremely troublesome from the religious point of view. For people are put to death merely on account of their *intentions* and their repentance is not accepted.

Another variety of political punishment concerns a group of Musalmans, who without any cause for *suspicion,* rebel against a caliph or king, who is neither a conqueror nor a usurper. They take up their swords, resort to force and fight battles and wage wars against the army of Islam; and without any necessity, they plunder the *ra'iyyat* so that the people are distressed and scattered. There is no difference of opinion among the scholars of the *shari'at* concerning those rebels who are killed in battles against the army of Islam. But there is a difference of opinion about this. If rebels are captured alive and repent of their rebellion, is their repentance to be accepted or not?

Now in such circumstances the judgment of the (average) king demands that in order to keep others on the right path by warning them, the repentance of captive rebels be not accepted and that they be put to death. But truly religious kings have had various opinions about the punishments of captive rebels. One opinion is that all captives should not be put to death and that a distinction should be made between wholesome and wicked persons. Thus they have set free people in whom the tendency to peacefulness had appeared and who had joined the rebels owing to necessity or in consequence of deception. This category includes camp-followers, slaves, servants, bazaar people and the like, who are collected together in all rebellions. The mischievous, again, have been divided into two classes. They have put to death zealots and wicked persons, who had repeatedly created disorder and rebelled and who had always been conspiring to revolt. On the other hand, they have not put to death but merely exiled or imprisoned in the custody of their officers those rebels whose repentance they considered worthy of acceptance and who had rarely rebelled in the past.

Religious kings have also distinguished between persons who, after rebelling and disobeying, have been content to withdraw themselves to a corner and persons who have shed blood, plundered cities and attacked the banner of Islam. They have mitigated the punishments of the first group in various ways. Persons of the second group have been punished by them in proportion to their misdemeanours, crimes, ravages, oppressions and cruelties. So far as setting matters right by other means has been possible, religious kings have not put captive rebels to death. They have refrained from killing and accepted the repentance of all believers in one God, who apart from merely rebelling and disobeying, have neither shed anyone's blood, nor plundered the wealth and the property of Musalmans, nor injured the wives and children of the people, nor attacked the banner of Islam.

The sons of Mahmud should know that love of power and desire for kingship belong to a world in which, at the time of issuing the orders of government, the *shari'at-seeing* eyeball is blinded; while fear of God, fear of the Day of Judgment and fear of being punished hereafter belong to a different world. But in whatever circumstances the king may be placed, the obligation of the true Faith do not permit that he should in his insolence turn his back on the laws of the *shari'at* and pass whatever orders his wrath demands concerning the honour (*furuj*) and the blood of the Musalmans.

The sons of Mahmud and kings of Islam should know that there are two categories of political offences—first, those from which there is a danger of the downfall of the state; secondly, those which bring the honour and dignity of kingship into disrepute. The tyrants and pharoahs of ancient days, who had turned aside their faces from the worship of God and had laid claims to divinity, inflicted capital punishments for both categories of political crimes. They put thousands and hundreds of thousands of men to death and had no hesitation or fear concerning the multitudes they slew. But the kings of Islam, who consider the state to be the sword of religion, must not follow the traditions of rebellious tyrants.

Early Muslim kings, who were remarkable for their Faith, reflected carefully about punishing Musalmans. Their punishments varied. They did not drive the mass of political offenders with the same stick; they hesitated and reflected over the matter in different ways and trembled even at the thought of depriving a Musalman of his life. When they found the offences of the criminals proved, and no appropriate way (could be found) by which their lives might be spared while it had been made clear that their offences were both wicked and heinous, then they put a few such persons to death as a warning to the public. And yet, so long as they lived they kept trembling at the punishments they had inflicted. If the innocence of a man was proved after he had been put to death, they contacted his heirs, gave his blood-money to them and nurtured them under their wings. They did not resort to the infliction of the death penalty under every pretext and they were not severe in their dealings. They did not kill ten men for the sins of a single person. Also, after having put a man to death for his offences, they did not cause any injury to his innocent relations, for the man who had been killed was guilty and not his relations. It is Godlessness and insolence towards the *shari'at* to ignore the Quranic verse—"No one bears the burden of another"[86]—and to overthrow and exterminate the (innocent) family of a man who has been put to death or to cast a hundred men or a thousand men into affliction for the sins of one man without paying any heed to the punishments of the next world.

Religious scholars have stated as follows concerning, the heinousness of putting a Musalman to death without the sanction of the *shari'at*: A strong religious king who is the protector of the Faith, firm in his creed and sound in his judgment, must have the fear of God and of the Prophet's *shari'at* in his heart, and the welfare of the inhabitants of the kingdom should be the object of his thoughts and actions. The preservation of his own person and his kingdom should not be the sole aim and object of his punishments, and his heart should be constantly supplicating to God. *He should be able to discern correctly those occasions of inescapable necessity when a Muslim king can order a capital punishment on his own responsibility.*

Muslim kings have kept in view many principles in inflicting the death penalty and other punishments for political offences. One principle they have kept in view is this. They punish a few persons in order that many may be warned and behave properly. But if they put a large number of people to death, viz. one hundred or two hundred or five hundred, then this would not be political punishment but disorder and tumult. Concerning political punishments (as already stated) there is neither any Quranic text nor any tradition of the Prophet nor have the (recognised) legists written anything clearly about it; they have not even cared to discuss about the qualifications of the king, who can have the right of legal interpretation.

The second principle to be kept in view in political punishments is this. If a number of persons accused of the same offence are brought before the king, the test of the king's discernment is, that he orders different punishments with due regard to the character of each individual. Concerning some he is content with exacting a money fine, for others he orders public imprisonment, and some he casts in fetters behind iron bars. He punishes some with kicks, others he exiles to distant places and some he puts to death.

4. Another kind of punishment is that which kings inflict owing to the perfection of their religion and concerning which they do not accept the repentance of criminals. Though there is a difference about the matter among religious scholars, nevertheless kings are rewarded by God for inflicting these punishments. Claimants to prophethood are to be put to death and their blood is to be shed without any hesitation. Similarly, if a man calls himself a Musalman but wags his tongue in abusing and reviling the Prophet and refers to him in insulting and contemptuous

terms, it becomes obligatory on the kings of Islam not to leave him alive on the earth for a single moment and to put him to death in the worst of ways. His repentance is not to be accepted under any conditions. Though some scholars have differed about the punishment to be given to a *zimmi* (protected non-Muslim) who reviles the Prophet, the correct opinion is that he should be beaten (to death) and not left alive. The death penalty and the shedding of blood have also been prescribed as punishments for abusing other prophets, but in this case there is a difference of opinion as to whether the criminals' repentance should be accepted or not. Further, if a Musalman tramples the Quran or a book of the Prophet's traditions under foot or insults them in any way, or drinks wine openly in the Juma mosque, or is guilty of adultery or sodomy in public, or drinks wine in public during the month of Ramazan, or has sexual relations with a child, or commits fornication within the prohibited degrees of relationship like the accursed *mulahida*—well, these groups of criminals have to be put to death in order to help the Faith and to warn the general public lest these practices become common. Persons eating during the month of Ramazan, even if they eat openly, are not to be put to death, for there is a possibility that they may have a legitimate excuse; such persons are, nevertheless, to be reprimanded and punished and not let alone. Concerning those who insult the traditions of Islam no kindness whatsoever has been prescribed.

5. As to the punishment for insulting the Sultan, if the insulter is a *kafir, mushrik* or *zimmi,* they have put him to death; but there are differences of opinion about it if he is a Musalman. It has also to be considered whether the matter comes within the scope of the *shari'at* or not. In either case, there is no death penalty. But concerning a *non-shari'at* matter, there is neither death penalty nor any punishment, but there is punishment with regards to matters coming within the scope of the *shari'at.* Also there is one kind of punishment for the select and a different one for the common people. In some contingencies the punishment for the select is severe, whereas for the common people it is mild; in other contingencies the punishment for the common people is more severe than for the select. The punishments for the select are also more varied as compared with those for the common people. A knowledge of the circumstances is necessary for properly punishing the insulter.

Religious scholars have said: If the abuser of the king or an insulter of his orders is also to be put to death, then there will be no difference in this respect between the kings and the prophets of mankind, and to ignore this distinction would be insolence against the *sunnah* (traditions). For the holy Prophet has said that "the abuser and reviler of the prophets is to be put to death, but the reviler and abuser of the Companions of the Prophet is to be thrashed and imprisoned." Religious scholars have concluded from this tradition that he who abuses Abu Bakr is to be first kicked and then imprisoned and that he who abuses Ayesha is to be put to death. Similarly, he who abuses the other wives of the Prophet is also to be put to death, for in the abuses of the Mothers of the Faithful the Prophet is also included and (in fact) it is he who is abused.

6. For misappropriation and other offences against the Public Treasury (*Baitul Mal*), in which all Musalmans are partners, there is neither death penalty nor amputation of hands.[87] If the charge is proved, the money should be demanded back. If in spite of being in possession of the money, the defaulter makes excuses, harsh treatment and punishments may be meted out to him. But in all such punishments, such as imprisonment, bonds and chains, due attention should be paid to the Quranic law. The crime should be estimated according to the good or bad character of the defaulter. There will be great loopholes in the Public Treasury if thieves are allowed to enter into its service in order to make the embezzlement and misappropriation of public money into a profession and the king knows of it and does not get back the money through imprisonment and chains. Further, if such things are allowed to happen, no public confidence will be left in the king, who is the custodian of the Public Treasury and to whose judgment and discretion the collection and expenditure of public money has been assigned. Lastly, (as a result of continued embezzlements) respect for the supreme command will vanish from the minds of the people. This will in turn lead to laxity in the enforcement of orders; no stability will be left in the affairs of government and there will be chaos in the administration of the country.

7. Another principle to which great kings have paid regard in their punishments and political penalties is keeping open the door of intercession (*shafa'at*), for owing to this a great hope grows in the hearts of the people, affection for the king develops

among the select and the commons, and the opponents of the king and fugitives from his territory do not give way to despair. But the king should keep certain conditions in mind when opening the door of intercession. The first condition is that if the person permitted to intercede happens to be one of the sons, brothers or high officers of the king, he must not be one who hates others, and no one should be nearer, dearer and closer to the king than him. The wise and the noble-born know well how small is the number of persons who have such a dignity. If the person interceding happens to be one of the *shaikhs,* he should be unrivalled in his status and no one should be higher and more respected than him. If the person interceding is one of the religious scholars (*'ulama*), he should be such that no one surpasses him in piety, honesty, excellence of behaviour and scholarship, so that his intercession may not be turned down, other persons may not set their hearts on the acquisition of the same dignity and the *amirs* and *wazirs* may not have an opportunity of interfering in the matter.

The second condition for opening the door of intercession is that this door should not always be kept wide open. Sometimes the king should lend a willing ear to intercessions, but if intercessions (concerning punishments) are continuously listened to and accepted, all offenders in administrative and revenue matters will seek this path and disorders will result. But the door of intercession concerning pensions, gifts, increase of salaries and offences not related to administrative and revenue matters should be kept more open. And the privilege of making such intercessions should be granted to a larger number of persons, so that needy supplicants may seek recourse to such intercessions as a means for attaining their objects. This procedure conduces to great advantages in the affairs of the government and the state.

[This Advice is supported by two illustrations. (1) It is stated on the basis of Imam Sualabi's *Tarikh-i Abbasian* (*History of the Abbasides*) that while the Caliph Mamun-ar Rashid was still at Merv, there was a rebellion at Baghdad. Ibrahim Mehdi, a brother of Harun-ar Rashid, was proclaimed Caliph, and Rabi bin Fazl, who had been Harun's wazir, joined the rebels. Mamun marched on Baghdad and the rebellion was easily quelled, Mamun forgave all rebels, including Ibrahim Mehdi and Rabi bin Fazl.[88] (2) The ancient rulers of Yaman bore the title of 'Tubbas'. One of them Tubba, the tyrant, marched on Rum (Byzantine) on hearing that a minor had been placed on the throne. He was overtaken by the rainy season (*birshikal*) and returned unsuccessful after two years. Meanwhile, in order to protect the kingdom the officers of Yaman had placed his brother on the throne. Tubba re-established himself in his capital, arrested four or five thousand men, who had supported his brother, and ordered five hundred of them to be put to death every day. After the first day's slaughter, the prisoners broke out of their prisons and slew Tubba, the tyrant, along with his family, relatives and kinsmen.[89]]

Advice XIV

On State-Laws (Zawabit)

Sultan Mahmud says: O sons! You should know that kingship is a responsible office and a great burden. And what an office it is that the affairs of the people, the enforcement of justice and equity in the world and the dealings of the sons of Adam with each other, their differences and their contentions, are all referred to the opinion, judgment, orders and directions of one man, and are thus stabilised and remain stable! And in consequence of this, order and good administration are established, the rules of the *shari'at* are enforced, the traditions of Islam are elevated, truth is established at the centre, merits are manifested, meannesses hide themselves, justice is enforced, munificence increases, oppression and cruelty are overthrown, there is blessing in corn and cattle, misfortunes and calamities decrease, the grace of heaven rains continuously and the rewards and recompense for good deeds are obtained! *But a great and responsible office like kingship cannot be established nor the affairs of men kept under control without permanent laws, concerning which knowledge and reason agree and which have also the benefit of the counsel and advice of men of learning and intelligence.*

A state-law (zabita) in the technique of administration means a rule of action which the king has imposed as an obligatory duty upon himself for realising the welfare of the state, and from which he absolutely never deviates.

To take an example. The object of all government measures is both immediate profit and ultimate-welfare; and wise men do not consider immediate profit to be of value unless it also leads to ultimate good. Now the honouring of the well-born and the degradation of the low-born is approved by both knowledge and reason. So the king makes it an obligatory duty on himself to give the posts and offices of government to the noble and the free-born only, and under no condition will he give government posts to ignoble, mean and low-born people. Even if he sees no immediate profit from the appointment of the well-born and can find immediate profit from the appointment of the low-born, he will not allow base and low-born men to come anywhere near government posts. And he will consider this principle so obligatory on himself that he will never deviate from it. *Such a rule is known as a state-law.* If the king gives a single office or post to a mean or base-born man, or allows any of the great officers of his state to do so, this law will not remain a law any longer and the object of enforcing it will not be attained.

In the affairs and policies of government and administration many laws are needed, so that the object of state-policies, which is immediate benefit as well as ultimate welfare, may be attained. *It is the duty of a king of perfect wisdom to enforce, if he can, those royal laws which have become proverbial owing to their principle of justice and mercy. But if owing to change of' time and circumstances he is unable to enforce the laws of the ancients, he should, with the counsel of perfectly wise men, who are also adorned with political experience and distinguished by their education for leadership, frame laws suited to his time and circumstances and proceed to enforce them.* Much reflection is necessary in order that laws suited to his reign, by enforcing which the objectives of his political policy can be attained, are properly framed.

So, O sons of Mahmud, it is your duty to consider the affairs of your administration to be in disorder unless your state-laws are enforced and stabilised. If it is possible for you, adopt the laws which religious kings have framed with the counsel of their wazirs and wise men. But if owing to change of circumstances you cannot act according to these laws, *collect the wise well-wishers of your kingdom and frame new laws. But these new laws, which will regulate the work of every government department, should be framed after careful reflection, consideration and discussion in which every aspect of the matter, present and future, is kept in view.* But for you, who are the sons of Mahmud it would be better to follow his laws, for if Mahmud is junior to others he is nevertheless senior to you. You should consider it your honour and glory to adopt his laws.

During the first year or two of his reign, Mahmud put himself to a lot of trouble in order to frame laws suited to his time and the circumstances of his reign. The blood of Ahmad Hasan, Ali Kheshawand and Abu Sahl Isfraini was turned into water in the reflections needed for the purpose. Thirty-six[90] years have elapsed since Mahmud has been administering the affairs of his state in accordance with these laws and because these laws were correct, his administration has been going strong and no grief or misfortune has overtaken it.

In case you wish to frame new laws and think that this is necessary for your political policy, then a slight reflection will convince you that it is necessary to keep the following *four* conditions in view:

First Condition

The provisions of state-laws should neither negative the orders of the *shari'at,* nor interfere with the commands of religion, nor lead to the degradation of religious affairs.

Second Condition

The enforcements of state-laws should lead to the increase of loyalty among the select and of hope among the commons, to the winning over of the good and to the frustration of the wicked. State-laws should not be a source of hatred, burden or trouble.

Third Condition

The precedents for these state-laws should be discoverable in the laws of religious kings, and their enforcement should not revive the customs and precedents of irreligious rulers or the traditions and ways of tyrants.

Fourth Condition

If there is anything in these laws against the sunnah and you find their enforcement to be nevertheless, necessary owing to the extraordinary lack of virtue or the extreme weakness of faith among the people, then you should not deem them to be right and correct. You should give plenty of charities in compensation and be afraid of the evil you are doing. It should be clear to you that the enforcement of these laws comes under the category of the shariat precept: "Necessities make lawful things forbidden." You should give plenty of charities in compensation and be afraid of your sins. Such, for example, are the laws of the courts of the ancient tyrannical kings concerning the manner of standing, placing the forehead on the ground and kneeling, which were intended to establish the king's unequalled status, supremacy and power, which later on became customary in the courts of Muslim religious kings.

O sons! You should know that the framing of state-laws is a very difficult task. Laws newly framed to suit the visible needs of the time and the occasion are not easily enforced. Unless the framers of new laws are adorned with perfect wisdom, discernment, knowledge and variegated experience and are acquainted with the laws of the past, the people will neither accept the laws made by them in their hearts nor conform to them outwardly.[91]

The passions and anger (of the law-makers) must be under the control of their reason, their desire for religion must be predominant over their desire for this material world, their feelings of envy and jealousy must have withered away, and good-will for the king and the *ra'iyyat* must have grown in their hearts; and they must for certain have discerned the inter-mixing of good and evil in their own lives and the inter-penetration of right and wrong in the affairs of state, and they should be capable of distinguishing the policy that leads to ultimate good from that which conduces to immediate profit only, and of keeping the former in view. *When (these conditions are fulfilled), the laws made by them will become stable and will be worthy of being followed by others.* But as to the framing of state-laws by the worthless, the ignorant and the worshippers of desire, whose greatest object is a passing benefit, or the welfare of a short period, it has been observed that laws made by them cannot remain firmly established for a week or even for a day. As a result, they produce more disorder than prosperity.

On the other hand, (ancient) tyrants who blackened their faces by claims to divinity and called themselves gods of the earth, also framed laws for controlling the world and its affairs and cast God, His prophets and the Day of Judgment entirely behind their backs in enforcing their laws. Their *first* law was this. Everyone was to obey them in everything. If they found disobedience in a hundred thousand or two hundred thousand persons, they put them all to death. Their *second* disgraceful law was that if they were pleased with anyone, they gave him a treasure, though he was not worth even ten *dinars.* If they found a thousand men worthy of death, they would set them free for their own purposes, while they slaughtered nations and peoples for no crime or misdemeanor.

Owing to such disgraceful laws, Godless tyrants have been able to reign and to exercise the powers of government. It has been possible for a time. But it is extremely difficult for religious kings to govern in this way, specially for kings of the Muslim faith. For the basis of the Muslim faith is forsaking this world and hating it. Also the Muslim *shari'at* declares that if a single drop of Muslim blood is shed without justification, then the shedder of it will be subjected to painful punishments for all eternity. *And there are sunnahs (traditions) in the faith which are all opposed to the customs and ways of royal government. Consequently laws which have to be promulgated among the Musalmans should be framed by the rarest of wise men, so that while secular affairs are properly managed and the people are kept in obedience, the Muslim religion is not injured and the rewards of the next world are not lost.*

Every wise and religious Sultan should carefully consider the following words of Mahmud, who has had experience in this affair, and he should carefully ponder over his own involvement in spiritual misfortunes owing to his kingship. He will then realise the value of the following statement of Mahmud and pray for Mahmud while he lives:

"All the arrangements about the people at the gate and the court of the kings, from ministers, officers, place-men, dignitaries to slaves and porters were organised firmly by the wise men of ancient days to ensure the dignity and the unique status of the king and to control the affairs of the state. They have remained operative since then. Nevertheless there is no verse of the Quran and no tradition (hadis) of the holy Prophet permitting the pomp, ceremonies, manners and customs of kings or all those actions of pride and power by which the terror of kings is engraved in the hearts of the subjects, both far and near, and which are a means for securing the enforcement of their orders. Also from the words and acts of the Pious Caliphs, which are worthy of being adopted by kings of the Muslim Faith, no precept (about the procedure of royal courts) has come down to us. Consequently, the framing of laws by the enforcement of which the affairs of the state are put in order and the world becomes

prosperous without the religion of the king and his affairs being ruined, is a difficult task."

[Barani Illustrates this Advice by referring to a meeting between Sultan Mahmud of Ghaznin and Qadr Khan, ruler of Khita,[92] in which the two *monarchs* inform each other of their laws. Since Mahmud died in 1030 A.D. and the kingdom of Khita (or Kara Khita) was not founded till 1123 A.D. no such meeting could have been possible. Also the title of the ruler of Khita was Gor Khan, 'Universal Lord', and not Qadr Khan. Superfluous sentences have not been translated in the following extract.]

When peace was concluded between Mahmud and Qadr Khan of Khita, Qadr Khan prepared a feast and came personally to invite Mahmud. Mahmud went with him to his army-camp. In the eyes of Mahmud and his officers the army of Qadr Khan seemed wonderfully well-equipped, well-prepared and numerous. Mahmud saw that Qadr Khan's soldiers were so obedient that thousands and thousands of men ran to do their duty merely at the hints of his officers and immediately executed every order that was given to them.

[Mahmud thereupon asked Qadr Khan about the laws according to which he had organised his government and Qadr Khan replied as follows.]

"No revealed book has come from Tingiri[93] (God) to my people and no prophet has been sent to us. My ancestors and I have governed through the strength of laws based upon reason. When a preceding ruler of my dynasty has governed the kingdom of Khita by laws based on reason, the affairs of state have been well organised and no harm has come to his sons after him. But if he has wished to govern according to his personal desires and self-will and to promulgate a new rule and a new custom among the people every day, no confidence in his words and deeds has been possible; he has sacrificed his life and the lives of his sons in the enterprise and he has perished in the worst of ways.

[Qadr Khan then proceeded to enumerate his twenty laws as follows:]

"(1) The king should not tell lies. I have considered everyone who tells a lie before me to be my enemy and I have not allowed him to approach the precincts of my court. Thirty years have passed since I became king and I have never told a lie. I have made it obligatory on myself not to tell a lie in any crisis, great or small.

(2) If any of my officers has been, guilty of embezzlement then, after taking back the misappropriated money, I have not given any office to him or to his sons.

"(3) If a rebel against me has been a stranger, I have put him and his officers, who were the instigators of the rebellion, to the sword along with their tribes and followers. If the rebel has been from among the partners of my kingdom (i.e. from my family), I have given him a little money and exiled him with his wife and children to a distant land, but I have put to death the leaders who had instigated him.

"(4) No low-born or common man is to have a status near the king or to get any post or office. I have not during this time given any post or office to a base, low-born or bazaar man. I have not permitted them to come near the high officers of my state or to attain to prosperity in my kingdom.

"(5) When I have seen one man oppressing another, I have transferred the house and property of the oppressor to the oppressed.

"(6) If a man has excelled in service at my court and has shown greater loyalty than his peers, I have not allowed the rights of his service to be ignored. I have promoted him grade by grade according to his ability. Owing to the enforcement of this law, oppression has decreased in my kingdom.

"(7) I have so suppressed the groups of merchants and shopkeepers in my kingdom that they do not resort either to the adulteration of goods or to cheating and profiteering in the purchase and sale of commodities; they do not attempt regrating in corn or anything else and are content with small profits. The cheapness of corn and cloth leads to the stability of the army.

"(8) I have throughout my reign been well-informed about my high officers, courtiers, tribesmen and followers as well as the officers of the army, governors of the territories and revenue-officers.

"(9) I have given army-commands to persons of virtue and good-will, to seekers of welfare, matured in experience, lion-hearted, well-behaved, loyal, afraid of God and modest.

"(10) Whenever I have heard that anyone has forsaken the world and devoted himself to Tingiri (God), I have honoured and respected him; I have gone to him and appealed to him to pray for the welfare of the people. I have bestowed gold and horses on men of learning and merit.

"(11) I have not neglected, or failed even by a needle-point, in protecting the dignity of the commanders of ten thousand (*umara-i tuman*), commanders of one thousand (*umara-i hazarah*), old and experienced men and persons of noble birth in the procedure of sitting and standing at my court, in honour and dignity, and in the bestowal of robes and gifts.

"(12) At the beginning of my reign I selected some wise and experienced men, whom I had found kind and affectionate towards me, for the sake of advising me in the affairs of government. I have promoted them in various ways, made them my counsellors of state and not deviated from their advice in any way.

"(13) I have made it obligatory on myself to inquire into the affairs of the army twice a year. I have shown favour to every army-commander and have raised him to the highest post, if I have found him to be a promotor of the welfare of the soldiers and if his troops have been ready and well-equipped. But if I have found his soldiers in distress and disorder, I have taken away my favours from him and transferred his soldiers to another. Owing to this policy the army has prospered.

"(14) I have not throughout my reign exacted a single copper coin (*dirham*) from the caravan-people and merchants of the neighbouring countries in taxes or other ways: on the other hand, I have favoured them with the bestowal of robes and cash-gifts and as a result of this grain and cloth have become cheap in my country. I have observed moderation in realising the tribute and the poll-tax (*jizya*) from the people.[94]

"(15) If a *ra'iyyat* was unable to pay even ten copper coins, which were due from him I have not insisted on exacting them. If a man has been loyal to me, I have remitted his taxes in proportion; and I have not considered it permissible to impose extraordinary levies or taxes, compulsory labour or night-work, whether light or heavy, on the *ra'iyyat*,

"(16) If I have promised favour or promotion to anyone, I have at the time of rewarding given more than I had promised. If

I have threatened anyone about anything, I have not, at the time of reckoning, hesitated in punishing where the crime has been political. But if the crime has appertained to revenue matters and I have found him short of the money he should have realised, I have inflicted a punishment milder than my threats. If the humility and the distress of the defaulter has become clear, I have forgiven him.

"(17) I have not acted perfidiously towards any man. But if any man has rebelled against me, I have left no trace of him on the face of the earth.

"(18) I have made the following arrangement about accusations made by jealous persons. If the accusation has been about revenue matters, I have not heard it against officers whom I have personally promoted; if it has been against persons unknown to me, I have left the investigation of it to my officers and have not given the accuser access to myself. If the accusation has concerned political matters and I have found the charge of the accuser to be correct, I have favoured him with gifts and honours; even if I have found such a charge to be false, I have not been very severe towards the accuser, so that this door of information may not be altogether closed.

"(19) I have for so many years, whatever the circumstances, lived with dignity among intimates and strangers, and with my wives, children, relations, near ones and loyal and chosen officers. I have not degraded the dignity of kingship by any word or deed which could lead to indifference or lack of regard towards me.

"(20) I have, so far as possible, not revealed the secrets of the kingdom to anyone. If I have revealed them, it has been only to persons concerning whom it could not be imagined that they would disclose them. If a person has revealed my secrets, I have never again given him a post of status near me. Lastly, I have not wavered even by a needle-point from any of these twenty regulations.

[Barani considered the Khitains to be a community who believed in one God (*Tingiri*) on the basis of reason but who had no religion. Qadr Khan's laws, as Barani describes them, are reactionary and autocratic but they are secular and not fanatical. Mahmud in reply to Qadr Khan's question enumerates his fourteen laws, which do not in Barani's opinion, violate the *shari'at* and which very well indicate the type of ruthless fanaticism which Barani approved.]

Mahmud said to Qadr Khan: "We belong to Mohammad's Faith; he was the last of the prophets. In every law, I frame concerning the affairs of my state, my real object is the enforcement of the Prophet's *shari'at,* to which my laws are not opposed.

"(1) The first law of my government is this. Thirty-eight[95] years have passed since I became king, and it has been my strong resolve and firm determination ever since my accession to put the opponents of the Prophet's religion to the sword, to take the orders of the Muslim *shari'at* to the ends of the earth and to illuminate all territories with the light of Islam.

"(2) I assign the duty of enforcing the orders of the *shari'at* to pious, religious and God-fearing men. I do not appoint any swindler, deceiver, greedy seeker of the world or a man of false faith as a *qazi.* I assign the secular offices of the state to men of noble and good birth only; no man of mean, base or ignoble birth is allowed to come near the offices of the religion or the state.

"(3) I do not degrade for every little fault an officer who after careful tests has been raised by me to a high status and put among the persons near the throne. No one's claims of service or loyalty are ignored. I do not overthrow persons promoted by me or by my[96] father for every little crime, embezzlement and oppression. I live with my sons and the supporters and well-wishers of my kingdom in such a way that my dignity is not lowered while their loyalty is increased.

"(4) Every year I have gold and silver piled up into heaps and distributed among the soldiers in my presence. The greater the amount distributed, the greater is the pleasure of my heart. I have never enforced, or even contemplated, any retrenchment in army expenditure. As far as possible, I have not permitted the soldiers to be humiliated.

"(5) I hold learning, wisdom, justice, piety, skill, virtuous behaviour, truthfulness and good conduct in great honour. I have raised persons possessing these merits to greatness and dignity without their possessing any means of access to me or any other recommendations, such as claims of old service and the like. I have granted them pensions, gifts, villages and gardens. So my kingdom has come to be adorned by persons possessing these merits. This fact has also contributed to my good name and reputation.

"(6) I am very well-informed about the condition of everyone in my kingdom from my sons, relations, courtiers, governors and rulers of territories to the land-owners (*zamindars*), village headmen (*muqaddams*) and the *ra'iyyat*. Consequently, I have found propriety and rectitude in the execution of orders.

"(7) I have apportioned my time properly in attending to affairs of state, so that my life may not be wasted in useless things while real worth remains undone.

"(8) Before determining upon any enterprise and undertaking its execution, I have carefully pondered over its achievement and consulted my advisers. After that I have made my determination firm. God has brought my enterprises to a successful conclusion with excellence and ease.

"(9) I have always treated the submissive and obedient *ra'iyyat* with affection and have nurtured the peaceful and the virtuous under the wings of my favour. In the collection of the tribute I have neither been so severe as to make the *ra'iyyat* poor and indigent, nor so lenient as to enable them to become rebellious and disobedient through excessive wealth. I have been hard-hearted in dealing with the fearless, the reckless, the brutish and blind adventurers, the Godless, the rascally, the deceitful, the shameless, the tyrannically-minded and the insolent; I have behaved towards such people with severity, firmness, terrorism and domination.

"(10) I have not been deceived by the flattering speeches of liars nor considered the misrepresentations of cheats to be correct. I have not become proud owing to the flattery of courtiers and poets.

"(11) I have not slept peacefully on my bed to my satisfaction for a single night from fear of God, the Prophet, the Day of Judgment and the claims of my opponents on that day. This has kept me back from cruelty, tyranny, oppression and inequity.

"(12) I have not overthrown defaulters, who have been guilty of embezzlement or other crimes in revenue-administration, in such a way that they cannot get on to their feet again. I have observed the *shari'at* limits in the matter of fining and confiscation of property. Inevitably no post or office in my kingdom has remained unfilled.

"(13) I have never forsaken the side of righteousness or taken to arrogant ways at any time or for any reason. This law is the basis of all my other laws. So Almighty God has vouchsafed success to my enterprises.

"(14) I have so carefully observed the above-mentioned laws that the thought of deviation from them has never entered my innermost heart.

"The observance of such laws", Qadr Khan remarked, "is only possible through the kindness of Tingiri." He embraced the Faith at the hands of Mahmud and became a Musalman[97].

Advice XV

On the King's High Resolve

[Though Barani does not say so in express words, his discussion implies a clear distinction between 'correct determination' (*azm-i durust*), without which no king can perform his normal duties or remain on the throne already discussed in Advice IV, and 'high resolve' (*ulu himmat, buzurg mansha-i, ulul azmi*) which is necessary for a king who wants to be distinguished and pre-eminent among the rulers of the earth. In the Persian text the argument of this Advice suffers from confusion and it has been found necessary to change the order of the paragraphs and to omit some repetitive sentences (169a to 170b). After these very necessary changes it will be seen that this Advice deals with the following topics: (i) High resolve is the distinguishing feature of a great king; (ii) The king with high resolve is characterised by his generosity; (iii) Miserliness is incompatible with high resolve; (iv) Wise men have enumerated eleven characteristics of a king with high resolve; (v) Praises of Sultan Mahmud; and (vi) five conditions which a king should observe when conquering foreign lands.]

1. Sultan Mahmud has said in his Testament[98]: O sons of Mahmud and kings of the earth! You ought to understand that the premier virtue of the king and the basis of the moral qualities of royalty is 'high resolve', Kingship and high resolve are necessary for each other, for kingship is the lieutenancy and the deputyship of God.

Great rulers have said: It is not possible for anyone who is not endowed with high resolve to exercise the powers of government, or to call himself the 'Deputy of God' and the 'Shadow of God', or to bring the people of the world beneath the wings of his affection and favour, or to expect the execution of his orders from the sons of Adam, or to elicit loyalty, sincerity and affection from the hearts of the nobles and the commons, or to bring the leaders of the people and great and distinguished men within the circle of his obedience and service, or to obtain supremacy over the world and its inhabitants, or to make the proclamation, "I and none other!" reach the ears of the people or to make his gate and his court the object of the petitions of the seventy-two communities or to treat his equals as his subordinates. Almighty God created the prophets perfect in knowledge and wisdom and flawless in their character and ways of life so that their teachings may establish themselves firmly in the hearts of men. In the same way a king of Islam must (for the proper performance of his functions) be endowed with manliness, eloquence, capacity of discernment and firmness of faith. For this reason the great men of the religion and the state have said: "Kingship is compatible with infidelity (*kufr*) and disease, but it is not compatible with miserliness, injustice, weakness of will and vileness of character."

Plato, Aristotle, Diogenese, Hippocrates, Socrates[99] and all wise men, ancient and modern, are agreed that kingship is the embodiment of high resolve and that men of base determination cannot attain to kingship. Now high resolve is the distinctive feature of prophets, saints and *hakims,* who have kicked off the temptations of the material world on account of its mean nature and ephemeral character and have turned their high resolve towards God, 'like whom there is nothing else.'[100] But the ruler, who aspires for religious and worldly perfection and strives to be distinguished among his fellow-men for having attained to the highest stages in both the worlds, must be—whether these two qualities can be combined or not—also a person of high resolve. No one can become a king without obtaining pre-eminence in secular affairs; but the distinctive feature of a king's high resolve is that just as he has become pre-eminent in his own dominion, he also flings the rope (*kamand*) of his ambition for the kingship of the inhabited earth in the attempt to become the greatest of rulers. But if this is not possible, he should at least attempt to be distinguished among the kings of the inhabited earth on account of his orthodox virtues, numerous soldiers and servants, and treasures and valuables beyond computation. A person without high resolve cannot attain that kingship which is the perfection of greatness.

2. If monarchs do not have high resolve, lofty determination and quest for greatness, they will not be able to discharge the duties of rulers properly. Their gifts will not reach the people; and if their gifts do not overflow to all the people of the country, regard for their dignity and greatness will not become firmly established in the hearts of the select and the commons. 'The gifts of kings are the kings of gifts'; they are larger and more valuable than the gifts of others; in addition to this they reach everyone. Just as the king should be distinguished from all other people of the kingdom by his capacity for leadership so that trust in him may grow in the hearts of the common people, in the same way his generosity—the bestowal of fine, costly and numerous gifts—should be considered a necessary feature of his royal position. In other royal distinctions, such as the possession of treasures, valuables, horses, camels, mules, and lofty palaces, which are necessary for maintaining the dignity of kingship, there is an element of selfishness and greed. But the bestowal of gifts is the result of high resolve only.

3. High resolve, greatness and the quest for greatness are incompatible with parsimony, avarice and miserliness of character. Kingship, which necessitates the control of men, is only possible if the king is superior to his fellow-men in dignity, power and status; such superiority is not possible for weak-willed, short-sighted, miserly and niggardly persons. Misers are always considered to be disgraceful, untrustworthy and of no account; hatred and contempt for them is implanted in the human mind. Now contempt for the king (on account of his miserliness) should not be allowed to grow in the hearts of the people for this will lead to laxity in the enforcement of state-orders. Conversely, the greater the public veneration and respect for the king, the easier will it be to execute his commands; and the more effective the enforcement of the king's commands, the greater will be the prosperity of the king and his subjects.

Kingship rests permanently on two pillars, mercy and terrorism but both mercy and terrorism are out of the reach of a miserly, and weak-willed king. An avaricious and miserly king is tempted by everything valuable or costly he sees in the possession of his subjects or even hears of their possessing it; so he tries by every means within his reach to get into his hands the goods and properties of his subjects. Unwilling to spend his treasures on the enterprises before him, he uses his royal authority for the permanent oppression of his subjects so that he may, without any just claim, seize their properties and belongings. Such actions are opposed to the natural character of kings and contrary to the virtues expected in a ruler. [A repetitive paragraph has not been translated here.]

A person without innate high resolve may attain kingship either by inheritance or by force and deceit; in either case plenty of treasures will fall into his hands. He will spend these treasures for the preservation of his kingdom, but in a troublesome way and without any definite policy. He will be generous and munificent but with great inner efforts and his ultimate end will be religious and worldly disgrace. Generosity with ostentation and liberality as a (political) policy are not the means to praise and glory. For merit is a necessary condition of high resolve, and only men of merit are honoured in this world and obtain salvation in the next.

4. Wise men (*hakims*) have attributed the following (eleven) characteristics to the king with high resolve: *First,* the kingdom of this world is nothing in his eyes; his efforts are directed entirely to the next world. But in case his ambition turns to this world, he aspires to bring the entire inhabited earth under his control. If this is not possible, he tries to be distinguished among the monarchs of the world by his orthodox virtues, plenitude of wealth and extensive territory. *Second,* he wishes to put the whole world under his obligation, but is unable to bear the obligation of anyone except God. *Third,* he desires that the good and charitable deeds of the whole world should be the work of his own hands, but he wants no reward for himself in this world or the next. *Fourth,* his constant desire is to take nothing from anybody and to be constantly giving to others. *Fifth,* he is always desirous of distinction in administrative affairs and also of the highest spiritual merits. His mind hates all defects, whether in the administration of the realm or in the character of individuals. *Sixth,* he wishes that all men and *jins* should dine at his dinner-cloth, that food to all beasts and birds should be served from his kitchen, and that the naked ones of the earth should wear clothes

from his clothes-store (*jamah-khana*). *Seventh,* he desires that the orders for the seven climes should issue from his lips. *Eighth,* by whatever extent his kingship increases, his heart is not content with it and he still wishes for something more. *Ninth* he wishes to be the means for fulfilling the needs of the people; he cannot bear that anyone should go back from his door without the attainment of his hopes. *Tenth,* he wishes that he and his government should be the means for the many missions of slaves, the relief of debtors and the rescue of the unfortunate; he cannot bear to see, or even to hear of anyone being overtaken by any calamity in his kingdom. *Eleventh,* when he has reached the stage of perfection, he strives for the impossible. He can find no peace in himself after having merely attained the possible.

The leading scholars of history have said that ancient kings followed the following custom. They would beat the drum when the king's dinner-cloth was spread and everyone who was hungry could come to the king's feast; at the time of their meals they had food loaded on four or five thousand camels taken to the steppe and scattered, so that animals, wild beasts and birds may also have their share of the king's bounty. If twenty thousand or thirty thousand persons sat down at their feast, there would be the same food, sweets (*halwa*) and sweet drinks (*sherbat*) for them as was served to the king himself. They said: "The dinner of the king is the king of dinners." During winter and summer the kings would not put on their one-fold cloak (*qaba-i yakta*) unless a hundred thousand persons had not put on their gift-robes. They said, "If the king has not the courage to do even so much, it is not lawful for him to govern the people of God and it is cruel to give him the title of a king".

[Here follow several paragraphs in praise of Sultan Mahmud, which it is unnecessary to translate as they are merely figments of our author's imagination. But among them we come across the following historically impossible statement: "On various occasions it came to Mahmud's mind that it was a very great misfortune that Qadr Khan was not a Musalman, that he did not believe in the correct Faith and that Islam was in danger from him[101]. Otherwise Mahmud would have called Qadr Khan and the great men of his kingdom as guests to his army-camp, and after presenting them with the territories of Ghaznin, Khwarazm, Mawaraun Nahr, Khorasan, Sistan, and the whole of Hindustan,

Mahmud himself would have wear the patched frock (*khirqah*) of a mystic (*darwesh*) and taken the road to Mecca."]

5. There are certain conditions which it is necessary for kings to observe in their campaigns for conquests; if these conditions are observed, their objects will be attained.

First, soldiers, who are appointed to accompany the royal stirrup, should in all respects have peace of mind concerning their tribes, followers, wives, children, property and goods. There should be no anxiety or worry in their hearts, even if the campaign continues for ten years.

Second, all those things, which are needed by the people of God or which their hearts long for and which they can find in the capital, should also be available in the army-camp. The king should arrange that all varieties of food, clothes, perfumes, fresh and dry fruits of all kinds, electuaries (*ma'jun*), sweetmeats, pickles (*achar*), medicines, beer (*bugni*), wines and bhang are available in the army-camp. Further, all groups without whom religion and amusements are not possible, such as religious scholars, mystics (*shaikhs*), jurisconsults (*faqihs*), physicians, astrologers, artisans, shopkeepers, merchants, caravan-people, courtesans, musicians, dancers, buffoons, tavern-keepers, jugglers (*bazigar*), story-reciters, wrestlers and jokers should be present in all long and distant campaigns. The soldiers on seeing them will think that they are in the capital; their hearts will not be depressed owing to their distance from their homes; they will not deem their exile to be an exile; and owing to the excess of all that is required by religion, worldly life, desires and passions, they will imagine the army-camp to be the capital, they will forget the pain of separation from their relatives on looking at the faces and seeing the performances of the above-mentioned groups.

Third, the king in his long and distant campaigns: should not be severe with his soldiers for the sake of one-fifth of the spoils[102] and should not resort to detailed investigations; for the enjoyment of beautiful slave-girls and handsome slave-boys, along with the goods and valuables which fall into their hands, causes the soldiers to forget their families and reduces their affection for their relatives in their hearts.

Fourth, the king in consultation with his wazirs and wise men should make arrangements so that the route for fast-runners (*ulagh*), footmen, (*paiks*), dromedaries and messengers from the capital to the army is not cut off by the enemy. Then the people at home and in the army will receive news from each other rapidly and this will lead to peace of mind on both sides. Owing to these arrangements the heart of the king will be at peace about his capital, the hearts of the soldiers about their wives and children and the hearts of the people at home about the army. This peace of mind on both sides will contribute to the success of the enterprise; and there need be no anxiety if the campaign of the army has to be prolonged.

Fifth, when the king has embarked on his campaign, his soldiers will see many new cities and new lands. Now the minds and tempers of the sons of Adam are variegated and different. Many of the new cities and lands which they see may suit the soldiers; they may find many things to their liking and wish to settle there. Also there may be personal embarrassments for the soldiers in their own capital owing to which they hate and detest it. So when they see another city, properly decorated and adorned they may wish to settle there. Consequently, the king should be so careful and vigilant during his campaign that not even an ant is allowed to desert the army in order to settle in another land. Rather, the king should by all means within his reach—by gifts, kindness and plenty of promises—bring skilled men, experts, and the well-born and the virtuous to his capital from all sides of the world.

[This Advice is illustrated by two examples: (1) The Sultanus Salatin of Herat (whom it is impossible to identify with any known king) attacked Iraq but was defeated. His opponent sold him to a merchant, who in turn sold him to Baghra Khan of Samarkand. Baghra was pleased with the services rendered to him by the Sultanus Salatin when his country was attacked by the ruler of Khwarazm and in recognition of these services Baghra Khan enabled him to recapture Herat. (2) Aristotle advised Alexander against world-conquest, "This world has not such permanence that one may waste one's precious life in conquering it." But seeing that Alexander was keen, Aristotle gave way. "The ways by which world-conquest is possible are not hidden from the mind of Alexander."]

Advice XVI

On the Diseases of the Kingdom

Sultan Mahmud has said: O sons of Mahmud and kings of Islam! You should know that kingship being the perfection of worldly good fortune is incompatible with the distresses of an evil day. If owing to changed circumstances, the administration is thrown into confusion and diseases in the kingdom appear, providing remedies for them is necessary. If in spite of these remedies the disease increases, death is inevitable. If the remedy is effective, it is a symptom of survival. Wise men have said: Kingship is good fortune incarnate; but on rare occasions a disease appears in the state or calamities and misfortunes befall it. If this disease is not cured quickly by wise judgments and correct designs, and if kings do not devote themselves to the removal of these calamities through the advice of ministers and wise men and persist in their negligence and carelessness, then the fall of the kingdom should be expected very soon. If a breach of even ten bricks occurs in the palace of the kingdom, then in the twinkling of an eye it will grow into a chasm and more breaches will occur; but if this breach of ten bricks is repaired and quickly filled up, then there will be no future fractures on any side.

One *variety* of state calamities are epidemics and famines. The efforts and designs of the king and his *ra'iyyat* are ineffective in both these cases. In famines nothing more than the following measures are possible. The king can help the people by reducing the tribute (*khiraj*) and the poll-tax (*jiziya*) or by advancing them loans from his treasury or by making a gift of what he can to the poor and the needy. He can, further, direct cash-loans to be advanced to merchants so that they may import grain from other countries and sell it to the *ra'iyyat* at the cheapest possible rates. If the famine is more severe, the king can remit the tribute and the poll-tax altogether and issue a general order to the rich men of the kingdom asking them to take charge of the poor and the destitute, so that the people may not perish in every tribe and locality. But the plans and efforts of the king are quite ineffective in cases of epidemics.

Another *variety* of the diseases of the kingdom is this. The confidence of the *ra'iyyat* in the king is shaken and the army and the people come to detest him on account of his policy and character—severe demands and minute claims, bad temper and harsh measures, excessive censures and punishments, lack of mercy and refusal to connive at defaults, low salaries and high taxes, and, finally, orders the execution of which causes great affliction to the people or is altogether impossible. Ancient kings and wazirs have considered this to be a very serious disease of the kingdom.... for the conflagration is due to a household fire. Owing to the hatred and ill-will of the subjects towards him, hatred of the subjects also grows in the king's heart; the bonds of good administration are loosened and the hatred of the two parties for each other makes the continued existence of the state impossible. Rebellions and revolts appear on all sides; obstinacy and disobedience grow; confusion and disorders increase; and government orders cannot be executed. The two pillars of kingship—the treasury and the army—are shaken to their foundations and begin to crumble.

It is extremely difficult to find a remedy for this disease as it is the fruit of the king's own character. Whenever the king treats his subjects in the ways mentioned above and the subjects discover his true character and aims, then even if the king gives up his policy and changes his character in order to reorganise the government and win over the subjects, the subjects will not trust him, their hatred for him will not decrease and they will attribute his (apparent) change of character to trickery and deceit.

Some kings, when faced with this misfortune of public detestation, which is indicative of a chronic disease of the state, have assigned the kingdom to their son or brother and sought seclusion in a monastery and thus remained safe from annihilation and disgrace; or else they have taken poison and preferred to sacrifice themselves, so that there may be no rebellion in which they would be slain along with their tribes and followers[103].

Another *variety* of state-calamity is this. A strong enemy who is superior to the king in every respect—in power, dignity, treasures, and military strength—invades his dominion and no opposition or resistance for the time-being is possible. They have considered this a great calamity and various devices—if practicable at all—have been suggested.

The *first* device is this. Gifts and presents should be sent by such means as may be available to the invader and his high officers, courtiers and army-commanders, and the evil that they can do should (for the time-being) be postponed by diplomatic means. The king should use this breathing space to collect a large number of soldiers and organise his defences. He should in such a contingency not only use his own treasures but call upon the people to give him their money, and everyone who has attained the age of discretion should be made a soldier of the king. Every attempt should be made to collect stores and strengthen the forts. [A scorched earth policy should be followed.]

Everything on the route of the invader should be desolated—houses should be pulled down, tanks emptied and fodder burnt. If a money-tribute, whether great or small, is promised to the invader, the king's prestige will be ruined. Consequently many kings have preferred wars and battles, which may lead to their ruination and annihilation, to submitting to the enemy and offering a tribute. In such a contingency the honour of the king demands that he should, with his helpers, supporters, well-wishers, partisans and lion-hearted warriors, come to grips with the enemy, risk his life and his kingdom, give no thought to the ultimate result and strike so hard at the enemy that he either goes back or refrains from advancing. There is danger in this contingency, and in danger there is either victory or defeat[104].

The *second* device for removing a, powerful enemy is a marriage-alliance. Kings have approved of such alliances, provided they are effective. But this device is not possible when difference of religion is a bar, for Muslim women cannot be given in marriage to a non-Muslim enemy. In such a contingency this design will not work.

The *third* device for removing a powerful enemy is winning over his highest officers and his army-commanders. If the enemy does not refrain from advancing in spite of the king's gentlemanly behaviour and the despatch of valuables, gifts and presents, some officers of his, who occupy the highest positions, should be won over confidentially and secretly by the payment of large sums of money. If the chosen and famous officers of the invader (owing to the bribes they have accepted) do not support him in his enterprise with their heart and soul and are really opposed to it, its successful conclusion will not be possible. This fact has been proved by experience.

The *fourth* device against a powerful enemy is a really desperate measure. If the enemy has obtained predominance over the kingdom and his determination has reached the extreme limit and no other means—war, marriage-alliances or winning over of his officers—are effective, the king should establish his capital in another territory. Chosen persons and experienced warriors from among the king's subjects should be taken to a place to, which the access of the enemy is difficult; they should be asked to leave their own country and settle there. This device has been described, but seldom adopted in practice, for the emigration of the people from their country is extremely difficult.

Another *variety* of state-calamities is this. The king is established at his capital with his army and treasures and two opponents both equal to him in strength, attack his kingdom simultaneously from opposite directions, e.g. from east and west or from north and south. If under these circumstances the king decides to fight one of his enemies and marches forward to meet him, the other enemy will get an opportunity of conquering his country. If he wishes to oppose both, his army will not be sufficient for the purpose. The king is really in a helpless position. In such a contingency, discretion and policy demand that the utmost effort be made to protect the capital and the great forts of the realm with all available resources till the campaigning season is over and both the enemies retire as a matter of necessity. The desolation of the kingdom, which is probable owing to the invasion of two enemies of equal power, can well be imagined. But such a calamity is rare.

Another *variety* of state-calamity is this. The equipment of the king has been wasted over an enterprise he had undertaken, and before he can provide the entirely new equipment his army needs, all enemy of equal strength marches against him well-equipped. In such a contingency also the remedy is to protect the capital and to seek refuge in the forts. The only alternative for the king is to protect himself and the nobles and commons by whatever means he can[105].

Another *variety* of state-calamity is this. The king has established his power over a newly-conquered dominion but has not as yet succeeded in winning over the officers of the enemy's *khalsa* (royal domain) or in overcoming the hostility and opposition of the army-officers of the conquered territory. At this moment an enemy attacks his kingdom. Resort to war and battles is inadvisable in such a contingency. There is no remedy for the king but to seek refuge in his forts, to protect his capital and to play for time.

Yet another *variety* of state-calamities is this. An enemy of equal power but ready and well-equipped attacks the king's dominion, and the king has not enough treasures to provide a well-equipped force to match the invader's army. Under these circumstances, the king should take the property of his subjects as a loan, whether they are willing or not, prepare the war-equipment he needs and march to face the enemy. "That necessity makes lawful, things which are prohibited" is a great basic principle. Lastly, if an enemy invades the country whom it is impossible to meet with the army in hand, and it is also impossible to obtain money for equipping a new and larger force, then this order of God should be obeyed: "March forth, whether lightly or heavily equipped, and fight in the path of Allah with your properties and your lives."[106] In other words, the whole *ra'iyyat* should be organised into an army.

O sons of Mahmud! You should know that from the view-point of wisdom and policy there is a grave danger in 'decisive battles' (*harbaha-i buzurg*). 'Decisive battles' is the name given to battles between two kings of equal power. Engaging in such a battle means risking the kingdom at a single stroke of the game. Far-sighted and wise men have said: "If avoidance by other means is possible, decisive battles should be shunned". True wisdom does not permit that the king should in a single moment risk his life, kingdom, wife, children, property and goods and engage in a decisive battle. A battle between parties of equal strength is like the movements of the two pans of a balance; owing to the greater weight of one balance, even if the difference be very slight, no weight or value is left in the other pan. Owing to the loss of a decisive battle the whole country is overrun, families and tribes are overthrown and fall to the lot of others, the government and the kingdom are torn up by the roots, and wives and children of the people, for whose security they are prepared to endanger their lives, fall into the hands of others.

This battle between two kings of equal strength, in which there is no possibility of retreat in case of defeat, is unlike other battles. In other battles only the superior army-officers of one of the parties are defeated, the kingdom is not lost, the situation can be retrieved, and distress and disorder are confined to the defeated army. But owing to the defeat and discomfiture of the king himself in a decisive battle, the whole kingdom is turned upside down, and there is no possibility of reconstruction and retreat and no hope of rehabilitation. Because in a decisive battle there is danger of universal public disorder and distress, great wazirs have said: "Avoid decisive battles in which in a single moment everything is altered".

Wise men have said: The king in his battles should not pay exclusive attention to the large member of his own army and the small number of the enemy or be deluded with pride. For Almighty God has said: "How often has a small army vanquished a large army by the help of God."[107] Also a king should not expect victory and success on the ground that he is on the side of righteousness while his enemy is on the wrong side, for the wicked have often been victorious over the virtuous. The victories and defeats of armies in battles are among the preordained orders of Divine destiny, the mystery of which is not possible for human knowledge or wisdom to unravel.

Engaging in decisive battles is not permitted by wise men. Foresight lies in avoiding such battles and not in seeking them; and regard for foresight, so far as possible, is obligatory on kings. But on occasions of necessity decisive battles are permitted. Hesitation and reluctance, it must be clearly understood, are only permitted in conditions where there is a choice and not in cases of necessity.

O sons of Mahmud and kings of the earth! Let it be known to you that wise designs, considerations of ultimate welfare concerning one's own safety, the well-being of one's wives and children and the survival of families and followers, love of one's country and kingdom, the promptings of passions and wishes for pleasures and comforts, greed for long life, longing for worldly wealth and goods, love for good-looking women and desire for high status—all these can only hold the skirts and cross the minds of lion-hearted warriors till the fire of battle is lighted and men in drawn ranks come face to face, while their eyes flash fire at each other. But when the fire of battle throws up its flames, the neighing of the horses strikes the ear-drums, the dust raised by the two forces commingles, the armies hear each other's shouts and war-cries, the bows are taken out of their cases and swords come out of their scabbards, the three hundred and sixty veins of the body are distended, eyes glow red, and the hair of the head and the body stand erect—then all considerations of security and welfare, love of women and slave-girls, and affection for brothers and sons disappear from the breast and all other enterprises are forgotten. At that moment nothing else comes to the mind except drawing the sword, shedding blood throughout the land, falling upon the enemy, taking life out of each other's bodies, raising Hell, making the earth and the sky into one and considering the sacrifice of life to be an amusement. It is only before the battle that designs and policies come to the minds of the courageous; but once the battle has begun, no precepts and sermons, no considerations of prudence and no fear of danger can, influence their hearts. If the enemies are thousands upon thousands, they seem small in their eyes. At the time of battle brave men do not search for allies or ask anyone for help and assistance. If a thousand men fall upon one really courageous warrior, he should attack them in return without any hesitation.

Now I have written for you what wise men and wazirs have said by way of caution and I have also explained to you how the bravest of brave men behave at the time of battle, so that you may be ready for what God has ordained during battles and do what may seem to you best. But that which has been prescribed by destiny will come to pass. All other talk is superfluous.

[This advice is illustrated by the cleverness of a king of Khwarazm.[108] This illustration is worth quoting as it shows Barni's stupendous ignorance of both history and geography.]

It is written in the *Tarikh-i Khwarazm Shahi* (*History of the Khwarazm Shahs*) that there was a Khwarazm Shah (King of Khwarazm) in the time of the Caliph, Mu'tasim, brother of Mamun.[109] There was, first, a dispute between him and the Caliphate. For four successive years—a wonder for the times!—calamities befall his kingdom and epidemics raged. But by his wise designs he tried to find remedies for these calamities and strove hard to meet his enemies and repeatedly prepared and equipped his armies.

The record of his calamities is as follows. One year the horses of his army were affected with a disease of the backbone (*tabaq*) and perished. Thus an enormous number of his mounted soldiers became footmen. Out of several lakhs of horses in his stables only a few thousand remained. The people of his kingdom also became indigent owing to the perishing of their horses. In that very year an army was appointed to march against Khwarazm from Baghdad. When this army entered the territory of Khwarazm like ants and locusts, Khwarazm Shah sent messengers to the commander of the Caliph's army and secretly promised to pay him two hundred thousand *dinars* of western (Roman) gold; he gave security to his own merchants for delivering this gold at Baghdad to the Caliph's commander. He had a daughter whom he sent to the *harem* of the Caliph. He also undertook to pay an enormous amount of cash to the Caliph every year, wrote a deed of promise to this effect and gave it to the Caliph's officers. In that year by these designs he solved the troubles of his kingdom and turned back the army of the Caliphate. He gave a lot of money to the Caliph's soldiers for their fodder; he also invited the leading men and officers of the Baghdad army as his guests and won them over by offers of presents. The army of the Caliph returned quite pleased with him and he was saved from such a great danger.

As the news of the destruction of the horses of Khwarazm Shah had spread far and wide, next year I-sikun, King of Khita, along with Bughra Khan of Samarqand invaded Khwarazm from opposite sides.[110] Khwarazm Shah reflected within himself: 'If I attempt to fight both these kings, I have not the power to do so; if I engage one of them in battle, the other will enter my capital and capture it'. So he gave up the idea of fighting and summoned the experienced warriors of Khwarazm to his four great forts. The women and children were put within the forts while the warriors encamped round them; if anyone attacked them, they were to repel him. They set free their cattle, so that they may divert the soldiers of the enemy; but cattle for whom fodder could be provided were brought within the forts. Khwarazm Shah, with the fort of Khwarazm behind his back, fanned his army-camp in the precincts of his capital and alighted there. An amount of fodder beyond computation was· collected in Khwarazm. The two enemy armies entered from opposite sides of the territory; they grazed their horses on the cornfields and seized the cattle. But though they greatly desired that Khwarazm Shah should offer them a pitched battle, he did not move more than a *farsang* from

Khwarazm and followed the strategy of the besieged for three or four months. When the campaigning season was over, both the invading kings found it necessary to return to their countries. Thus Khwarazm Shah remained secure from such a calamity.

In the third year the king of the Franks (Firang) invaded his territory and the Franks entered Khwarazm numerous as ants and locusts.[111] Khwarazm Shah ordered the whole territory of Khwarazm to be laid waste. Horses and herds of cattle were sent in various directions to be sold at whatever prices people cared to offer. He ordered the rich men of Khwarazm to come within the great forts while the poor and destitute people of the country were asked to go to the neighbouring lands and live there for a few months. He reduced the fodder (of Khwarazm) by every means he could. He ordered the excess grain of the country to be buried in the steppe and forests in such a way that no foreign army could find it. All grass was set on fire and burnt. The cattle were slaughtered and eaten or else taken to other lands from where their dried meat (*qadid*) was brought to the capital and put in the great forts. He had a wooden rampart built at a distance of one *farsang* round the capital. Then he entered the inner fort with his soldiers and did not go anywhere near the Franks. The king of the Franks, who had entered the territory of Khwarazm with his numerous army, remained there for a month. But he was reduced to distress from lack of fodder; his soldiers became helpless from hunger while the horses of the Frankish army began to perish for lack of grass. As a matter of necessity the King of the Franks withdrew from the territory of Khwarazm, and Khwarazm Shah and his subjects escaped from such a calamity, This firm policy of Khwarazm Shah, which has been followed by later kings, has been recorded on the pages of time and proves his great wisdom and intelligence.

In the fourth year a king from among the well-known kings of Egypt and Syria attacked Khwarazm.[112] No money was left in the treasury of Khwarazm Shah owing to the excessive expenditure of the past years. So Khwarazm Shah ordered everyone who had any money in his kingdom to bring it (as a loan) before the door of his court and pile it up there; the return of the loan was promised within three years. He wrote a general deed to this effect with his own hand and ordered it to be read from the pulpits of the mosques and to be shown in the bazaars and the assemblies. As the people of Khwarazm had faith in the spoken and written word of Khwarazm Shah, they divided their wealth without any hesitation into two halves and brought one half of it before the court of Khwarazm Shah and piled it up there. Khwarazm Shah equipped an army with this money, marched against the enemy but did not risk a battle. Ultimately the King of Syria (Sham) was reduced to distress; his soldiers began to desert and he returned home. Thus this year also Khwarazm Shah escaped a great calamity through design and policy.

In the fifth year he collected and equipped so many soldiers in Khwarazm that the desire of conquering his kingdom disappeared from the minds of his rivals. He remained secure on the throne of Khwarazm for years.

Advice XVII

On the Advisability of Forsaking Severe Exactions

Sultan Mahmud says: O sons of Mahmud and kings of Islam! You should know that the foundations of public administration are friendliness, affection, kindness and mildness. If a king understands well the moral basis of government and treats his subjects with kindness, his kingdom will be soon put into order and his reputation will last for a long time. He should also have a correct understanding of human nature. For man has been created helpless, poor, needy, indigent and fearful; love of ease, comfort and softness are ingrained in his nature; he detests difficulties, hardships, labours and afflictions, and runs away from them or tries to remove them. Consequently, if the king gives his subjects orders to which before that time they had not been accustomed, and there are difficulties, hardships and afflictions in .carrying them out, and if in spite of all this, the king is still exacting and severe in his orders and keeps the subjects in affliction for the performance of duties beyond their powers and the subjects are unable to execute his commands—then it will become necessary for the subjects to remove their neck from the yoke of obedience. Under these circumstances the king will become the enemy of the people and the people will become enemies of the king. The affairs of the supreme command will fall into disorder; revolt and disobedience will appear on every side and the authority of the government will vanish.

If the king in the affairs of government follows the traditions (*sunnah*) of Almighty God, he will realise that the kingship of a mere human being, though, phenomenal (*majazi*) and temporary, has nevertheless the dignity of the deputyship and vice-regency of God; and God has forbidden excess even in religious matters. "Do not resort to excess in your religion[113]", the Quran has ordered; and as to the removal of hardships, the Quran has said: "God does not impose upon a person (*nafs*) a duty beyond his powers[114]". In addition to this, with reference to every command that God has given to man through heavenly inspiration and every order obedience to which He has made obligatory—and the Islamic religion is bound up with submission to these orders—a number of exceptions (*rukhsats*) have been permitted. Thus theism (*tauhid*) is the basic principle of Islam and the basis of theism is gnosis (*ma'rifat*).[115] But attaining gnosis is difficult and laborious. So out of regard for the ease and convenience of the Musalmans, they have considered traditional theism, which is based on hereditary faith and is unrelated to gnosis, to be sufficient, and have thus brought the mere follower of theistic tradition (*muqallid*) within the circle of Islam and the Muslim community. Similarly concerning prayer, which is the essence of all obedience and devotion, and the obligatory character of which has been inculcated with great and extreme firmness, the number of genuflections has been reduced from four to two in case of travellers, who have to face sufferings and hardships. On rainy days, which cause difficulties, it is permitted to say two prayers together—i.e. the early afternoon (*zohr*) with the later afternoon (*asr*) prayer and the evening (*maghrib*) with the night (*isha*) prayer. If a man cannot say his prayer owing to some insuperable difficulty and the time for it has passed, then a belated prayer (*qaza*) is permitted in its place at a later time.

All such orders have been given for the lessening of afflictions and hardships and with a view to ease and comfort. For the sake of his convenience a traveller is permitted to eat during the fasting month and the same privilege has been extended to pregnant women, nursing mothers, and to sick and, very old people, for whom fasting would be an insuperable burden. On the same principle the duty of paying *zakat* (obligatory charity) has been imposed only upon the wealthy, who possess something beyond their own requirements. The Haj pilgrimage is not binding unless the routes are safe and unless a man has the means of performing the long journey and has obtained the permission of his parents. The object of these exceptions is that there may be no superhuman difficulty in the performance of those religious duties on which Islam is based; otherwise the Musalmans would be spiritually ruined owing to their incapacity to perform them in commenting upon the ease and comfort, which God allows in the Muslim faith the holy Prophet has said by way of glorification: "I have been sent with the correct religion of leniency and ease".

Further, concerning punishments prescribed by the *shari'at,* which are tortures entailing danger to human life and a great affliction and burden on men's souls, the holy Prophet has said: "Avoid punishments on grounds of doubts". In other words, since Almighty God transcends all elements of vindictiveness while mercy is a necessary attribute of His Divinity, fear of punishment on account of the violation of God's rights (*hudud*) is to be removed from the minds of men on the ground that there may be doubt about the guilt of the accused[116]. Thus, the creatures of God, in spite of the fact that they are guilty, will not be subjected to the hard and severe punishments prescribed by the *shari'at.*

My reason for referring to the mildness of *shari'at* rules, while discussing the king's commands, is this. The basis of public administration (as already stated) are friendliness, kindness, courtesy and forgiveness; severity and excessive demands are against the correct principles of governance. A royal order, obedience to which causes plenty of afflictions and hardships, will ultimately lead to a situation beyond the endurance of the people. Consequently, if the king is not mild in punishing the offences of the people and is harsh in exacting obedience to the orders of God or to his own orders; and completely gives up pardoning crimes and totally forsakes the virtues of gentleness, compassion, affection, humanity, forgiveness and connivance at faults; and orders the most difficult tasks and demands obedience and submission to his commands to the utmost bounds and insists on exacting to the full the amount that is due to him and also makes inquiries into details, and considers shortcomings and negligences to be great crimes both in his officers and subjects; and is harsh in his demands and does not condescend to hear apologies or excuses; and behaves with harshness and ill-temper both towards the select and the commons and refers every revenue-matter for investigation to the auditors (*mustaufir*)—there will inevitably be disorders in the administration, the people will be heart-broken, the hope of the subjects will change into despair and loyalty to the king will vanish.

With the select and the commons driven to despair, the government cannot be stabilised or made permanent. For permanence in the enforcement of royal orders depends upon the elements of hope and fear in the hearts of the people; and they have only been able to stabilise the affairs of administration successfully on the principle that *the best of actions is the middle path.* Extreme demands and severe exactions have been considered wrong in all religions, and they have also been declared injurious to the stability of the state. Wise kings have treated their subjects with leniency and gentleness; they have distinguished between acts of service and obedience and acts of wickedness and treason in such a way that no weakness or impotence of any kind has appeared in their supreme command and their royal prestige has not suffered, while on the other band, loyalty for them has increased in men's breasts and fear and reverence for them have been established in the minds of the select and the commons. Thus, while the subjects have become habitually obedient to the king owing to his power and terror, the king's government has attained glory and honour owing to the good-will and loyalty of the subjects; and the affairs of the administration have been stabilised in a proper way.

This type of administrative stability, which is the fruit of the king's contrary qualities, becomes a means for his salvation and his eminence in the next world. It is, therefore, obligatory on kings of perfect judgment and great eminence in all their varied relations with their high officers, courtiers, soldiers, subjects, select men as well as the commons to act on the principle that 'the middle course is the best'. They should neither be negligent, careless, indifferent and remiss in enforcing the confirmed claims of Islam, nor resort to extreme and severe demands, which are great defects in a king. Among the Qaisars of Rum they had a precept: 'The king should neither be like sugar, which they may lick completely, nor like poison that kills everyone who eats 'it'. In the *first* case, when the king seeks exclusively to please the subjects, the result is the degradation of his status; the prestige of the supreme command withers away and becomes tasteless. In the *second* case, when the king treats all his subjects with harshness and ill-temper and is extreme and severe in his demands, hatred for him is roused among the subjects. But whenever the king adopts moderate ways and does not resort to extremes either for pleasing or for terrorising the people, and puts ointment (*marham*) where ointment is needed and cauterises where cauterisation (*dagh*) is necessary, the state is put into order and organised—the submissive become well-wishers, rebels become obedient, enemies become friends, deserters return, the abhorrers of the king become inclined towards him, the hearts of the people are at rest and their minds at peace. The forgiveness and leniency of the king raise the hopes of the people while his power and terror cause them to be afraid. Consequently, whenever owing to fear and hope, which are contrary to each other, the minds of men are properly balanced, the affairs of the administration are settled in the best ways, and the rulers and the ruled obtain the greatest advantage from their work.

[This Advice is illustrated by two examples. (1) Barni states on the authority of the book, *Sharhus Sunnah* (*Commentary on the Prophet's Traditions*), as follows. An Arab cohabited with his wife during the day while fasting in the month of Ramazan and was filled with deep regret after the act. His tribesmen disowned him and he appealed to the Prophet, who asked him to fast for forty days continuously in compensation for the sin he had committed. 'Prophet of Allah', said the Arab, 'My body becomes so excited during fasting that I cannot restrain myself from cohabiting with my wife'. The Prophet, as an alternative, asked him either to set free a slave or to feed sixty beggars. The Arab said that he had no slave to manumit and that he could not feed sixty beggars, as he was the poorest man in Medina. At that moment someone brought several loads of dates to the Prophet. 'Take these dates', the Prophet said to the Arab,' You and your family are to eat them in compensation for your sin'. Barni adds that, according to the *faqihs*, this order of the Prophet was exclusively for that Arab and must not be taken as a precedent.]

[(2) The emperor Yazdjurd[117] was extremely prodigal; he spent five and even ten lakhs of *dinars* daily while only one lakh of *dinars* came into his treasury every day. His wazir, who attempted to warn him, got a scolding. Yazdjurd lived like this for twenty years; then a rival king attacked him. Yazdjurd, who was sixty by now, got rid of this rival somehow and then attempted by harsh exactions to fill the ancestral treasury he had depleted. He used to put two hundred or three hundred men of all ranks to death before his court every day. The people, sick of his exactions and his punishments came to his palace and tore him to pieces.]

Advice XVIII

On the Contradictory Qualities of the King

Sultan Mahmud says: O sons of Mahmud and kings of Islam! You should understand that God has formed man of contradictory qualities. In every living creature that has been taken out of circle of animals and put into the group of human beings, the contrary qualities of contraction (*qabz*) and expansion (*bast*),[118] terrorism and mercy, generosity and niggardliness, pride and humility can, for certain, be seen and witnessed. That human nature should develop these contrary qualities is a wonder! In the king, in particular, these opposite qualities should be developed to perfection to enable him to act as the 'deputy' and 'vice-regent' of God. For Almighty God has created men with different tempers and characters and variegated wills and motives. The external form and features of one man are never like those of another; and the same is true of the mental and moral qualities of men. The actual differences in human character are immense, Though all men are compounded from the contrary qualities of virtue and vice, yet there is a different mixture of vice and virtue in every man, so that the vices and virtues of one man never totally or entirely resemble those of another. In some men—but they are few among the very few—virtue has so overpowered vice that vice is as good as non-existent and no meanness is visible. In other men vice has so overpowered virtue that either no excellence is seen, or if any kind of excellence appears, it will be found on critical examination to be meanness which has put on the external form of excellence. Such people are plentiful and abundant. In a few men sometimes excellence and sometimes meanness can be witnessed. *But most, in fact the greater number of men, have been created unspeakable brutes ('haiwan ghair natiq'); they have been brought within the circle of animals and beasts of prey and deprived of every excellence; and their existence and their being, their lives ana their deaths, are all in meanness.*

In the sphere of public administration, the king's court deals with all the subjects of his territories and the king is the commander and ruler of them all. Consequently, terror and kindness, prestige and affection, strength and compassion, pride and humility, severity and gentleness, wrath and mercy, generosity and hardness of heart, which are all contradictory qualities, should be developed in the king's character to a perfect degree and should also find expression at appropriate occasions. With this perfection of his character it is possible for the king to deal with thousands and thousands of men, who are quite different from each other in their moral qualities, characters, temperaments and natures. If there is only terror in the king and no kindness, what will happen to the submissive, the helpless and the obedient? How will they be able to withstand a policy that is entirely, or even predominantly, terroristic? If there is kindness alone in the king, and no terrorism, he will not be able to check the rebellious, the contumacious, the refractory and the disobedient. He will not be able to reduce them to subjection, submission and impotence through kindness alone. It is the same with the other contradictory qualities of the king.[119]

It is a wonder of the wonders of creation that the king's contradictory qualities should be perfect and that they should be expressed at appropriate and proper occasions! Thus there should be no severities at the occasions for mercy, nor mercy at the occasions for severities. A king so endowed has a proper share and portion of Divine attributes. *Only a person whose contradictory qualities are innate, and are not only developed to perfection but also express themselves at proper occasions for dealing with the virtuous and the wicked, the peaceful and the disobedient, the submissive and the rebellious, is entitled to that kingship, which is the 'deputyship' and 'vice-regency' of God; and the kindness of God shines on the forehead of such a king. In this world such kings have the status of the axis of the earth (qutb-i 'aim) and in the next world they will find a place in the shadow of the Divine Throne.* Recounting their praises and good deeds is a source of salvation and not a cause of ruin. The precept, "An hour of justice is better than seventy years of devotions", has been propounded with reference to the justice of such kings, and the Prophet's tradition, "The *sultan* is the shadow of God on earth and all the oppressed take refuge with him", has been laid down with reference to them. *Religious scholars have said, "A king who has no share or portion of God's qualities and attributes will make himself and others fit for the fire of Hell on account of his undesirable actions and words, regardless of the fact that he is a usurper or a ruler by hereditary succession".*

From the Prophet's traditions—"The sultan is the shadow of God on earth and all the oppressed take refuge with him" and "If there was no *sultan,* some men would destroy others"—it is made clear that the salvation and the spiritual eminence (*darajat*) of kings are dependent upon their contradictory qualities, and that by the manifestation of these qualities on appropriate occasions they become worthy of Paradise. All those qualities that are needed and necessary for kingship and conquests, and without which the affairs of state cannot be put right, are comprehended in the aforesaid traditions. The traditions of the Prophet are brief in words but comprehensive in meaning. If scholars devote themselves to commenting on these two traditions, at least a volume could be written, though even then it would not be possible to discharge the duties of a commentator properly.

All kings in whom virtue predominates over vice and in whom excellences of character are innate, display justice and kindness in their administrative dealings with the people. Though love for the kingdom is predominant in their minds, and no one to control them has been appointed on behalf of the Faith, nevertheless owing to their inborn good nature they do not resort to wickedness, oppression, cruelty, misplaced terror, hatred, violence, unkindness, or insensate destruction in their dealings with the people, and the inhabitants of their realm pass their lives in prosperity and happiness. *Such kings have a good reputation in this world, and in the next world they attain salvation or at the least, their punishments are lessened.*

Further. kings of Islam, who are needed by the true religion and are endowed with excellences of character and firmness of faith, manifest their kindness and terror, wrath and gentleness, strength and compassion, severity and mildness in their dealings with the people only for the sake of God and the Prophet's creed; and the permanence of their power is of value to them only for this purpose. If they are merciful, it is for God and the Prophet's creed only; if they resort to terror, their object is to serve the Faith. Their royal power, which is based on their contradictory qualities, is exercised for the protection of Islam; and their lives are dedicated to glorifying the True Word, to elevating the traditions of the Faith, to executing the commandments of the *shari'at,* to enforcing 'the order for the good and the prohibition of the evil', to honouring Islam and the Mussalmans and to degrading infidelity and idolatry. Inevitably, they have a good reputation in this world, praises of their good deeds will continue till the Day of Judgment, and then they will rise up from their graves among the prophets.

But the vices of those kings of Islam, who have not been created with excellences of character, inevitably predominate over their virtues. Their belief in the Faith is not firm and their (apparent) excellences are due to policy and design. Their eyes and their minds are set only on the preservation of their persons and their power, and they exercise their contrary qualities only for these two objects. *Their real aim is prosperity and power in this world and they subordinate their religion to this aim.* They are fierce or mild, as the case may be, only for the preservation of their persons and their power. If they are kind, their object is personal gain; if they resort to terrorism, it is for the same purpose. When they bestow favours or show tolerance or refrain from molesting people, their object is not the protection of the Faith but the preservation of their persons and their kingdoms; and for the same objects they will also molest others or resort to violence and terror. Consequently, in both cases they will be held responsible and denied the blessings of the next world. (A paragraph of no significance to the author's argument has been omitted here).

O Sons of Mahmud! If they have adorned you with innate excellences, strive to make the protection of the Faith the end and object of your valour and courage, and exercise your contradictory qualities exclusively for this purpose. Consider the preservation of your state and power to be subordinate to this aim so that you may obtain salvation. But if, on the other hand, excellences of character are not innate in you, then act in accordance with the tradition of the Prophet: "Create (in yourself) in the moral qualities of Allah". You should by your efforts change your vices into excellences; for man has been created capable of improving his moral qualities. Other people may or may not improve their moral qualities, but the king, whose contradictory qualities affect the whole world, cannot maintain his kingship without improving his character; for both religious and worldly affairs are thrown into disorder owing to the mean character of the king. And as to your religious faith in Islam, test yourself by this touch-stone. If you see that the exclusive aim of your valour and courage—the object and end of your state and your power—is the protection and promotion of the Faith, the glorification of the True Word, the elevation of the traditions of Islam, increasing the honour of the Musalmans and the overthrow of idolators and idolatry, and that your sole object is not the preservation of your kingdom and your person, then you can be certain that you are a true Musalman. But if this is not the case, then you should be afraid concerning your faith and not be proud in self-admiration.

The Real King of all kings and rulers is God Almighty, who maintains the world through His terror and kindness, severity and mercy; their effects are visible both on the good and the bad. He has created Paradise for the good and the obedient and promised it to them. He has created Hell for the wicked and the disobedient and threatened them with it. He has created Rizwan, the keeper of Paradise, with the eye of kindness and Malak, the guardian of Hell, with the eye of terror. *The phenomenal king should follow the traditions (sunnah) of the Real King, and he should deal with the inhabitants of the kingdom according to his contradictory qualities, which are necessary for the affairs of state.*

Now just as the king, on the one hand, has no alternative but to appoint officers remarkable for their good manners, sweet tempers, generosity, modesty and tolerance at his gate and portal, so that his good and obedient subjects may feel that these virtues are the virtues of the king himself and that his administration will be inspired by them owing to the officers in charge; similarly, on the other hand, he has no alternative but to instal harsh and merciless officers also at his gate and portal in order to control his wicked and rebellious subjects. The qualities mentioned here are contrary to each other and among the officers of the king both these contrary qualities should be found. If this is the case, all the inhabitants of the realm will have respect for the king, the administration will be efficient, the houses and farms of the people will increase, virtue will overpower vice, and the good and virtuous subjects of the king will be satisfied and prosperous. (Respect for the traditions of the English language has prevented me from translating more than one hundred adjectives which Barni has put into this paragraph.)

Barni once more returns to his low estimate of human nature. *There are in this world plenty of wicked men—sons of Adam with the character of Satan, sons of demons (does) with the qualities of Iblis, rapacious men with demonic tempers, and men who have the characteristics of the carnivori and seem to have descended from wild beasts. Now if in the court of the king there are not officers with the requisite power and terror, how are these groups to be subdued?* And unless they are subdued, how are the king's obedient and submissive subjects to be protected from their rapacity and beastliness? There can be no liberation for the weak and the helpless unless such persons are brought under subjection. It is, therefore, necessary that in the court of the king there should be prisons, prison-officers, overseers (*sarhangs*) and cruel men, who are ready and well- equipped for the infliction of punishments; so that from fear and dread of prisons, chains, injuries, afflictions and hardships, the disobedience and dishonesty of the people may decrease and the orders of the government may be enforced.

The object of these preliminary remarks is this. The king should possess contradictory qualities in perfection, his excellences should be innate in him and his devotion to religion should reach the extreme limit, so that the country may be properly administered, the government conducted according to the orders of God, the True Word glorified, the correct Faith made predominant over the false creeds, the orders of the *shari'at* enforced and truth established at the centre. Then both the king and the subjects will gain an advantage from the obedience of the latter; the king will be raised to spiritual eminence in the next world and his subjects will be saved from calamities and misfortunes.

(Barni offers two illustrations for this Advice. (1) The Second Caliph, Umar bin Khattab, is praised for helping the Musalmans and overthrowing other creeds. (2) The following account of Sultan Sanjar is worth quoting as another example of our author's colossal ignorance of history.)

As to the extremely benevolent attitude of Sultan Sanjar towards the obedient and the submissive and his severities towards the refractory, his secretary, Muin Asam, has stated in the *Tarikh-i Sanjari* (*History of Sanjar*) as follows:

Owing to the authority and power of Sultan Sanjar most kings of the inhabited globe, who belonged to non-Muslim religions, were overthrown along with their women, children, families and followers, and the commandments of false religions were erased. The slaves of Sultan Sanjar became kings in the territories and lands of his opponents. He enforced the rules of the *shari'at*; idolatry was liquidated in the cities, and idolators and polytheists were overthrown. Men of bad dogmas and bad communities hid themselves in snake-holes during his reign. No one had the courage to observe openly the rites of a creed opposed to Islam; no man of bad religion and bad faith could be honoured and respected in the cities of the Musalmans; and no enemy of the Faith could be exalted over the Musalmans in any respect. If a man of bad dogmas or an opponent of the Muslim faith came to live among the Musalmans, he was degraded and made of no value and account, so that no one paid any heed to his life.

The pomp and grandeur of Sanjar had reached such a height that thirty thousand horses, mules and camels used to travel with his court-pavilion. Courtiers, poets, *qawwals* (reciters of mystic verses) and musicians were given seven hundred caparisoned horses at the time of starting on the march from the royal stables every day. Yet in spite of this grandeur, power and prestige, Sultan Sanjar had such a compassionate heart that his eyes were filled with tears after he had recited his obligatory prayers, and he wept a lot on hearing sermons and advices. He went on foot at night to the houses of religious devotees and other persons who had forsaken the world. He considered the days passed with pious and holy men to be a blessing. Once every week, he used to go to the houses of two shoe-makers, who were inspired mystics and worked miracles. So they have said: "Sultan Sanjar used to go to *salaam* two shoe-makers once a week."

He showed great courtesy to the slave-officers of his father and used to sit respectfully before them; he considered them to be in the place of his father, brothers and sons. On occasions of festivities and marriages he went as a guest to the houses of his relatives and slaves; and in spite of the great prestige of his kingdom, he went twice as a guest to the house of the poet, Anwari.

Owing to his excessively kind and compassionate nature, Sultan Sanjar would not permit any Musalman to be put to death for political or revenue offences. "I cannot kill a Musalman for a crime against my kingdom", he would say, "for I will not be able to answer God for his death." If a relative or high officers of Sanjar rebelled in his territory and they brought him bound as a prisoner before him, Sanjar would set him free immediately. He would only say so much in the presence of the captive, "I forgive you this time; do not rebel and throw yourself into the danger of annihilation again." Owing to the blessings of his good deeds and the excellences of his character, his orders were enforced over the whole world. He lived for ninety-five years and reigned happily for seventy or eighty years.

Note on Sultan Sanjar

It is useless protesting against Barni's ignorance of history and his ignorance of his ignorance A defender of Barni may justify his story of the 'king of Khwarazm' in the preceding Advice as an illustrative fiction. But such a justification is hardly possible for Barni's wholly erroneous picture of the reign of Sultan Sanjar.

In his *Tarikh-i Firoz Shahi* (p. 216), Barni makes the following statement on behalf of Ahmad Chap in his conversation with Sultan Jalaluddin: "Why does your Majesty not follow the traditions and customs of Sultan Mahmud and Sultan Sanjar, who were pillars of the Muslim faith and who conquered the world *and kept it*?" The assumption here is that the unfortunate Sanjar was a successful conqueror like Mahmud. In this Advice Barani reveals his hand and attributes the following achievements to Sultan Sanjar—(a) that he overthrew most non-Muslim kings; (b) that he suppressed the opponents of the orthodox faith; and (c) that he kept the government strong and the people prosperous. Now Sanjar tragically failed in all these matters and there can be no two opinions about it.

Sultan Sanjar son of Malik Shah was born at Sanjar in Syria in 1086 A.D. and died at Merv in 1157 A.D. at the age of seventy-two (lunar) years and ninth months. (*Rauzatus Safa,* p. 114). For twenty years he was governor of Khorasan on behalf of his brothers, the emperors Barqiaruq and Mohammad, and he reigned as an emperor for fifty-nine (lunar) years (1119–1157 A.D.). It has to be admitted candidly that Sultan Sanjar occupies a unique position in Persian literature, which prefers to refer to him, in spite of his misfortunes, as the *Sultan-i Sa'id* (Fortunate King). Nevertheless it is a sad fact that Sultan Sanjar inherited a great empire extending from Turkestan to Anatolia and when he died broken-hearted at Merv in 1157, the great Seljuq empire had completely vanished.

"Sultan Sanjar", says the *Rauzatus Safa,* "fought nineteen battles and was victorious in seventeen of them". Among other things, he subdued Bharam Shah of Ghaznin, Alauddin Jahansoz of Ghor and Ahmad Khan, governor of Mawaraun Nahr. But his repeated campaigns against Itisiz, the governor of Khwarazm, failed, and Itisiz was able to lay the foundation of an independent royal dynasty, which was destined to inherit the Seljuq dominions.

The two defeats suffered by Sultan Sanjar were decisive.

"In 1141 A.D. the Gor Khan of Kara-Khita marched with a strong army against Sultan Sanjar. The Khorasanians in their insolence thought that a hundred Gor Khans would not be able to stand against them. But when the armies met, it was found that the soldiers of the enemy were beyond computation. They surrounded Sanjar on all sides; a great defeat befell the army of Islam and thirty thousand Muslim soldiers were martyred. Sanjar was perplexed. Ultimately one of his officers, Tajuddin Abul Fazl, said to him, 'We should try to escape, for it is impossible to fight'. Sanjar escaped with ten or fifteen persons to the fort of Tar (?Atrar), where he was joined by the remnants of his wounded and distressed soldiers... In this battle some ten thousand, distinguished warriors of the Sultan were killed and his wife, Turkan Khatun, fell into the hands of the enemy along with many of his distinguished *amirs...* Owing to this defeat the dignity and prestige of Sultan Sanjar vanished from the minds of men and the wealth he had collected during his reign was lost". (*Rauzatus Safa,* Vol. IV, pp. 112–113)

In the decade that followed, Sanjar strove hard to build up his reputation but then a greater misfortune befell him. His officers through their aggressive behaviour drove the Ghazz Turks—a group of some forty thousand families who lived round about Balkh and Khatlan—to desperation. The very humble submission and compromises offered by the Ghazz were rejected and Sanjar, at the insistence of his officers but against his better judgment, marched with an army against them. "When the Ghazz tribes despaired of the mercy of the Sultan, they determined to risk their lives and fight... In a short time the Sultan's army was defeated and took to flight. The Ghazz followed in pursuit and killed many of the fugitive soldiers". (*Rauzatus Safa,* p. 114).

Since Barni insists on considering Sanjar as the great protector of his people, it is necessary to give some account of what the people really suffered at the end of his reign. "The Ghazz pursued the Sultan, captured him, placed the crown on his head, kissed his feet and took him captive to Merv. The city was full of wealth, for the people had lived in peace from the time of Chaghr Beg. The infidel-minded Ghazz plundered it for three days and nights; then they tortured the citizens into revealing their buried treasures. After this they proceeded with the Sultan to Naishapur. The people of Naishapur killed some of their Ghazz opponents in the first attack and then, like animals destined for slaughter, they admitted defeat and fled for refuge to their Juma mosque.

The infidel and sinful Ghazz pulled down the door of the mosque; and making no distinction between men and women, old and young, pious and sinful, they caused the blood of all of them to flow in the courtyard of the mosque like the waves of the Oxus. After sunset the Ghazz proceeded to another high mosque where the flames of its burning ornamented pillars were rising so high that the whole city was illuminated; so with the help of the light from the burning mosque-pillars, the Ghazz proceeded to capture and plunder the inhabitants. (After everything on the surface of the ground had been seized, the Ghazz proceeded to torture the inhabitants by thrusting earth into their noses and salt into their mouths to compel them to give up their buried treasures.) The great *ulama* and *shaikhs* of Khorasan fell into the clutches of these rascals and were martyred. Among them Imam Mohammad bin Yahya, who was distinguished for his learning and piety, was also tortured to death under the rack. Every inhabited place in Khorasan was plundered by the Ghazz." (*Rauzatus. Safa*, Vol. lV, p. 114)

Many other provinces and cities of the prosperous Seljuq empire were plundered in the same way, but the examples of the Merv oasis and Khorasan should suffice to show what Sanjar's subjects suffered.

After about three years of captivity, Sultan Sanjar managed to escape from the Ghazz. "He crossed the Oxus, encamped by the side of the river to enable his followers to collect under his banner and then proceeded to his capital. But on reaching Merv he found the treasury empty, the country desolated and the people scattered. His mind became clouded with pain and sorrow; and he was overpowered by some illness—the last he was to face—and died in 1157 A.D." (*Rauzatus Safa,* Vol. IV, p. 114).

Though Barni seems to have known nothing about it, the greatest challenge to orthodoxy in Sanjar's reign came from the Ismaili assassins of Alamut. The founder of this movement, Hasan bin Sabbah, lived till 1124 A.D.—i.e. till the fifth year of Sanjar's reign. The Seljuq emperor was quite unable to meet the challenge.

It is impossible to prove that Sanjar had no secretary called Muin Asam. But no secretary of Sanjar could have made the erroneous statements repeated by Barni. Also since Barni was so well acquainted with Persian poetry and definitely refers to Anwari, why did he not recall to mind Anwari's *Tears of Khorasan* written while Sanjar was a prisoner? (Browne, *Literary History of Persia,* Vol. II, pp. 385–389). One can excuse Barni for not having within his reach the historical material which the wazir, Amir Ali Sher, placed at the disposal of the author of the *Rauzatus Safa,* but he cannot be excused for not knowing what the *Tabaqat-i Nasiri* could have told him about Sanjar and his contemporaries. In his *Tarikh-i Firoz Shahi* he claims that he is continuing that work. [H]

Advice XIX

On the Noble Birth of the Supporters of the State

Sultan Mahmud has said: O Sons of Mahmud and kings! You should understand the Quranic verse in which God has declared; "Obey Allah, obey the Prophet and obey the rulers that be from amongst you,"[120] and the tradition in which the Prophet has said, "All of you will be called and all of you will be questioned about your *rai'yyat.*" You should carefully consider that God has put the status of the orders of the supreme ruler (*ulul amr*) parallel to His own orders, though He is the Lord of eight thousand worlds, and to the orders of the Prophet, who is the distinguished one of men and *jins,* and the beloved of the two eternities (*azal wa abad*). How can a helpless son of man repay such an obligation? Further, the holy Prophet has said, "Every Musalman is the shepherd of his own house and he will be questioned about the *ra'iyyat* of his household". Consequently, on Judgment Day, when a man will be unable to answer questions concerning his own life, let alone questions about his household, how will a king, who is the ruler of a whole country and responsible for its welfare, be able to answer for the actions of his subjects?

The king cannot be sufficiently grateful for God's favours to him. At the same time the duties of his high office, that is of conducting the government in accordance with the *shari'at,* cannot be discharged by him without loyal supporters and officers adorned with noble lineage and merits of character. He cannot with the assistance of the worthless and the shameless, or the cooperation of the Godless and the wicked, live with the seventy-two communities in such a way that he can take responsibility for all his subjects before God and be among those who attain salvation.

The wise men of the world are agreed that the king cannot personally discharge all the duties of the administration and that he cannot admit unknown persons into partnership in the affairs of the supreme command. It becomes, therefore, necessary for him to delegate the work of administration to his helpers, supporters and partisans and to assign the posts of governors and *amirs* to those who are closest to him. If he directs a stranger to look after the affairs of his government, he cannot be certain of his loyalty; also a stranger will have no anxiety about the king's business.

Now whenever a king's supporters, helpers, well-wishers, partisans and followers are base and mean, and are characterised by ignoble qualities and have no share or portion of religion, they throw the affairs of government into disorder and undertake enterprises which bring distress to the religion and the state. *Even if they put the affairs of the world right, well, the affairs of the world are set right by the enemies of God also! But the worthless, the shameless, the low-born, the mean and the Godless can accomplish no enterprises, the final end (aqibat) of which is good or owing to which the king is honoured in the next world.*

The following principle has been proved by experience to hakims, scholars and wise men of ancient as well as modem communities and no disagreement about it is possible—that the base, the low-born and the Godless cannot accomplish any work, religious or secular, which is approved by knowledge or reason. Whenever the king appoints this wicked group to offices in the religion or the state of the Prophet, and as the supreme commander, which is a great favour of God on him, not only makes these people, who have been rejected and cast off by the spiritual world, his partners but also gives them a free hand, he will have to answer before the Divine Throne for all things they do on his behalf. Is it not a curious position that the advantages and luxuries of office should be enjoyed by these low-born officers, while the king has to answer for their misdeeds before God?

But if the king appoints the free-born (*ahrar*), the noble and the possessors of merits as his officers and supporters, then since owing to their nature and character their action as his agents are bound to be praiseworthy, he will not on the Day of Judgment be distressed and bewildered at having to answer for so many thousands and thousands of his subjects—though on that day the prophets and saints, who are among the near ones of the Court of God, will exclaim, O my soul!' 'O my soul!' (*Nafasi! Nafasi!*) and devotees, hermits, *abrar* and *akhyar* will be unable to answer for themselves and for the members of their households.

The sons of Mahmud are to know that the injuries, both religious or secular suffered by kings have been mostly due to their bad supporters, helpers and partisans. In the intoxication of their royal power, they have not taken care about preventing the promotion of the worthless; the sincerity and the loyalty of the mean and the base-born have succeeded in blinding their discerning eyes and their desire for immediate prosperity has prevented them from considering ultimate results. So owing to the supreme command, which has come to them as a gift of God, they have made worthless people their partners and have disgraced themselves in this world and the next owing to the deeds of these people.

If the king is the victim of low and forbidden vices but his helpers and supporters who are his partners and confidential officers in his administrative policies, are endowed with high birth, noble lineage and merits of character, the work of the government will not become unstable, disorders will not arise and the threads of the administration will not be loosened. And the king owing to their achievements will not be punished in the next world. On the other hand, if the king himself is adorned with noble qualities and the fear of God predominates in him, but his helpers, supporters, governors (*walis*) and revenue-officers (*amils*) are the victims of vices, then in consequence of their wicked deeds the affairs of the administration will fall into disorder. And the king himself, on account of their words and deeds, will be disgraced in the next world.

All wise men of ancient and modem times are agreed on this fact—that the merits or vices of the supporters, helpers, high officers and partisans of the king are a conclusive proof of the merits or vices (as the case may be) of the king himself. A king endowed with merits will not, owing to his nature and character, enrol anyone, who is a victim of vices, among the high officers of the administration or the helpers and supporters of his court. Similarly, a king of mean character will not, in consequence of his nature, be able to bear the sight of anyone gifted with merits or to make such a man a helper, supporter or high officer of his state. For the fact of belonging to the same category, whether of vice or virtue, creates affection, desire for company, courtesy and harmony between men, while between virtue and vice there is both contradiction and opposition. And both with reference to merits and vices, the superior officer may be trusted to act according to his character and not the inferior officer; it is owing to this that a man of merit cannot bear the sight of a vicious man or a vicious man the sight of a man of merit. They deem each other to be enemies and they remain enemies.

The government of the Kisras extended for a very long period from Kaimurs (son of Adam) to Khusrau Parwez. The greatest cause of this was that the Kisras did not permit any means, low-born or wicked man, or any man who was a captive of vices, to obtain a position near to themselves; they did not enrol the worthless and the sons of the worthless as their helpers and supporters. And as they had been of noble and royal descent from the time of Kaimurs, while greatness, royalty, supreme status and capacity for leadership had permeated their veins and sinews, no base or low-born man was enrolled by them among the officers of their government and their partners in the supreme command or even permitted to approach the precincts of their court. And as they appointed the high-born, the noblest and the best of people to be their helpers, supporters, partisans, well-wishers as well as the governors and revenue-officers of their territories, the royal power remained in their dynasty for several thousand years. Their greatness and the greatness of their kingdom were inscribed in the hearts of the peoples of the world and the praises of their good deeds were recorded in books.

O sons of Mahmud and kings of Islam! You should during your phenomenal kingship of a few days follow the traditions of the Real King of kings in selecting virtuous persons for appointment as your confidential officers and partners in your supreme command, so that you may be honoured owing to their actions in this world and the next. Almighty God selects only possessors of merits and virtuous characters for nearness to His Court; he distinguishes them with prophethood and saintship and raises them to high grades and great spiritual status; he makes them honoured, great, distinguished and noble. They do not permit any man who is wicked, unclean, or victim of vices and meannesses, to occupy a place of nearness and distinction before the Divine Throne. Whenever a king possesses good fortune and perfect wisdom, then for his rule of a few days he adopts this tradition of Almighty God. He enrols men of merit, skill and wisdom in the country as the helpers and supporters of his government, appoints the highest and best men of the land as the chief officers of his court and assigns governorships, offices and posts only to the distinguished persons of his country.

Though the leader (*qibla*) of the highest and the best will not condescend to serve the king[121], still by varieties of favours, kindness, affection, courtesy and gifts the king, can make the select and the chosen people of the land into the well-wishers of his state; but he should not make such people subordinate either in dignity or in office to the ignoble and the worthless. Wise kings have not, either as a general rule or in special cases, had any hopes of good and virtuous achievements of a permanent character from groups of mean and Godless people. From these low people, even if they have a hundred successes, there can be no honour to the king in this world or the next.

[Nausherwan, the Just, emperor of Ajam, is declared to have said in his Testament to his successors: 'Adorn in your kingdom those whom God has adorned... You can adorn those selected by you with the goods of this world only; you cannot embellish them with the qualities of merit. Your kingdom can never be set right by those you have yourself chosen, but those whom God has embellished can organise your administration properly.']

[In a sermon in the Juma mosque of Kufa the Caliph Ali was trying to incite his reluctant army-commanders to march against the rebel, Mu'awiya. They were slack in marching to Syria against him and made lame excuses. A Companion asked, "The legitimacy of your Caliphate is not doubted by any Musalman. Why then is your Caliphate not stable like the Caliphates of Abu Bakr and Umar?" The Caliph replied, "The stability of a kingdom depends upon its supporters. The supporters of Abu Bakr and Umar were people like Abu Ubaidah Jarrah, Usman son of Affan, myself, Abdur Rahman bin Auf, Sa'd bin Wiqas, Talha, Zubair, Salman Farsi, Abu Zar Ghaffari, Abdullah Masud, Khalid bin Walid, Ma'az Jabal and all the Immigrants and Companions.... During their Caliphates a whole world came under the banner of Islam and the frontiers of the Faith were pushed forward. But how can the administration be stabilised or rebellions suppressed or the countries of Islam cleared of opponents with the supporters I have? You see them in this assembly. In this war against Mu'awiyah, whose rebellion has become widespread, they are putting forward every variety of excuse and are guilty of every default."]

Religious kings have observed and kept in view certain principles in testing and selecting their helpers and supporters:

First, the person selected should be one in whom the quest for religion predominates over the quest for the goods of this world, even though it be by a needle-point. If all his efforts are directed to seeking the goods of this world only, be should not be put among the helpers and supporters of the king, for he will not in that case be useful even in worldly affairs. And the greatest mistakes, which religious kings make in this respect, is that in the selection of their helpers and supporters they think exclusively of their loyalty and devotion to themselves. Without clearly reflecting from the very beginning that a man whose loyalty is dependent on the material advantages he obtains from them and who is, therefore, a slave of this world and from whom, consequently, nothing can be expected the ultimate end of which is commendable, they appoint such a man to high office in the government; and deciding about his merits from his words and actions only, they expect from him good work, fulfilment of promises and loyalty to themselves both while he is present with them and away from their court. In the garden of religion no fruits can be plucked from a tree the roots of which are strong and have gone to water-depth owing to greed for this world; and a man who is not trustworthy in religious matters cannot be worthy of trust in affairs of the state.

Second, the person selected should for certain have the advantage of free, gentle and noble birth, even if this advantage happens to be very meagre; for to promote base, mean, low-born and worthless men to be the helpers and supporters of the government has not been permitted by any religion, creed, publicly accepted tradition or state-law. Even if a man of base or low birth is adorned with a hundred merits, he will not be able to organise and administer the country according to expectations or be worthy of leadership and political trust.

Third, when a man has been selected as an officer and supporter of the government and admitted to the secrets of the state, he should not be punished except for political crimes and rebellion. Punishing him for inefficiency, negligence, oversight and attention to private affairs (leading to the negligence of public duties)—offences from which there is no danger to the state or to human life—is not desirable. In short, he should not be disgraced for faults, whether great or small, which appertain only to the administration.

Fourth, the king should observe moderation in the matter of promotions, favours, kindness and benevolence to his helpers and supporters. He should always keep them in the hope of an increase in the grades of their dignity and not raise one of them suddenly to an office above which there is no higher office than that of the king. But if the king shows excessive favour in the official promotion of one of his supporters, then he should, thereafter, neither be angry with him too often, nor reject every advice he gives, nor permit him to be disgraced or dishonoured in any way. For if the honour and dignity of those who have reached the highest grades of the official hierarchy is injured even to the extent of a sand-grain, their loyalty ceases to be firm and, in fact, begins to decline. Loyalty to the king disappears from the minds of high officers so treated; they begin to act like flatterers; and this leads to ultimate injury. Also, owing to the king's excessive favours to some of his supporters, the loyalty of others, who are their equals and colleagues, declines; their self-respect and sense of honour are injured; and on account of their envy and jealousy they become enemies of each other.

[This Advice is illustrated by a reference to Bahram Gor, 'the great hunter' of Fitzgerald. We are invited to believe that the world has never been so prosperous since the time of Adam as in the earlier reign of Bahram. "Even the misfortune of death had, disappeared," and as a result there was such an increase of population that in a country, which is mostly steppeland, "houses had so increased owing to excessive population that men went from one city to another by jumping from roof to roof and no plot of unbuilt land was to be seen even in dreams"... But Bahram appointed a wazir who was mischievous, cruel, beastly, merciless, destructive, mean born and of law origin; and the wazir, as was to be expected, appointed oppressors, rascals, sinners, liars, destroyers, reprobates, base, mean and low-born men as the helpers and supporters of the state and as governors and *qazis* of the country. "The injustice of these officers affected even wild animals and birds, trees and wooden beams". The soldiers did not get their salaries and went their own way, and rivals began to attack the frontiers of Bahram's territory.

[Bahram in his distress crossed the great wilderness between India and his country, and entered the service of the Rai of Kannauj and took his salary along with the *rawats.* The Rai was impressed by Bahram, called him to a confidential interview and Bahram told him everything about himself. The Rai descended from his throne, paid respects to Bahram and made him sit near his throne. He gave his daughter to Bahram in marriage, placed thirty thousand horsemen and thirty thousand footmen under him and presented him with a treasure of valuables, twenty elephants and ten thousand horses. He advised Bahram to recapture his country, put the wazir and his co-workers to death, and then to call the *hakims* of Ajam and order the scribes to note down the qualities which these hakims considered necessary for the officers of the king. Bahram was to give up wine, music and hunting entirely till his government had become stable. Bahram reconquered Ajam and acted on the Rai's advice. The qualifications which the *hakims* of Ajam considered necessary for the king's officers are given by Barni; they are about 120 in number (if the repetitions put in by the copyist are included) and contain all the relevant adjectives in the Persian language. For any practical purpose such a list is useless.[122]]

Advice XX

That No One Should Have Ascendancy Over the King

[The greater part of this Advice seems to have been lost and the third paragraph here has been apparently written by someone who tried his hand at restoring Barni's lost passages but gave up the attempt after he had written a few stupid lines. Both in his *Tarikh-i Feroz Shahi* and the other *Nasihats* of this work Barni leaves us in no doubt that ascendancy over the king is usually obtained through two means—efficiency of service and loyalty, which may be sincere or deceptive. But enchantments, necromancy, alchemy and medicines for increasing sex, potency and curing leprosy have never helped anyone to gain political ascendancy over a ruler. The term, *Din-i Ilahi* (Religion of God), which occurs in the last paragraph here, is generally used with reference to Akbar's creed; I have not found it is used by Barni anywhere else. Very probably this paragraph was interpolated into the text after Akbar had promulgated his *Din-i Ilahi*. In any case the *Din-i Ilahi* of Akbar has nothing to do with the religion of Mazdak.]

Sultan Mahmud says: Sons of Mahmud! You should know that *kingship means the control which a man obtains over a territory by power and force.* He may be entitled to it (by inheritance) and may be thus maintaining what is his own or he may have obtained it by usurpation and without any right. *In either case they call him king on account of his control of the territory.*

Now if someone from among the sons, high officers, wives and slaves of the king obtains such influence over him that the king is unable to reject his advice or go against his wishes, then the situation is reversed; the ruler becomes the ruled, the superior becomes the subordinate and the attributes of the ruler change into the qualities of the subject. Further, whenever a man succeeds in obtaining such an ascendancy over the king, kingship really vanishes (*lacuna*).

The causes of the influence of a man over the king are these. A man of bad faith or bad religion can obtain influence over the king by showing him enchantments, by necromancy, by imparting to him knowledge of magic or alchemy or by (providing him with) medicines for increasing sex-potency or curing leprosy. Such a man deceives and captivates the king and spreads his own religious cult. He misguides the king and shakes the foundations of his faith. Thus Mazdak, the *ibahati*, deceived Qubad, the father of Nausherwan, with necromancy and magic and published the *Din-i Ilahi* (Religion of God).

[This Advice is illustrated on the basis of the *Ghadrus Siyar* by misfortunes, ultimately leading to his martyrdom, which befell the Caliph Usman on account of the influence his relations had obtained over him. It is not necessary to translate Barni's account of these events, the substance of which will be found in any book on the history of the Pious Caliphate.]

Advice XXI

On the High Born and the Low Born

It has been said that all men have been created equal; that they are equal in form and appearance; and that every difference that appears between men is due to the effect of their character and the consequences of their actions. (But Barni does not agree with this doctrine of equality and proceeds to give his own views.)

The merits and demerits of men have been apportioned at the beginning of time and allotted to the souls. The acts and deeds of men are due to Divine Commandments; whenever Almighty God instils goodness or wickedness, virtue or vice, in a man. He also endows him with the faculty of giving expression to that goodness or wickedness, virtue or vice.

When during the first generation the children of Adam were born and grew in numbers and the world came to be inhabited, men needed everything for the sake of their existence; and the Eternal Designer inspired men's minds with the arts they needed. Thus some minds were inspired with the art of letters and writing, others with horsemanship, and yet others with weaving, smith-craft and carpentry. *So all the arts, fine and coarse, from writing and horsemanship to hair-cutting and tanning—in accordance with the merits and demerits which by their basic nature had been allotted to their souls—were communicated to the minds and breasts of men. The minds of the possessors of merit, owing to their meritorious nature, were inspired with fine capacities, while to minds involved in meanness, owing to their low natures, only capacities for the baser arts were communicated.* In this way the angels inspired the minds of men with various arts and men adopted different professions and followed them. The arts, crafts and professions for which men have been inspired are practised well by them, and they are only able properly to practise their specific arts.

This aptitude for arts, fine and coarse, is hereditary. It has been inherited by the descendants from their ancestors and in every generation the descendants have, in accordance with their quickness of intelligence and acuteness of mind, added somethings that are fine and desirable to the professions of their ancestors, so that every art, craft and profession on the produce of which mankind depends has attained perfection.

And as excellences have been into those who have adopted the nobler professions, they alone are capable of virtues—kindness, generosity, valour, good deeds, good works, truthfulness, keeping of promises, protection of other classes, loyalty, clarity of vision, justice, equity, recognition of rights, gratitude for favours received and fear of God.

They are, consequently, said to be noble, free-born, virtuous, religious, of high genealogy and pure birth. These groups alone are worthy of offices and posts in the government of the king, who owing to his high position as the supreme commander, is distinguished as the leader and chief of men. As a result of their actions the government of the king is strengthened and adorned.

On the other hand, the low-born, who have been enrolled for practising the baser arts and the meaner professions, are capable only of vices—immodesty, falsehood, miserliness, misappropriation, wrongfulness, lies, evil-speaking, ingratitude, dirtiness, injustice, cruelty, non-recognition of rights, shamelessness, impudence, blood-shedding, rascality, jugglery and Godlessness. *So they are called low-born, bazaar-people, base, mean, worthless, plebeian, shameless, and of dirty birth. Every act which is contaminated with meanness and based on ignominy comes elegantly from them.*

If the king as the supreme commander honours by the conferment of posts in his court and government those people in whose original nature not only were meanness and wickedness ingrained but have also been developed by heredity, then as a consequence of their actions the court and the high position of the king will be disgraced, the people of God will be distressed and scattered, the objectives of the government will not be attained, and, finally, the king will be punished on the Day of Judgment. *The promotion of the low and the low-born brings no advantage in this world, for it is impudent to act against the wisdom of Creation.* You should not deviate from the wisdom of Creation or be insolent in the affairs of government. You should adorn the offices of your state with persons whom God has created with the eye of favour, to whose souls He has allotted excellences and whom He has brought into this world for virtuous behaviour and good actions. On account of their just and equitable dealings with the people and their virtuous behaviour, you may hope for good reputation in this world and for salvation in the world to come.

(Here follows another paragraph in which Barni using a mass of adjectives once more warns the ruler, in view of his interests in both the worlds, to appoint only the high-born to government posts and to keep the low-born in their place. *"Do not owing to the words and actions of the base and the low-born, obtain a bad reputation in this world or put yourself into trouble in the world to come. Do not make the people of God captives under their command, rule (imarat), government and control. Do not let them come near your religious and administrative offices. Do not be captivated by the cleverness and the agility of the low-born and the mean, for their excellences are imitative, and not real, excellences."*)

The holy Prophet has said respecting the well-born and the low-born—The vein is deceptive, i.e., the good vein and the bad vein draw towards virtue and vice. The meaning of this metaphor is that in the well-born and the noble only virtue and loyalty appear, while from the men of low birth and bad birth only wickedness and destruction originate.

As to what the Holy Quran has said: "Indeed, those honoured from amongst you before Allah *are the pious amongst you"—it ought to be known that in the impure and impure-born and the low and low-born, there can be no piety. If they see piety in a baseborn bazaar-man, then indeed the blood* (*arq*) *of his ancestors must have coming led with noble blood.*[123]

O sons of Mahmud! You should know that the majority of *hakims* and wise men, ancient and modern, have declared on the basis of observation and experience that the great duties of the administration have not been well discharged by the low-born and the base. If a base-born man has become a ruler, he has striven, so far as he could, to elevate the low-born and the base and to overthrow men of good birth. The ultimate work of the low-born has never come to any good and they have not been capable of loyalty in any contingency. Though some kings have been captivated by the flattery, agility, apparent intelligence and jugglery of mean and low-born men and have made these people their colleagues and the confidential officers of their kingdoms, yet in this world, both during their lifetime and after their death,[124] they have suffered such wounds and received such injuries from them, that regret for having appointed them will not diminish in their minds during all eternity.

Further, if mean, low, base, and sordid men along with bazaar-people and cowards are established on the pillows (*masnads*) of high offices and are successful in their work, then according to the principle that 'every group is inclined to itself', they will make people of their own kind their helpers, supporters, colleagues and assistants in their consultations as well as in their work of ordering and command. They will make the lowest and the meanest their partners and their intimates and assign a part and portion of their administrative authority to them. They will not, owing to their nature and their character, allow nobles and free-born men and men of merits to come anywhere near the affairs of their government; they will consider them their enemies and keep them their enemies. They detest the noble-born and will strive for their degradation and overthrow with their hearts and souls. Thus owing to the promotion of one base and low-born man, many base and low-born men will get offices and be respected and honoured on that account. Many chasms will appear in the work of the administration in consequence of the words and actions of these low-born men; a number of honourable and meritorious persons will be dishonoured and made of no standing and account; the noble and the free-born will be degraded and persecuted; and meannesses will be manifested while merits are suppressed and compelled to hide themselves.

[Our author in a somewhat longish paragraph refers once more to the history of the Saffarid brothers—Yaqub bin Lais and Amr bin Lais. But this time he quotes the *Tarikh-i Khorasan* (*History of Khorasan*) as his authority. The two brothers are accused of enrolling only the low-born in their service. During the period of their power, the noble and the free-born found it necessary to leave Khorasan and migrated in various directions. Yet in their hour of misfortune the low-born men whom the Saffarid brothers had promoted did not prove loyal to their patrons. Those very low-born men and bazaar-people, who had become the helpers, supporters, officers and workers of the two carpenter-boys, became the leaders on behalf of the Samanids for overthrowing and uprooting their families, followers, women and children.]

[This Advice is illustrated by a fictitious anecdote about Sultan Mahmud of Ghaznin. Once the Sultan while entering the precincts of Ghaznin saw some fifty or sixty women. They were dressed in tattered clothes, and holding their locks in their hands, they cried: "Redress! Redress!" Their complaint was against the wazir Isfraini[125]. "For six months he has locked up our sons, brothers and husbands in the prison of the Ministry of Revenue (*Diwan-i Wizarat*). He treats them severely without any right; he has taken from them all that they had and demands more by kicks and blows."].

[Mahmud ordered the women to be put in an empty house and supplied with food and drink. All night Mahmud wriggled like a snake. "If this is the condition of Ghaznin", he thought, "where I myself reside, what will be the condition of far-off places?" He determined to take stern steps against Isfraini if the charge was proved.]

[Next morning Mahmud summoned an assembly or *mahzar*. The women repeated their complaints. Mahmud asked Isfraini to stand up before the women and answer their charges. Isfraini, smiling and quite unperturbed, replied: "If these women can prove against me one-hundredth of the complaints they have made to the king, I will consider the shedding of my blood to be lawful". But he claimed that complaints by the women were not enough; the real complainants—their male relations—should be brought. The prominent persons in the assembly agreed with the wazir and Mahmud summoned the prisoners.]

[But the prisoners, when brought before the king, hung their heads in shame and could only answer after a long time, 'The Wazir has done us no injustice... Money of the Ministry of Revenue was due from us; therefore we are in fetters.' Mahmud asked whether Isfraini was demanding from them the money they had collected from the tax-payers or asking them to give him money from their own salaries. 'We have received all our dues, allowances and salaries', they confessed, 'this money is due to us from the original collections (*asl mal*).']

[The prisoners further confessed that sums of fifty thousand, sixty thousand and seventy thousand were due from each of them, and that they had spent the money in paying their creditors, in the marriages of their sisters and daughters, in sin and inequity and in showing themselves off so that men of good birth, who were poor, may give them their daughters in marriage.]

[At the request of the wazir investigations were made into the origin of these people and it was found that they were the sons of tavern-keepers, butchers and weavers. Isfraini apologised for the appointments he had made. "They served me for years and showed themselves to be capable. They executed quickly and before my eyes every order I gave them. I was deceived by their cleverness and was not cautious about their origin and birth. I accept a fine for this fault and will undertake to do what is ordered." Mahmud set the prisoners free. But he directed a deed to be taken from them that they would not in future come near the Ministry of Revenue, that they would cast off from their heads the vain arts they had learnt and that they would devote themselves to agriculture and spend the rest of their lives as villagers]

Note on Sultan Mahmud's First Wazir, Abdul Abbas Isfraini

The difficulty with Barni is that he only knows the names, but not the full names, of a few officers of Sultan Mahmud, and nothing about their work or careers. This Illustration of Barni would be meaningless unless Isfraini had served Mahmud for a considerable time; the revenue-officers, we are told, had been in prison for six months, and Isfraini confesses that he was responsible for their appointment and that they had 'served him faithfully for years'. But Isfraini was Mahmud's wazir only during the first two years of his reign and the manner of his dismissal and murder (for there can be no other name for it) does no credit to Mahmud.

In his carefully prepared account of the wazirs of Sultan Mahmud, the author of the *Hahibus Siyar* (Persian text, Vol. II, p. 140) writes: "According to the consensus of all historians, the first wazir of Sultan Mahmud was Abul Abbas Fazl Ahmad bin

Isfraini. In his early career Abul Abbas was the secretary and *naib* of Faiq, a great Samanid *amir.* But when the sun of Faiq's good fortune began to decline, Abul Abbas joined the service of Amir Subuktigin and became his wazir. Sultan Mahmud on succeeding his father confirmed him in his post. Abul Abbas was not distinguished by scholarship or learning, but he showed great merit in managing the affairs of government and in looking after the army and the *ra'iyyat.* But after two years his star declined and Mahmud dismissed him. Some historians have described the cause of his fall as follows. Sultan Mahmud was very fond of good looking slaves and Fazl bin Ahmad, in this matter, acted on the principle, 'Men follow the religion of their kings.' Fazl happened to hear of a remarkably handsome boy at some place in Turkestan; he sent his agent there and the agent purchased the boy and brought him dressed as a girl to Ghaznin. Mahmud heard of this through a mischief-maker and sent a man to the wazir to demand the Turkestani boy. Fazl denied the fact. Mahmud found an occasion for visiting Isfraini's house and Isfraini welcomed him with respect and humility. But at that moment Mahmud's eyes fell on the Turkestani boy and he found in this an excuse for ordering the plunder and confiscation of Isfraini's property. Soon after this Mahmud started on a campaign to India and during his absence his hard-hearted officers in their attempt to wring all his property from Abul Abbas, put him to such tortures that he died. It is stated in the *Jamiu't Tawarikh-i Jalali* that Abul Abbas had a son named Hajjaj, who was distinguished among his contemporaries for his learning and wrote fluent *ghazals* and also a daughter from whom they have quoted traditions." [H]

Advice XXII

On the Advantages of the King's Protecting Old Families

[This Advice really deals with two problems—the impermanence of the ruling dynasty and the impermanence of the governing class. Barni, who believed that everyone should be compelled to follow the profession of his ancestors, is unable to suggest any remedy for the first evil. Six dynasties had ruled northern India since the second battle of Tarain—the Ghorians, the Qutbis, the Sharnsis, the Balbanis, the Khiljis and the Tughlaqs—and none of them except the first could claim a respectable, princely origin. But a change of dynasty generally meant the overthrow of the governing class of the former dynasty and the formation of a new governing class on which the new dynasty could rely. Barni fails to consider the contingency when it was not the king who created the governing class but the governing class that created the king, like the Deccan officers who rebelled against Mohammad bin Tughlaq and elected first one king and then another. Throughout this work Barni attributed to the king a power he could in practice seldom exercise, and so he talks as if the governing class was entirely the king's creation. Barni could hardly deny that the history of Islamic lands, even as he knew it did not substantiate his doctrine that God had created two grades of souls, one to command and the other to obey. But the Advice here only poses the question—*what is to be done with a governing class which has been overthrown?* Barni tries to find an answer to this in his first illustration. *The old governing class should be deprived of its political power but not of its material prosperity.* But in view of Barni's own emphatic statement that those deprived of power will not rest content until they have overthrown their successors or been totally annihilated by them, it is doubtful whether in his days the plan he propounded would have been workable in practice. It was never tried.]

It has been said that in ancient days and old times kingship was confined in Ajam, Rum, Yaman, India, Syria, and Egypt to the royal dynasties of these countries and the desire for usurping the throne did not come to the heart of the members of any other group[126]. Thus in Ajam, the people would not obey any ruler who did not belong to the dynasty of the Kisras. Similarly in Rum, if a ruler did not belong to the dynasty of the Qaisars, the Rumis would neither bow their heads before him nor obey him. *Whenever this principle becomes accepted and customary among the people for generations and ages, usurpation becomes impossible, no one from any other group can raise a tumult and seize the country by force. Further, since kingship was hereditary among the ancients, when a king died he was succeeded by one of his sons on the basis of hereditary right and appointment by his father; the new king would naturally keep all the previous helpers and supporters of the state in office and inflict no injury on any leader, tribal chief or clan.*

This mode and custom was extremely desirable. But after the rule of these monarchs in whose dynasties monarchy had become permanent came to an end, kingship was established by usurpation and force, and no attention was paid to the origin and descent of the kings. Any person who by any means whatsoever could obtain the necessary prestige, power and followers was able to establish his authority over the country, overthrow its previous ruler, take possession of the royal power and call himself its king.

Now, whenever a usurper attains kingship, inevitably his partisans, helpers, well-wishers and near-ones collect round him; and owing to those who have already joined him, still more tribes and families are gathered in his support. Some fifty thousand persons, more or less—men and women, old and young, slaves and youths—became of one heart and one speech owing to his royal favours; they become the pillars of his authority and it becomes possible for him to rule with their support.

Now kingship with this evil practice arose and became customary among the kings of Islam from the time of the Yazidis and the Marwanids. If a king was removed from the throne by natural death or killed and another king established himself on his throne, with or without any hereditary right, it was not possible for him to reign with security unless he had overthrown the helpers, supporters, tribesmen and families of the preceding king, plucked off their wings and feathers and organised his own partisans to take their place.

If, on the other hand, he retained the partisans and helpers of the previous king and confirmed them in their offices and dignities in the state, they would not become the supporters of his government but would, in fact, strive for his ruin and destruction. They would repose no trust in the new king or the new king in them. The above-mentioned calamity has become known to men of wisdom by observation and experience.

Among the Musalmans this calamity came through the Umayyad Sultans, who have been called Yazidis and Marwanids. During the generation of the Companions of the Prophet the government of the lands of Islam belonged by right to the Pious Caliphs (*Khulafa-i Rashidin*) on the basis of appointment by their predecessors and the agreement of the people. The Caliphate came from the Commander of the Faithful, Ali, to the Commander of the Faithful, Hassan son of Ali. Ali and Hassan belonged to the Bani Hashim tribe, Mu'awiyah, Yazid and the Marwanids were only able to govern for eighty years because by every means in their power they had overthrown and suppressed the Bani Hashim and all their supporters and well-wishers and blackened their faces in this world and the next. *Similarly, the Caliphate of the family of Abbas at Baghdad could not be firmly established till Abu Muslim Maruzi had taken revenge for the family of the Prophet from the Umayyad Sultans and totally overthrown and uprooted the supporters of Mu'awiyah, Yazid and the Marwanids.*

Mahmud says: O sons of Mahmud and kings of Islam! If you claim to belong to Mohammad's faith and consider yourself to be true believers and Musalmans, *you will consider this custom of kingship to be a grievous calamity and misfortune.* Reflect with a clear mind on how this bad practice and wicked custom has become prevalent among the kings of Islam. *First they seize a territory without any right, international* (*khariji*) *or domestic* (*dakhili*)*; then on account of their political or religious policy they obtain permission for this usurpation and conquest from the capital of the Caliphate. In addition to this, by every means that comes to their hands, they overthrow and reduce to poverty and distress many families, clans and tribes of the preceding king merely for the preservation and protection of their lives,* which are in any case doomed to be terminated by death. *Some they spare, others they kill; some they imprison, others they exile; and some they deprive of their properties.* Owing to the weakness of their faith, they do not care for Islam and the rights of the Musalmans, and the answer that they will have to give on the Day of Judgment never crosses their minds. *To this kind of 'overthrowing' they give the designation of 'political expediency'.*

The love and desire for kingship so blinds them that they never pause to consider that if they overthrow the wives, children, tribes, followers, friends, and well-wishers of another for no political or *shari'at* crime and adhere to such a (wicked) custom, the person who takes their place after them will in his turn do what they have done. So you may say that by continuing the ways and customs of the Godless, they have, in effect, overthrown their families, followers and adherents with their own hands. What notorious crime they are guilty of in overthrowing the innocent! Neither they, nor their power, nor their supporters will last forever as a result of this plan which they designate 'political expediency'. But their necks will be responsible on the Day of Judgment for those whom they have destroyed.

At the time of overthrowing the old families, the king who overthrows them seems to declare by his action (*zaban-i hal*): 'The king who succeeds me should overthrow my supporters and followers in the same way as I have overthrown the supporters and followers of my predecessor; if he does not do so, my followers will not permit him to reign for a single day. He should have the same regard for 'political expediency' as I have had (*lacuna*).'

The king should not overthrow so many families on mere suspicion. He should not for the welfare of a few days send the enemies of his life and his property to complain against him on the Day of Judgment. He should not be deceived by world-worshipping religious scholars, who give a judgment (*fatwa*) against the commandments of God and the Prophet to the effect that the king can kill and imprison Musalmans for the sake of his state-policy. And if he has sanity of judgment he will realise at least so much that others will in their turn treat his sons, women, helpers and supporters in the same way as he has treated the family and followers of another; that they will play the same game as he has played (*lacuna*).

How sweet it seems and how pleasant to the soul when a new king makes a few of his greatest well-wishers sit before him in a Confidential Council (*Majlis-i Khilwat*)! One of them takes ink, pen and paper in his hands to write down a list of those who are to be overthrown. Another says: "That man ought to be overthrown along with his family and followers as he will for certain never become one of us; he should be put to death and his wife and sons given to another; his tribe and followers ought to be scattered; his property and goods should be given to that trustworthy man who is among the well-wishers of this government, so that his power and dignity may increase, for this will conduce to the increased power and dignity of the king. Political policy demands that this be done." Another person reminds them of another confidential officer of the former king, has his name also written in the list of those who are to be overthrown and gives reasons based on state-policy for doing so. The king on hearing the conversation of those sitting before him becomes assured of their loyalty and concludes that they are his chosen supporters, while they, on their part, are strengthened by his kindness and favours and proceed to buttress the ramparts of their loyalty by overthrowing others.

To this meeting they give the name of Council of State-Policy (*Majlis-i Rai Mulki*). Many people are excluded from this Confidential Council (*Majlis-i Mahram*), and mere sight-seers are sorely grieved by the desire to become acquainted with its secret discussions. But they do not know, and owing to the blindness of their eye-balls they cannot see, that the doors of Paradise are closed (on the members of a meeting) owing to the discussions of which it is finally decided to overthrow a group of Musalmans notwithstanding the commands of God and the Prophet; and that the faces of impudent persons who design and act in violation of the *shari'at* and the *sunnah,* of the Prophet become black on the Day of Judgment.

(It has been necessary to eliminate many repetitions from the following paragraph, the substance of which is, nevertheless, of considerable significance.)

And Time laughs at them and says with the language of experience: "O fools, *ignoramuses,* proud and blind fellows, who are intoxicated with power! (You should know that others will in due course inflict on you and yours the sufferings you are now inflicting on others.) Before long they will make plans and designs against you and your wives, children, tribes and followers in just the same way; and they will do exactly what you are doing. Then why do you wield your two-handed sword for your own destruction by considering that your welfare lies in the destruction of the Musalmans and in completely crushing your predecessors? Inevitably, others will also be able to obtain judgments (*fatwas*) for the destruction of your people and act according to them. *Why, then, O fools, do you not think of a policy* (tadbir) *owing to which Musalmans may be able to survive and their families and followers may not be deprived of their lives and properties, scattered and ruined.* Then your families also will escape this fate. [The punishments that will be meted out to you in the next world are a separate issue. But you and your group will, within a short time in this world, be overthrown and subjected to the same kind of sufferings as you are now inflicting on others, unless a policy of the type here suggested, can find universal acceptance.]

The great men of the religion and the state have said: The decline of the power of a king should be considered near when he feels strong because no partner, opponent or molester of his kingdom has been left and when he has removed all those from whom there was any fear or danger of opposition. When he reaches that position of security, his trust in God declines and he feels less need of Divine assistance. All his calculations about keeping the country clear of his enemies are then based on the strength or his own supporters (*lacuna*).

No greater calamity can befall you than that you should overthrow the helpers, supporters, tribes and followers of Mahmud, for they can all become your helpers and supporters[127]. Mahmud has no more fear from you than this—that your own old followers will creep before you and claim to be like the Masudis and Mahmudis. They will give to the officers of Mahmud, everyone of whom is hillock of religion and of loyalty, the designation of 'Mahmudis'. They will put into your mind the idea that Mahmud has plenty of sons and grandsons; that if one of the Mahmudi princes captures and part of the country, the Mahmudi officers will put him on the throne; that you should organise your own helpers and supporters, and that owing to this danger you should overthrow the helpers and supporters of Mahmud. But you will never be able to find helpers and supporters who are so loyal and faithful as my supporters.

This advice of Mahmud is meant for the monarch, whose father and grandfather have not been kings and who, having obtained the kingship by usurpation or the agreement of the people, desires on account of his shallow opinion to completely overthrow the helpers and supporters of the old regime and to put his own men in office in order to strengthen his government. This advice of Mahmud is also intended for the monarch whose kingdom is old and hereditary but into whose mind Satan has put the thought that, to ensure the permanence of his dynasty and to prevent the kingship from passing to another family, he should so arrange matters that all the officers of the kingdom are his slaves and thus belong to a single family (*khandan*).[128]

[This advice has two illustrations—Mahmud's treatment of the Simjuris, the dynasty from which the territory of Ghaznin came to Mahmud; (2) Alexander's treatment of the *Shahzadas* of Azam. The account of Mahmud and the Simuris deserves to be translated in full as it displays Barni's frightful ignorance of the real Mahmud of history and also because Barni attempts in this

Illustration to give an answer to a terrible problem of the middle-ages—how a new and successful governing group was to treat the governing group it had overthrown].

O Sons of Mahmud! You should know that the territories of Ghaznin and Khorasan came to Mahmud from the Simjuris. The father and grandfather of Mahmud were not kings. God granted victory to Mahmud over the Simjuris and a mandate (*manshur*) of kingship in the name of Mahmud came from Baghdad, the capital of the Caliphate. So Mahmud was established on the throne of Ghaznin.[129] Before that the Simjuris had held the kingship of Khorasan and Ghaznin for years. There was no difference of opinion about the fate of such Simjuris as had rebelled against the Caliphate and were killed in battles and skirmishes. But Mahmud was hesitant about the treatment to be meted out to the helpers and supporters of the Simjuris, who had survived along with their tribes and followers, horsemen and footmen. The tradition of kings of weak faith is to consider religion a child's play, to shed the blood of thousands of innocent persons out of love for their kingdom and its security, to seize the property and goods of the Musalmans for their treasury, and to give the properties, women, children, slaves and slave-girls of the supporters of the preceding regime to their own supporters, so that with this wealth the latter may become powerful and dignified. They reduce the tribes and followers of their predecessors to dust and ashes, and consider this to be necessary for the preservation of their power and the strength of their government.

Now if Mahmud had behaved towards the Simjuris according to ways of Godless kings, his sincere faith in the Prophet's creed and in the obligations of Islam would have caught hold of his skirt and shaken his beard. But if he left the Simjuris in their prosperity and did them no harm, he felt afraid; for his kingdom had been newly acquired, none of the policies of his government had yet matured, and the wings and feathers of his supporters had not yet grown. Many Simjuris had survived and their distinguished clans and families were numerous and prosperous. May be, they would raise a tumult, upset the administration and overthrow Mahmud, for they had held the country for a generation or two and the subjects were loyal to them and praised them. Such being the position, the fire of their mischief could soon be lighted and would rapidly burst into flames.

Mahmud spent several days in reflection. Ahmad Hasan, Arsalan Jazib, Altun Tash, Ali Kheshawand and other confidential officers of Mahmud discussed this matter with him, every day. Mahmud owing to his insight into their honesty saw that they also were not pleased at the idea of suppressing so many illustrious houses and families; and that it was only out of regard for political expediency that they said that the Simjuris should be overthrown. Ultimately a list of the names of the surviving Simjuris was drawn up. Mahmud ordered them to be divided into groups and a different order was given for each group. Thus, for example, two hundred persons from among their leaders and distinguished men and some three or four hundred persons from among their courtiers, officers and chosen people were selected for being put to death. About three or four thousand persons—men and women, young and old—were selected for being exiled to distant lands. Some six or seven hundred persons from among the revenue collectors (*amils*), office-holders, *gumashtas* (agents) and junior officers (*paiwasthgan*) of the Simjuris were arrested for being chained, imprisoned and fined. The names of seven or eight thousand persons from among their wives, children, slaves, slave-girls, relations and kindred were noted in the list for being transferred from various tribes (*khail*). The names of the *harems* (of the Simjuri kings), their sons, daughters, grand-daughters, followers, relatives and kindred were listed separately and a plan for dealing with them was prepared. Their properties, estimated at one or two thousand villages and gardens and one hundred or more large houses were to be confiscated by the Sultan. Their movable property—e.g. golden vessels, woollen clothes and other valuables was collected.

This plan of destroying, scattering, killing and exiling the Simjuris and their followers appeared extremely onerous to Mahmud. His heart was not satisfied with inflicting punishments on the basis of doubts and suspicions only, and the humility of the Islamic faith made the taste of kingship bitter in his mouth. Finally, on a Friday night he got up according to his habit and devoted himself to his post-midnight (*tahajjud*) prayer. He rubbed his forehead in humility on the ground and prayed and cried during his prostration (*sijdah*). At that moment a voice from above him, from his right-side and from the direction of the Qibla declared: "O Mahmud! There is a tomorrow after today, and there is a recompense for every good and bad act". Mahmud realised that it was a heavenly voice and that Almighty God had good intentions towards poor Mahmud, and, therefore, he was given this advice at a time when he was thinking of overthrowing so many people. Thereafter he did not sleep till dawn.

When the day dawned, Mahmud called the leading mystics (*shaikhs*), religious scholars (*alims*) and distinguished men of Ghaznin and held a meeting (*mahzar*). In the presence of all them he took the Holy Book in his hands and in the name of God, the holy Prophet and all other prophets (*nabis*), the angels and the saints, he took an oath to the effect that so long as he was alive he would not shed the blood of a Musalman and a theist merely for the preservation of his kingdom and that he would not behave arrogantly towards the wives, sons, and children of the Musalmans. He then placed this record (*tazkirah*) of Godless and un-Muslim designs before the assembly of the great men.

[Mahmud then proceeded to give his modified orders.] First, he restored their wives and children to those who had been selected for capital punishment; he gave them the expenses of their journey and exiled them in groups of forty and fifty to distant and foreign lands. But he took a deed from them that they would be deserving of death if they did not leave the country or tried to return to it. Next, he assigned to the various loyal governors of his extensive provinces groups of two hundred or three hundred of those persons whom it had been decided to exile; they were to be given sufficient food, clothes and other necessities of life and were to be confined within the areas of distant cities.

Concerning (officers) who had been separated from the rest for chains, fetters and imprisonment on account of revenue-claims, Mahmud ordered that they should submit their accounts to the *Diwani* (Revenue Ministry) in the usual manner, but if anything was due from them out of the capital collections, they were to pay it. But for three or four years, that is, till the new officers of the government were firmly established, they were not to evince any desire for government service (*amal*) and were to remain idle in their corners. [The plan of transferring some seven or eight thousand persons from their tribes was also altered.] Mahmud ordered the chiefs of his own tribes and his helpers and supporters to form marriage alliances with the families of the Simjuri tribal chiefs in accordance with the *shari'at* and thus to assimilate them through family relationships, kindness and favours. He ordered the *harems* of the former kings—their daughters, grand-daughters and women related to them—to be kept in forts near the capital; all that these delicate women needed for their food and clothing was to be supplied to them, but apart from a limited number of slaves and slave-girls no one was allowed to go to them or to come from them. The sons and sons-in-law of the former kings, along with the sons of their sisters and brothers, were sent to the extremity of India. Mahmud wrote to the governors of India that they were to be kept separately in various cities and towns and that one or two villages were to be assigned for their maintenance. Horsemanship, riding and hunting were prohibited to them but not the practice of other arts. Finally, Mahmud ordered his chiefs to hold as trustees the properties, gold, buildings, valuables and houses of the Simjuris. But after a few years had elapsed and all ideas of greatness and leadership had vanished from their minds, while at the same time the hearts of the inhabitants had been reconciled to the government of Mahmud and his kingdom had become firm, the property of the Simjuris was to be returned to their owners.

After Mahmud had settled the above-mentioned plans concerning the Simjuris in the presence of the assembly, he performed a prostration (*sijdah*) in thankfulness that even in such a contingency the blood of no Musalman had been shed, that he had not resorted to any unlawful aggression, and that no attempt had been made to deprive the people of God of their lives. He saw the following tradition of the Prophet with the eyeball of insight: "Man is the building of God; he who destroys man, destroys the building of God." And God blessed Mahmud all his life in reward for not shedding the blood of the Musalmans at the beginning of his reign; for never in future had he to face a contingency in which merely for the preservation of his kingdom it became necessary for him to smear his hands with blood without the permission of the *shari'at*.

[After he had overthrown Dara and conquered the whole of Iraq and Ajam, Alexander wished to put to death the *shahzadas* of Iraq, to uproot totally families with a standing of five hundred to one thousand years and to put his own men in their place. And as he proceeded to conquer more countries, Alexander wished to follow the same policy. But Aristotle protested against this uprooting of old families and trusting to untried men, and Alexander gave up his design on reading Aristotle's letter. Alexander divided the territories of Iraq into several parts, allotted them to the *shahzadas* and assigned to them kingships on his own behalf. He did not overthrow any illustrious family or clan. The sultans and their sons whom Alexander appointed are referred to in history as the *malikut tawaif* (tribal kings). Owing to the treatment which he meted out to the *shahzadas,* Alexander's reputation has remained among mankind.]

Note on Sultan Mahmud and the Simjuris

In his Illustration to this Advice, Barni makes the following statements: (i) The Simjuris were kings, a royal dynasty, who had ruled 'Khorasan and Ghaznin' for two or three generations. Barni does not name any Simjuri kings, for the simple reason that he did not know. (ii) The Simjuries had a large following—200 or 300 leaders, 400 courtiers, about 600 or 700 revenue collectors and other officers, about 3,000 or 4,000 followers deserving the punishment of exile and some 7,000 or 8,000 prominent tribesmen. In addition to this, it is assumed that the Simjuri royal family was fairly large. (iii) 'The father and grandfather of Mahmud were not kings.' (iv) Mahmud, at the order of the Caliphate, overthrew the Simjuris and established a new administration in place of the Simjuri regime. There were conflicts in which the Simjuris were killed and Mahmud's government, to start with, was weak.

Now Mahmud's grandfather was certainly not a king, for Mahmud's father, Subuktigin, started his career as a slave. But Subuktigin became an independent king and Barni is forgetting that he has already referred to him as such.

There were no Simjuris at Ghaznin at any time

The origin of the Ghaznavide kingdom is well known, and Barni could have found the facts from the *Tabaqat-i Nasiri.* Alptigin, the governor of Khorasan on behalf of the Samanid kings, took the wrong side on the succession question and, unwilling to rebel against his new Samanid overlord, Amir Mansur son of Nuh, he marched, to Ghaznin, drove away its ruler, Amir Anuk (or Lawik) and established a principality, which in theory, though not in practice, remained loyally subordinate to the Samanid kingdom as long as that kingdom lasted. Alptigin died after a reign of eight years and his son, Ishaq, could only enjoy a troubled reign of one year. Then two Turkish officers governed the territory—the first, Bilkatigin, was a good man and reigned for two years but his successor, Pirey, was a tyrant. The people overthrew Pirey and placed Subuktigin 'under the red canopy' in 977 A.D. Subuktigin reigned for about twenty years and extended his kingdom. After his death there was a war of succession between his two sons, Mahmud and Ismail. Mahmud was successful and ascended the throne. So far as Ghaznin is concerned, the Simjuris do not come into the picture at all.

The Simjuris were a troublesome family of Samanid officers, whose main theatre of action was Khorasan. But at no moment did they attain to the stature of kingship; also Subuktigin had succeeded in completely crushing them before his death and they had been effectually liquidated before Sultan Mahmud ascended the throne of Ghaznin.

Abu Sa'id Gardezi in his *Zainul Akhbar* condescends to note four generations of Simjuris. (i) The Samanid ruler, Abu Nasr Ahmad bin Isma'il (907–914), appointed Abu Imran Simjuri who had formerly been his *Dawat-dar* (Inkpot-bearer) as governor of Sistan (p. 24), (ii) Abu Imran's son, Ibrahim, was appointed governor of Naishapur by the Samanid ruler, Nuh bin Nasr, in 942–3 A.D. (iii) But the person who brought the family into real prominence was Ibrahim's son, Abul Hasan Simjuri, who according to Gardezi was 'cunning and crafty'. On being appointed governor of Naishapur in 959 A.D., Abul Hassan behaved so badly that the Samanid king, Abdul Malik bin Nuh, found it necessary to relieve him of his post after a year. But on being reappointed to his old post in 961 A.D., Abul Hasan behaved remarkably well and everybody was pleased. But later on he was accused of slackness in his military enterprises (pp. 44-46). Still the new Samanid king, Nuh bin Mansur, extended three honours to him—he gave Abul Hasan the title of *Nasiruddoulah,* offered to marry his daughter and made him commander-in-chief and governor of Naishapur, Herat and Qahistan. But Abul Hasan quarrelled with Amir Nuh's wazir, Abul Husain 'Utbi, and an order of dismissal was sent to him: "Put on your cloak and sit in your house." Abul Hasan first showed fight but soon yielded and handed over the army command to his son, Abu Ali Simjuri. Amir Nuh had ascended the throne as a minor; the royal power had grown weak and Abu Ali Simjuri and a Samanid officer, Faiq, obtained the real control of the kingdom. It was decided that Tash Hajib was to have Naishapur, Faiq was to have Balkh, Abu Ali Simjuri was to have Herat, while Badghis and Qahistan along with some other territories were to go to Abul Hasan Simjuri. Abul Hasan was also to have the military command of Khorasan. Abul Hasan Simjuri died while sleeping in his garden with a favourite slave-girl in 988 A.D. and the fortunes of the Simjuri family were left in charge of his two sons, Abul Qasim and Abu Ali Simjuri (p. 52). (iv) Abu Ali was then at Herat and Abul Qasim took the treasures and slaves of Abul Hasan to his brother. "Amir Nuh gave Abu Ali the command of his father along with the standard, *Khila'at,* and the title of *Imadul Mulk*". Then Abu Musa Harun, son of Ilak Khan of Turkestan, attacked Bokhara; but he had to retire on account of his bad health due to piles, and the only effect of his invasion was to weaken the power of Amir Nuh still further and to strengthen Abu Ali Simjuri. "The treasure and army of Abu Ali increased. He extended his power over Khorasan and seized Mawaraun Nahr. He got complete control of the revenue, expenditure and all affairs of the Samanid Kingdom. He took the title of *Amirul Umra supported by Heaven* and inflicted every possible insult on Amir Nuh. Only the Friday sermon was left in Nuh's name." (p. 53)

To make a long story short, Amir Nuh appealed to Subuktigin, and Subuktigin and Mahmud inflicted a signal defeat on Abu Ali at Herat. Abu Ali fled to Naishapur and thence to Gurgan. He apologised for his past behaviour but his apologies were ignored by the victors. Nuh gave the title of *Nasiruddin wad Daulah* (Supporter of the Religion and the State) to Subuktigin and appointed Mahmud governor of Khorasan in 997 A.D.

Then Nuh returned to Bokhara and Subuktigin to Herat, while Mahmud remained at Naishapur to settle the affairs of that territory. While he was so engaged, Faiq and Abu Ali Simjuri advanced against him with a large army. Mahmud retreated to his father at Herat and summoned support from every side. At a second battle at Tus the power of Abu Ali was finally crushed (p. 56).

It remains to give an account of the real end of the Simjuris. In spite of his desperate condition, Abu Ali Simjuri came to

Naishapur for the sake of a woman and was duly imprisoned by Sultan Mahmud. But he succeeded in escaping to Khwarazm. From here he was induced to come to Bokhara. "The moment he entered the palace of Amir Nuh, Abu Ali Simjuri was arrested with his eighteen brothers and officers (*sarhangan*). They were all tied up and taken to Qanduz in 998 A.D. When Amir Subuktigin heard of the arrest of Abu Ali Simjuri, he demanded him of Amir Nuh. Amir Nuh sent Abu Ali Simjuri along with his slave, Il Man Ku, Amirak Turi and Abul Husain son of Abu Ali Simjuri to Subuktigin. Amir Subuktigin sent these four persons to the fort of Gardez and kept them imprisoned there. In 998 A.D. all of them were put to death." (pp. 58–59)

Advice XXIII

Meannesses Which Do Not Assimilate with Kingship

[There are, according to Barni, five mean qualities which are incompatible with that nobility of character which a king needs for the proper performance of his duties—(i) Falsehood, (ii) Changeability, (iii) Perfidy or Deception, (iv) Wrathfulness, and (v) Promotion of the Unjust. But this obvious fact is driven home with unnecessary repetitions and tiresome platitudes. I have not translated sentences and paragraphs which merely repeat what Barni has said elsewhere. Also all paragraphs concerning the effect of the character of the king on the *morale* of the people have been put by me at the beginning.]

Since kingship is due to the favour of God, this Divine favour will not assimilate with meannesses; if they are found combined in any ruler, he is a usurper and not a king.....

If Almighty God looks upon a people with the eyes of wrath and wishes them to remain in toils, troubles and sufferings, he appoints over them a king who is a slave of innate meannesses, so that in consequence of his depraved behaviour they are desolated and scattered. Further, owing to the meanness of the king, the mean qualities of the subjects increase....till meanness becomes so common that people cease to consider it a defect, and even people of merit become depraved. A long time has passed since the two following proverbs were framed—"People follow the religion of their rulers", and "People are inclined towards those of their own disposition and character". A mean king is drawn towards depraved persons in accordance with the principle of 'inclination to the same type'. [The depravity of the officers appointed by the king, in turn, affects the public.] Evil and wicked things increase from time to time among the generality of the people; rectitude is overpowered by corruption, good by evil, obedience by sinfulness, justice by cruelty... The evil seeks precedence over the good, and owing to the preponderance of wickedness and corruption, virtue and rectitude almost cease to exist. Finally, owing to the inauspicious effects of the vice and, wickedness with which the world has been filled, calamities and misfortunes rain from the sky again and again. "People become sick of their existence; life and death seem the same to them; in fact, since their lives have been divested of all joy and comfort, they begin to long for death...

And the *hakims* of the past and their successors have written: Every merit and demerit of the king will be adopted by the subjects. The elect among the subjects will try to cultivate every virtue the king possesses, whether be orders them to do so or not, so that according to 'the principle of inclination to the same type (*hukm-i jinsiyat*)', they may be accepted and loved by the king. And the king's vices have the same effect..... Thus if the king is given to religious devotions, all the distinguished men of the country will strive for devotion and piety. If the king is a good calligraphist, the select men of the kingdom will try their hands at calligraphy. If the king has a poetical mind and composes verses, all men will take to poetry and the composition of verses. If the king is a scholar, all persons will try to get educated, whether they are granted bread and stipends for their education or not. And the same is the case with the king's vices. If the king is a liar, then he will inevitably give preference to liars and most people of the country will take to speaking lies. If the king is an excessive drinker, all those who had refrained from wine will begin to drink.

As the character and actions or the king influence the subjects, the Pious Caliphs have said: "The good acts of the rulers (*amirs*) warn the governed from things unlawful more than their words." For example, if the ruler drinks wine, speaks lies, breaks promises and commits injustices, but forbids drinking, lying, promise-breaking and injustice to the people, no one will lend ears to his advice or be warned. But if he does not drink or lie or break promises or behave unjustly, his virtuous actions will keep most people away from these vices, even if he does not so command.

And one wisdom in the principle that the true Imam should be 'innocent' (*ma'sum*) is that his orders will be obeyed. The prophets have been created innocent (*ma'sum*); therefore they deserve to be followed. If the king, who in the *shari'at* is the deputy of the Imam, is not innocent[130], he should at least be protected (*mahfuz*), so that people may follow his words and deeds; if he is not even protected, then the minimum needed for the function of kingship is that he should not be a slave of vices. For kingship, in reality, is the deputyship and vice-regency of God; and such a high office is not compatible with those low qualities which are the negation of this office.

1. The *first* mean quality, which can never be assimilated with the dignity and high position of the king—and if mixed with it creates distress—is *Falsehood.* Falsehood is considered blameworthy in all religions and is one of the greater vices...And wise men and *hakims* have said: "A man lies either owing to a meanness, which is in this character, or from necessity, want or frustration." But for a king, who has been endowed with power and honoured by success, there is no necessity to lie. His lying is, therefore, a meanness which has become his habit... The holy Prophet has said: "The true believer commits adultery and theft but he does not lie"... Also the trust of the people in the word and the pen of the king is the basis of the work of government and the pillar of the policy of the state; whenever this basis is shaken, all the affairs of the kingdom are thrown into disorder... One great advantage of kingship, both for the king and subjects, is that everything done before the king is done righteously and owing to the fear of his authority, no falsehood is possible before him. But if the king himself is a liar, this advantage is turned into a misfortune both for him and his subjects. The object aimed at is inverted.

2. The *second* meanness which does not assimilate with the high quality of kingship is *changeability* (*Inqilab*). The meaning of changeability is turning aside from one's words or actions. According to scholars and wise men, both ancient and modern, firmness (*sabat*) is a necessary condition of kingship and an ornament for kings, while changeability is the opposite of firmness. They have considered the unity of opposites to be among the impossibilities. And as firmness is one of the necessary qualities of kingship, they say that a changeable person is not worthy of

the office of king; and if he establishes himself on the throne of the kingdom without any right, the select men, the commons and the *ra'iyyat* of the country will repose no trust in his words or deeds. Kingship is trust personified; if this trust vanishes, kingship becomes vain and futile. And great kings have said: "The signs of kingship are manifested by the king's words and deeds. If the king is not firm in his words and deeds—if his words are not like inscriptions on stones and his determination firm as a mountain—then the subjects will not obtain happiness or felicity from him or he from them." [Barni here refers to the fact that the Caliph Umar sent a Companion of the Prophet to the King of Egypt[131]. But the Companion came back without delivering the Caliph's letter to the King of Egypt as he found the King to be too changeable.] The kings of ancient days persisted in, and faced, the consequences of their errors so that the *ra'iyyat* of their country may consider them to be firm and not accuse them of changeability. But the great men of the religion and the state of the Prophet have said: "Persistence and firmness in error is itself an error; and turning back from an error is sheer righteousness." So the king of perfect wisdom is firm in all his words and acts and does not turn back from what is good and right; nevertheless, he has no hesitation in turning back if he discovers that he has made an error. He does not wish to be punished for disobeying the commandments of religion and prefers the principles of the Faith to the traditions of rebellious sultans.

3. The *third* meanness which does not assimilate with the high quality of kingship is *'Perfidy* (*ghadr*) *or Deception* (*Makr*)'. 'Perfidy' and 'deception' are allied in meaning. The basis of 'perfidy' is Godlessness and pride while the source of 'deception' is hypocrisy and falsehood... Great kings have owing to necessity resorted to perfidy, duplicity, ambushes and night-attacks on their enemies during wars and battles. But they have not put such acts in the category of 'victory and success' and have not boasted on account of them. They have considered the attainment of an object through low means to be worse than a hundred failures... [There must be consistency in the king's actions.] If the king looks towards anyone with the eye of favour, or gives him a robe of honour, or praises him, or for any reason whatsoever behaves towards him with kindness or affection, or condescends to talk to him, then the significance of such actions is that the person so

treated has received security for his life, property and goods. If he has sinned in a hundred ways and has been put in the list of criminals for political or revenue offences, the moment the king turns kindly towards him all these offences are deemed to have been forgiven. The real significance of such behaviour on the king's part is well-known to a ruler in whose blood and sinews kingship has come through inheritance. If the king for any cause or reason shows favours to anyone and after that arrests him, or puts chains on his feet, or has him poisoned secretly, then that king has not recognised the dignity of kingship; he is a worthless and disgraceful usurper of whom no trace will remain on this earth. And wise *hakims* have said: A man of perfidy, deception, hypocrisy, lies, trickeries and fraud is for certain not worthy of kingship.

4. The *fourth* meanness which does not assimilate with the great virtues of the kingship and is a great defect in a king is *'Wrathfulness'* (*Ghuzub*). Wrathfulness (*ghuzub*) and anger (*ghazab*) are different things. Anger and ill-temper are natural in man; and anger manifested at the proper occasion is a virtue. But when 'anger' overcomes all other qualities in a man, then the man becomes 'wrathful' and anger personified, and this is a vice. For anger is a medium quality while wrathfulness is its extreme limit. *When any quality of man is in a middle position, it is reckoned to be a virtue.* Thus one extreme limit of generosity is prodigality and the other limit is parsimony and miserliness, Generosity itself is in a middle position. If there had been no anger in man, he would not have rid himself of his dangerous enemies, and no resentment would have been excited in him at the sight of things forbidden... [There is a *lacuna* here and then we find Barni describing the man who is the victim of his own wrath.] The fear of religion disappears from the heart of the wrathful man owing to his overpowering anger; in that condition, when he is overcome by wrath and merely seeks to satisfy his anger, he forgets God, the Prophet, the orders of the *shari'at* and has no fear of the Day of Judgment. Till he has satisfied his anger and revenged himself on the object of his wrath, be he in the right or in the wrong, he finds no peace within himself and his anger keeps on surging in his heart from time to time; even though he may consider it to be undesirable, yet his anger raises its head and demands satisfaction. It often happens that owing to his excessive anger the wrathful man can attend

to nothing else while attempting to seek revenge; he cannot, for example, ease his anger by laughing, eating and enjoying. If he has not the power of wrecking his anger on the object of his wrath, he falls ill or his mind gets deranged.... or he remains in sorrow, melancholy and anxiety. Kingship cannot remain stable with this desire of wrecking vengeance on people. For kingship, for the most part, consists in showing affection, mercy, kindness and forgiveness and wrathfulness cannot assimilate with these virtues.

5. The *fifth* quality that does not assimilate with the essential virtues of kingship—and if mixed with it is a cause of trouble, distress and disgrace—is the *'Promotion of the Unjust and the Nurture of the Cruel'*. [Barni's sentences here are mostly repetitive]... There is an opposition between injustice and justice; if the virtue of justice really exists, the nurture and promotion of injustice is an impossibility... Whenever an unjust man is favoured, the promotion of injustice follows as a consequence; and with the promotion of injustice, justice packs up its belongings and disappears from the earth.... It is a long time since they have said, "The state can coexist with infidelity but it cannot coexist with injustice"... There is no clearer symptom of the king's injustice than his promotion of the unjust. [A reference is here made to the promotion of Hajjaj by the Umayyad Caliph, 'Abdul Malik bin Marwan. 'Hajjaj bin Yusuf did great harm to the family of the Prophet; he burnt the holy Kaaba and destroyed it with catapults'.]

[Barni illustrates this Advice by an incident which, he says, is recorded in the *Tarikh-i Nausherwan* (*History of Nausherwan*). The Qaisar of Rum (i.e., the Byzantine emperor) broke the treaty of peace between the two countries and plundered the frontiers of Ajam. Nausherwan wanted to march against the Qaisar, but his wazir, Buzurchemehr, advised him that 'as the territory of Ajam has not yet been consolidated, it would be wiser to send an ambassador in the first instance'. A suitable ambassador was sent and the Qaisar received him well. The Qaisar set free the prisoners he had taken but apologised about the booty. There would have been no difficulty about returning it had it been with me, he explained, but it has been divided by the soldiers amongst themselves. Further, a treaty drawn up on the lines desired by Nausherwan's ambassador was signed by the Qaisar. Nevertheless, the ambassador sent a code-message with the courier who brought the treaty to Nausherwan: 'Tell my family to prepare for the marriage of my sons, for on returning I will go to Khorasan for their wedding. Nausherwan guessed that the ambassador's mission had failed and ordered arrangement to be made for the march of his army. On returning to Nausherwan his ambassador stated: "The Qaisar is a speaker of lies, changeable, wrathful (*ghuzub*) and a promoter of the injust; he is also perfidious and deceptive."]

Note on the Theory of the Imam

It is curious to find such an Ismaili doctrine creeping into Barni's ideology. According to the Sunnis and the Asna Ashari Shias the king represents no one but himself; there can be no two opinions on the matter. It is not claimed, for example, that Shah Ismail Safavi or Mahmud of Ghaznin acted on behalf of some unknown but in innocent Imam. Whenever in the *Shari'at* books of the Sunnis reference is made to the Imam the actual responsible ruler is meant and no innocence is implied. But the Ismaili sects believed that when the Imam was hidden (*makhfi*), a *Dai* (or Propagandist) worked on his behalf. But the *Dai* was an agitator for the Imam rather than a ruler or king. A *Dai*, who became a ruler after agitating for an unknown Imam, would be inclined, like Ali Zikrahus Salam of Alamut, to declare himself both king and Imam. This theory of 'the innocent Imam', whom the king represents, is so inconsistent with the general tenor of Barni's thoughts that I am inclined to discard this sentence as a later interpolation. [H]

Advice XXIV

The Basis of All Advice—That the Salvation of the King Depends Upon the Supplication That Fills His Heart

[To understand this Advice what Barni has already said about monarchy should be remembered. *First,* the virtues inculcated by Islam are directly opposed to the qualities which a king must possess if he is to perform his functions properly; in acting as a king he clearly seems to claim Divine attributes. *Secondly,* all the institutions of monarchy are opposed to the *sunnah* of the Prophet and the Pious Caliphs. Now Barni hopes that the king will, nevertheless, attain to salvation if he follows the policy that Barni has prescribed. But external acts are not enough; the king should be conscious of his sinfulness and properly repentant.]

Sultan Mahmud has said: O Sons of Mahmud and kings of Islam! You should understand that Adam and the sons of Adam have been created for worshipping God, for the holy Quran says: "We have only created *jins* and men so that they may worship Us."[132]

Now the necessary virtues of devotion are supplication, helplessness, poverty and humility. But the qualities of kingship are opposed to, and the very reverse, of these virtues. Terror, prestige, pride, high status, domination and superiority, which are attributes suited to God only, are also among the necessary qualities of kingship.

There can be no greater difficulty for a human being than that he should live sharing the attributes of the Lord of eighteen thousand worlds, and lay aside all human qualities, in order to conduct the affairs of government. But if in this condition, when the king tries to adhere to the attributes of God and owing to this finds himself deprived of all human qualities, he always feels that his heart is full of excessive supplication (*nizamandi*) and humility, which are the special attributes of man and of his devotions and are opposed to the qualities of kingship, and if in spite of his practice of contradictory qualities, he finds himself a humble supplicant before the Divine Throne, then this is a sign of his salvation and high grades in the next world. The traditionalists (*ghair ma'qulaat*) consider the miracles of the saints to be due to this humility and supplication.

[This Advice is illustrated by three examples. (1) The *Tarikh-i Umamul Awwalin* (*History of the First Communities*) is quoted as an authority for the following statement. Adam had two sons, Shis and Kaimurs, who were twin brothers. Adam received God's command to the effect that Shis and his descendants would be prophets and would lead people on the right path while Kaimurs and his sons would be kings and keep the world in order. Kaimurs found that his character was degenerating on account of his kingship and wept bitterly before his brother. But Shis consoled him: "Do not despair, for you too have been created with the eye of Divine favour. Owing to your terror, prestige, domination and dignity, the world has become prosperous and the people are kept in proper order. The commands of the *shariat,* that come to me by inspiration, cannot be enforced unless society has been organised properly. It will not be possible to invite men to the path of religion if they are confused and scattered, poverty-ridden and distressed." To Kaimurs' further question as to what was the sign (*alamat*) by which he could be sure of his salvation, the prophet Shis replied: "If your heart is repelled by worldly affairs and inclined towards God and the other world, and you are convinced that attaining God and high grades in the next world is not compatible with the successes of worldly life, and your heart begins to supplicate to God and this supplication constantly fills your heart then you may consider this supplication to be a sign of blessedness and salvation."

[Sultan Mahmud has attained this spiritual condition after an effort of twenty years. Both supplication and humility have so overpowered Mahmud that he does not feel them absent from his heart for a single moment; owing to this a stream of tears flows from his eyes at the time of prayer (*munajat*).]

[The following statement is made on the basis of the *Tarikh-i Sikandari* (*History of Alexander*). Alexander after conquering the inhabited globe realised that this world was not at all permanent. His heart was repelled from the work of government and conquests; application to state-affairs began to sadden and disgust the mind of Alexander. The great conqueror was overpowered by the desire for God and for high spiritual status but at the same time it was not possible for him to retire from the work of government. So he summoned his leading religious scholars and *hakims* and asked them: "What should I do in order to combine the perfections of this world with the perfections of the next world?" They replied in accordance with their customary precepts: There is an opposition between the perfections of religious life and worldly life, and the unity of opposites is inconceivable to human intelligence." Ultimately Alexander was advised to visit two monks in Yaman, who after a brief conversation said to him: "Be happy Alexander, that in spite of your royal dignity, you find yourself in such a spiritual condition that supplication fills the whole of your breast. We have read in revealed books: 'Supplication cannot be combined with kingship; nevertheless if through Divine favour the desire for God so overpowers the heart of the king, and supplication fills his breast in such a way that it is not free from this supplication for a single moment, then this is a sign of his promotion to high stations in the next world.'"]

[Ziauddin Barni's Epilogue]

Hoping in Divine mercy I end this book, which I have named the *Fatawa-i Jahandari* in an excess of supplication. I pray to the Lord of the eighteen thousand worlds that He may hold my helpless hands and pull me out of the whirlpool of my sins and make me reach the shore of salvation through His universal mercy. And that just as through His universal kindness, He has filled my breast, a house of sorrow, with supplication, humility and helplessness, so may my end, and the end of all Musalmans, be on this Oath of Affirmation—"There is no god but Allah and Mohammad is the Prophet of Allah."

By the honour of the pure Oath of Affirmation, I am extremely perplexed, broken-hearted, helpless and needy. But in spite of my poverty, this is my appeal to the masters of knowledge and wisdom in religion and the state. Preceding writers and authors have compiled many books about the science of government and the commandments of the state. They have done justice to the traditions of learning and eloquence; they have displayed marvels in composition and literary contrivances and have adorned their works with poems and quotations in prose and verse. But they have confused the commandments of government, which depend upon the words and deeds of kings, *wazirs, maliks and amirs*—and this is the essence of the supreme command with the commandments of other groups.

And wise men will come to *know* that they cannot find among books a work with the order, form and plan according to which the *Fatawa-i Jahandari* has been written; I have discussed within it, from the beginning to the end, all the commandments of government and state-affairs with reference to principles as well as illustrations and examples.

Such a (poet as) Khusrau does not exist in every city, and if he does, he will not be so sweet.

I have taken great trouble in the composition of this book and reflected in a variety of ways.

I had to make my body and soul into ropes
Before I could bring up the Water of Life.

God be praised! *Wazirs, maliks,* the lords of discernment and policy, and efficient counsellors of the state and the kingdom—those of the present generation and those who will come after one another from the Unseen World till the Day of Judgment—will not withhold their justice and praise when they honour the *Fatawa-i Jahandari* by studying it and understand what I have said openly and by insinuations concerning principles, illustrations and examples.

I appeal like a beggar to all my readers, both during my life-time and after my death, for their sincere prayers (*fatiha*) to God for the forgiveness of my sins. They should help me with the affection that is expected from the greatness of the great. Help me, people of God, and may God help you also, for I am quite helpless and impotent, ruined and sinful. *What should I say about my condition before the people? I am a sinner, I am a sinner, I am a sinner. I have no place of refuge except in the forgiveness of God: I have no asylum except in the veil of God, the Veiler of Sins.*

REFERENCES

1. The Prophet of Islam has been called by many names, Barani generally prefers to call him 'Mustafa'; I have referred to him as 'Mohammad' or, more often, as 'the Prophet.'
2. That is, the court of Firoz Shah Tughlaq.
3. The first page of Persian manuscripts generally begins on the right side. The next page is not, therefore, a part of the same paper, and it is possible for the succeeding pages to be taken out while the first page remains. Here the first page ends in an incomplete sentence, while the next page begins with the end of a sentence "...and all his plans are erroneous." We are left to guess what Barani might have written in his *Preface.* Still if another manuscript of the *Fatawa-i Jahandari* is found, it will probably contain the whole of Barani's *Preface.*
4. In the Illustration which follows, Ismail Samani is made to tell his followers not to be afraid because he was under the protection of the Quranic *Sura* (No. LVIII)—"Indeed God has heard," In this *Sura* (among other things), Allah warns the hypocrites (*munafiqin*) that He is present everywhere and

knows about their conspiracies. The Quranic threat ends with the statement: "God has said, I and my apostles will prevail."

5. For an account of the Saffarid dynasty, see the *Zainul Akhbar* of Gardezi (Dr. Nazim's edition, pp. 10–21), the *Rauzatus Safa* of Mirkhond (Newal Kishore edition, Vol. IV, pp. 5–9), the *Habibus Siyar* of Khondamir (Vol. .IV, pp. 125–129, Tehran edition, 1371 H), and the *Siyasat Namah* of Nizamul Mulk (Schefer's edition, pp. 11–17). Short accounts in English will also be found in Sir Percy Sykes, *History of Persia* (Vol. II, pp. 11–21) and Professor Browne, *Literary History of Persia* (Vol. I, pp. 353–354). An examination of these authorities will show how inaccurate was the knowledge of our author about the two Saffarid brothers.

6. *Sons of Mahmud.* By the term, 'Sons of Mahmud', here and everywhere else all Muslim Kings arc meant. The last princes of the Ghaznavide dynasty were exterminated by the Ghorian brothers, Ghiyasuddin, and Shahabuddin, in 1201–1202 A.D. (*Tabaqat-i Nasiri,* pp. 26–27).

7–8. *Grades of saints—Ghaus, Qutb, Abdal, Autad, Akhyar, Nuqaha,* etc. According to a generally accepted postulate of medieval Muslim mysticism or *tasawwuf,* the world was kept in order by Muslim saints or *walis. Wali* means 'friend' and the Quran says, "Indeed, the friends of Allah, there is no fear for them and no regrets." (Sura X, verse 62). At the bottom of the grades or saints, it was said there were four thousand saints called *maktums* (hidden), who were not aware of each other. The highest saint was called *Ghaus* or *Qutb* (Axis) or *Qutbul Aqtab* (Axis of the Axes). Between them were the grades of *abdal, autad, nuqaba,* and *akhyar.* Mystic writers differed about their numbers and grades Shaikh Ali Hajwiri puts the *akhyars* as 100, with three *nuqaba* and one *qutb* or *ghaus* at the top (*Kashful Mahjub,* Discourse on the Affirmation of Saintship, p. 168, Lahore, 1931 edition). [H]

9. *Shari'at,* literally means 'path', i.e. 'the path of the Prophet'. As used by Barani, here and elsewhere, it means religious laws as developed by the great *mujtahids* or legists of Islam and is contrasted with state-laws or *zawabits,* which are the responsibility of the king and his officers.

10. *Sunnah. Sunnah* means tradition—i.e. following what has been done in the past. The three most important *Sunnahs* are—the Sunnah of Allah, the Sunnah of the Prophet and the Sunnah of

the community. Our knowledge of the Sunnah of the Prophet is based upon the traditions or reliable accounts of what the Prophet said or did. In this respect the Arabic terms, *hadis, khabar* and *rawayat,* are equivalent. I have translated them as 'traditions.'

11–12. For *Muhtasib* and *Amir-dad,* see notes at the end of this Advice.

13. Here and everywhere else, the 'capital' referred to by Barani is Delhi and not Ghaznin.

14. *Bid'at. Bid'at* technically means a novelty—doing something that the Prophet and his Companions did not do or thinking as they did not think. "All novelties are errors"—"*Kullu bid'atun fi zalal.*" Still many novelties could not be avoided. So *bid'ats* or novelties came to be divided into two kinds—good novelties (*bid'at-i hasanah*) and bad novelties (*bid'at-i sayyiah*). But still no external criterion was possible except the public welfare and fanatics could condemn almost everything in life as a 'novelty' according to their sweet will. [H]

15–16. For the *Mu'tazila* and Shaikh Bu Ali Sena see the notes at the end of this Advice.

17. No people so curious are referred to by any known historian.

18. *Dahriyat.* The term *dahriyat* is derived from the Quranic verse: "And they say: There is no life but this earthly life or ours; we live and we die; and nothing destroys us but time (*dahr*)" (*Surah XLV,* verse 24).

19. Fuzail bin Ayaz is a well-known mystic of the early period (*See,* for example, *Kashful Mahjub,* biographical note on Fuzail bin Ayaz, p. 78, Lahore text, 1931, and the *Tazkiratul Aulia* attributed to Shaikh Fariduddin Attar, No. 10). But while all other authors declare that Fuzail scolded both Harun and his wazir, Barani makes Fuzail talk to the Caliph like a courtier.

20. Abu Sa'id Abdul Malik bin Kuraib al Asma'i was born at Basra in 740 A.D. and died there in 828 A.D. The Caliph Harun Rashid brought him to Baghdad as tutor to his son, Amin. He retired with his savings to Basra. He was primarily a philologist. No book on the history of the Abbaside Caliphs is attributed to him (*Ency. Islam,* Vol. I, p. 490).

21. The Quran, *Sura* III, verse 159.

22. *Jamshed.* The first legendary dynasty of Persia is known as the Peshdadian (Early Law-givers), Jamshed was its last ruler. "*Jam* (*Yam*)," the *Rauzatus Sofa* tells us, "was his name

and *Shed* (Sun) was his title." It is not difficult to see in him the Indian god Yama. He degenerated in his later days, got drunk, claimed divinity, etc., and in spite of his flight to Sistan and thence to India, he was captured by his relentless enemy, the tyrant Zuhhak, a Syrian prince, and sawn into two pieces (See *Rauzatus Safa,* Vol. I, pp. 172–176, Persian text; also Sykes, *Persia,* Vol. I, p. 134).

23. *Kaimurs.* Kaimurs, to whom our author refers repeatedly, was the founder of the Peshdadian Dynasty according to Persian legends. People finding the affairs of the world in disorder, the *Rauzatus Safa* tells us, elected Kaimurs as their king. "The first king who governed mankind," says Firdausi, "was Kaimurs, the leader of all kings." Kaimurs means 'the father of mankind.' But in order to coordinate Persian and Jewish traditions, Kaimurs was declared to be a son or Adam and a twin brother of the prophet, Shis; he was made king by Divine order and on the principle of hereditary succession and the fact of his election was forgotten. "The scholars of history," *Rauzatus Safa* tells us, "have differed about his descent. One school of scholars declares *him* to *have* been the *eldest* son of Adam and Imam Ghazali in his *Nasihatul Muluk* supports this statement." (See *Rauzatus Safa,* Vol. I, p. 166).

24. *Lauh-i Mahfuz.* Reference is to the Quranic verse: "Indeed it is the glorious Quran in the Preserved Tablet," (*Sura* LXXXV, verses 21–22). The Divine Idea as revealed—and revealable—to man is the Quran and the revealed books preceding it; the Divine Idea in the Divine Mind, not revealable to man, is the *Lauh Mahfuz* or the Preserved Tablet. No human eyes, according to Muslim tradition, can reach the Preserved Tablet—not even the eyes of the king's courtiers. [H]

25. *'Muqam' and 'Hal'. Muqam* (station) is a mystic term correlated with *hal* (state). It was attempted to map out the spiritual progress of the soul towards God; the starting point, according to all mystics, was *tauba* or repentance. The last point, so far as it could be reached, was *raza* or submission to the Divine will. Now at every 'point' in its march the human soul could be surveyed in two ways—with reference to the progress it had made and the place at which it was (station, *muqam*) or with reference to its spiritual condition (*hal*). Of course, no eminent mystic of that period would have recognised that the king's counsellors had any spiritual station or *muqam*—let alone

anything like the *muqam* of the prophets. Their *muqam* was that of pre-repentance and their *hal* was sinfulness. [H]

26. *Alexander, the Great.* The Alexander of Persian legends is not to be completely identified with the Alexander of Greek history. The Persian people had no living memory of Alexander and no traditional hatred for him. Their knowledge of Alexander came to them from foreign sources. Firdausi and the poets—above all Nizami Ganjavi through his two *Sikandar-Namas*—did the rest. The matter has been discussed by Professor Browne in his *Literary History of Persia* (Vol. I, pp. 118–120).

27. *Ardsher Babakan.* Ardsher Babakan or Artaxcrxess, reigned from 240 A.D. to 266 A.D. He put an end to the Parthian rule over Persia and founded the famous Sasanian dynasty.

28–29. *Nausherwan* (531–578 A.D.) and *Buzurchemehr.* Nausherwan was the last of the great emperors of the Sasanid dynasty. He was reputed for his justice, but his justice seems to have been class-justice. His resistance to all attempts to better the lot of the masses left them discontented and made the Islamic conquest of Persia inevitable. As for Buzurchemehr (or Buzurgmehr). Sir Percy Sykes says: 'This remarkable man first attracted the royal notice when acting as a tutor to his son, Hormuz, who at first resented the tutor's zeal, but finally showed him intense respect and attention. Buzurgmehr was soon made wazir, and many of Nausherwan's reforms may be attributed to his signal capacity.' (*Persia,* Vol. I, p. 460).

30. *Majlis-i Rai.* This *Majlis-i Rai* is the same as the *Majlis-i Khas* to which Barani and other historians of the Sultanate period refer so often. At the *Majlis-i Am* or *Bar-i Am* the king transacted business in public. At the *Majlis-i Rai* confidential matters were discussed between the king and the high officers whom he had summoned. Barani often gives us the substance of these discussions in his *Tarikh-i Firoz Shahi.* Such a council is necessary whenever the supreme power is concentrated in the hands of one man. Barani in the course of this work also gives other equivalent names to the *Majlis-i Khas.*

31. *Waqidi.* A well-known Arab historian who was born in Medina in 130 A.H. He was a qazi during the caliphate of Mamun and may also have been appointed a qazi by Harun Rashid. He appointed the Caliph Mamun the executor of his will, and his eminence may be estimated by the fact that the great Caliph performed these duties personally. A book by the name

of *Tarikh-i Mukhtasar* does not occur in the works ascribed to Waqidi by the famous *Fihrist* of Ibn-i Nadim. But such a summary may have been prepared on the basis or Waqidi's *Tarikhal Kabir.* "Only his *Kitabul Maghazi* has survived as an independent work." *But Ibn-i Sa'd* in his *Tabaqat* and Tabari in his *Maghazi* have drawn very largely on Waqidi's lost work. (*Ency. Islam,* Vol. IV, p. 1105; also *Ibn-i Khallikan's Biographical Dictionary, Slane's translation,* Vol. III, p. 61).

32. This statement of Barani is probably correct. (See *Al-Fakhri,* translated by C.E.J. Whitting, p. 75; also Muir, *Caliphate,* p. 98).
33. Barani is probably mistaken in putting these persons as advisers or Hazrat Ali. Sa'd bin Wiqas, Abdullah bin Umar and Usama bin Zaid were definitely neutral in the Ali-'Mu'awiya struggle. (*Ency. Islam,* Vol. III, p. 787). Mughira bin Shubah had been appointed governor of Kufa by the Caliph Umar; and when Mughira died in 50 or 51 H., he was succeeded by the famous Ziyad, 'son of his father' (Muir, *Caliphate,* p. 220 and 295). [H]
34. Barani, like other Muslim writers, uses the term 'Kisra' for the pre-Muslim emperors of Iran and the term 'Qaisar' (Caesar) for the emperors of Byzantine.
35. *'Cancelling'* and *'cancelled' verses of the Quran.* There has been great controversy about this matter among Muslim theologians. In view of the emphatic and clear declaration of the Quran—a well-known verse which Barani proceeds to quote—the principle that some orders of the Quran have cancelled previous Quranic orders (as well as the previous commands of the Prophet and earlier revelations) is generally admitted. But controversy has raged on the question as to what orders have been cancelled. [H]
36. *Sura II,* section 13, verse 106.
37. This is a well-known incident of early Islamic history. The apostates demanded a reduction of taxes along with a reduction of religious devotions, but the Caliph Abu Bakr refused all suggestions about a compromise because if Islam (after the death of the Prophet) started with compromises, it would in due course be compromised out of existence. He was determined to fight and won. (See *Muir, Caliphate,* pp. 18–38, and *Al Fakhri,* pp. 70–71).
38. See Muir, *Caliphate,* pp. 515–516, *Al Fakhri,* pp. 229–230.
39. A figment of Barani's imagination, not based on any records.

The march to Somnath has been described by many historians and none of them refers to a fall of hail-stones.

40. *Khusrau Parwez.* The Sasanian Emperor, Khusrau Parwez (590–628 A.D.) started well, but degenerated during the later part of his reign. He was deposed by his officers and put to death with tortures. (See Sykes, *Persia,* Vol. I, pp. 478–787, *Rauzatus Safa,* Vol. I, pp. 265–266).

41. *Ibahatis. Ibahatis* would literally mean persons who permitted that which was not permitted. Barani and his contemporaries use the term for the Ismaili groups, against whom the charge was made that they permitted incest. Thus Amir Khusrau referring to the terrible punishment of these Ismailis by Sultan Alauddin Khilji says: *"Massacre of the fraternity of incest* (*ashab-i ibahat*) *when punishment for their deeds was meted out to them.* Next the pious supporter of the Shari'at ordered all members of the 'fraternity of incest' to be brought before him. Truthful inquisitors were appointed to catch every one of them and to make thorough inquiries into their assemblies. It was discovered that among these shameless wretches, mothers had cohabited with their own sons and aunts (mother's sisters) with their nephews, that the father had taken his daughter for his bride and there had been a connection between brothers and sisters. Over the head of all of them, men as well as women, the saw of punishment was drawn....The saw with its heart of iron loudly laughed over their heads with tears of blood. Those, who by a 'secret stroke' (*zarb-i pinhan*) had become one, were now openly sawed into two, *and the soul that had sought union* (*wasl*) *with another soul was now compelled to leave its own body."* (The *Khazainul Futuh* of Khusrau, Professor Habib's translation p. 12). Ziauddin Barani refers to the same punishments in the *Tarikh-i Firoz Shahi* (Persian text, p. 336). But the charge though widely made was without any foundation. For a short account of the Ismaili movement, see Professor Bernard Lewis, excellent monograph, *The Origins of Ismailism;* O' Leary, *History of the Fatamid Caliphate,* also gives an account of the origin of the Ismailis and the Carmathians (pp. 1–50).

42. *Seventy-two Communities.* The term 'seventy-two communities', has been used to indicate both the seventy-two sects of Islam or the seventy-two religions of the world. Barani seems to use it in the latter sense.

43. Sura LI, verse 56.
44. The *Ulama-i Dunyavi.* Medieval Muslim thought divided the *ulama* or religious scholars into two groups—(a) religious (*dinavi*) and (b) worldly (*dunyavi*). All scholars who made their religious learning a means of livelihood were classified as 'worldly religious scholars' and were charged with having sold their religion for worldly goods, specially if they entered the service of the state as *qazis, sadars,* etc., for in that capacity they had to issue religious judgments or *fatwas* according to the demands of the king and the high officers. Muslim mystic literature is full of condemnation of scholars in the service of the state. [H]
45. *Aflatun-i Ilahi.* Almost all important Greek works were translated into Arabic, mostly during the period of the great Abbasides. The political works of Plato and Aristotle evoked no response among the Musalmans. These two great thinkers of antiquity considered the city-state to be the final form of political organisation and dismissed all non-Greeks as barbarians. Such postulates were meaningless for medieval Musalmans. Still it was known that they had speculated on politics and every Persian author was free to attribute to them any statement he liked. On the other hand, Aristotle's works on scientific subjects, and in particular his *Logic,* become the starting point of Muslim secular speculations. Plato's influence was not so wide, but his doctrine of knowledge and his doctrine of Ideas (Forms) had a profound influence on the highest sphere of Muslim thought. He was called 'divine' because he was the leader of the Musalmans in the sphere of *ilahiyat* or speculations about things divine. (See *Kitabul Milla-l wan Nahl,* Persian Translation, pp. 364–370). [H]
46. Aristotle in his *Ethics* lays down the principle that virtue is a mean between two extremes. But many thinkers, quite independently of Aristotle, have laid down the same postulate. Barani is quite fond of expounding this idea.
47. The argument of this paragraph can only be understood with reference to the discussion between Sultan Alauddin Khalji and Qazi Mugheesuddin of Bayana. (*Tarikh-i Firoz Shahi,* Persian Text, pp. 293–294).
48. *Shaikh.* A Shaikh, in the technical language of the mystics of those days, meant a *sufi* or mystic whom his master or *pir* had, on behalf of a recognised *silsilah* or mystic order gives a

'certificate of succession' (*Khilafat namah*) authorising him to enrol disciples. If the Shaikh was a Saiyyed (or descendant of the Prophet) he was entitled to be called Khwaja. [H]

49. *Khanqah.* According to Maulana Jami (*Nafahatul Uns,* Persian text, pp. 31–32), the first *khanqah* was built for Muslim sufis by a Christian prince at Ramla in Syria (*circa,* 150 A.H.) During the Sultanate period we find mystic houses of two types—the *jama'at Khanas,* consisting of a single hall in which all disciples lived, and the *khanqahs,* a more elaborate structure in which separate rooms were provided for the leading mystics at least. The Chishti mystics declared that living in a *khanqah* was not permitted, but the Suhrawardi mystics defended their *khanqahs.*

50. After the famous general, Khalid bin Walid, had won the decisive battle of Yarmuk (656 A.D.) against the Byzantine army and secured Syria for the Caliphate, he was directed by the Caliph Umar to hand over charge to Abu Ubaidah Jarrah (Muir, *Caliphate,* p. 130; *Al Fakhri,* p. 72). The great Caliph's act in dismissing Khalid after such a brilliant victory has been discussed in many works on Islamic history.

51. The Caliph Umar did not (as Barani thinks) divide the whole Muslim community into castes or grades, but only fixed a principle for the division of spoils, particularly the hoarded wealth of the Persian emperors. A Persian satrap explained to the Caliph how the pay registers of the Persian emperors were prepared and his suggestion was adopted. "Next Umar decided to allocate pay emperors to precedence in faith and the assistance given to the Prophet in his battlefields and wars." The Caliph instructed the scribes: "Begin with 'Abbas, uncle of the Prophet, and the Bani Hashim, then with those after them, category by category, and put the family of Khattab where God put them." (*Al-Fakhri,* pp. 80–81).

52. *Kai-Khursrau.* According to Persian legends, Zuhhak, the Syrian prince who had overthrown Jamshed, the last of the Peshdadian emperors, misgoverned Persia for about a thousand years. Then *Kava,* a blacksmith of Isfahan, led a successful insurrection against him and used his blacksmith's apron as a revolutionary flag. But *Kava* realised that the government of men was not his proper business and placed Faridun, a descendant of the old royal dynasty, at the head of the insurrection. Faridun overthrew Zuhbak and founded the

second royal dynasty of Persia, which is called '*Kiyani*' after *Kava,* the blacksmith. Kai-Khusrau, (son of Siyawash son of Kai-Kaus), figures as the greatest emperor of this dynasty. He overthrew Afrasiyab, the Turkish emperor, and the famous Rustam was one of his officers. "It may be said without exaggeration," the *Rauzatus Safa* declares, "that whatever adjectives are used in praise of Kai-Khusrau's virtues and good deeds, they will fail to do him justice." (See *Rauzatus Safa,* Vol. I, pp. 196–198; Rogers, *The Shah Nama of Firdaust,* pp. 203–279).

53. *Ariz-i Mumalik.* The title of *Ariz-i Mumalik,* during the Sultanate period, was given to the Minister of War. He was one of the four great ministers of the state and his chief function was the control of the *arz* or the examination of every soldier at least once a year. The soldier's salary and the price of any equipment he had purchased was only paid to him if he was found efficient in this review (*arz*); it was also understood that if a soldier's horse perished or his arms were lost through no fault of his own, they would be replaced at government cost. All the civil affairs of the army were under the control of the *Ariz-i Mumalik.* If he happened to be a military man, the king could put him in charge of a campaign. There was no officer equivalent to the commander-in-chief during the Sultanate period or the Mughal empire. The *Ariz-i Asl* (Central Ariz) is only a variation of the term *Ariz-i Mumalik*—the *Ariz* of the whole empire. During the Mughal period the *Ariz* was replaced by the *Bakhshi,* a purely civil officer. There was a *bakhshi* for every province and also a *bakhshi* for the whole empire.

54. Our authorities often refer to soldiers coming for *arz* or review to Delhi. Standing on the Tughlaqabad fort one can see a space of several square miles enclosed by a crumbling wall. Very possibly this is the spot where the review was held. The review had to be finished at one stretch to prevent the arms, and possibly also the horse, of one trooper being presented again by another. [H]

55. A note on the Kara-Khita is given at the end of this Advice.

56. Firoz Shah Tughluq, as is well known, collected a large number of slaves. What was its purpose? Is Barani hinting that the object was to create a body of devoted men to check the 'arrogance' of government servants?

57. Alauddin Khalji, according to Barani, put thirty thousand Mongols to death on a single day and directed their property to be confiscated (*Tarikh-i Firoz Shahi*, p. 336). Barani condemns this tyrannical act as most of the persons slaughtered were innocent of the alleged conspiracy. No such opinion concerning the Mongols is expressed in the *Tarikh-i Firoz Shahi.*

58. Obviously, soldiers not recruited by the king will be recruited by rebels. During the days of Barani, it seems clear, there were more soldiers than could be employed by the king. One of the curious features of the time is the ease with which rebels, who had not the slightest chance of success, could enlist soldiers to follow their fortunes.

59. For Mazdak, see a note at the end of this Advice.

60. The word *barid*, according to Hitti, is not derived from the Latin *veredus* or the Persian *birdan;* 'a swift horse' but from the Arabic *birdhawn*, 'a horse of burden'. The Caliph Mu'awiyah is said to have been the first ruler who established the Department of Post (*Diwan-i Barid*) for the official communications of the far-flung Caliphate. But the *Barid* in the time of Barani meant not the officer who was in charge of communications, but the officer who collected confidential information and sent it to the king. Unlike the secret and unknown spy (*Jasus*), the *barid* was a publicly appointed officer of whose authority and functions everyone was aware.

61. Part 26, *sura* XLIX, verse 12. The whole verse reads as follows: "True Believers: Avoid most suspicions, for some suspicions are sinful, and do not spy (on each other), and let not some of you speak ill of others behind their backs. Would any of you like to eat the flesh of his brother? You would abhor it. So fear God, God is forgiving and merciful." It is impossible to accept the interpretation Barani puts on this verse in his attempt to deify the royal authority. He was more sensible when he said in his second Advice: "What is private and secret should not be revealed and published."

62. Referring obviously to the fact that religious Musalmans of the highest calibre—and the Chishti mystic group to which Barani had at least been formally inducted—considered it a sin to enter the service of kings.

63. Barani has no clear idea of Sultan Mahmud's wazirs and high officers. In the popular parlance of the middle ages, Khwaja Ahmad son of Hasan Maimandi was generally referred to as

the wazir of Sultan Mahmud, though he only served Mahmud for seventeen years. After the former wazir, Abul Abbas Fazl bin Ahmad Isfraini, had been put to death (with tortures), Sultan Mahmud appointed Ahmad son of Hasan Maimandi to succeed him. Ahmad was a foster-brother and class-fellow of the Sultan, and his father, Hasan Maimandi, was stationed at Bust for the collection of taxes on behalf or the Ministry of Revenue. The report current among the people that Hasan Maimandi (the father of the wazir) was also a wazir is quite incorrect. Khwaja Ahmad, son of Hasan Maimandi, was distinguished by religious devotions and scholarly merits. He was at first in charge of the Departments of *Insha* (Secretariat) and *Risalat* (Correspondence); but Sultan Mahmud regarded him with favour, the collection of the revenues of Khorasan was added to his other responsibilities and he discharged his duties with remarkable efficiency. When Sultan Mahmud was displeased with Abul Abbas Isfraini, he assigned the wizarat permanently to the efficient hands of Khwaja Ahmad son of Hasan Maimandi. For seventeen years the Khwaja looked after the political and military affairs of the country. Then a number of great *amirs*, like Altuntash Hajib and Amir Ali Kheshawand, began to lay complaints against the Khwaja before the Sultan. Their words had effect on the Sultan; he dismissed the Khwaja and imprisoned him in a fort in India. When Sultan Mas'ud ascended the throne after Mahmud's death, he set the Khwaja free and appointed him wazir once more. The Khwaja performed the duties of the wizarat till his death in 1031 A.D. (*Habibus Siyar*, Vol. II, p. 140, Persian text. Tehran edition). [H]

64. The facts are briefly as follows. The Caliph Harun Rashid died at Tus (Mashhad) in 808 A.D., after having sent Mamun with an army to Merv. A civil war followed and Mamun's general, Tahir, overpowered and slew Mamun's rival, Amin, after capturing Baghdad. Now Mamun at Merv was far removed from the Abbasides of Baghdad and he appointed Imam Ali Raza, the eighth Imam, who was twenty-two years older than him, as his successor. It is generally assumed that Mamun did so owing to the influence of his wazir, Fazl bin Sahl. But this was more than the Abbasides and other vested interests of the Caliphate could permit. At Baghdad, Ibrahim son of Mahdi (Mamun's uncle) was proclaimed Caliph and Mamun's governor, Hasan bin Sahl (brother of the wazir), was forced to retire. Mamun at length realised what was happening and

started for Baghdad. At Sarakhs (in northern Persia) the wazir, Fazl bin Sahl, was found murdered in his bath, and at Mashhad Imam Ali Raza died of eating grapes. The rebellion at Baghdad collapsed at Mamun's approach; but he has been accused by many of having planned the assassination of his wazir and the poisoning of the Imam. These circumstances make it very unlikely that Fazl bin Sahl could have given Mamun the advice Barani has attributed to him, for Fazl's interest was to keep Mamun ignorant of affairs. Mamun during the later part of his residence at Merv (808–811 A.D.) seems to have lost touch with the affairs or the Caliphate, but contemporaries held Fazl bin Sahl responsible for this.

65. In order to understand this Advice, Barani's account of the economic regulations of Alauddin Khilji should be borne in mind (*Tarikh-i Firoz Shahi,* pp. 303–319). But two other considerations have also to be kept in view. *First,* in spite of what Barani says about the 'general markets', some scholars have concluded that Alauddin's economic regulations were exclusively a military measure. Barani here makes it quite clear that price-control is meant for the benefit of both the army and the people. *Secondly,* both Barani (*Tarikh-i Firoz Shahi*, p. 305) and Amir Khusrau (pp. 12–13) affirm that so long as Alauddin lived, there was no rise in the price of grain and other commodities. But Barani assumes even in the *Tarikh-i Firoz Shahi* that this was a peculiar achievement of Sultan Alauddin Khilji and quite beyond the reach of other kings. Here this fact is candidly admitted.

66. It is a favourite idea of Barani that the prices of all things should be fixed according to 'production-cost', or, in the more exact terminology of Karl Marx, by the 'socially necessary labour time' of the immediate producer. Thus in the *Tarikh-i Firoz Shahi* (p. 316) he writes: "In order to enforce the aforesaid regulations of the general markets, the benefit of which accrues to the common people, Sultan Alauddin strove day and night and inquired about the production (*baraward*) of everything, even of things so insignificant as needless, combs, socks, shoes, bowls, jugs and cups. He fixed the price of everything in his own presence on the basis of production-cost (*nirkh-i baraward*) of commodities and the profit of the producer. The tariff of the prices fixed before the king was handed over to the *Diwan-i Riyasat*."

67. In his *Tarikh-i Firoz Shahi,* Barani only describes the economic regulations of Alauddin Khilji with reference to Delhi. He is silent about the provinces, except for the statement that grain was obtained from there and that the *naiks* had the exclusive privilege or duty of bringing it. This paragraph of the *Fatawa-i Jahandari* leaves the impression that Alauddin's economic measures were extended to the cities of the Empire.

68. Musalmans generally divide all acts, whether sinful or virtuous, into two categories—first, those acts which affect a man himself and are a matter only between him and his God; secondly, acts which affect others. So far as injuries to the rights of others are concerned, it is feared that even Divine forgiveness may be conditional on the forgiveness of the person injured.

69. *Regrating:* Regrating meant buying a commodity from outside, or purchasing it in the market, when prices were low and selling it when prices were high. Regrating was made possible by two *facts—first,* the insecurity of the roads, the inclemencies of the weather and the cost or transit; *secondly,* monopolies created by the combination of the transport-merchants and the market-merchants. Many Muslim theologians were so afraid of the sin of regrating that they ordered Musalmans not to deal in grain. In any case, trading in grain during the middle ages was entirely in the hands of the Hindus, and Alauddin Khilji, when inaugurating his economic regulations, depended entirely on the Hindu *naiks* organised into a corporation (*yak-jeht*), for implementing his measures. Since grain trade was entirely in the hands of the Hindus, they alone were in a position to resort to the regrating of grain. The addition of Magians (*Gabrs, Parsis*) by Barani is quite superfluous. [H]

70. The reference is to the school of Imam Shafi'i, whose doctrines with reference to those non-Muslims, who had no scriptures to which the Quran has referred, Barani has both misunderstood and misrepresented. The matter has been discussed in a note at the end of Advice XI.

71. Prices will be low in case of abundance, provided there is (a) free competition and (b) proper facilities for transport. This would be a simple economic proposition today. But Barani abuses the character of men and does not even refer to transport facilities. This is primarily due to the fact that in the middle ages the transport of merchandise was the hereditary

business of particular communities, and members of these communities by arrangements with each other could keep prices at a high monopolistic level. Barani's primary demand is that the authority of the state should crush monopoly-prices and enforce prices which would have obtained had there been free competition. The government could easily fix fair or competitive prices by adding the cost of transport and normal mercantile profits to the prices at which the transport-merchants themselves had purchased their commodities in the countryside or in other cities. [H]

72. *Imam Mohammad Ishaq*: Imam Abu Abdullah Mohammad Ishaq is one of the earliest writers on the biography and the *ghazwas* (campaigns) of the Prophet. The Imam's grandfather, Yasar, was captured and brought from Iraq to Medina in 633 A.D. and the Imam grew up in Medina and collected the material for his books there. But the criticism of some theologians, who declared him to be a Shia, compelled him to migrate to Egypt; later on the Caliph Mansur invited him to Baghdad and he died there about 767 A.D. The Imam is said to have prepared two volumes on the biography of the Prophet and also written a history of the early Caliphs. Unfortunately no work of his has survived, But Tabari in his famous *Tarikh* has preserved considerable extracts from Imam Ishaq's work and Ibn-i Hisham, who knew the works of Ibn-i Ishaq through a pupil of his, also utilised Ibn-i Ishaq's works in the preparation of his famous *Kitab-i Sirat-i Rasullallah* (*Ency. Islam* Vol. II, 389–390). Barani is obviously referring to some later compilation attributed to Imam Abu Ishaq. The conversation of Abu Hazifa with the Byzantine emperor is referred to in many books of early Islamic history.

73. *Hududallah*: The Quran says, "These are the limits ordained by Allah (*hududallah*), so do not transgress them, and if any (persons) transgress the limits of Allah, they are *zalims* (unjust)." (*Sura* II, verse 229). All crimes, the punishment of which is prescribed by the Quran, are distinguished from other crimes, because they violate the *hududallah* or the limits prescribed by God. [H]

74. *Birshikal:* The monsoon or rainy season (*birshikal, barkharut, barsat*) is a peculiarity of India. There is a weak monsoon in the Iranian province of Fars, but in the rest of Persia as well as in Afghanistan, Central Asia and Turkestan the monsoon is

quite unknown. According to the records kept by the British consulates the average rainfall in this region is about four inches a year and it is cyclonic in character. Any immigrant from these regions could have informed Barani of this well-known fact. And many persons had come to India from Ajam owing to the Mongol terror. Nevertheless Barani is so ignorant or forgetful that he refers to *birshikal*—not to rainfall but to monsoon in its Indian form—four times in the course of the *Fatawa-i Jahandarl.* [H]

75. The Quran, *Sura 51,* verse 49.
76. The Quran, *Sura* 32, verse 13.
77. Charitable kitchens for feeding the poor, also called *langar khanas,* were maintained during the Sultanate period by kings and high officers; they were also maintained by mystics and *qalandars,* who spent in the maintenance of these kitchens the presents (*futuh*) they got from the people. [H]
78. Both in his *Tarikh-i Firoz Shahi* and the present work, Barani assumes that the Hindus, unlike 'the people of the book', are not entitled to peaceful life on the payment of the *jizya.* His view is clearly against the doctrines of Imam Abu Hanifa, but Barani assumes that Imam Shafi'i had permitted no alternative for them except 'Islam or the Sword'. The doctrines of Imam Shafi'i on the matter are discussed in a note at the end of this Advice.
79. For the religious attitude of the Caliph Mamun and the three eminent persons mentioned here, see note at the end of this Advice.
80. The Omayyad Caliph Umar son of Abdul Aziz (717–720) is regarded by many Muslim historians as having followed the principles of the Pious Caliphate.
81. Nizamul Mulk gives a similar advice to kings in his *Siyasat Nama.* "There is no choice for the king but to sit for two days in the week for the hearing of complaints, so that he may punish wrong-doers, administer justice, and hear the statements of his subjects with his own ears. Some cases, which are of importance, should be placed before him and should formulate an order about all such cases. When the news, that the king personally summons the injured and seekers for redress before himself twice a week and hears their complaints, spreads through the realm, all oppressors will be afraid and restrai' their unjust

hands and no one will be able to resort to oppression and cruelty from fear of the king. (Schefer's text, p. 10).

82. The Quran, *Sura XL,* verse 3.
83. The Quran, *Sura XXXV,* verse 45.
84. A concept like the '*Sunnah* of God' cannot be discussed properly in a footnote, but there are two references in the Quran to this concept.—(a) *Sura XVII,* verse 77: "The Sunnah which we sent with our apostles before you and you will find no change in Our Sunnah." (b) *Sura XLVIII,* verse 23: "The Sunnah of God concerning what has happened before you and you will find no change in the Sunnah of God."
85. References here and in the succeeding paragraphs are to the Quranic injunctions, *Sura IV,* verse 13: "A true believer ought not to kill a true believer, but if it happens by mistake... If anyone kills a true believer intentionally, his reward is living eternally in Hell."
86. The Quran, *Sura VI,* verse 164.
87. The Quranic punishment of amputation of the hands (*Sura V,* verse 41) was not to be *inflicted on persons who stole from the public treasury because they were guilty of 'misappropriation'* but not of 'theft'. Thus according to the *Tarikh-i Firoz Shah* (p. 292), Qazi Mugheesuddin of Bayana said to Sultan Alauddin Khilji: "If the revenue officers do not get enough for their maintenance and steal from the public treasury, which is filled by taxes from the *ra'iyyat,* or take bribes or (give to the government) less than the money and *khiraj* (collected), the ??????? to his discretion, inflict on them fine, imprisonment, or other punishments. But the ?????? has not been prescribed for such a theft (*duzdi*) as stealing from the public treasury."
88. As explained in a previous note, there was a rebellion at Baghdad while Mamun was at Merv. Mamun's uncle, Ibrahim son of the former Caliph Mahdi by an Abyssinian slave-girl, was placed on the throne in July, 817, and he was supported by Fazl bin Rabi, an ex-wazir of Harun. Mamun recognized the error he had committed and refrained from punishing the rebels." (Muir, *Caliphate,* 498–501; *Al-Fakhri,* pp. 116–219; *Ibn-i Khallikan,* note on Ibrahim, son of Mehdi, Vol. I, p. 16).
89. Yemen in south Arabia had an ancient civilisation, some account of which will be found in Hitti, *History of the Arabas* Chap. V. But by the seventh century A.D. no living memory

of this ancient civilisation had remained among the Arabs, though there were traces of it everywhere. The Quran twice refers to 'the Tubba people'. "Are they better than the people of Tubba and those who were before them? We destroyed them because they were guilty of sin." (*Sura XLIV*, verse 37)." "And the companions of the wood and the people of Tubba; they rejected the apostles and (Our) warning was fulfilled." *Sura L*, verse 14. Barani's Tubba, the tyrant, is manufactured on the basis of these Quranic lines. But he could not have attacked the Byzantine empire, since it did not exist in his days, nor could he have been overtaken by the monsoon rains (*birshikal*), which are not found in those regions. [H]

90. Here as elsewhere, Barani is confused about dates. The *Tabaqat-i Nasiri* says that Subuktgin died in 387 H and Mahmud in 421 H. It also declares, "Mahmud died at the age of sixty-one after a reign of thirty-six years." So the thirty-sixth year of Mahmud's reign would be the last year of his life—the year in which, unable to manage the affairs of western Persia or to suppress the Seljuq menace and paralysed by the advance of galloping consumption, Mahmud assigned the affairs of western Persia to Masud and returned to die at Ghaznin. But this is not all. Later on, in this very Advice, Mahmud is made to state that he has been reigning for thirty-eight years. [H.]

91. Of the rulers reviewed by our author in his *Tarikh-i Firoz Shahi*, only the state-laws of Alauddin Khilji were framed and implemented in the way Barani desired (*Tarikh-i Firoz Shahi*; see pp. 282–289 for *zabitas* about Alauddin's land-revenue and administration and pp. 302–319 for his *zabitas* for price-control).

92. The author of the *Tabqat-i Nasri* (p. 11) writes about the later part of Mahmud's reign: "Mahmud constructed a bridge over the Oxus and took his army to the land of Turan. Qadar Khan met him. The Khans of the Turks also came to see him, and paid him homage and offered their allegiance. At their request, Mahmud transferred the son of Seljuq, against whose courage all the Turkish khans were helpless, across the Oxus to Khorasan along with all his tribesmen."

    Now it is impossible to identify the Qadr Khan of the *Fatawa-i Jahandari* with the Qadr Khan of the *Tabaqat-i Nasiri.* The Oadr Khan of the *Fatawa-i Jahandari* has the following features—(a) He is a non-Muslim; (b) he is a Kara-Khitain (and could not, therefore, be a contemporary of Mahmud); (c) he acknowledges God under the Mongol name of 'Tingiri'; (d) and he is equal, if not superior, to Mahmud in prestige and power. Barani, it seems, remembered the name of Qadar Khan from the *Tabaqat-i Nasiri* or some other history and then compounded a fictitious figure by adding to Qadr Khan some of the features of Changiz Khan. But Changiz Khan was a law-giver of a type Barani did not approve of and a meeting between Changiz Khan and Mahmud could not have been postulated, for there was a known difference of some two centuries between them. The Khitains, on the other hand, hovered on the dim horizon of the Muslim historians, and it was easier to frame a fictitious ruler for them.

93. *Tingiri.* It is said that *Tingiri* in Mongolian means Sky or Space. It is the Mongol term for God, and the Mongols after conversion to Islam kept on using the term *Tingiri*, I-I *Tingiri* and *Tingiri Ta'ala* as equivalent to Allah or Khuda. [H]

94. *Jizya.* In the technique of the Shari'at the jizya is a poll-tax which a Muslim ruler levies from the people on their subjects. But what was, one may ask, the sense in which the term *jizya* was used in ??? throughout the *Fatwa-i Jahandari* talks of taxes as divisible into *khiraj* and *jizya*, and he speaks of the *jizya* as being levied by pre-Muslim kings on their subjects and by Hindu rajas on their Hindu subjects (*Advice XI*). And there are also instances where Amir Khusrau and Amir Hasan Sijzi have referred to *jizya* being levied from the Musalmans. There is good reason for thinking that during the Sultanate period the *jizya* in the sense of a poll-tax on non-Muslims simply did not exist and that while the term *khiraj* was used for land-revenue, the term *jizya* was used for all other taxes, which were not taxes on land, regardless of the persons paying the taxes. [H]

95. This was impossible for Mahmud reigned only for thirty-six years. See note (1) of this Advice.

96. This clearly implies that Mahmud's father was a king. But in Advice XXIII Barani quite forgets what he has told us here and elsewhere and makes the astounding statements (a) that "the territories of Ghaznin and Khorasan "came to Mahmud from the Simjuris and (b) that "the father and grandfather of Mahmud were not kings." [H]

97. But see the next Advice (No. XV) in which Barani declares that Qadr Khan is not only a non-Muslim but a danger to Islam.

98. Strictly speaking, Sultan Mahmud left no will or testament about general advice or instructions for kings but the habit of framing testaments and attributing them to kings of the past had become widespread in Barani's days.

99. To the highest Muslim scholars, like Farabi and lbn-i Sena, the philosophical systems of Plato and Aristotle were well known. Even theological writers of the higher type had some clear views about the general trend of the thought of Aristotle to whom they referred with reverence as the First Teacher or *Mu'allim-i Awwal* and the Great Philosopher. (See, for example, the Persian translation of Shahrastani's *Kitabul Millal-i Wan Nahl* (*'Book of Religions and Sects'*) by Afzaluddin Sadr Turkah Isfahani, edited by Syed Mohammad Raza Jalali Naini, pp. 328–470). But the average Muslim historian had the vaguest idea of the great Greek thinkers. A very good example is the account given of them by Mirkhnd in his *Razuatus Safa* (pp. 224–236), which leaves a modern reader smiling and perplexed. But in view of Barni's habit of putting Aristotle as the wazir of Alexander and an adviser to kings in general, it is necessary to point out that Aristotle in his *Politics* (Book III, Chap. 16) definitely rejects monarchy as a proper form of government. [H].

100. The Quran, *Sura XLII,* verse 11.

101. Barni has apparently forgotten that at the end or the preceding Advice (No. XIV) he has converted Qadr Khan to Islam.

102. Reference is to the Quranic order (*Sura VIII*, verse 41), "You are to know that if you acquire anything as war-booty, then, one-fifth of it is for Allah, for his Prophet and for near relations, the orphans, the destitute and the traveller."

103. It is impossible to resist the conclusion that in describing the ruler who drives his subjects to despair by his harsh measures, Barni had Sultan Mohammad bin Tughluq in mind. He tells us in his *Tarikh-i Firoz Shahi* (pp. 521–522) that in one of his conversations with the Sultan he suggested the Sultan's retirement or abdication as a means for solving the troubles of the kingdom. But whether from discretion or fear, Barni did not suggest suicide as a final and effective remedy for the troubles of Mohammad bin Tughluq.

104. Barni here may have been thinking of the conversation of his uncle Alaul Mulk, with Sultan Alauddin Khilji on the eye of the battle of Kili. Alaul Mulk hinted at some compromise with the Mongol prince Qutlugh Khwaja, possibly a payment of tribute, but Alauddin declared that the time for compromises had passed and decided to fight. (*Tarikh Firoz Shahi*, pp. 254–259).

105. This may be a reference to the situation in which Alauddin Khilji found himself when after returning victorious from Chitor, he suddenly found that the Mongol general, Targhi, had reached Delhi (*Tarikh-i Firoz Shahi*, pp. 299–302).

106. The Quran, *Sura IX*, verse 41.

107. The Quran, *Sura II*, verse 249.

108. If the (our military dangers contemplated by Barni are to be overcome by a king in four successive years, then no historical king is available to whom such an achievement can be attributed. Barni should have given us a fictitious king with no reference to any contemporary kings or known geographical places. But, unfortunately, he found a very stupid story in a very stupid book, and owing to his ignorance or failing memory, he did not realise the historical and geographical errors of this Illustration. [H]

109. During the Caliphate or Mu'tasim (833–842) the city and territory or Khwarazm was a directly administered area. The governor was appointed and removed by the Caliph. The ancient ruler of Kath was allowed to keep the title of 'Khwarazm Shah' but he did not govern the city or the territory (Barthold, *Turkestan*, p. 147). [H]

110. Not possible. The kingdom of Khita, as already explained, was not established till 1123 A.D. There was no Bughra Khan of Samarqand at the time. According to the *Zalnul Akhbar* (p. 20), Saman Khudat, the ancestor of the Samanids, came to the Caliph Mamun and accepted Islam at his hands. Saman had a son, named Asad, whom Mamun favoured. Later on the governor of Khorasan, Ghassan son of Ibad, at Mamun's suggestion, assigned various territories of Mawarun Nahr to the sons of Asad. Samarqund was put in the charge of Nuh son of Asad. Later on the Tahirids assigned Samarqund to Nasr, son of Ahmad, son of Asad, son of Saman Khudat. But these persons were only officers of the Caliphate; the *imarat* or kingdom of the Samanids was not established till the time of Ismail, son of Nasr. (See also Barthold, *Turkestan*, p. 210).

Lastly, two armies marching on Khwarazm from Khita and Samarqund would not approach it from opposite directions, but from the same direction—that is from the east. [H]

111. This is absurd. Apart from the proved historical fact that the Franks or Europeans did not attack Khwarazm in the time of Mu'tasim, they could have only reached Khwarazm by either overthrowing the Baghdad Caliphate or by marching across Russia and Siberia—achievements quite beyond the capacity of Europeans in the ninth century. [H]

112. This also is absurd. There was no king of Egypt or Syria at the time. Both territories were directly governed from Baghdad. The first Egyptian dynasty—the Tulunid—did not start its career till the time of the Caliph Mutazz (866–869). Babykital, the leading Turkish officer at Baghdad, was appointed governor of Egypt, but he preferred to perform his duties as governor of Egypt through his deputy, Ahmad ibn-i Tulun. "Tulun at last threw aside the yoke of the decrepit Caliphate and became independent ruler of Egypt (868–883 A.D.)." Secondly, "a king from among the well-known kings of Syria and Egypt" could not reach Khwarazm without first overthrowing the Caliphate of Mu'tasim on his way. [H]

113. The Quran, *Sura IV*, verse 249.

114. The Quran, *Sura II*, verse 171.

115. *Ma'rifat*. The *Misbahul Hidayat*, quoting the famous *Awariful Maarif* of Shaikh Shahabuddin Suhrawardi, explains *mu'arifat* or gnosis as follows. You are reading my book; it is in Arabic. If while reading the book you are simultaneously conscious of all the rules of Arabic grammar and their application to every word, then you have gnosis of grammar. Now if you have a similar knowledge of the totality of existence, then you have gnosis (*marifat*) of God. [H]

116. The matter cannot be discussed in detail here. But humanitarian considerations, in fact, necessity required the avoidance of punishments laid down by the Quran under conditions of life which had passed away. So the qazis followed two methods. *First,* they sternly restricted the definitions of crimes enumerated by the Quran. *Secondly*, they made the rules of evidence so strong that unless such a crime had been committed in the market-place or the king's highway, proof of it was practically impossible. Indirect evidence was not admitted; four witnesses were required to prove every crime

and if there was the slightest difference in their evidence, the accused was set free. As a result these crimes had to be tried according to state-laws. [H]

117. *Yezdjurd.* There have been three Yezdjurds in the Sasanian dynasty. Yezdjurd I, the wicked (399–420) who succeeded Bahram IV; Yezdjurd II (440–457) son of Bahram Gor; and Yezdjurd III who was overthrown by the Arabs (Sykes, *Persia*, pp. 429–430; 435–436; and 489–502). None of these Yezdjurds met their death in the way described here.

118. *Qabz and Bast. Qabz* and *Bast* are mystic terms, which have really no place here. Normal human beings have the experiences of pain and pleasure, joy and gloom, fear and hope. Among the higher mystics, whose spiritual nature is developed, these contrary experiences take the forms of *bast* (expansion), when they feel the highest possible happiness because they are in contact with the Absolute, and of *qabz* (contraction) when their frustration is great because they seem to have been cut off from tho source of Divine inspiration. [H]

119. There is nothing mysterious in the contradictory qualities which Barni attributes to the king with such vehemence, assuming that this is unique phenomenon confined to the character of kings. These contrary qualities are found in every man and, consequently, in every organised society or state—in a constitutional government even more than in a monarchy. It only means that the state or government should have different types of organisations (or treating different types of people. The attribution of contradictory qualities to God is a highly disputed theological postulate. The highest thinkers of most religions are of opinion that there can be no contradictions in God. "You cannot understand the nature of God," says an Arabic proverb attributed to Hazarat 'Ali, "unless you transcend (*tanzih*) His attributes." [H]

120. No other verse of the Quran has been more misrepresented by the flatterers of political authorities, Muslim and non-Muslim, throughout the whole history of Islam. There can be no comparison between God and His Prophet, on the one hand, and the 'rulers that be from amongst you' on the other. The injunction to obey the former is unconditional, while obedience to the ruler is limited and conditional. But a wholly wrong impression of the Quranic injunction is given if only the first part of the verse is quoted and the rest of it is left out.

The whole verse runs as follows: "True Believers, Obey Allah, obey the Prophet and obey the rulers that be from amongst you, but if you disagree about any matter, then refer it back to Allah and His Prophet." (*Sura IV*, verse 59.) [H]

121. Referring to the fact, already discussed, that the principles of most mystics did not permit them to enter the service of the government.

122. *Bahram Gor.* All writers on the subject, Firdausi, Tabari, etc. bring Bahram Gor to India. But, as the *Rauzatus Safa* points out, they bring him to India in different ways. It is useless investigating a mere romance.

123. The Quran, *Sura XLIX,* verse 13. This is one of the basic verses of the Quran; it means very plainly that the most pious Musalmans are nearest to God, regardless of all other considerations. Barni's claim that only well-born Muslims (*like him*) could be pious is only one of the innumerable examples that show how the basic principles of Islam were shamelessly misinterpreted in the interest of the governing classes and the pseudo-Islamic ideology that had been manufactured to support them. [H]

124. Meaning their families after their death, as in the case of Alauddin Khilji and Mubarak Shah Khilji.

125. For the career of Isfraini see note at the end of this Advice.

126. Barni expresses the same idea in his *Tarikh-i Firoz Shahi* (p. 71): "In the *Diwans* (Empire) or the Kisras of Ajam from Kaimurs to Khusrau Parwez, kingship went by descent to kings, the wizarat by descent to wazirs, the office of malik by descent to maliks and nobility (by descent) to the nobles." But even on the basis of such world history as was within Barni's reach through works like the *Shah Nama* and the *Tarikh-i Tabari,* such an interpretation of it was absurd. Thus in Ajam alone (ignoring minor cataclysms) the Peshdadians were said to have been overthrown by Zuhhak. Zuhhak by Faridun, the Kiyani dynasty of Faridun by Alexander, the successors of Alexander by the Parthians (Ishakanians) and the Parthians by Ardsher Babakan. But Barni is so obsessed by the idea of all offices devolving at all times by birth that he forgets that he has himself stated facts in contradiction with his theory, e.g. in his Illustration concerning Bahram Gor. [H]

127. Mahmud in this paragraph is obviously addressing a person who will overthrow his dynasty and his officers and he also assumes that Mas'ud will be his successor. Was Barni really unaware of the fact that Mahmud had ignored the claims of Mas'ud and appointed Mohammad to succeed him, and that Mahmud's dynasty lasted at Ghaznin for quite a long time? If Barni had ever read the *Tabaqat-i Nasiri*, he seems to have completely forgotten it.

128. Obviously by appointing his slave-officers to all high offices. In his *Tarikh-i Firozshahi*, (p. 27), Barni condemns 'slave purchased by cash' (*dirham-kharida*), who suppressed the free-born officers of Shamsuddin Iltumish and established their rule in northern India.

129. For Barni's errors and contradictions about Mahmud and the Simjuris, see the note at the end of this Advice.

130. For the theory of the Imam, see note at the end of this Advice.

131. This is absurd. Egypt at the time of the Caliph Umar had no king of its own; it was a province of the Byzantine empire. This is made clear by such a well-known book as Bilazuri's *futuhul Bulden*, which states that the highest authority against whom Amr binul As fought in Egypt was 'the king of the Greeks' (the Byzantine emperor). Bilazuri gives the name of al-Muqauqis to the governor of Egypt on behalf of the Byzantine emperor. European scholars are inclined to identify him with Cyrus, the Viceroy and Archbishop of Alexandria under Heraclius (See Hitti, *Origins of the Islamic State* being a translation of Bilazuri's *Futuhul Bulden*, Vol. I, pp. 335–345; see also Muir, *Caliphate*, pp. 158–167).

132. The Quran, *Sura LI*, verse 56.

Life and Thought of Ziauddin Barani

by

Mohammad Habib

CHAPTER I

Introduction

"Speak well of the dead," says a well-known Arabic proverb; and following this universally accepted principle Barani's junior contemporary, Syed Mubarak Kirmani, generally known as Amir Khurd, penned a biographical note about him in the fifth chapter of his *Siyarul Auila,* which is the standard work on the history of the Chishti Mystic Order (*Silsilah*) in India.[1] Amir Khurd who was some twenty years younger than Barani knew him personally, but their ways had parted. The mystics in general were against having any contacts with the government and its officers and, Shaikh Farid and Shaikh Nizamuddin Aulia were particularly insistent on this principle. Shaikh Nizamuddin (so the *Siyarul Aulia* tells us) took back from Mohiuddin Kashani his *khilafat-nama* (certificate of succession) simply on the ground that Sultan Alauddin (on hearing that Mohiuddin was starving) had sent him a letter of appointment to the Qaziship of Awadh, which was his hereditary post, along with *in'am* and land grants.[2] The only livelihood the Chishti mystics permitted to their higher disciples was newly-cultivated land (*zamin-i-ahya*) or *futuh,* the unsolicited charity of neighbours. But after the death of Shaikh Nizamuddin ('the great Shaikh'), Sultan Mohammad bin Tughlaq made up his mind to bring all mystics under his control; and the threats and the temptations of the Sultan succeeded in breaking up the circle of the great Shaikh. His senior *khalifas,* like Shaikh Nasiruddin Chiragh, Shaikh Shamsuddin Yahya, Shaikh Qutbuddin Munawwar and Maulana Fakhruddin Zarradi refused to waiver from the moral principles of the great Shaikh; they would have nothing to do with the government, which they considered to be a sinful organisation; they did not want the Sultan's favours and they were not afraid of his wrath. But the temptations of the Sultan succeeded in winning over the smaller fry. Among them Amir Khurd was offered a post in the Deccan, but when Sultan Mohammad's government in the Deccan collapsed, Amir Khurd had no alternative but to return to Delhi. He confesses to the consciousness of a great sin but does not tell us what that sin was. But this sin-consciousness disappeared after he had seen the great Shaikh in 'a complete dream' exactly at the spot where he used to sit on the roof of his *jama'at khana*;[3] he then presented himself before Shaikh Nasiruddin Chiragh, who under very changed circumstances was trying to continue the traditions of the great Shaikh, and re-entered the mystic path.[4]

Khwaja Ziauddin Barani was appointed a courtier by Sultan Mohammad bin Tughlaq in the tenth year of his reign and fell from grace under circumstances that will be described later after Sultan Mohammad's death. But for Barani no return to the mystic circle with its principles of poverty and spiritual independence was possible, and to the last, though sternly excluded from the Court, he kept hankering for pension or office and appealing to Sultan Firoz and the high officers of the state who turned a deaf ear to his sad and pathetic appeals. Barani refers to Shaikh Nasiruddin by name as one of the leading men who were responsible for the election of Firoz Shah, but there is no evidence of his meeting the Shaikh after the latter's return to Delhi. They must have been acquaintances in the past, but now they belonged to different worlds. The saint insisted on maintaining his independence and condemning the existing administration, though in consonance with mystic tradition he does not name the reigning Sultan.[5] Barani, on the other hand, was writing book after book to attract the Sultan's attention.

It is in the light of these circumstances that Amir Khurd's biographical note on Barani should be examined.

"And among (the disciples and friends of Shaikh Nizamuddin) was Khwaja Ziauddin Barani,[6] unrivalled in grace and pleasing to the spiritual-minded. He was admired by the select and the commons. He had plenty of wit and humour; in all social gatherings in which he was present, the attentive ears of everyone were turned to his soul-refreshing words. He was an encyclopaedia of humorous remarks and stories. He had in fullness the good fortune of associating with religious scholars (*alims*), eminent mystics (*shaikhs*) and poets, and was gifted with high resolve. All this was due to the fact that owing to the affection of his father, who belonged to a noble family, he was blessed with the discipleship of Shaikh Nizamuddin and had placed his forehead in sincerity at the Shaikh's heaven-like threshold. He settled down at Ghiyaspur and, as he himself hints in his *Hasrat Nama* (*Book of Regrets*); he had obtained a position of status and nearness to the great Shaikh. Later on, as owing to his elegant mind he had no equal under the blue sky in the courtier's art, he was well-established and confirmed in the Court of Sultan Mohammad bin Tughlaq (May God illuminate his proofs) and during his reign, Barani received an abundant portion and full share of this fraudulent, faithless and deceitful world. When he reached the age of seventy and odd years, he retired to a corner on receiving at his request (*ba iltimas*) the necessaries of life from the eternal government of Firoz Shah (May God perpetuate his government and sultanate) and devoted himself to the writing of his unrivalled books such as the *Sana-i-Mohammadi* (Praises of the Prophet Mohammad), *Salat-i Kabir* (The Great Prayer), *Inayat Nama-i Ilahi* (Book of God's Gifts), *Ma'asir-i Sada'at* (Good Deeds of the Saiyyids), *Tarikh-i Firoz Shahi* and others. He brought them to *completion.*

"This gentleman (*buzurg*) was often in the company of the sultan of poets, Amir Khusrau; and the king of scholars, Amir Hasan, and obtained great benefits from their company. In addition to these merits, love for the descendants of the Prophet (saiyyids) was firm in his heart. Ultimately, he was ill for a few days and then went with the courage of a lover from this world to the next. He had no *dang* or *dirham*[7] with him at the time of his death; he had even given away his clothes in charity. There was only one piece of cloth (*tau*) over his dead body and only a piece of gunny-cloth (*buriya*) under it. Inevitably the influence of the company of the great Shaikh (i.e. Nizamuddin Aulia) overcame the influence of the company of kings and his end was good. He went out of this world in poverty as a man should. He was buried in the mausoleum of the great Shaikh at the foot of the grave of his noble father (Mercy of God upon him!)."

It was no credit to the government of Firoz Shah that it had purposely left the great scholar to die in such distress but Amir Khurd had to wield his pen with care and draw a veil over the whole affair. The statements that Barani retired from service at his own request and that he got a pension from the government of Firoz Shah are both incorrect. The circumstances of his fall will be discussed later but many paragraphs in the *Tarikh-i Firoz Shahi* make it quite clear that he lived during the reign of Firoz Shah in great poverty and was probably avoided by people because the government, which he insisted on praising, continued to regard him with disfavour. He returns to the subject of his helplessness and poverty again and again. The following quotations from the *Tarikh-i Firoz Shahi* will give some idea or the conditions under which he lived after Mohammad bin Tughlaq's death.

1. "If I describe in detail how the wicked sky and discordant time have played with the author, I will have to compose two volumes of complaints and write down various disloyalties to the sky." (*T.F.* p. 69).

2. "The Sky has treated me in a way that is not permitted in any infidel land." (*T.F.* p. 114).

3. "And in addition to the regrets which I have expressed in these lines, a still greater regret awaits me. The king of my time and generation—May he live for a thousand years!—is greatly interested in history and is blessed with accomplishments in this science (*'ilm*). But what am I to do? My enemies have thrown me far from his Court and his presence. It is not possible for me to place this *History* (*Tarikh-i Firoz Shahi*) before his august eyes. If this *History*, which I have not only honoured with his august name, but in which I have recorded some of his good deeds along with his charities and virtues and the events (of his reign), is placed before his throne and is perused by him, I will be freed from all my regrets, and every desire which crosses my heart owing to the lack of the assistance of good fortune will vanish. By Allah, the forgiving and the powerful, I am in great distress, and in this distress I appeal to Almighty God and pray: O Lord! Out of regard for my distressed mind and my condition of helplessness and poverty, provide a means so that this *History* of mine may be placed before the eyes of his Majesty, the king of mankind, Firoz Shah Sultan (May his kingdom and sultanate last for ever!) so that

all this labour of mine may not be wasted. And this is easy for Allah, and He is omnipotent in the acceptance of prayers." (*T.F.*, p. 125.)

4. After describing the general prosperity of the country in the reign of Firoz Shah in hyperbolic terms our author adds: "I am not prosperous or rich, well-provided or happy in the august reign of Firoz Shah, for in this respect I stand solitary and distinguished from all other inhabitants of the country. The following line is correct with reference to me but not with reference to anyone else—*Even the birds and fish are happy in their homes but I am not.*"

5. The substance of Barani's complaint against his fate is summarised in the following two sentences: *"I have neither attained eminence in my religious affairs, nor have I obtained in my worldly life the prosperity that could satisfy a refined and cultured mind,* and now I am old and blind and confined to my corner, helpless and poor, with nothing but my regrets to feed upon and nothing to carry with me to the other world except my unfulfilled desires."

These lines were penned in the sixth year of Firoz Shah's reign when Barani's age was seventy-four (lunar) years. Had he died before Mohammad bin Tughlaq, he would have been satisfied with what fortune had given him. His life till then had been happy and aristocratic.

REFERENCES

1. In the fourth chapter of his *Siyarul Aulia,* Amir Khurd gives an account of tea *Khalifas* or successors of Shaikh Nizamuddin Aulia, whom the great Shaikh had authorised to enrol disciples. In the fifth chapter he gives biographical notices of twenty disciples of the great Shaikh and then adds a list of nineteen other disciples about whom he only jots down a sentence or two. A page is given to our author (pp. 312–313). The Persian text of the *Siyarul Aulia* was printed by Chiranji Lal, a Jain gentleman of Delhi, in 1861 on brown paper. This work is difficult to find. An Urdu translation by Molvi Ghulam Ahmad Biryan was printed at Lahore. I am indebted to Mr. Khaliq Nizami for the loan of Chiranji Lal's Persian text.
2. Shaikh Nizamuddin Aulia, who died in 725 A.H. (1325 A.D.), is sometimes referred to as 'Dehlavi', or as 'Ghiaspuri' after the suburb of Delhi in which he lived, or as 'Badauni,' after

his birth-place. At present he is generally known as Shaikh Nizamuddin Aulia. This designation is not correct for *aulia* means saints—not a saint. Writers of mystic annals have loved to coin titles for the greatest of Indo-Muslim mystics. Amir Khurd gives him the designation or *Sultanul Mashaikh* (Sultan of the Shaikhs). I have preferred to follow the custom of my Aligarh colleagues and have referred to him as 'the great Shaikh'.

Amir Khurd's grandfather, who was a merchant, became a disciple of Shaikh Farid. After the death of Shaikh Farid, the Kirmani family came to Delhi and attached itself to his senior disciple, Shaikh Nizamuddin. Amir Khurd confesses that he was made a disciple of the great Shaikh when he was too young to understand mystic principles; nevertheless the *Siyarul Aulia* is mainly devoted to Shaikh Farid and Shaikh Nizamuddin, about whom the author had learnt a lot from the senior members of his family and the surviving disciples of the two great mystics. In addition to this, the great Shaikh's conversations were summarised in five thin volumes by the famous poet, Amir Hasan Sijzi, and published under the name of *Fawaidul Fuwad.* This work is authentic; it narrates no miracles and it was revised before publication by the great Shaikh himself.

Shaikh Nasiruddin Chiragh of Awadh is generally considered to have been the senior disciple of the great Shaikh. One hundred conversations of Shaikh Nasiruddin have been recorded by Hamid Qalandar in a book called the *Khairul Majalis.*

3. *Jama'at khand* means a house of mystics; if it is a large building, presumably with a separate room for each mystic; it is called *Khanqah.*

4. *Siyarul Aulia*, Chapter IV, No. 2 (Shaikh Nasiruddin Chiragh).

The *Fawaidul Fuwad* has been printed by Newal Kishore and other presses and it has been translated into Urdu by Molvi Ghulam Ahmad Biryan. An excellent edition of the Persian text of the *Khairul Majalis* has been brought out by Mr. Khaliq Nizami for the Aligarh History Department.

Apart from the biographical note in the fifth chapter, the *Siyarul Aulia* notices Ziauddin Barani at two other places—it quotes a conversation of Barani and the great Shaikh from Barani's extinct *Hasrat Nama* and also states that Sultan Mohammad bin Tughlaq sent Barani along with Firoz Shah with a great amount of cash to Shaikh Qutbuddin Munawwar of Hansi. But whatever the reason, the name of Barani does not occur either in the *Fuwaidul Fuwad* or the *Khairul Majlis*.

5. The *Fuwaidul Fuwad* gives the dates of all conversations—3 Sha'ban, 707 A.H. (January 29, 1307) to 11 Rajab, 722 (July 27, 1322)—but none of the persons present refers to the reigning Sultan Alauddin Khilji, either directly or indirectly. But the great Shaikh refers unhesitatingly to Balban and others kings of the past. Similarly, in the conversations recorded in the Khairul Majalis neither Shaikh Nasiruddin nor any of the persons present refers to Firoz Shah. But Shaikh Nasiruddin is quite free in his criticism of the conditions of the age and praises Alauddin Khilji and his reforms.
6. Our author always calls himself Zia-i Barani, but his full name, as Amir Khurd knew it, was Ziauddin Barani.
7. That is, no copper coin.

CHAPTER II

Literary Works

At the age of sixty-nine Barani was overtaken by a great misfortune; and this misfortune, which deprived him of almost all the material goods of life, made him an inveterate scribbler, a famous author and a powerful, though in some respects a misguided, thinker.

The details, of Barani's fall in 1351 A.D. will be discussed later. The main facts are: Mohammad bin Tughlaq died on the bank of the Indus and three days later Firoz Shah was elected Sultan. Meanwhile at Delhi the Wazir, Khwaja-i Jahan Ahmad Ayaz, acting on wrong information, placed a boy on the throne, alleging him to be the son of the late Sultan. When Firoz Shah approached Delhi, the so-called rebellion collapsed and the Khwaja-i Jahan committed suicide. Barani either fled to the fort of Bhatnir or was taken there, and he spent five months in suspense awaiting the decision of his case by the government.

In this terrible position Barani, like a good Musalman, thought of his past sins and came to the conclusion that the only means by which he could attain salvation was writing a life of the Prophet. So in great haste he composed the *Sana-i Mohammadi* or *Na't-i Mohammadi.* This work has not been published and not much should be expected from it as far as accurate information about the life of the Prophet is concerned, though it may throw much light on Barani's own life. Barani had to depend entirely upon his memory; he had no authorities within his reach; and no scholarly work was possible under these circumstances. Nevertheless the effort of composing the *Sana-i Mohammadi* turned Barani, who had hitherto been a *dilettante* and a gentleman of leisure, into a professional author. In spite of his old age and poverty, book after book was composed by him in the next six or seven years. At the age of sixty-nine (lunar) years he became conscious of a profession as well as a mission. Very few authors in world history have begun their life's work so late.

Of the nine books written by Barani after his sixty-ninth year, only two have been printed apart from the *Fatawa-i Jahandari*—the *Tarikh Baramakah* and the *Tarikh-i Firoz Shahi.*[1] The conditions under which Barani worked have been already indicated. He had no library and no resources. He could translate a book which he possessed or could borrow; he could write a book of his own based upon another man's book; he could tax his memory and give his reader what he found there mixed inevitably with something that his feverish imagination had created; and he could expound at length postulates which he considered to be the final achievements of human wisdom. But it was not within his power to undertake any investigation or research. Even well-known works on Islamic history and Indian history were not within his reach. He had no means of making sure of a date or a fact. A related question also arises—*For whom did Barani write?* That some of his books were intended for Firoz Shah is obvious. *But at the same time he leaves us in no doubt that he wrote for all eternity, though only for the noble and the well-born.* But did Barani also write for the booksellers? The balance of evidence is in the affirmative. He delights at the idea that the books of people, whom he does not like, have no sale. "What men worthy of reliance have written in their histories has been deemed worthy of credence by others. But what self-made men and people of low birth have written has not been trusted by the wise. Histories written by persons of no standing and account (*bi sar wa pa*) become old in bookshops; they are then given back to the paper-merchants and the paper is washed white."[2] Also some of his books, like the *Tarikh-i Baramakah,* could not have been written without a view to the book-market.

The way in which the Caliph Harun-Rashid overthrew the Barmakides (or Baramakah) is well-known. For several years all persons connected with the fallen family lived in constant fear and it was dangerous to praise the Barmakides. But after the passage of some thirty years, one Abul Qasim Taifi ventured to take up his pen and wrote an account of the fallen family of the great wazirs. Barani says that the author's father may have talked to a freed-man of Jafar Barmaki, but an author writing within thirty years of Jafar's death could have also found many other sources of information.[3] Taifi's Arabic book, apparently the first on the 'subject, was later on enlarged by one Abu Mohammad Ubaidullahul Asari.[4] Asari's enlarged work was translated into Persian by Abu Mohammad bin Abdullah bin Mohammad in the time of Sultan Mahmud of Ghaznin and may have been placed before him. The author of the Arabic text is Abu Mohammad Obaidullah bin Mohammadul Asari and the servant, Zia-i Barani, has translated his Arabic in a pleasing Persian style." Obviously the translation of Abu Mohammad was available in the Delhi market, but its style was out of date and Barani considered himself justified in translating Asari's work afresh. "The servant, Zia-i Barani," our author states, has seen great advantage in narrating the account of the Barmakides and has therefore, translated it from Arabic into Persian; though before this time a Persian translation has been made, just critics are invited to compare the two translations.

The *Tarikh-i Baramakah* of Barani gives the history of the Barmakide family in the barest outline and concentrates its attention on one feature only—the generosity of the Barmakides to all and sundry. It is a well-known and hackneyed theme. Stories of Barmakide munificence follow each other in serial succession; they are a challenge to revenue calculations and common sense and quite impossible to swallow. Barani quotes the high authority of Sultan Mahmud to justify the nonsensal stories that had gathered round the Barmakides in the century and a half after their fall. "It is no secret to the world that Sultan Mahmud, a religious ruler and a holy warrior, was fond of truth and quite sensitive about the matter; no one in his extensive dominions could have had the courage to translate false stories about the generosity of munificent persons and place them before him. Till the correctness of every fact (*hikayat*) had not been agreed upon, it was not translated."[5] Still it has to be remembered that the total resources of the Abbasides were limited to the surplus value of the labour of the peasants and the workers of their empire, and the gifts attributed by Barani to the Barmakides far exceed this amount. Owing to its services to philosophy and culture and to the development of Muslim religious sciences, the Abbaside Caliphate occupies a historical position far higher than the Delhi

Sultanate. Nevertheless the larger part of the Abbaside Caliphate was a desolate steppe with a cyclonic rainfall of about 4" a year; there were a few favoured tracts like the Nile banks and the south Caspian region, but elsewhere the people were dependent entirely upon artificial irrigation. A halo of romance surrounds the Baghdad of Harun Rashid which medieval Delhi cannot seek to rival. But so far as the vulgar things of life are concerned—corn, cash, commodities and cattle—the empire of Alauddin had a larger area of arable land and produced more grain than the Abbaside Caliphate, and the money that Mohammad bin Tughlaq threw away in his meaningless gifts far exceeded what the Barmakides had ever possessed. But Barani after his fall was anxious to record the munificence of the great, and he found in Asari's Arabic book a composition suited to his purpose.

In the Introduction to his *Tarikh-t Baramakah,* Barani refers to the fact that he had been reading the *Tarikh-i Mahmudi* of Qaffal. He also refers to the *Tarikh-i Mahmudi* (without naming Qaffal) in his *Tarikh-i Firoz Shahi* as one of the books with which Sultan Mohammad bin Tughlaq was well-aquainted.[6] No manuscript of this book has survived, but in view of the fact that it seems to have been the only book on Mahmud within Barani's reach, that it gave him very meagre facts about Mahmud's career and a lot of erroneous information, and of Barani's statement that Mahmud was a Shafi'i[7] and, therefore, not bound to respect the rights given to non-Muslims by the Hanafi *shari'at,* the matter deserves a careful examination.

Ibn-i Khallikan (1211–1282 A.D.) gives the following information about Qaffal in his *Biographical Dictionary:*[8] "Abu Bakr Abdullah ibn-i Ahmad ibn-i Abdullah al-Qaffal al-Maruzi (native of Merv), a doctor of the sect of as-Shafi'i was the paragon of his time for legal knowledge, traditional learning and self-mortification... Great numbers studied with profit under his tuition, and among the numbers were Abu Ali as-Sinji, the Qazi Husain, and Abu Mohammad, al-Juwayni, the father of Imamul Haramain. All these persons became *imams* of great note; they composed most instructive works, propagated as-Shafi'i doctrines in the different countries of the Muslim empire and taught them to others, who in their turn became eminent as *imams.* Al-Qaffal was already advanced in years when he began to study the law; he had spent his youth in making locks (*qufl*), an art in which he attained great skill and it was for this reason that he was surnamed al-Qaffal (the locksmith). It is said by some that he was thirty years of age when he commenced learning jurisprudence. He composed a commentary on Ibnul Haddad al-Misri's treatise on the secondary principles of the law, a work which has been commented upon also by Abu Ali as-Sinji and by Abu Tayab al-Tabari... Al-Qaffal died in the year 417 H (1026-27 A.D.) at the age of ninety and was buried in Sijistan, were his tomb is still well-known and continues to be visited as a place of sanctity. Ibn-i Khallikan attributes no book on Mahmud to Maulana Qaffal; had such a book existed, Ibn-i Khallakan would not have been ignorant of it.

The gross trick by which Sultan Mahmud was converted to the Shafi'i sect is described by Ibn-i Khallikan on the authority of the *Mughisul Khalq fi Ikhtiarul Haq* (Assister of God's Creatures in the Selections of What is Fittest, Vol. II, p. 26) of the Imamul Haramain, whose father was a pupil of Qaffal. In order to decide which of the two sects was correct, Sultan Mahmud, it is stated, convened a meeting of Hanafi and Shafi'i doctors at Merv. "These doctors," Ibn-i Khallikan writes, "agreed that a prayer of two *rak'ats* (according to the two sects) should be recited in the presence of the Sultan, so that he may examine and reflect, and choose that which was better. These prayers were said by al-Qaffal al-Maruzi.[9] Qaffal said two *rak'ats* of prayer with great care and decorum in accordance with the Shafi'i rules. He then commenced a prayer of two *rak'ats* such as was allowed by Abu Hanifa, and, having clothed himself with the curried skin of a dog, and daubed one-fourth of his body with an impure matter, he made an ablution with date wine. (It being the heart of the summer in the country, he was soon surrounded by flies and gnats.) After performing the ablution in the contrary way,[10] he turned towards the *qibla* and began the prayer without having manifested the intention (*niyyat*) of doing so whilst making the purification; he then pronounced the *takbir* in Persian, after which he read this verse of the Quran in Persian, *do bargak-i sabz* (two green leaves), and stood and bowed towards the ground twice, like a cock picking up corn, without leaving any interval between these motions; he then pronounced the profession of faith (*tashahhud*) twice and finished by breaking wind backwards, without even marking the intention of pronouncing the salutation.[11] 'Such', he said, 'O Sultan, is Abu

Hanifa's mode of prayer.' The Sultan replied, 'If it be not so, I will put you to death, for no religious man would authorise such a prayer.' The Hanafite doctors denied it to be their master's, on which Quffal ordered Abu Hanifa's books to be brought in and the Sultan ordered a Christian scribe to read aloud the system of each *imam.* It was then found that the mode of prayer as represented by Qaffal was really authorised by Abu Hanifa, and the Sultan abandoned the Hanafite rite for that of as-Shafi'i."[12]

This incident, if it has been correctly reported, does no honour either to Sultan Mahmud or to Maulana Qaffal. But in the legends that grew round Sultan Mahmud, his conversion to the Shafi'i sect was attributed to Maulana Qaffal and someone had the bright idea of writing a book on Sultan Mahmud in the name of Maulana Qaffal. Like the other fabricated histories of the period, it circulated for a while and it probably inspired Barani into giving his *Fataw-i Jahandari* the form it has. But it was not accepted by the learned and disappeared from the market. Later authors, like Nizamuddin Ahmad Bakshi and Ferishta, do not refer to the *Tarikh-i Mahmudi.*

Ziauddin Barani's fame as a historian during the last six centuries has rested entirely on his *Tarikh-i Firoz Shahi,* which covers the history of the Delhi Sultanate for a period of ninety-five years, from the accession of Balban to the sixth year of Firoz Shah's reign. It has grievous shortcomings; on some very important matters it has misled almost every later historian and yet it is difficult to find any Persian history of medieval India that one can place by its side. The reason for this is simple and clear. For Barani history was not a record or a chronicle or a story; it was very definitely a science—the science of the social order and its basis was not religion or tradition but observation and experience. This cannot be said of any earlier Muslim historian. Very few later historians have come up to Barani's standard. This does not mean that we are under any obligation to accept either Barani's basic principles or his conclusions. But we have to credit Barani with the fact that he made a sincere effort to understand the social order in a scientific way. His personal misfortunes had brought him a curious insight.

The *Tarikh-i Firoz Shahi* is best understood if we begin by examining its two vital defects.

(1) Barani says that he finished writing the *Tarikh-i Firoz Shahi* in 758 A.H. (1357 A.D.), some six years after his fall when he was living in great poverty. The question naturally arises—had he collected any documents, kept a diary or prepared any memoranda from time to time for the writing of his proposed history? The answer has to be in the negative. Barani had no idea of writing any history of this period till after his fall. He tells us in the Introduction to the *Firoz Shahi* that his original intention was to write a world-history from the time of Adam to his own time, and to dedicate it to Firoz Shah. "But while contemplating this, I recollected that the Sadar-i Jahan Minhajuddin Jurjani has written the *Tabaqat-i Nasiri* at Delhi with surpassing excellence."[13] The *Tabaqat-i Nasiri* consists of 23 Sections (*Tabaqat*) covering the history of mankind from Adam to the time of Sultan Nasiruddin. Barani very rightly concluded that if he merely repeated the facts of the *Tabaqat-i Nasiri* in his own language, his labour would be wasted; and that if he wrote something different, "people would consider him insolent and presumptuous and he would also be casting doubts in the reader's mind about the correctness of the *Tabaqat-i Nasiri.*" To understand the full implication of this remark we must remember that the facts of Islamic history collected by Barani from the fabricated histories then current directly contradicted the *Tabaqat-i Nasiri.* So Barani wisely decided to begin where the *Tabaqat-i Nasiri* had ended. Barani very often records long conversations and advices, but they are not based on any records he had kept. "The facts of history, he says, "are not based on evidence (*sanad,* documentary proofs)."[14] It is not possible to accept this precept as general principle. But a non-official historian, like Barani, who records contemporary events and is unable to reach the government archives, has no alternative but to record popularly known facts or what he had learnt from individuals, whose names he may not be in a position to mention.

(2) Barani refers again and again to the great historians of Islam, like Tabari, Baihaqi, Utbi, etc. It has to be confessed with great regret that he has either not read them in the original or forgotten them completely. The matter has already been discussed. With reference to the history of the Delhi Sultanate, Barani refers to the four following authors as authentic—Khwaja Sadr Nizami, the author of *Tajul Ma'-asir*; Maulana Sadruddin Awfi, the author of *Jamiul Hikayat*; Minhajuddin Jurjani, the author of *Tabaqat-i Nasiri;*

and "Kabiruddin Iraqi, son of Tajuddin Iraqi, who has written the *Fath-Namas* (*Books of Victories*) of Sultan Alauddin during his life-time and worked miracles".[15] Of these only the last appertains to the period covered by the *Tarikh-i Firoz Shahi.* But there were other works also—the *Historical Masnavis* of Amir Khusrau and two prose-works of the same author, the *Khazainul Futuh* and the *Ijaz-i Khusravi* (5 Vols.). The *Diwan* of Amir Hasan and the four *Diwans* of Amir Khusrau with their prose introductions would have been of help to him. Did Barani ever look up any of these books to make sure of a date or ascertain a fact?

Again the answer has to be in the negative. Had Barani studied the *Khazainul Futuh* at the time of writing, he would have given us a more accurate account of Malik Kafur's southern invasions; the same book with the help of the earlier part of Khusrau's *Dewal Rani Khizr Khani* would have enabled Barani to give us a less obscure account of Alauddin Khilji's conflict with the Mongols.[16] The *Tarikh-i Firoz Shahi* does not use any available material, either books or public documents, like the official *Fath Namas* (Messages of Victory), which had been published widely, on the period it covers. The author had nothing but his memory and his pen, ink and paper.

Still the *Tarikh-i Firoz Shahi* is a great work and it is instructive to look at its positive aspects.

(a) The *Tarikh-i Firoz Shahi* is a remarkable feat of memory. The author records everything that he had himself witnessed and everything he had learnt front the preceding generation. There are, of course, shortcomings. Barani forgets some important events, like Tarmshirin's invasion of India. At other times his memory plays him false, as in his account of the battle of Kili.[17] Similarly his story that Sultan Alauddin wanted to establish a new religion is either a figment of the feverish imagination of his old age or else is based on wrong reports given to him in his youth.

We have Barani's own authority that though Alauddin knew how to say his prayers, he never fasted and did not even attend the Friday congregation, a duty which very few Muslim kings have had the courage to ignore. Barani and Khusrau both affirm that Alauddin was a stern persecutor of the Ismaili heretics (*ibahatis*), and that whenever an Ismaili was discovered, his body was sawn into two parts in accordance with the Sultan's orders. Alauddin may have been negligent in fasting and prayer, as Barani regrets, but he was sound in doctrine. "Alauddin," Barani says, "had a firm faith in traditional Islam, like ignorant people; he neither knew nor heard, nor repeated the dogmas of men of bad faith or bad religions."[18] Obviously a man so true to orthodox and traditional Islam could not have dreamt of overthrowing it. A critical reader will find many errors of the same kind throughout the *Tarikh-i Firoz Shahi.* Barani's dates are inaccurate and very often he gives no dates at all. This shortcoming can be made up by reference to other works; we can also put in chronological sequence events which he has described in the wrong order. Our real difficulty arises when events, which had become fixed in Barani's mind in the order of cause and effect are described without any reference to sequence or chronology. This is particularly distressing in respect of the reign of Mohammad bin Tughlaq, concerning which Barani says: "I have not cared as to which victory, rebellion or event came first and which came later, and I have not adhered to the chronological sequence of events, so that wise men may obtain warning and wisdom by observing the affairs of the state in their totality."[19] There was a terrible famine in the land, one of the worst our country has ever seen; simultaneously, Mohammad bin Tughlaq embarked on a series of novel measures and he had to face a number of rebellions. Barani describes the famine but does not correlate it with the other events, and wishes us to accept his own interpretation of the reign—that all misfortunes were due to the inventions or reforms (*aslub*) of Mohammad bin Tughlaq, to his hardheartedness, which Barani attributes to his faith in rationalistic philosophy, and to his reckless generosity. 'Modern historians have succeeded in putting the wars and rebellions of Mohammad bin Tughlaq in their chronological order, but not his reforms or *aslub*. Concerning other matters—like the Khorasan campaign, the token currency, the Department of Agriculture, etc.—Barani has forgotten to tell us the whole story and this has led to widespread misunderstanding.

It is necessary to insist on the shortcomings and defects of the 'Tarikh-i Firoz Shahi,' which are due to Barani's lapses of memory and the tricks it played with him, because no historian, medieval or modern, has had any suspicion about the matter. In fact it is only a study of the *Jahandari* that reveals to us that Barani's remarkable memory was failing, and if we approach the *Firoz Shahi* with this suspicion in mind, the suspicion is confirmed. Some events are quite forgotten; others are incorrectly related; and in some cases Barani's fixed opinions play havoc with his memory. It is not possible here to point out all the errors of the above-mentioned type in the *Tarikh-i Firoz Shahi,* this would mean an independent work by itself.[20] But an examination of one problem—the token currency of Mohammad bin Tughlaq—will explain what is meant. Hitherto, thanks to Barani's incomplete narrative and a memory that played him false, all historians have been writing as if Mohammad bin Tughlaq was stark mad and behaved like a perfect idiot in the matter.

To avoid misunderstanding, an exact translation of Barani's account is necessary. "The third design of Sultan Mohammad, which contributed to the ruin of the country, to the strength and courage of the rebels of Hindustan, and to the greatness and prosperity of *all* Hindus in the matter of buying and selling, was the issue of the bronze coin (*sikka-i-mis*). Because his high courage incited him to conquer the whole world and bring it under his control, and for this impossible enterprise an army beyond all computation was necessary, and such an army is not possible without an unlimited treasure, and the royal treasury had been greatly depleted, Sultan Mohammad issued the bronze coin. He ordered the bronze coin to be made current in buying and selling in place of the gold and silver coins.[21] As a result of this measure, the house of every Hindu became a mint and the Hindus of the empire had lakhs and crores of bronze coins minted; they used them for their expenses; they bought horses, arms and valuables of all kinds with them and *havalgan* (?), *muqaddams* and *khots* attained to power and dignity through the bronze coin. A great misfortune overtook the country. Before long persons in the distant provinces exchanged the bronze coin according to the amount of its bronze. But in regions where they were afraid of the Sultan's order, the silver *tanka* exchanged for one hundred bronze *tankas.* Every goldsmith (*zargar*) struck bronze coins in his house and the (royal) treasury was filled with bronze coins. The bronze coins were so degraded and disgraced that they became as valueless as potsherds and stone-pieces. The old coins, owing to their dignity, rose to four and five times their value. When the operations of buying and selling began to collapse everywhere, and the bronze coins became worthless like clods of earth, Sultan

Mohammad cancelled his order about the bronze coin, and, with great wrath in his heart, ordered that anyone who had a bronze coin was to bring it to the treasury and to take the old gold coin in exchange for it. Many thousands of people *of various groups,* who had these bronze coins in their houses and had given them up as valueless or had kept them for making bronze vessels, took them to the treasury and brought gold and silver *tankas* or *sashganis* and *duganis* (silver pieces) in return to their houses. Such a large number of bronze coins were brought to the treasury that they were piled up in heaps, like hillocks, at Tughlaqabad. In return for these bronze coins a very large quantity of (silver) coins went out of the treasury. One of the great disasters that overtook the treasury was the issue of these bronze coins".[22]

The whole world is living on token currencies today, but in many countries token currencies have led to disaster at some time or other. It is unfortunate that the account we have of the first token currency in India should be so erroneous. The word *mis* in Persian means either copper or bronze; for the wrong translation of *mis* as copper Barani is not responsible. Copper is an element; bronze is an alloy.

Two contradictions and errors in Barani's account are obvious. (1) The reference to Hindus is wholly irrelevant and is due to "Barani's unsoundness of mind concerning the Hindus." Only goldsmiths, whether Hindus or Muslims, could have forged the bronze coin. Maybe, the majority of goldsmiths were Hindus then. But *all* Hindus could not have forged the bronze coin in their houses, because they did not know the art. On the other hand, the order to forge bronze coins could have been given to the goldsmiths both by Hindus and Musalmans. The phenomenon of rising prices has been carefully studied in modern times; creditors lose, debtors gain; the producers also gain at the cost of the consumers. Nobody's religion or community has anything to do with the matter. (2) Secondly, if there was not much money in the treasury when the experiment started, how was Mohammad bin Tughlaq able to redeem the bronze coins forged and uttered on such an extensive scale? The fact that the Sultan could not possibly have redeemed all forged coins—in addition to the fact that plenty of these coins have survived to our days—throws a doubt on Barani's whole account. Modern governments redeem their depreciated currencies at their market value. Why did the

Sultan not follow this policy? *What sense was there in paying full value to the holders of the depreciated coins, who had purchased them at their depreciated value?*

Barani's account would have been complete if he had added the following:

(i) The mint had a special type of bronze alloy for the coins, which could be easily distinguished on the touchstone; but the secret of the proportion of the metals in the bronze coins could not be discovered by the goldsmiths.

(ii) When people took gold and silver coins in those days, they had the coins weighed (to make allowance for clipping) and also tested on the touchstone for purity of metal. The Sultan expected the public to follow the same practice in regard to his token coin. But in this matter the public failed him. Consequently many forged coins got mixed with the treasury coins; and as the forged coins became current and the government was unable to prevent this, more and more coins were forged.

(iii) A bronze coin would be at least worth in weight its bronze—i.e. about 50 bronze coins would be normally equal to one silver *tanka.* But forging the bronze coin was an offence. So a forged bronze coin may meet any fate, for a new element—fear of punishment—also entered into the determination of its value. In the distant provinces it circulated at one-half of its usual metal value in terms of the silver *tanka;* in the Capital people would be afraid of being found in possession of forged bronze coins. They would throw them away or keep them in order to melt them into bronze vessels later on.

(iv) The whole operation got beyond the control of the government. Too many forged coins got into circulation and the failure of the experiment caused havoc. In the market, it was not possible to punish those in actual possession of the forged bronze coins, because they were innocent. In fact strangely, nobody was punished.

(v) It was understood from the very beginning that the treasury would redeem every bronze coin it had issued. The Sultan now ordered this to be done. People brought to the treasury the bronze coins they had. *The treasury redeemed the bronze coins it had issued as a matter of treasury-conscience; it rejected the false coins but did not punish their owners because they were* 'bona fide' *possessors.*

Heaps of these rejected bronze coins, which were probably melted later on, could be seen at Tughlaqabad. But forged bronze coins not brought to the treasury continued to circulate at their metallic value and have survived to our days.

These additions would have made Barani's account correct and complete. Paper currency for government purposes only was used by the Chinese and also by the Mongol emperors. The Il Khans of Persia were tempted to issue a paper currency for public use, but their advisers decided against the experiment. The government of Mohammad bin Tughlaq could not manufacture a special quality of paper; so it decided to use a special bronze alloy. Ferishta says that Mohammad bin Tughlaq's experiment was suggested by the paper currency (which he calls *sikka-i chau*) of China. It is easy to prove these statements for a large number of the forged coins are found in our museums. The silver coin of the period was known as *tanka* and the copper coin as *jital.* The forged coins, which this experiment produced, are of bronze and easily distinguishable from all other coins by their remarkable superscription. On one side the superscription in Persian reads: "This *tanka* has become current (*raij shud*) in the time of the servant hopeful (of Divine favours), Mohammad bin Tughlaq Shah." The language of all other coins of the Sultanate period was Arabic, but here is a bronze *coin* (*jital*) declaring in the Persian language that *its circulation value* is that of a silver coin (*tanka*). However, the superscription on the other side is in Arabic: "He who obeys the Sultan, obeys God (*Rahman*)."

The fact that all these coins are forged is also easily proved. Take five or six of them, rub them on a stone, and see the rubbed parts of the coins in bright light. They will have different colours showing that in everyone of them the proportion of the metals is different. None of them therefore, can be from Mohammad bin Tughlaq's mint.

It has been necessary to discuss the token currency of Sultan Mohammad bin Tughlaq to warn students of the *Firoz Shahi* that Barani's lapses of memory must be constantly kept in view along with his inflexibility of thought and the predominance of fixed ideas, which are often the concomitant of old age.

(b) In his Introduction to the *Tarikh-i Firoz Shahi,* Barani lays down the following canon for the guidance of the historian: "One of the principles in the writing of history is this. It is the obligatory duty of an honest *historian* to record the excellences, charities, justice and kindnesses of kings and great men, but (on the other hand), he should not seek to hide their wickedness and meanness; he should not practice flattery in the writing of history. If he considers it advisable, then openly, otherwise by hints, insinuations and indirect speech, he should convey the correct information to the discerning and the wise. If the historian is unable to write in this way (i.e. convey the correct meaning by insinuations) owing to the terror and fear of his powerful contemporaries, in that case he is excused. But concerning the rulers of the past, he should write openly and truthfully."[23] Further, if the author has been injured or favoured by the king or a powerful officer, he should not allow this fact to colour his narrative. In examining Barani's flattering chapters on the six years of Firoz Shah's reign, what he says here should be borne in mind. He is excused.

(c) All readers of the *Tarikh-i Firoz Shahi* during the last six centuries have been captivated by Barani's remarkable Persian prose style, which is simple, direct and effective. Persian histories before Barani's time were either written in a highly ornate style, full of allusions, figures of speech, etc., like the *Tajul Ma'asir* of Nizami and gave the minimum of facts with the maximum of words, or they specialised in a plain blue-book style, like the *Tabaqat-i Nasiri,* and merely recorded facts. In Barani's hands history became literature—literature in our modern sense. The *Tarikh-i Firoz Shahi* reads like a novel, with passages of surpassing excellence scattered throughout the work. No Indo-Persian history equals the *Tarikh-i Firoz Shahi* either in the analysis of characters or the delineation of scenes. Nowhere does Barani make an unnecessary show of learning. He writes so as to be understood with the least amount of effort on the reader's part; current tradition (if one may judge from the works of Amir Khusrau) required simplicity in poetry and ornateness in prose. On the other hand, one has to deplore Barani's fondness for abusive words and phrases.[24] So far as the persons damned by the *Tarikh-i Firoze Shahi* are concerned, they could not rise from their graves to answer Barani's abuses and misrepresentations. But it appears from his own confession, as we shall see later, that one of the charges brought against him before Firoz Shah was the persistent use of 'poisonous words'.

(d) Barani belonged to a family of high officers and he was a courtier for over seventeen years. One of the distinctive features of his work is the careful account he gives us of state-laws (*zawabit*) and government orders (*aslub*). Later historians, in this respect, have greatly improved on Barani's work. But Barani's achievements should not be underrated. To take an example: Chengiz Khan was, a great figure and eminent Persian historians have written about him—Ata Malik Juwaini, Rashiduddin, Wassaf, Mirkhond, Khondamir and others. But none of these authors have described the *yasas* or laws of Chengiz Khan with the clarity with which Barani has described the economic regulations of Alauddin Khilji.

(e) Barani had a very high opinion of his work and declared that 'he had won the ball of distinction from Persian historians'. "I have taken great trouble in writing this work and I expect appreciation from the just. This book has many virtues. If you consider it a history, you will find in it an account of kings and *maliks*. If you search in this book for laws, government regulations and administrative affairs, you will not find it without them. If you want precepts and advice for kings and rulers, you will find them more plentiful and better in this book than in any other. And because everything I have written is true and correct, this history is worthy of credence; also I have put a lot of meaning in very few words and this example of mine deserves to be followed. It would be true and correct if I recited the following quatrain about my *History: If I say there is no history* in *the world like mine, how will a person who is ignorant of this science agree with my statement*?" And elsewhere he says: "I know, and critics of history, who in these days are rare like alchemists and the mythical bird, Simurgh, also know that during the past thousand years no historian has been able to write a history like the *Tarikh-i Firoz Shahi,* which also includes information about principles of administration. I have really worked wonders."

The great claim Barani makes for himself is that of the wisest thinker on state affairs. Till about the time of Sher Shah, everyone who read the *Firoz Shahi* acknowledged Barani's wisdom. Then the circumstances of the country and the thoughts of educated people changed. Barani, though still valued as a historian, was ignored as a political teacher. Today no precept of Barani has any practical value. But the wisest of political thinkers—Plato,

Aristotle, Machiavelli, Karl Marx—are only wise for their time. No one is wise for all times. Barani's political wisdom is confined to the period of the Delhi Sultanate.

REFERENCES

1. So far as we can gather, Barani wrote the following books: (1) *Sana-i Mohammadi,* (2) *Salat-i Kabir,* (3) *Inayat Nama-i Ilahi,* (4) *Ma'asir-i Sadaat,* (5) *Tarikh-i Firoz. Shahi,* (6) *Lubbatut Tarikh,* (7) *Torikh-i Baramakah,* (8) *Hasrat Nama,* and (9) the *Fatawa-i Jahandari.* The *Fatawa-i Jahandari* probably Barani's last work, was unknown to Amir Khurd. Amir Khurd also writes as if he did not know all the works of Barani. The *Tarikh-i Baramakah* has been lithographed in Bombay. The *Tarikh-i Firoz Shahi* was edited by Sir Syed Ahmad Khan for the Asiatic Society of Bengal in 1862. Both books are out of print. The Persian text of the *Tarikh-i Firoz Shahi* is being edited by my esteemed colleague, Professor S.A. Rashid for the Muslim University History Department, and Vol. I (covering the *Muqaddama* or Introduction and the reigns of Balban and Muizuddin Kai-Qabad) is available.
2. *Tarikh-i Firoz Shahi,* p. 14.
3. At one place Barani makes Taifi quote an incident from his father who has heard it from Yaqub bin Ishad Ibrahim (bin Salih bin Mihran), who was a high officer of Harun-Rashid (p. 43). At another place Taifi's following remark is quoted: "I have not seen them (the Barmakides), for over a *qarn* (thirty years) has passed since the brave fellow (*jawan mard*), who called himself 'Caliph', overthrew these generous people." (p. 60)
4. There is reason for thinking that Asari revised and enlarged Taifi's text about one hundred and fifty years after the fall of the Barmakides, for Barani's *Tarikh-i Baramakah* contains the following sentence: "Till today one hundred and fifty years have passed since that event. There is no stability left in the government of the Abbasides. Every region has falled into some one's hands and only Iraq and Egypt, owing to their religious rulers, have remained subordinate to the Caliphs. All rights of governance and direct administration have completely vanished." (p. 86)
5. *Tarihh-i Baramokah,* p. 112.

6. Ibid., p. 465.
7. This sentence has been omitted in Afsar Begam's translation by an unfortunate oversight.
8. Translated from the Arabic by B.M.G. De Slane, and published by Bernard Quaritch, 15 Piccadilly, London, 1868, Vol. II, p. 26.
9. Ibn-i Khallikan's *Biographical Dictionary,* De Slane, Vol. III, p. 334.
10. That is, in the reverse order, beginning with the washing of the feet and not with the washing of the hands.
11. *Ibn-i Khallikan,* Vol. III, p. 336. The chief features in Qaffal's parody of the Hanafi prayer are explained by Dc Slane (Vol. III, p. 336) as follows: "According to the Hanafite doctrine the tanned skin of every animal, except the hog, is pure. The expressed juice of every plant and fruit is impure, except the juice of the date (*nabiz*)." (Qaffal reversed the usual order of washing the hands, face, feet, etc. on the ground that in Hanafi law a change in the order of washing does not invalidate the ablution. According to the Hanafi's it is better to express the intention to pray in words, preferably in one's mother-tongue, but unpronounced intention is enough). The words, *the green leaves,* are an inadequate translation of *mudhammatan* (Quran, 64 verse of the 54 *surat, Ar Rahman*). Imam Abu Hanifa specifies three Quranic verses as the minimum required for a rakat, but Qaffal interprets him to mean three words." The Hanafites have permitted prayer in one's mother-tongue, though this is not generally done. The Shafi'ites do not permit the use of the translated Qaffal verses in prayer. The passing of wind invalidates prayer in Hanafi law; Qaffal is misrepresenting the Hanafis in this matter.
12. *Ibn-i Khallikan,* Vol. III, pp. 334–335.
13. *Firoz Shahi,* pp. 20–21.
14. *Tarikh-i Firoz Shahi,* p. 13.
15. *Firoz Shahi,* p. 14.
16. Ziauddin Barani, after praising the volumes of the *Fath-Namas* which were composed by Kabiruddin Iraqi, points out the following shortcomings:—(a) Kabiruddin only gives an account of Alauddin's victories and says nothing about his defeats; (b) he has resorted to praise and flattery and not followed the traditions of historians, who record both the good

and bad acts of men; (c) since every volume of the work was written in Alauddin's reign and was placed before that ruler, he had no alternative to flattery; (d) Barani praises the excellence of Kabiruddin's Persian and Arabic prose, but implies that this is not the proper style for historical works. Now Amir Khusrau's *Khazainul Futuh* (which has been translated into English by me under the name of Campaigns of Alauddin Khilji) is in its earlier part a summary of Kabiruddin's work but in its later part it gives a detailed account of Malik Kafur's Deccan campaigns. Very probably Kabiruddin had died and Amir Khusrau, either at his own initiative or at Alauddin's order, continued his work; it is certainly written as if it had to be placed before the Sultan. The *Khazainul Futuh* by Khusrau has all the defects of Kabiruddin's work. Barani had no books with him, but he apparently remembered enough of the shortcomings of Khusrau's work to make up for them by giving us a detailed account of the invasions of Qutlugh Khwaja and Targhi. Khusrau has simply ignored these invasions both in his *Khazainul Futuh* and the *Dawal Rani*.

17. Isami in his *Futuhus Salatin* makes it clear that Zafar Khan, who commanded the right wing of the Delhi army, attacked the army of Qutlugh Khwaja at his own initiative and in direct contravention of Alauddin's stern order that, in view of the very delicate military situation, when not only a defeat but a drawn battle would have meant complete disaster, the enemy should not be attacked without his permission. "If any officer moves forward without the ruler's order, his head would be severed from his body," Alauddin had commanded. No blame attaches to Alauddin or to Ulugh Khan for not following up Zafar Khan after he had broken through a part of the Mongol lines; for their primary duty was to protect the unfortified city of Delhi and they could take no risks. "Even if I break my way back through the enemy ranks," Zafar Khan said to his officers, "how are we to show our faces to our master?" So they decided to die fighting. (*The Futuhus Salatin of Isami*, Dr. Mehdi Husain's edition, pp. 249–261).

18. *Firoz Shahi*, pp. 388–389.

19. Ibid., p. 467.

20. This work, I hope, will be undertaken by my colleague, Professor S.A. Rashid, in the Introduction to his edition of the *Tarikh-i Firoz Shahi*.

21. The word 'gold' in this context is quite superfluous; the bronze coin was to replace the silver *tanka* only.
22. *Tarikh-i Firoz Shahi,* pp. 475–476.
23. Ibid., pp. 15–16.

    It was a generally accepted principle of medieval history that criticism of the powerful rulers of the day and their officers should be made indirectly. Thus Mirkhond (a contemporary of Babur) in the Introduction to his famous *Rauzatus Safa* writes: "The second condition is that the historian should describe all aspects of every affair. In other words, just as he recounts the merits, charities, justice and mercy of great men, similarly he should describe, and not seek to hide, their wicked and mean acts. If he considers it prudent, he may describe the latter (wicked acts) openly; if not he should resort to hints, insinuations and indirect remarks. A hint to the wise is enough." (*Rauzatus Safa,* Newal Kishore edition, Vol. I, p. 6)
24. Many of these abusive words and phrases are only intelligible if translated into Hindi or Hindustani.

CHAPTER III

Ziauddin Barani: Family and Early Life

"The father of this weak individual," Barani writes, "was a man of status.[1] I am the son of a munificent man and the descendant of munificent ancestors."[2] Barani's claim to good birth cannot be denied, though it is unfortunate that his pride of it so deeply coloured his life and vitiated even his religious outlook. His mother's father, Sipahsalar Hisamuddin, was the *Vakildar* or Deputy of Malik Barbek Bektars Sultani,[3] the *Hajib* (or Chamberlain) of Sultan Balban; and Barani quotes Hisamuddin as declaring that Malik Bektars was 'the highest, the closest and the most trusted of Balban's officers'. Seniority of status among Balban's officers, however, belonged to Malikul Umara Fakhruddin, the Kotwal of Delhi. When Balban started on his three-years campaign against Tughril, the rebel governor of Bengal, he took Malik Bektars with him but left Fakhruddin as his *Naib* (Deputy) at Delhi with power to decide all matters in his discretion without referring them to the distant Sultan. When Balban marched from Lakhnauti against Tughril, he appointed Sipahsalar Hisamuddin to the office of *shuhna* (kotwal) of Lakhnauti with the instruction to forward information from Delhi along with the *arzdasht,* (reports) of the *maliks* and *amirs* of Delhi to the Sultan three or four times a week. Malik Bektars was sent forward with an advance-guard of seven or eight thousand courageous horsemen against Tughril and his scouts succeeded in capturing and killing him. Barani declares that Sipahsalar, Hisamuddin was a man of intelligence, sound judgment and tact, and that he had a high status and position before Sultan Balban.

In his account of the Saiyyids of the reign of Alauddin Khilji, Barni praises the Saiyyids in general—'for the world exists owing to them'—and the Saiyyids of Kaithal in particular. "My father's mother was the daughter of Saiyyid Jalaluddin, who was among the dignified and prominent Saiyyids of Kaithal. She was a pious Saiyyid lady, capable of performing miracles, which were witnessed by chaste women."[4]

Barani's father, who had the title of Moidul Mulk, was the *Naib* (Deputy) of Arkali Khan, the second son of Sultan Jalaluddin Khilji. Jalaluddin invited his officers to build their houses at Kailugarhi, and Moidul Mulk (Barani tells us) built a large and high house there. Barani does not tell us what office his father had held in the reigns of Balban and Kai-Qabad, though he quotes his father and his teachers 'who were the great scholars of the time,'[5] as his authorities for that period. Moidu, Mulk did not go with Arkali Khan, when he was appointed governor of Multan nor was he among the loyal officers who fled from Delhi to Multan with the Malka-i Jahan (Sultan Jalaluddin's widow). The reason for it was simple. Moidul Mulk's brother, Alaul Mulk, was one of the five highest officers of Alauddin Khilji. Consequently, Moidul Mulk was appointed *Naib* and *Khwaja* (governor) of Barani (the present Bulandshahr in UP) by Sultan Alauddin. Our author took his Surname 'Barani' from Baran, but he shows no knowledge of the place nor any affection for it either. We are left to assume that he was in Delhi all the time, and that his father could perform his duties through agents.

Barni condemns his uncle, Alaul Mulk, for having been a party to the murder of Sultan Jalaluddin. But Alaul Mulk's high status, diplomatic tact and efficiency cannot be denied. When Alauddin marched against Deogir without the permission of Sultan Jalaluddin (his uncle and father-in-law), he left his governorship of Karra (Allahabad) and Awadh in charge of Alaul Mulk; later on, when after the murder of Sultan Jalaluddin, Alauddin marched on Delhi, Alaul Muik was again left in charge of these two provinces. In the second year of Alauddin's reign, Alaul Mulk was called from Karra and appointed Kotwal of Delhi. It was a very responsible post. In spite of the rise and fall of kings and the changes of dynasties the Kotwalship of Delhi had for over eighty years remained in charge of Malikul Umara Fakhruddin and his father; father and son had made their post secure by not meddling in politics and intrigues and confining themselves to administration. In the struggle between Jalaluddin Khilji and the old Turkish nobility led by Aitmar Kachchin and Aitmar Surkha, the sons of Fakhruddin Kotwal had sided with the Khiljis (1290 A.D.). No reference thereafter is made to Fakhruddin, but the administration of Delhi seems to have remained in charge of officers appointed by him. They were all now, put under the control of Alaul Mulk along with the City, the *harem* and the royal treasures.[7] The Sultan said that Alaul Mulk deserved to be his wazir, but could not be appointed to that post on account of his extraordinary corpulence. When marching to Kili against Qutlugh Khwaja, Alauddin left the City and everything else in charge of Alaul Mulk and instructed him to kiss the keys of the City-gates and the treasury and place them before the victor, whoever he might be, and be loyal to him thereafter. Barani says that none of those who took part in the assassination of Jalaluddin, with the exception of Sultan Alauddin himself, were destined to live for more than three or four years. Alaul Mulk seems to have died soon after the battle of Kili.

Barani at two or three places refers to his grandfather—obviously paternal grandfather—as a person from whom he had obtained information about the past. His paternal grandfather also must have been a high officer, for Alauddin in the council held before the battle of Kili declared: "You all know that Alaul Mulk is wazir and a *wazir-zada*." The two terms are used figuratively, but they do imply that Barani's grandfather was an officer of distinction.

This is all that Barani tells us about his family in the *Tarikh-i Firoz Shahi*. If he had brothers, sisters, wives and children, we know nothing about them at present. The *Tarikh-i Firoz Shahi* is the composition of a very solitary soul. But it is probable that if his autobiography or *Hasrat Nama* is discovered, we will know more about his family.

Barani was a precocious child. He declares in the *Firoz Shahi* that what he has written about Balban and Kai-Qabad is based on what he had heard from the senior members of his family, his teachers and others.[8] But from the reign of Sultan Jalaluddin—and he was only about six years old at the time of Jalaluddin's accession—he claims to have written everything on the basis of his own observations and facts he had himself collected. He adds that during Jalaluddin's reign he had finished the Quran, was learning Arabic word-meanings (*mufridat*) and trying his hand at composition. The way in which he wrote about the dancing-girls of Jalaluddin's court some sixty years later also seems to show that he had a very prematurely developed sex-impulse.

Barani insists that he had eminent teachers. The best teachers of that time taught in their own houses or in mosques or other public places; they did not go about teaching gentlemen's children in their homes. Still Moidul Mulk did probably get fairly competent teachers for him. They taught him good Arabic and traditional logic, but his complete ignorance of philosophy and science—and his fanaticism against both—proves that he was taught no book on either subject. Islamic history, as is well known, was not a part of the medieval syllabus but only that portion of it—the period of the Prophet and the Pious Caliphs—which is concerned with theology and theological controversies. Barani in his old age could remember quite well the facts of early Islamic history as it was taught to the sons of the orthodox, but he was all at sea concerning the period after Hazrat Ali. "My life," he writes, "has been passed in the study of books. I have read many books of ancient and later times in every branch of knowledge; and after the sciences of *tafsir* (Quranic commentary), *hadis* (the Prophet's traditions), *fiqh* (law) and the *tariqat* of the Shaikhs (mysticism, *tasawwuf*), I have found no science so useful as the science of history."[9]

Barani was acquainted with the first three subjects listed here, but in regard to these he was merely a creature of tradition; he refused to think for himself and repeated platitudes. Barani's ignorance of Islamic history has already been proved in the notes on the *Fatawa-i Jahandari*. Of mysticism or *tasawwuf* his ignorance was even more profound. He repeats some platitudes he had heard in the *khanqah* of the great Shaikh or learnt from cheap books—e.g. that religious scholars are of two types, those who seek this world (*ulama'i dunyavi*) and those who seek the next (*ulam-i dinavi*) and that the latter do not flatter kings and their officers for posts and pensions; and he puts these platitudes in the mouths of his heroes again and again. But the unfortunate fact is that he never understood the ABC of mysticism—its cultivation of God-consciousness as the primary objective of life; its rejection of all the trammels of the material world to the extent that they were a hindrance in this path; its dismissal as mere allegories of the joys of Heaven and the tortures of Hell, which to Barani were things of such hope and fear; its determination to remain aloof from the medieval class-state because it was an organisation of exploitation and sin; its tolerance of all creeds; its innate pacific and forgiving character, and its principle of selfless service in the sphere of social life. *Barani's God, as is quite clear from his works, has two aspects—first, He is the tribal deity of the Musalmans; secondly, as between the Musalmans themselves, He is the tribal deity of well-born Muslims.* No conception of God could have been more anti-mystical. Also to the very end of his life, *tasawwuf* meant nothing more to Barani than continuous fasting and numerous prayers. And his conception of religious devotions was purely mechanistic. Thus in estimating the influence of the great Shaikh[10], he only refers to the mechanistic elements of religion and has no idea that the Shaikh's mission, though it included formal devotions, was for something really higher. Barani admits that Sultan Alauddin and his family were believers in Shaikh Nizamuddin. This is correct. But it is curious to find him adding: "What a heart was Alauddin's and how negligent and reckless! People came to see Shaikh Nizamuddin from two thousand and three thousand *farsangs,* and the young and the old, the literate and the illiterate from the City tried to present themselves before the Shaikh by every means they could. But it never came to Sultan Alauddin's mind that he should pay a visit to the Shaikh or invite the Shaikh to meet him."[11]

Barani, the ex-courtier who was trying to be readmitted to the royal circle, seems to have thought that the great Shaikh would have gone running to the Hazar Sutun Palace, if he got Alauddin's invitation. But Alauddin knew better. Nothing but force could have taken the great Shaikh to the Royal Palace and nothing but force could have enabled Sultan Alauddin to break into the Shaikh's *khanqah*. The spiritual elements in Barani's life are not worth considering.

Still no one would go to Barani for the principles of religion. What makes Barani important for us is the fact that he concentrated his attention *on the basis of experience* on three important political problems—(a) the state laws, (b) the governing class and (c) the monarchy. It will conduce to clarity if we first discuss his theories of state laws and the governing-class, and examine his theory of monarchy after giving an account of his career.

REFERENCES

1. *Firoz Shahi,* p. 350.
2. Ibid., p. 204.
3. The term *Sultani* after the name of an officer means that he was a slave of the Sultan; but some people also adopted this title out of excessive loyalty.
4. *Firoz Shahi,* p. 32.
5. Ibid., p. 350.
6. Ibid., p. 127.
7. Ibid., pp. 248 and 255.
8. Ibid., p. 127.
9. Ibid., p. 9.
10. Ibid., pp. 341–47.
11. Ibid., p. 366.

CHAPTER IV

State Laws

It has been the habit of the Musalmans to talk as if the Muslim community did, or could, guide all its affairs in accordance with the *shari'at,* which is believed to be based on the Quran, the Prophet's precepts and *qiyas* (analogy). At the same time it is claimed that the door of *ijtihad* (or the formulation of new *shari'at* laws) was closed after the period of the great Abbasides (754–861 A.D.). Both postulates are incorrect. Early Muslim society was changing rapidly; the Pious Caliphs felt the need of new laws and had no hesitation in framing them. But the laws of the Pious Caliphs have been accepted as an integral part of the *shari'at* by the orthodox and so no difficulty arises. A very good example is the Caliph Umar's prohibition of temporary marriages.

The time of the Umayyads was a period of sectarian controversies and political conspiracies, which were brutally suppressed; and whether they liked it or not, a very stem political authority kept the Musalmans of the world together. By the end of the period of the great Abbasides, the standard collections of the Prophet's *hadises* had been made and the four schools of Sunni *shari'at* had been consolidated. At the same time the Central Caliphal power vanished; Islam expanding into foreign lands had to face new social conditions, which the *shari'at* had never contemplated and to which it could not be applied without disastrous consequences. Meanwhile monarchy, for which there could not be any pretence of 'general acceptance' or 'succession to the Prophet', arose in the lands of the Persians and the Turks, primarily because it meant a centralised authority for the public welfare. These newly-risen kings had to define their attitude towards religion and to declare what laws they would enforce. The easiest way of solving the first problem was to accept the religious sect, rites and traditions of the people and to employ a body of religious scholars, with decent salaries and proper honours but dismissible at will, for the religious and semi-religious functions of the state. These pliable, state-controlled *mullahs* have been called externalist scholars (*ulma-i zahiri*).[1] We must not forget that this was about the only well-paid profession open to the educated men of those days, regardless of their class origin. *The second problem led to a perplexing contradiction. The basis of 'shari'at-law' was canonical authority; the public good was not a relevant consideration.* If fornicators are to be thrashed, they must be thrashed everywhere, regardless of persons and traditions. If women have a right to inheritance, this right must be given to them everywhere, regardless of the fact that owing to local condition and traditions, such as the purdah-system, it is not possible for them to manage their properties. *But the basis of kingship was the public good; it could have had no other basis.* It is a brutal fact that the larger number of Muslim kings have come to a sad end, because lack of public support gave an opportunity to their opponents. Under these conditions wise kings adopted a policy of compromise and moderation. They paid lip homage to the *shari'at* and admitted their sinfulness if they were unable to enforce any of its provision; they kept the state-controlled *mullahs* disciplined and satisfied; over the whole field of administration concerning which the *shari'at* is silent or nearly silent, they made their own laws; if the traditional customs of the people were against the *shari'at,* they allowed them to override the *shari'at* under the designation of *urf. Thus state laws, called zawabit, grew under the protection of monarchy.* If these laws violated the *shari'at,* the principle of necessity or of *istihasan* (the public good) could be quoted in their favour. *And the back of the shari'at was broken for the primary reason that it had provided no means for its own development.* The great authority of Imam Ghazzali was quoted, correctly or otherwise, in favour of a compromise. Monarchy may be an illegitimate institution; the officers in charge may be bad men; but the affairs of the Muslim community had to be carried on. The fact that the imam (prayer-leader) of my mosque has been appointed by a bad king does not invalidate the prayers I say behind him. I can take my case to a *qazi* in spite of the fact that the country is governed by a bad king. It is an achievement of Barani that he has found a solution for this problem. Unfortunately, while his thoughts are clear, his words are conflicting. *Still he is the first theoretician to justify secular laws among the Musalmans and he deserves full credit for this achievement.*

In the time of Sultan Shamsuddin Iltutmish there flourished a great ecclesiastic, Saiyyid Nuruddin Mubarak Ghaznavi, who was generally called *Mir-i Delhi* (Leader of Delhi). Shaikh Abdul Haq in his *Siyarul Abrar* lists him among the mystics, but he was one of the *ulama-i zahiri* (externalist scholars) and represented their conscience, such as it was. Some fundamental postulates of his were reported to Barani and deeply influenced his young mind.

"I heard," Barani writes, "from my grandfather, Sipahsalar Hisamuddin, who was the *Vakildar* of the *Barbek* (Chamberlain)[3] of Sultan Balban that Balban repeatedly told his sons and confidential officers that he had twice heard Saiyyid Nuruddin Mubarak Ghaznavi make the following statements in his sermons to Sultan Shamsuddin Iltutmish:

"In all that the kings do concerning the necessary rules (*umur*) of kingship—the way in which they eat, drink wine and wear their royal robes, the manner in which they sit, get up, and go out riding, the order in which they sit on their thrones and compel the people to sit and perform the *sijdah* (prostration) before them—they follow with their hearts the customs of the *Kisras* (Persian emperors), who were rebels against God. In all their dealings with the people of God they claim super-human status (*fard*) for themselves; this too is opposed to (the teachings of) the Prophet; it is a claim to partnership in the attributes of God and a cause of damnation in the next world.

"Owing to the commission of the above acts, which are against the will or God and the traditions of the Prophet, the salvation of kings is not possible except by the implementation of the following four policies for the protection of the Faith:

"'*First,* the kings should protect the religion of Islam with sincere faith. They should utilise the power, dignity and prestige of their kingship, which is against the (moral) character of (God's) creatures, in establishing the supremacy of the True Word in elevating the customs of Islam, in enforcing the commands of the *shari'at* and in glorifying 'the order for the good and the prohibition of evil'. And kings will not be able to perform the duty of protecting the Faith unless, for the sake of God and the Prophet's creed, they overthrow and uproot *kufr* and *kafiri* (infidelity), *shirk* (setting partners to God) and the worship of idols. But if the total uprooting of idolatry is not possible owing to the firm roots of *kufr* and the large number of *kafirs* and *mushriks,* the kings should at least strive to insult, disgrace, dishonour and defame the *mushrik* and idol-worshipping Hindus, who are the worst enemies of God and the Prophet. The symptom of the kings being the protectors of religion is this. When they see a Hindu, their eyes grow red and they wish to bury him alive; they also desire to completely uproot the Brahmans, who are the leaders of *kufr* and *shirk* and owing to whom *kufr* and *shirk* are spread and the commandments of *kufr* are enforced. In order to maintain the honour of Islam and the prestige of the true Faith, they do not permit a *kafir* or *mushrik* to live with self-respect or to attain honour and independence among the Musalmans, or to pass his time in luxuries, enjoyments and pleasures, or to become the ruler of a people (*qaum*), group (*garoh*), territory (*wilayat*) or province (*iqta'*); also owing to the fear and terror of the kings of Islam, not a single enemy of God and the Prophet can drink water that is sweet or stretch his legs on his bed and go to sleep in peace.

"'The *second* policy necessary for the salvation of Muslim kings is this. The open display of sins and shameless deeds and the publication of forbidden things should be suppressed among the Muslim people and in the cities, territories and towns of Islam through the terror and power of kingship. Sinful and shameless deeds should, by excessive punishments and warnings, be made more bitter for sinners than poison. Persons who, in spite of their claim to be Musalmans, make dirty and shameful sins their livelihood and profession, and practise them all their lives, should be reduced by the kings to such distress that the world appears to them narrower than the circle of a finger-ring, and they are compelled to leave their professions and find other means of livelihood. If prostitutes, who work for hire (*mustajira*), are not prepared to give up their sinful ways, they should practise their profession secretly and not openly and proudly. But if prostitutes practise their profession in their own disgraceful quarters, and do not come out into the public, the practice of their profession should not be prohibited; for if the prostitutes are not there, many rascals driven by their sex-impulse will attack (Muslim) *harems.*

"'The *third* principle for the protection of the Faith, which leads to the salvation of kings, is this. The duty of enforcing the rules of the *shari'at* of the Prophet should be assigned to pious, God-fearing and religious men; dishonest and Godless people, who have no regard for the fights of others as well as cheats, swindlers and self-seekers—in fact all men who are in love with this world—should not be allowed to sit before the *mamad* (*pillow*) for enforcing the *shari'at* or given leadership in matters appertaining to the *tariqat* (mysticism) or assigned the duty of giving *fatwas* (legal opinions) or the teaching of religious sciences. Philosophers and believers in rationalistic philosophy should not be allowed to live in the land; the teaching of philosophical sciences should not be permitted under any circumstances. The kings should strive to insult and degrade men of bad sects, bad dogmas and the opponents of the orthodox Sunni creed; and none of them should be given any office in the government.

"'The *fourth* principle, which is necessary for the protection of the true creed and the salvation of kings, is the administration and enforcement of justice. The kings will not have performed their duty in this respect unless they strive to their utmost in the enforcement of justice and are just in every matter; and, owing to the fear of the authority of the kings, oppression and cruelty are eliminated from their kingdoms and all oppressors are overthrown.

"'Whenever (Muslim) kings implement these four policies with firm determination and sincere faith and establish truth at the centre through the terror and prestige of their royal authority, *then even if their souls are polluted by sinful desires and in the necessary acts of kingship they have even acted against the Sunnah, their status will be among the religious people and owing to their protection of the Faith, their place on the Day of Judgment will be among the prophets and saints.* On the other hand, if a king recites a thousand *rak'ats* (genuflections) of prayer every day, fasts all his life, does not go near things forbidden and spends the whole of his treasure in charity, but neither protects the Faith by using his royal power and authority for overthrowing and uprooting the enemies of God and the Prophet, nor glorifies the orders for the good and the prohibition of the evil in his provinces and territories, nor tries to enforce justice to the greatest extent possible his place will be nowhere except in Hell.'"

The words and style are Barani's but the ideas might well have been the ideas of Nuruddin Mubarak, which went deep into Barani's mind and found expression later on in the *Fatawa-i Jahandari*. The only important element which Barani added to these postulates was the right of the noble-born to govern the country.

The basic principles of the great ecclesiastic's thoughts deserve to be carefully examined: (a) All non-Muslims are classed, not as co-worshippers of God but as His enemies; *so Allah,* whom the Quran calls 'the Lord of the Worlds' 'on whose nature mercy is engraved[4], *becomes the tribal deity of the Musalmans.* (b) *This conception is further strengthened by the theory of Islam as a plundering creed, which was to proceed entirely by force.* There is no question of any discussion with the non-Muslims or of persuading them in any way; the resort is to be entirely to war and force, through the royal authority, (c) *Still the most terrible 'kafirs' of the day were the Mongols,* who had slaughtered the inhabitants of one Muslim city after another and were hovering on the frontiers of India. Whether Nuruddin Mubarak's precious sermon was delivered in the reign of Chengiz or Ogtai is immaterial. Iltutmish was in no position to challenge the Mongol empire; and severe Mongol attacks of the type which Alauddin Khilji managed to survive would have crushed Iltutmish completely. He had neither the administrative capacity and driving power of Alauddin nor his military genius, and it was no secret that he had sought to avoid a conflict with Chengiz Khan by refusing to offer an asylum to Jalaluddin Mankbarni. *So Nuruddin Mubarak selected the Hindus as the easier target. It was a cowardly choice.* But would the Delhi empire survive an anti-Hindu policy of the type demanded by him? The answer of responsible kings, as Barani admits, was in the negative. (d) *The king's office, though a violation of the 'shari'at', is recognised and he is authorised to act against the sunnah; still if he fights the non-Muslims in a manner that (according to the highest authorities of the Muslim religion) would have horrified the Arabian Prophet, he is to rise from the dead among the prophets and saints.* The dignity of the *shari'at* is affirmed and there is no reference to royal laws (or *zawabit*); *still the power of the king to override the shari'at is admitted.* (e) *The 'shari'at' punishments for the professions of sin are completely ignored;* the necessity of the continuation of these professions—in any case of the profession of prostitutes defined as women who live by the wages of sin (*mustajira*)—*is* emphasised; their profession is to be degraded and continued under state-control.

Barani, after expanding the precepts of Nuruddin Mubarak in Advice XI of the *Fatawa-i Jahandari,* complains that Muslim kings had no intention of following his directions. This is certainly true of Balban. He was frankly not in a position to march against the Hindu Rais from fear of the Mongols and made this fact clear to his high officers.[5] And Alauddin, who could fight both the Mongols and the Rais, wisely kept the public opinion of his Hindu subjects on his side.

Barani continues: "Balban repeated these precepts of Saiyyid Nuruddin Mubarak Ghaznavi to Sultan Shamsuddin Iltutmish, which he had himself heard, again and again, before his sons, nephews and officers and wept bitterly. *'I cannot fulfil the duties of protecting the Faith,' he told them, 'and how can I entertain such an ambition when my masters[6] themselves were unable to protect the Faith.* But I can at least come to the rescue of the oppressed and have no regard for any man in the enforcement of justice. You, my sons and relations, should take care of your steps.

If I come to know of your oppression of any weak person, I will punish you for it. In most cases I will put the murderers of innocent persons to death.[7] Your near relationship to me and your claims of service will not prevent me from administering impartial justice.' "

The problem of state-laws, so far as the *Tarikh-i Firoz Shahi* is concerned, is illustrated by the discussion between Sultan Alauddin and Qazi Mughisuddin of Bayana. But Barani had no access to Alauddin's court and he is mistaken in thinking that Alauddin's economic reforms were due, in the first instance, to his desire to bring the prices of commodities within the compass of the salaries of the soldiers. The real reason that inspired Alauddin is given by Shaikh Nasiruddin Chiragh in his *Khairul Majalis* on the authority of Qazi Hamid Multani.[8] Qazi Hamid on entering the Sultan's chamber one day found him sitting on the throne (*tang*), beating the ground with his feet, bare-headed, bare-footed and wholly absorbed in some thought. The, Qazi went before the Sultan but the latter did not notice him. He came out and informed Malik Qara Beg. Then the two entered the chamber and Qara Beg engaged the Sultan in conversation. Later on, Qazi

Hamid asked the Sultan what he had been thinking about. 'Hear me!' Sultan Alauddin replied, 'For some time a thought has been coming to my mind. God has so many people in this world but He has put me in command of them. *Now I should do something so that the benefit of my work may reach all mankind.* But what can I do? If I distribute all the treasures I have—and a hundred times more—they will not suffice for all. If I add all the (royal) villages and provinces to them, this too will not suffice. I have been thinking what to do so that I may benefit all men. Just now a thought has come to me, which I will explain. If I reduce the price of grain, the benefit of it will accrue to all. But how is the price of grain to be reduced? I will order the *naiks* or the provinces (*atraf*) to be summoned, so that they may bring the grain of the provinces to Delhi. Some will bring grain on 10,000 and others on 20,000 beasts of burden. I will give them robes of honour, silver and the expenses of their families, so that they may bring grain and sell it at the price I fix.'

The *Khairul Majalis* stops here, but it appears that Alauddin kept on thinking of the measures that were necessary for securing his main objectives—the elimination of famines and the establishment of economic security and stability on the principle of production-cost. It was not possible to work miracles. But he could ensure the safety of roads, see to the proper transport of commodities, crush monopolies, prevent regrating, and ensure that the prices fixed by him on the principle of production-cost were strictly maintained. Since most commerce and industry was in the hands of certain Hindu classes, he would work through them and control them. It was a strange dream, which no Muslim king has had before or since. But Alauddin was a man of action and the economic system he built up lasted during the remaining ten years of his life.

The laws of the *shari'at* were irrelevant to the objectives. Alauddin had in view and he paid no attention to them. He also paid no attention to the *mullahs* in state-service and, their doctrines, and left Qazi Hamid Multani to manage them on behalf of the state. But from where did Alauddin get this curious idea of serving all people? From a direct study of the Quran and possibly the teachings of Shaikh Nizamuddin Aulia.[9]

For the Quran, read in the original or in translation but without the misinterpretation of the commentators, will convince anyone that it is deeply concerned with the removal of human distress. The Prophet, as the head of the state, demanded taxes, or rather alms (*khairat*), for the expenses of the state and assistance to the distressed groups specified in the Quran—orphans, travellers people in temporary distress (*masakin*), poor persons who are incapable of working (*fuqra*) and persons who, though in great want, had too much self-respect to ask any individual for assistance. For the Prophet the only justification for the taxes or alms demanded by the government—and for him the distinction between taxes and alms was immaterial—was that the government would spend them in the relief of distress. 'Take from the rich and give it to. the poor,' was his instruction to the governor of Yemen. His own standard of living in house, clothes and food was roughly equivalent to that of a moderately provided Indian peasant of today, and a very important aspect of his life was his struggle with the material distress around him. Our modern conception of a welfare state depends upon our hope of improving the material and cultural conditions of the people by improvements in the instruments of production. No such conception was possible in the seventh century. All that the Prophet could visualise was that the government should be a machinery for relief and rehabilitation. But though the taxes had to be low, the object was attainable, and to a very great extent if was attained with reference to Arabian standards of life.

Now the great 'mujtahids' of Islam, who deserve to be highly respected and who should not be blamed in the matter, completely overlooked this aspect of the *Quranic teaching and the Prophet's state.* They merely laid down the principle that a man who had a good income should give 2½ per cent of it in charity for the removal of immediate distress; it was a religious obligation and the government had nothing to do with if. If a man gave more in charity, it was commendable but no binding. They could not possibly have expected that this small amount would suffice for relieving the distress of the classes mentioned by the Quran. But the conditions of the time should not be forgotten. *Monarchy, miscalled Caliphate, had come with the Umayyads and the Abbasides,* and *it* was supported by a well-organised bureaucracy whose members were appointed and could be dismissed by the ruler. *The taxes were taken for the expenditure of the government and not for the public welfare.* The government was expected to do something for education and culture, but this depended upon its discretion; and the government naturally spent money on this head in a way calculated to strengthen its own power. Now the great *mujtahids* lived during the period of the early. Abbasides (754-861 A.D.), and though there are some stories connecting Imam Shafi'i with Harun Rashid, the other founders of the Sunni schools were independent of the government. Also it was, as Shaikh Junaid said, a time of terror (*azmana-i wahshat*). It is conceivable that the great *mujtahids* could have framed laws for securing the objectives of the Quranic injunctions and the Prophet's state under these changed circumstances, and advised their successors to do the same from time to time. This would have given us a developing *shari'at.* But it is very doubtful if anything the *mujtahids* said about the state would have been considered binding by the rulers and the governing class or changed the course of history. In any case, as Barani correctly points out, the founders of the four schools decided to ignore all matters concerning the state, and no real guidance from them was available except for the fact that they recorded what the Prophet and the Pious Caliphs had done and said under very different conditions of life. *So quoting the 'shari'at'—as promulgated by the acknowledged 'mujtahids'—with reference to state-affairs was absurd.* The *ulama-i zahiri*, like Saiyyid Nuruddin Mubarak Ghaznavi, may promulgate their personal interpretations with a view to the welfare of their own class and profession. But there is no authority for such cheap postulates. "The government of the modern world, and in particular of Hindustan, is not possible in accordance with the *shari'at,*" Ferishta, who had witnessed the reforms of Akbar, declared while speaking of the reforms of Alauddin. The orders of the *shari'at* were, of course, still binding in the sphere of personal laws, e.g. inheritance, marriage, divorce and some other matters such as the prohibition of usury or interest.

Seen in the perspective of history, it appears clear that if a well-defined Quranic objective, specially in the social sphere, came into conflict with a law of the *shari'at* or even a law of the Quran itself, *the Quranic objective should have prevailed.* For law has no meaning except with reference to an end or object; also the law has been made for the fulfilment of man and not man for the fulfilment of the law. A non-Muslim might imagine that according to the general faith of the Musalmans, a Quranic injunction would cancel a *hadis* and a *hadis* would cancel a precept of the *mujtahids.* That should have been the normal procedure, whether we consider the *authority* that gives an injunction or *the proofs available* of that injunction having been given. The Quran has been preserved with absolute correctness, but too many unauthentic *hadises* have been set afloat, while for many precepts of the *mujtahids* we have only an indirect evidence and not their written word. But the medieval *mullahs* looked at the matter from a different angle. They did not—and they could not—prevent an educated Musalman from reading the Quran and guiding himself by his own interpretation of it in the realm of faith. But in the sphere of the *shari'at* it was different. The basic claim of every school was that its *mujtahids* could not have committed any error. If an injunction of the Quran or a *hadis* seemed on the face of it to contradict the precept of a *mujtahid,* it had to be reconciled with that precept by means of strained interpretations called *ta'wil. Consequently the shari'at of Islam is what the 'mujtahids' of the period of the great Abbasides* (754-861 A.D.) *have made it. There has been no 'ijtihad' since then.* Later law-books, like the great *Hidayah,* are really compilations. But the greatest of human thinkers, as the late Mr. H.A.L. Fisher remarks in his *History of Europe,* cannot anticipate all the capacities of life to present new formations. With the passage of time a great change took place. *To say that the door of 'ijtihad'* (*legislation*) *was closed would not be correct; that door can never be closed. But the power of 'ijtihad' was taken from the 'ulama' by a greater authority. The new 'mujtahid' was the state.* The door of the old type *ijtihad* had to be closed so that the door of the new *ijtihad,* state legislation, might be opened. But the stupid prattle about the *shari'at* has continued. It was, and has been, the duty of a good Musalman to praise the *shari'at* and demand its enforcement, but there has been an even greater duty to evade its enforcement on the basis of 'practical reason'.

These considerations should be kept in mind in examining the conversation which Barani records as having taken place between Sultan Alauddin Khilji and Qazi Mughisuddin of Bayana. The conversation turned round four questions asked by the Sultan.[1]

(1) *The position of the Hindus as tax-payers.* The Qazi repeated with reference to the Hindus what text-books like the *Hidayah* written in Iraq, Persia and Central Asia had said about insulting the helpless non-Muslim minorities in those lands. But Alauddin

was not concerned with Hindus in general but with the Hindu *chiefs—chaudhuris, khots* and *muqaddams—who* had not been paying him taxes. This point has been clarified by Mr. Moreland in the *Agrarian System of Moslem India.*

(2) *The 'shari'at' punishment to be meted out to government servants guilty of corruption, bribery, making up false accounts, etc. The Qazi declared that the matter had not been discussed by the 'shari'at' and he had not read about this question in any book.* So the Sultan could punish the defaulters in such a way as he deemed fit; but the *shari'at* punishment of cutting the hand was not applicable to those who stole from the public treasury.

(3) *The treasures brought from Deogir.* Alauddin had kept them separate from the public treasury on the ground that they had been acquired by him before his accession to the throne. The Qazi declared that hey were acquired through the strength of the army of Islam and should, therefore, belong to the public treasury. But since the Sultan controlled the public treasury in his discretion, the point was purely academic.

(4) *The claim of the Sultan and his family on the royal treasury. The 'shari'at' is silent on the matter and there had been no 'shari'at' restrictions on royal expenditure at any time.* Whatever the Qazi said was on his own responsibility. There were four alternatives: (a) According to the traditions of the Prophet and the Pious Caliphs, which no king had followed, the Sultan could take the salary he gave to his well-equipped troopers (i.e. 234 *tankas* a year). (b) In the alternative he could take the salary he gave to his highest officers. (c) Thirdly, worldly religious scholars (*ulama-i dunya*) had permitted a Sultan to take, for the maintenance of his dignity, an amount substantially higher than he gave to his highest officers. (d) But more than this could not be justified except on the ground of state policy (*maslahit-i mulki*).

The Sultan then gave an account of the punishments he had been inflicting. 'Are they all against the *shari'at*?' he asked. The Qazi replied, 'They are all against the *shariat;* for it has not been declared in the precepts of the Prophet or the judgments of the *ulama* that the head of the state (*ulul amr*) can do whatever he likes for the execution of his orders.' The Qazi's contention was that Alauddin's severe punishments were not authorised by the *shari'at;* he could not say what punishments should be inflicted in accordance with the *shari'at*, for the *shari'at* was silent. The whole conversation assumes that the king has the power of making laws, but that severe punishments, unless authorised by the *shari'at*, should be considered a violation of the *shart'at* because they are a violation of humanity.

Barani discusses at some length the laws (*zawabit*) as well as the new designs (*aslub*) of Mohammed bin Tughlaq. But he does not raise the question of *shar'iat-law* v. state-law in his account of that Sultan, and only comments on the practical consequences of his measures.[11]

Barani's final opinion on the state and its laws is to be found in the thesis he puts in the mouth of Bughra Khan: "Only that ruler can in truth and justice be called and deemed a king in whose territory no man goes to sleep naked and hungry, and who makes laws (*zawabit*) and frames measures (*mawazin*) owing to which no subject of his has to face any material distress (*darmandgi*) from which there is a danger to his life."[12]

This may be considered his last word in the matter; there was nothing more that could be expected under medieval conditions of production.

REFERENCES

1. The late Maulana Abul Kalam Azad calls them *ulama-i su* or the *'wicked mullahs.'*
2. *Firoz Shahi*, pp. 41–44.
3. That is, Malik Bektars.
4. *Kataba ala' nafsihir rahmah.*
5. *Firoz Shahi*, pp. 50–51.
6. Masters here would mean Shahabuddin Ghori and Iltutmish.
7. That is, he would not allow a murderer to escape the death penalty by paying money compensation to the heirs of the murdered man. *Firoz Shahi*, p. 44.
8. *Khairul Majalis*, ed. K.A. Nizami, p. 241.
9. Barani greatly underrates Alauddin's knowledge of Islam. He was surrounded by educated people and must have learnt the contents of the Quran and the Islamic creed from them. Shaikh Nuruddin Chiragh, who was then in charge of the

great Shaikh's charities leaves us in no doubt that Alauddin's reforms were cordially approved by the circle of the great Shaikh.

10. *Tarikh-i Firoz Shahi*, pp. 289–296.
11. It was not to be expected, however, that the *ulama* would not object to the Sultan's measures. The Sultan during the famine ordered wells to be dug outside Delhi and provided all the necessary requisites for agriculture. Maulana Afifuddin Kashani, a famous legist, objected to it because this agricultural work was being done by compulsion for the royal granaries. Sultan Mohammed imprisoned him and then set him free. But some time afterwards the Sultan heard that he had spoken against him to two other legists and he had all the three put to death. (Ibn Batuta, *Ajaibal Asfar*, Urdu tr. by Khan Saheb Muhammad Husain, Vol. II, p. 142)
12. *Firoz Shahi*, p. 148.

CHAPTER V

The Governing Class

No person could have obtained the position of Sipahsalar Hisamuddin in Balban's court unless he had been of pure Turkish birth, for Balban was a faddist on the question of birth and genealogy, and so probably were the senior members of Barani's own family. They seem to have cruelly driven it into his young mind that owing to his high birth he was above the mass of mankind. Personal misfortunes drove him to make this childhood conceit into a philosophy of life, and though he could never find a single theological text in support of his birth-theory, he nevertheless called in religion and the Divine design to support it. (Advice XXI) The Turkish officers at the time of Barani's birth were divided into two groups—those who had attained to high office as slaves, and sometimes called themselves *'sultani'*; and those who had entered government service as free men. Barani's family seems to have belonged to the latter group, for at some places he refers to the cash-purchased (*zar-kharida*) slaves with contempt.

But his family must have been living in India for many generations and lost all contacts with foreign lands, long before these relations were severed by the Mongol invasions. Unlike his friend, Amir Khusrau, he shows no knowledge of Turkish; and there are no Turkish words in his works except the titles in general use. His ignorance of the geography of Central Asia and Persia is surprising. Barani nowhere calls himself a Turk in the three works of his that are available, and in his modes of thought and feeling he is hundred per cent Indian. His governing class theory, though he is unaware of the fact, is the philosophy of the popular Hindu caste-system put into a Muslim mould. The mould, as we shall see, did not fit in popular Hinduism postulated that God had created men in separate castes and that it was the duty of the law to prevent 'a mixture of castes'. Nothing equivalent to it is found in the scriptures of the Jews, the Christians and the Musalmans. Only a person very deeply imbued with the traditions of the Hindu caste-system, like Barani, could have had the courage to state that piety was only within the reach of persons of good-birth. Today we only know of the Turks who settled in India from our records. They are not to be found anywhere in the country. Probably even in the time of Barani the process of the merger of the Turks with the Indian Muslims had already begun, though in the sphere of politics they were distinct and hostile groups. The Turks could only have maintained their separate social entity by refraining from marrying Indian women, but this they refused to do; so while many persons claimed to be Turks on their paternal side, their homes and with it the ideology of their children became more and more Indianised with every generation.

Islam taught that all men were equal and brothers, and it secured this equality within the Islamic fold to an extent that had not been possible for any group before. Nevertheless, the old ideas persisted; also no government could exist without a governing class before modern inventions made democracy possible. Consequently the whole of Persian literature is full of contemptuous references to the lower orders on the ground of birth. It was the same in the conversation of well-born persons. Still too much insistence should not be laid on this fact, for a very important section of the Muslim intelligentsia came from the lower middle class or the upper working classes.

Barani's theory of birth has a basic contradiction of which he was not conscious. The only nobility that mattered to him was the official bureaucracy of a unified state. He did not care for merchants and other classes, however prosperous, nor did he know of any such social order as the feudal aristocracy of medieval Europe; when he saw something similar to it, he condemned it like most Muslim political thinkers as *tawaiful muluki* or oligarchic anarchy, for it was incompatible with the implementation of state-laws and, in fact, with the state.

With reference to pre-Muslim times, it was easy for Barani to say that every government office was hereditary, though a slight reflection would have convinced him that such an arrangement would have led to the disintegration of the state. Barani has a very clear idea of the Umayyads and Abbasides as governing class states, the latter having been built on the ruins of the former. Then his knowledge becomes dim, but as he surveyed the Sultanate of Delhi for a century and a half, he saw the governing groups being overthrown one after another. The picture in Advice XXII is fairly well drawn, but it is based primarily on the experience of the Delhi Sultanate.

In order to understand Barani's ideas, the three principles that lay at the basis of the normal Muslim state should be borne in mind. The Prophet and the Pious Caliphs appointed officers for specific duties; their office ended when their duties had been discharged but they could also be dismissed at the discretion of the head of the state. Amir Mu'awiya established the system of Muslim monarchy. *First,* he organised a bureaucracy or governing class from the noble Arab clans; all officers were appointed by the head of the state and they could at any time be dismissed by him, *Secondly,* the head of the state had the right to nominate his successor, or series of successors, but the person nominated would only ascend the throne if accepted by the high officers; if dissatisfied, these officers could select another person from among the sons and brothers of the late ruler. *Thirdly,* when Islamic religious sciences had been reduced to writing in the time of the great Abbasides and their teaching had been put on a proper basis, a group of officers for religious and semireligious functions—*the ulama-i zahiri* or state-controlled scholars—was also organised on the same lines as the bureaucracy; its members were appointed and dismissed at his discretion by the head of the state.

This framework lasted so long as the Muslim monarchy lasted, but within this framework any number of revolutions were possible. Nevertheless Muslim states, generally speaking, have never tolerated a hereditary bureaucracy or a hereditary ecclesiastical class though the head of state was expected to have due regard for the relations of his deceased servants. They have also not tolerated a hereditary landed aristocracy (barring some exceptions such as the *dihqans* of Persia and the *rais, ranas* and *rawats* of the Delhi Sultanate); a landed aristocracy, when it appears, is generally due to the fact that the officers have seized the land assigned to their charge and the state is disintegrating.

After postulating that (a) nobility goes by descent because the sons of the nobles alone are noble and (b) that the nobles have the exclusive right to government offices, Barani finds it impossible to define a noble family. The governing groups had been destroying each other too rapidly. All that Barani could have meant by a noble family was a family the members of which had held high offices for three or four generations; conversely, if a family was effectively and permanently deprived of high offices, it ceased to be noble and took its place with the masses.

The main bureaucratic revolutions noted by Barani are the following:

(1) Shahabuddin was succeeded by his slave-officers, but Shamsuddin Iltutmish had to overthrow Yilduz and Qubacha and their officers in order to establish his power.

(2) Iltutmish organised a part of his bureaucracy from the old slave-officers of Shahabuddin and their descendants, but in order to balance them, he formed another wing of his bureaucracy from the noble-born and educated men who had fled to his capital from Muslim lands conquered by the Mongols.

(3) The death of lItutmish led to a conflict between the two wings. During the reign of his successors, the great Turkish slave-officers, known as the *Chahalgani* (or the Forty), obtained control over the affairs of the government and removed the free-born *maliks* and nobles. "The people of the time saw clearly that till great men and nobles are not overthrown, worthless and cash-purchased slaves do not attain to high office and leadership."[1]

(4) Since all the Chahalgani Turkish officers considered themselves equal to each other and everyone of them proclaimed, 'I and none other,' there was a period of anarchy for some thirty years (1236-1266) and the authority of the central power vanished. Balban (1266-1287) restored the authority of the central power by annihilating his rivals; still he was a great faddist for birth and kept the Turkish aristocracy intact. But during the reign of Kai-Qabad, his minister, Malik Nizamuddin, though himself from an old Turkish stock, had many Turkish officers executed by the Sultan's orders. Thus the backbone of the remnant of the old Turkish slave-bureaucracy was broken, and Aitmar Kachchin and Aitmar Surkha were unable to prevent the accession of Sultan Jalaluddin Khilji. But Jalaluddin was not the man to push a revolution to its

inevitable conclusion and he confirmed many Turkish officers of the old regime in their posts.

(5) Alauddin won over the officers of the uncle he had murdered through offers of gold and re-appointment to their posts. "But in the second or the third year of his reign, when his authority had been fully established, all the former officers of Jalaluddin, who had deserted their old master's family and joined Alauddin and taken *mans* of gold and offices and territories from him, were seized in the City and the army. Some were thrown into forts and imprisoned; others were blinded or killed. All the money they had obtained from Alauddin, along with their own wealth, houses and properties, was seized. Their houses were made *state-property* (*sultani*), their villages were brought back to the *khalsa*, and nothing was left for their children. Their soldiers and servants were put in the charge of Alauddin's officers and their families were overthrown."[2] Three of the old officers, with the surnames of Alvi, Khilji and Rana, Barani tells us, were spared[3]; the rest were totally uprooted. Most of the officers thus punished must have been the descendants of Balban's officers—men of true Turkish blue blood whose ancestors had come into prominence as slave-officers, Alauddin demanded efficiency and obedience; blue blood meant nothing to him. Also these officers of the old regime were accustomed (as Barani himself makes clear) to conspiring against the king. The new schemes Alauddin had in mind would have failed if officers of the old regime, accustomed to considering themselves as God's chosen families, had been kept in office. This is the greatest single act of suppression of the *amirs* or officers of a former regime that took place in the history of the Delhi Sultanate and it was very thorough. The suggestions for treating a fallen official regime with which no compromise is possible, offered by Barani in Advice XXII, may have been suggested to him by this situation.

(6) Barani, curiously enough, does not bring the charge of low birth and mean origin against the officers of Alauddin Khilji. Their fathers and grandfathers had not held high offices but they may have worked in the lower government posts which were open to non-nobles. Alauddin's control was stern, but his officers were able men and he gave them the discretionary powers they needed. Barani divides Alauddin's officers into three

generations. The first generation, led by the six, officers who had conspired to assassinate Sultan Jalaluddin, was brilliant. The second generation was competent and able, and Barani has great respect for it. In the third generation of Alauddin's officers too many 'Yes men' had crept in while for reasons unknown he put to death his great Minister of Revenue, Sharaf Qaini. Still, subject to the mishaps of medieval politics and in spite of the enormous strain put on it during the reign of Mohammad bin Tughlaq the continuity of Alauddin's bureaucracy was maintained till the end of Mohammad bin Tughlaq's reign. Thus at the beginning of Alauddin's reign we find Mohammad Ayaz Kotwal of Siri; his son, Khwaja-i Jahan Ahmad Ayaz, was Mohammad bin Tughlaq's *Naib* (Deputy) at Delhi when the Sultan died. Qutbuddin Mubarak Shah, to the surprise of all, re-appointed the high officers of his father, and they maintained his empire intact for him. Ghiasuddin Tughlaq Shah was himself a bureaucrat, and as far as possible he maintained the status and dignity of his former colleagues. Two royal favourites, Malik Kafur and Khusrau Khan, whose stories are well-known, tried to dominate the bureaucracy, but the main body of *maliks* and *umara* managed to survive both.

Mohammad bin Tughlaq's policy towards the bureaucracy can only be briefly reviewed here. All the three great authorities on his reign—Barani, Isami and Ibn-i Batuta—are firm in stating that he was a great shedder of blood.[4] There was something in his ways and manners that excited the suspicion of even his highest officers from the very beginning of his career. Thus when he was besieging Warangal in the reign of his father, four great *maliks* of his army—Tamar, Tigin, Mal Afghan and Kafur Muhrdar—marched back from the fort with their men because Ubaid, the poet, had convinced them that, since they were Sultan Alauddin's officers of standing and presumably co-partners in the kingdom, Mohammad bin Tughlaq (who had the title of Ulugh Khan at the time) would seize and behead them all on the same day. Similarly when the Sultan, owing to the famine, had moved to Sargdwari along with the inhabitants of Delhi, he was so pleased with the efficiency of Ainul Mulk in providing grain for his men that he decided to promote him from the governorship of Zafarabad to the Viceroyalty of Deogir in place of his former teacher, Qutlugh Khan. But Ainul Mulk got frightened, and though not a fighting man, decided to rebel.[5] The rebellion of Bahram Aibah (Kishlu

Khan), the governor of Multan, who had been a comrade in arms of Tughlaq Shah and was one of the senior-most officers of the empire, was due to a similar misunderstanding. Bahram was driven to take firm steps against an agent of the Sultan on account of his insolence. The Sultan refused to hear any explanations and marched against Bahram, and Bahram considered it a point of honour to die fighting.[6] *Still the Sultan succeeded in keeping the majority of the officers, high and low, of the homelands of the empire loyal to himself.*

It was otherwise with the lower officers of the distant provinces of the empire. When the Sultan appointed Aziz Himar, 'the Iow-born', governor of Dhar and the whole of Malwa, he instructed him as follows: 'I hear that everyone who rebels does so owing to the support of the *amiran-i sadah* (*sadah amirs:* commanders of one hundred) and the *amiran-i sadah* support him owing to their anger (at the imperial policy) and love of plunder'. Aziz Himar summoned eighty-nine *sadah amirs* and ordered their heads to be cut off.[7] This started the conflagration which cost the Sultan all his Deccan possessions. "It did not occur to the mind of this doomed and low-born man (Aziz Himar)", Barani remarks, "that if being an *amir-i sadah* was a sufficient offence for the infliction of the death-penalty, then wherever there are *sadah-amirs*—in Deogir, Gujarat and elsewhere—they will all be embittered and rise in rebellion. And how will the army of the country be maintained, if the *sadah-amirs* are embittered and rebel? The news of the slaughter of the *sadah-amirs* of Dhar, on account of their being *sadah-amirs,* reached Deogir and Gujarat. Consequently the *sadah-amirs* of these two provinces became vigilant and made preparations for rebellion."[8]

The term, *amir-i sadah,* has not been used by other historians of the reign, but their position is not difficult to understand. In the advice he puts in the mouth of Bughra Khan, Barani explains the organisation of the army as follows[9]: "A *sarkhail* commands ten chosen horsemen; a *sipahsalar,* ten *sarkhails;* an *amir,* ten *sipahsalars;* a *malik,* ten *amirs,* a *Khan,* ten *maliks;* and a king should have at least ten *Khans* under his command." An *amir,* properly so-called, would be a commander of one thousand horse; and the higher bureaucracy consisted of *khans, maliks* and *amirs* only. The *amir-i sadah* of Barani are the *sipahsalars* of Bughra Khan. The strength of their position lay in the fact that they constituted the backbone of the army that had conquered the Deccan under Alauddin Khilji and were under no obligation to Mohammed bin Tughlaq.[10] When the Deccan territories were annexed, they would be spread out on the land. It there were ten horsemen at a *thana* or military post, an *amir-i sadah* would be commanding ten *thanas* or a territory of the size of a *parganah.* They maintained the whole administration of the conquered lands, and the Bahmani kingdom originated owing to their revolt. They could not have been men of noble birth and do not evoke Barani's sympathy.

Barani's great complaint against Mohammad bin Tughlaq is that he appointed Hindus and men of low-birth to high offices. "I have served the Court of Sultan Mohammad bin Tughlaq and obtained plenty of gold owing to his constant *inams* and gifts. I am surprised at the contradictory qualities of that king, who was a unique product of creation. During all this time I heard from his sacred lips stories concerning the contemptible and worthless character of men of low and mean origin. He would prove with arguments and illustrations that men of mean origin are ungrateful, untrue to their salt, mischievous and wicked. He talked as if he hated low-born people more than he hated idols. Nevertheless I have seen him promoting Najba, the low-born son of a musician, to such an extent that he rose higher in status than many *maliks;* for Gujarat, Multan and Badaun were put in his charge. Similarly, he raised Aziz Himar[11] and his brother, Firoz *Hajjam* (the barber), Manka *Tabbakh* (the cook), Masud *Khummar* (the vintner), Laddha *Baghban* (the gardener), and many other gems of low-birth (*jawahir lotrah*) to a high status and gave them offices and territories. He gave Shaikh Babu, the son of a Nayak weaver (*Nayak bachcha julaha*), a position near himself and elevated the ranks and position of such a low-born man among mankind. He assigned the *Diwan-i Wizarat* (Ministry or Revenue) to Pera *Mali* (the gardener), the *lowest* of the low-born and mean-born men of Hind and Sind, and placed him over the heads of *maliks, amirs, walis* and governors (*maqta's*). He assigned to Kishen (Krishna) Bazran Indri, who was the meanest of the mean-born, the territory of Oudh. To Muqbil, the slave of Ahmad Ayaz, who in appearance and character was a shame for all slaves, he gave the *wizarat* (governorship) of Gujarat, which had been a post for great *khans* and *wazirs.* It was strange how he gave high offices and governments of extensive territories and great provinces to men of low and mean birth."[12]

The professions indicated in the above surnames are the ancestral professions of the officers mentioned; the officers themselves, it has to be assumed, were highly educated and efficient men. Looking back at the matter through the distance of six centuries, we cannot but admire Mohammad bin Tughlaq for the breadth of his vision. The rapidity of the Turkish conquest of India, as I have tried to prove elsewhere,[13] was due to the fact that Hindu society was divided into two sections, between whom there was an impassable gulf—the four Aryan castes and the non-caste groups, the latter being the basic workers of India; also the fact that Muslim kings could sit on Indian thrones for five centuries after Shahabuddin Ghori was primarily due to the fact that their position was a guarantee to the working classes that the worst features of the caste-system would not return.

Barani conveys to us a wisdom of which he is himself unaware. India could not have been properly governed without help from the sons of the soil. The Slave Kings, unable to obtain that cooperation, merely made arrangements for the payment of revenue with the existing Hindu chiefs—*rais, ranas, rawats,* and (lower than them) the *chaudhuris, khots* and *muqaddams.* The government of the Delhi Sultanate could not be carried on without a knowledge of Persian as well as the local dialect just as the British Indian government needed a knowledge of both English and the provincial language. It is also obvious that while government work at the lowest level—e.g. that of the *patwari*—had to be carried on in the local language, for the higher officers a knowledge of Persian and of Muslim ways of life would be necessary.

But what *groups* of Hindus would be incited to learn Persian immediately after the Ghorian conquest? Not the great *rais,* who could employ interpreters for their slight administrative contacts with Delhi. The great merchants and bankers could employ interpreters, but they would find a knowledge of Persian at the conversational level useful. Now knowledge of conversational Persian is not hard to acquire for a north Indian; Persian verbs differ from those of the Indian languages, but a small percentage of nouns is the same, and the construction of sentences is similar. An illiterate Indian (whether Hindu or Muslim), if taken to Persia and compelled to shift for himself in a purely Persian environment, can learn to express himself in Persian in six to eight weeks. A Hindu in Alauddin's Delhi could have learnt to speak Persian almost effortlessly in five or six months.

But Persian at the clerical and, later on, at the literary level would be learnt by all members of the non-caste groups (whether converted to Islam or not) who were determined to better their lot by cooperating with the government of the day, which according to all sane calculations had come to stay. We find clear indications of progress in this respect. A new middle-class man emerges—the *nawisandah* or clerk. If Sharaf Qaini had the central revenues compared with the *patwari's* papers and exacted every *jital,* he must have had a large bilingual staff. If the number of *nawisandahs* undergoing punishments for their offences varied from 7,000 to 10,000, their total number (even if these figures are somewhat exaggerated) must have been fairly large.[14]

The membership of a governing-class, whatever the character of that governing-class, requires not only a common language and culture but also a common way of life—or at least a knowledge and tolerance of each other's ways of life. During the period of the Slave Kings, membership of the higher bureaucracy was dangerous for an Indian Musalman and impossible for a Hindu. But the Khilji Revolution seems to have brought about a change. Amir Khusrau in his *Khazainul Futuh*[15] tells us that Sultan Alauddin sent an army of thirty thousand horsemen under a Hindu officer. Malik Naik, the *Akhur-bek Maisarah,* against the Mongols, Ali Beg, Tartaq and Targhi. The position of low-born men (whether Hindus or Muslims) in the government of Mohammad bin Tughlaq was the natural culmination of a process covering a century and half. The list given by Barani is only of 'precious specimens' and not complete. Isami mentions Kandi Rai among the leading officers of Qutlugh Khan, the Viceroy of the Deccan, he also refers to the fact that a Hindu by the name of Bharan was the governor (*maqta'*) of Gulburga.[16] And even Barani can record a fact like the following without comment: "A *mehta* (Hindu administrative officer) was appointed to Kamal and its Rana, Kankhar, was brought captive before the Court."[17] But Barani (for good reasons as we shall see) had not the courage to name the greatest man in the list—Kanna, a Hindu convert, whom Mohammad bin Tughlaq promoted gradually to the post of the Naib Wazir of the empire.

These facts cannot fail to suggest some reflections. If every Rajput Rai had kept a composite government, inclusive of the non-caste groups, like that of Mohammad bin Tughlaq, a truly national resistance to the Turks would have been possible and Shahabuddin Ghori would have failed; and, in any case, the Turkish power in India would have been shortlived like the Mongol (or Yuan) dynasty of China. Secondly, these low-born men were a source of strength to the Sultan; even Barani's hostile account leaves us in no doubt about their loyalty. Thirdly, these low-born men were the only Hindus whose cooperation the Sultan could get. The *Rais* of his day would not have been willing to enter his service as imperial officers like the Rajput princes of Akbar's time. The fourth point is only a matter for speculation, but perhaps we are on the right track. The functions of the Kayasthas in the administrative and revenue history of India are well known. But it is said, perhaps correctly, that they are a profession and not a caste. Will we be justified in finding the origin of the Kayasthas in those Hindus who regardless of caste, began learning Persian in the thirteenth century, gradually acquired the culture of both the communities and ultimately made themselves indispensable in revenue and accounts?

Mohammad bin Tughlaq's relations with the mystics and the *ulama* need not be discussed here. Barani does not raise the question, and though some of them refused to serve the Sultan and others were tempted into his service, their careers as administrative officers were temporary and tragic. Mr. Khaliq Nizami after examining the whole evidence available comes to the following opinion: *It seems obvious that Mohammad bin Tughlaq wished to exact the same work from religious scholars and mystics as the Pious Caliphs had demanded from the learned and the pious—the service of the state.*[18] This is correct. But it was nevertheless an error. "Our religious scholars," Ibn-i Khaladun remarks, "are farthest removed of all men from political affairs."[19] Persons taken from religious circles, whether academic or mystic, as Mr. Khaliq Nizami frankly admits, could give no help to the Sultan in his administrative affairs, while some of them perished in the course of their service. An example should suffice. The Sultan, who was a *murid* (spiritual disciple) of Shaikh Alauddin, a grandson of the famous Shaikh Farid of Ajodhan, appointed Shaikh Muizzuddin, son of Shaikh Alauddin to the governorship of Gujarat. In consonance with Chishti mystic principles, the appointment should have been refused. But the temptation of becoming a provincial governor was too great. The Sultan ordered Muizzuddin to be given two lakhs of *tankas* so that he could organise a body of two or three thousand well-equipped horsemen and march with the royal standard. On reaching Anhilwara the Sultan ordered Muizzuddin to establish himself there with his officers while the Sultan himself marched to Mount Abu. But later on, when the Sultan had marched to the Deccan to suppress the first rebellion of the Deccan *sadah amirs* under Ismail Makh Afghan, Taghi, a shoemaker and a former slave of Safdar Malik Sultani, rebelled with the assistance of the village-headmen (*muqaddams*). His first step was to capture Anhilwara; he put to death Malik Muzaffar, who was a counsellor of Muizzuddin, but it suited his purpose to keep Muizzuddin and his officers as prisoners and hostages. Taghi had only a small and mobile army of rebels and Shaikh Muizzuddin's defence of Anhilwara must have been tragically inefficient. Later on, when the Sultan was hot in his pursuit, Taghi came to Anhilwara and put Muizzuddin and all his officers to death.[20] It is a sorry tale, which proves the correctness of Ibn-i Khaladun's remark. The *ulama,* in general, have confined themselves to the wiser policy of declaring academically as to how affairs should be conducted instead of undertaking the harder and more dangerous task of conducting them.

To sum up: The great-test of truth is experience. Barani's theory about state laws (*zawabit*) is correct because it was based on the administrative experience of the Delhi Sultanate. But it is not possible to discover any value, practical or theoretical, in his doctrine that the offices of the state should be the monopoly of the well-born and go by descent from father to son. He admits again and again that his doctrine will not work, but attributes its failure to the wickedness of Time and the revolving Sky!

REFERENCES

1. *Firoz Shahi*, pp. 26–27.
2. Ibid., pp. 250–251.
3. The surnames prove that they were not of Turkish descent.
4. The following paragraphs will give some idea of the impression left on Barani's mind by the bloodshed of

the regime: "Everyone of the aforesaid designs, when implemented in practice, led to disturbances, distress and ruin; the hearts of the select and the commons were filled with hatred of Sultan Mohammad; and firmly established regions and territories went out of hand. As his orders were not carried out in the way he wanted, the temper of the Sultan became worse and worse; and owing to the changed temper of the Sultan, people were beheaded like herbs and radishes. This work of killing Musalmans, who believed in one God and were Sunnis, was taken up by a body of wicked men, the like of whom have not been created from the time of Adam till today and even Hajjaj bin Yusuf did not deserve to be their slave or servant in the matter of wickedness—such were Zain Banda Mukhtasul Mulk; Yusuf Bughra; Khalil, son of the *Sar-Davatdar*; Mohammad Najib; the accursed Shahzada Rahwandi; Qaranful Sayyaf (Swordman); the accursed Aibah; Majir Abu Rijah, on whom be a hundred thousand curses of God; the son of Qazi Gujrat Ansari; and all the three wretched sons of Thanesari. They devoted themselves to nothing else except the killing of Musalmans. By God, it is my firm conviction that if twenty prophets had been assigned for being put to death to Zain Bandah, Yusuf Baghra and the worthless Khalil, they would not have allowed a night to pass before executing the order. The king was engaged day and night in the design of punishing the mischievous (*sharir*), and thousands of accused were put to death under this charge. The few above-mentioned persons, who have been the worst of men in this world and the next, were the chosen and specially trusted officers of his Court." (*Firoz Shahi*, pp. 471–472).

"With my own eyes I have seen that no day passed without Sunni Musalmans being beheaded like herbs and radishes, and a stream of Muslim blood being made to flow before the royal gate. They had organised a Department of Punishment and some wretched, irreligious people were appointed jurists (*mufti*) of this Department, while other persons, who were apostates and infidels in temperament, were appointed its officers, controllers and investigators. The work of punishment was carried to such an extent that the sky and the earth, the heavens and the angels, became sick of it and began to hate it." (*Firoz Shahi*, p. 497).

Under these circumstances Isami, a hostile critic, naturally reflects: "If the people of the country become of one mind and rebel with a united heart and suddenly attack this enemy of the Faith, it would not be surprising if they are able to throw his (severed) head on the ground." (*Futuhus Salatin*, p. 436). But not even an attempt to assassinate Mohammad bin Tughlaq has been recorded, and we always find him surrounded by officers sternly loyal.

5. *Tarikh-i Firoz Shahi*, pp. 489–491.
6. Isami, *Futuhus Salatin*, pp. 420–421.
7. *Tarikh-i Firoz Shahi*, pp. 503 and 507.
8. Ibid., p. 504.
9. Ibid., p. 145.
10. Thus 'Isami,' their spokesman, while condemning Mohammad bin Tughlaq, shows the greatest respect for Alauddin Khilji.
11. *Himar* literally means 'the ass'; this title was given to people out of regard for their physical stamina. But with the addition of a dot, it may be read as *Khummar*, meaning vintner.
12. *Tarikh-i Firoz Shahi*, pp. 504–505.
13. *Introduction to Elliot and Dowson*, Vol. II, Cosmopolitan Publishers, Badar Bagh, Aligarh. For the condition of the non-caste groups about 1030 A.D, see Sachau's translation of *Alberuni's India*, Vol. I, Chapter IX and Vol. II, Chapter LXIV. It is not certain when the *Manusmriti* was written, but the position it prescribes for the *chandalas* or non-caste groups is not substantially different from the account given by Alberuni on the basis of his personal observations. (*Code of Manu*, Buhler's translation, Chapter X).
14. *Tarikh-i Firoz Shahi*, pp. 296–296. Alauddin says: "Owing to the thefts of clerks (*nawisandahs*) and revenue-officers, perhaps I have reduced ten thousand clerks to destitution in the City and put worms into their bodies." See also p. 382, where Sultan Mubarak Shah is said to have set free six thousand or seven thousand prisoners of Alauddin Khilji at Delhi and sent fast runners with instructions to set free those in the provinces.
15. My translation, *Campaigns of Alauddin Khilji* (pp. 26–27). In his *Dawal Rani Khizr Khani*, Khusrau definitely declares that Malik Naik was a Hindu servant (*banda*) of the august Court. Barani also refers to Malik Nayak *Akhur-bek*, (p. 320) but does not definitely state that he was a Hindu.

16. Isami, *Futuhus Salatin,* pp. 457 and 464.
17. *Firoz Shahi,* p. 523.
18. *Religious Tendencies of the Delhi Sultans* (Urdu), p. 366.
19. *Muqaddama,* Ibn Khalddun (Urdu Translation, 1904), Vol. III, p. 216. "*Al ulama ab'adun nas 'nis sayasiyat.*"
20. *Tarikh-i Firoz Shahi,* pp. 508–518.

CHAPTER VI

Ziauddin Barani: Youth and Age

I

Ziauddin Barani talks as if he was the chosen victim of fate, but his life till his fall in 1351 seems to have been fairly comfortable. We do not know when his father died, but such indications about his life, as he has left us, make it clear that till about his fiftieth year he lived like a gentleman of leisure, leading that double life which till the last generation or two our Indian society considered to be the proper thing for rich citizens, and which as a general rule was not only tolerated but approved. His father had left him a large, perhaps a palatial, house at Kailugarhi, a suburb of Delhi which Sultan Muizzuddin Kai-Qabad had laid out as more suitable for his gay life. It is quite likely that after Kai-Qabad's death many dancing-girls, buffoons, musicians, *bhands* (jokers), etc., went on living in that suburb, where, they had built their houses. There was no prohibition of a gay life under Jalaluddin or Alauddin, provided law and order were not disturbed. According to Ferishta the rates for dancing-girls were also included in Alauddin's comprehensive tariff, so that the lives of young men might not be ruined. Here our author seems to have kept his slave-girls and musicians. For the more respectable aspect of his life, he built a house for himself at Ghiaspur, where he met his literary friends and where he led that life of externalist religion, which was necessary in the neighbourhood of the great Shaikh.

We have only Barani's own word for saying that he had led a life of pleasure; but he insists on the matter and there is no reason for disbelieving him. "On reading my own narrative of the pleasures enjoyed by that king (Kai-Qabad)", Barani writes in his *Tarikh-i Firoz Shahi.*[1] "and of the sensualists (*ayyash*), beauties, habitual lovers and heart-throwers of that reign, I become unconscious. And in my present condition, when owing to old age and weakness not a single tooth has remained in my gums, and I am distressed in mind and a victim of my opponents and bowed down by the kicks and blows of my enemies and rivals, I recollect my youth again as well as the pleasure-parties and enjoyments of the past, which I partook with noble-minded persons of high resolve. *In my 'majlis' (parties) there were plenty of beauties, witty persons, unrivalled humorists, women with excellent looks, rose-faced (beauties) with silvery shanks, cypress-statured 'saqis', young boys with sugary lips, distinguished musicians and ghazal-reciters.*[2] *It stings my heart!* Owing to the scarcity of these groups and owing to my lack of silver and gold, I am confined to my laborious and disgraced corner, afflicted, valueless and without a purchaser. What am I to do? To whom am I to take this *History* and ask for justice? I have, however, written these few pages about the events and memories of the Muizzi period. I have (also) composed with reference to the pleasure and enjoyment of Sultan Muizzuddin and his contemporaries a volume of *ghazals* (*ghazalha-i diwani*) in praise of the elegance of beauties and named it the *Qubbatut Tarikh.*[3] Had it come before the literary critics or the literary geniuses of the past, this cloud of sorrow would have been removed from my breast and the pain of my heart cured owing to their praise and justice. And by the soul of those masters of literature,[4] who were once my friends and companions, in the whole of Hindustan no literary man of eminence or master-author comes to my mind to whom I may take my works and owing to whose praise and justice I may feel satisfaction and peace in my dry and desolated heart. And if I try to send the aforementioned pages from every word of which enjoyment increases, to a man of wealth, who has a desire for the enjoyment (of the company) of men of wit and elegance or has the high resolve of noble souls, *then by that God, who has honoured me at the beginning and disgraced me at the end of my life,* I do not see such a cultured, aesthetic, courageous and noble-born person anywhere. And if in my impotence and helplessness I wish to find a *Khanzada* or a *Malikzada* who is cultured, desirous of pleasure, dissipated and capable of providing the means of comfort to others and who owing to his refined and cultured mind can obtain pleasure from the above-mentioned vain words of love and enjoyment, so that

I may deceive him and get gold out of him, then I swear by the nature and faces of coquettes (*nazninan*) and the grace and glances of moon-faced women that I can find no such young man or any trace of him. So helplessly I weep over my life and pass my days somehow. The despair that is in my heart flows in tears of blood from my eyes; a wave from the river of blood pours out of my eyes, drips from my pen and stains the paper."

It is a relief to look at the other side of Barani's life. He did not get any post in the reign of Alauddin Khilji; still he had access to all circles, except the highest Court circles, but even of these he came to know a lot. His father and uncle had been among the highest officers of the land and no house would close its doors to him. He was, for example, on intimate terms with officers like Malik Lara Beg. He had access to Shaikh Nizamuddin Aulia and his circle, and Amir Khurd in his *Siyarul Aulia* quotes a conversation between him and the great Shaikh from his extinct *Hasrat-Namah.* Our author gives the highest praises to the scholars of Alauddin's reign in the traditional as well as the rational sciences, and after giving a list of forty-six leading scholars of Delhi, he adds: "The forty-six scholars, whose names I have given are those with whom I have studied or before whom I have presented myself; I have met most of them at meetings and parties or have seen them when teaching."[5] Similarly when writing about the Saiyyids he observes: "The author of the *Tarikh-i Firoz Shahi* has had the good fortune of meeting Saiyyid Tajuddin and Saiyyid Ruknuddin and has performed the rite of kissing their feet. I have seldom seen Saiyyids with such dignity and orthodox virtues."[6] Our author lived at Delhi through the stormy reign of Alauddin Khilji, seeing everything, observing everything and discussing everything. Though occasionally he forgets the sequence of events, his account of Alauddin's reign is more complete than that of any other king. It was a period of terror, of achievement, of cultural advance and of material prosperity; and all its features sank deep into Barani's mind.

From his literary friends of the past, our author's memory selects two for special note, of whom anyone would have been proud—Amir Khusrau and Hasan—though one cannot but regret that Barani so completely abandoned their ideals after they were dead.

"In the time of Alauddin Khilji," he tells us,[7] "there were poets such as the eye of time has not seen since then—or even before. The incomparable Amir Khusrau has been the king of poets, ancient and modern.[8] He has no rival either in the number of his writings, the invention of new ideas or the explanation of hidden meanings. If the masters of prose and verse have been unrivalled in one or two branches, Amir Khusrau excelled in all branches.[9] Such a master-poet, who excelled in all branches of poetry, has not been seen in the past and may, or may not, be seen till the Day of Judgment. Amir Khusrau has written a whole library of prose and verse and has worked wonders in the art of composition. Khwaja Sanai[10] may have written the following verse in praise of Amir Khusrau: *By God, if under the blue sky there is, has been or will be anyone like him !*

"And in addition to his learning, literary excellences, art and eloquence, he was a *sufi* (mystic) of stable spiritual position. Most of his life was spent in fasting, prayer, devotions and the reading of the Quran. He fasted continuously and was one of the chosen disciples of Shaikh Nizamuddin. I have not seen another disciple with such firm faith in the Shaikh. He was unrivalled in the performance of obligatory as well as superogatory devotions. He had a commendable portion of spiritual love and affection (*'ishq wa muhabbat*): he loved mystic songs and was a man of ecstasies and delights. He excelled in musical performances as well as musical inventions.[11] Almighty God had created him eminent in all arts that appertain to a refined and aesthetic mind. His was a unique existence and a wonder for these later times.

"The second incomparable poet of the period of Alauddin was Amir Hasan Sijzi.[12] He has many works in prose and verse. His compositions were considered models owing to the excellence of their literary construction and fluency of style. As he has written plenty of fluent and emotionally inspired (*wajdani*) *ghazals*, they have called him the Sa'di of India. And among persons endowed with excellence of character, I have seldom met anyone like him in relating anecdotes and making witty remarks at parties, in ready information about the Sultans, dignitaries and great scholars of Delhi—in stability of reason, in living according to the principles of the *sufis* (mystics), in the necessary virtue of contentment, in pure faith, in living happily and spending time happily without any worldly means and in leading a celibate existence free from worldly connections.

"There has been affection and friendship between me and Amir Khusrau and Amir Hasan for years. They could not live without my company and I too could not forsake their company. Owing to my friendship with them, these two masters also became friends and began to visit each other at their houses.[13]

"Owing to the great faith which Amir Hasan had in Shaikh Nizamuddin, he has collected in several volumes all the conversations of the Shaikh exactly as he heard them during the period of his discipleship and given them the name of *Fuwaidul Fuwad.*[14] In these days his *Fawaidul Fuwad* has become the text-book of true disciples. Amir Hasan has several *diwans* (of *ghazals*), letters (*sahaif*) in prose, and many *masnavis* (romantic poems). His conversation in society was sweet and witty; also he was a pleasant companion, capable of understanding the minds of others, and excellent in manners and good form. I have found more happiness and good cheer in his company than in the company of anyone else."

II

It must be remembered that Barani was very much younger than his two great friends. Amir Khusrau died a few months after Shaikh Nizamuddin (1325 A.D.) in the early months of the reign of Mohammad bin Tughlaq. Amir Hasan went with the Sultan to Deogir and died there. Both Amir Khusrau and Amir Hasan were in government service, and the direct confessions of the former and the indirect remarks of the latter leave us in no doubt that they found it a hideous burden and a degradation. Barani, coming from a family of old officers, probably felt differently. He was convinced that the well-born had a right to high government posts, and the fact that he was not given any office till his fiftieth year may have further incited him against the mean and the low-born. However in the autumn of 1334 A.D. Sultan Mohammad bin Tughlaq appointed Barani as his *nadim* or courtier. It was an office of much profit but no responsibility and not suited to a man with self-respect.

The great Seljuq Wazir, Nizamul Mulk Tusi, in his *Siyasat Nama*[15] has given an account of the courtier's position and duties.

These duties would naturally differ according to character of the king; but judging from Barani's own confessions, the description of the *Siyasat Nama* applies to him:

"The king", says Nizamul Mulk, "has no alternative but to employ courtiers so that he may be frank and intimate with them. Associating for long with the great *amirs* and generals of the army injures the prestige and dignity of the king, for it makes them bold. In short, if the king appoints a person to an office or an administrative duty (*amal*), he should not make him a courtier; if he appoints anyone a *nadim* (courtier), he should not appoint him to any office (*amal*), for owing to the freedom he has on the king's carpet, he will become aggressive and do harm to people. The officers should be always afraid of the king. The courtier should be bold, so that the king may obtain delight in his company; the king's mind is put at ease owing to the courtier. The courtiers should know their time; when the king has adjourned his court (*bar*) and the great officers have retired, that is the time for the courtiers.

"There are some advantages in employing the courtier. First, he is a friend of the king. Secondly, since he is with the king day and night, he is in the position of a bodyguard for the king. Thirdly, if a danger arises, the courtier sacrifices his life and makes his body a shield for the king. Fourthly, it is possible (for the king) to say a thousand things in jest or in seriousness, to the courtier, which it is not possible (for him) to say to the wazir and to the great officers of the government, for they are holders of high posts and managers of his affairs. Fifthly, they inform the king of the actions of the *maliks,* like spies. Sixthly, they can speak boldly about all sorts of things and, in sobriety and during intoxication, they can explain the good and bad (affairs of the state) to the king; and in this there are many advantages of policy.

"The *nadim* (courtier) ought to be well-born, accomplished, good in manners, pleasant in appearance, orthodox in faith, worthy of confidence and pure in his ways. He should be able to tell plenty of stories, jocular as well as serious. He should remember many proverbs. He should always speak well (of people) and be a bringer of happy tidings. He should know *nard*[16] and chess. If he can play on musical instruments and wear arms, it is better. He should (always) agree with the king. When the king brings anything to his lips and speaks, he should say, 'Bravo! Excellent!'

He should not tell the king: 'Do this'; 'Do not do that'; 'Why have you done that?' 'This should not be done'. Such speech appears difficult to the king and he dislikes it. It is proper for the king to arrange with the courtiers whatever appertains to drinking, enjoyment, displays, *majlises,* hunting, playing the ball[17] and the like. But it is better for the king to arrange with the wazir, the high officers of the state and experienced old men whatever appertains to the government, battles, campaigns, administration, revenue, marriage alliances, journeys, stoppages, army, *ra'iyyat* and the like, for they are his partners in these things. Thus every matter will be properly arranged..."

By the tenth year of Mohammad bin Tughlaq's reign, when Barani was appointed, the objectives of the Sultan's policy and the methods by which he sought to govern were well-known to all. Barani fully accepts before God and man his responsibility for his actions as a courtier. He was throughout loyal to his Sultan, but there were many aspects of the Sultan's policy that distressed and horrified him, and the most horrifying thing to him was the constant shedding of Muslim blood under all kinds of pretexts. "The killing of the Musalmans and believers in one God," Barani tells us, "had become a part of the Sultan's character and habit. He had put to death a large number of *ulama* (externalistic religious scholars), *mashaikh* (mystic leaders), saiyyids, *sufis* (mystics), *qalandars,* clerks (*nawisandah*) and soldiers (*lashkaris*). No day or week passed but the blood of a number of Musalmans was shed and a spring of blood was made to flow before the entrance to the royal gate."[18]

"And I, an ungrateful wretch, who had read many books and had a portion of the knowledge that edifies, practised hypocrisy and obtained a position near the Sultan. I had not the courage to speak to the Sultan in the matter of capital punishment, which is a violation of the *shari'at.* I was afraid on account of my life, which is sure to end, and for my wealth, which is sure to depart. My silence in the matter would have been a lesser offence; but for the sake of *tankas* and *jitals* and the desire for a position near the king, I became an accomplice in the matter by giving assistance to the violations of the *shari'at* and reciting worthless precedents. I do not know what will happen to others like me. But I, on account of the evil things I said and did, have become disgraced, contemptible, valueless and unworthy of reliance in this world.

I have become dishonoured from door to door on account of my poverty. I do not know what will be my fate in the next world and what punishments await me."[19] The Sultan, it is needless to add, felt quite convinced that his continuous death-penalties and other punishments were justified, and to the very end of his life neither his conscience nor his judgment troubled him about the matter.

Barani must have had many opportunities of conversation with the Sultan but he only gives us an account of four conversations:

1. The Sultan's ex-teacher, Qutlugh Khan, had been an efficient Viceroy of Deogir. He was firm, tactful and solicitous for the public good. He had suppressed rebels like Shahab Sultani and Ali Shah of Kara (a nephew of Zafar Khan, Sultan Alauddin's *Diwan-i Arz*) and sent them to Delhi[20]. But his ways were very different from those of the Sultan; the Sultan recalled him and appointed his brother, Maulana Nizamuddin Alimul Mulk, temporarily in his place. When the *sadah-amirs* of Baroda and Deohvi revolted and defeated Muqbil, the naib-wazir of Gujrat, the Sultan made up his mind to march against the rebels. At this juncture Qutlugh Khan sent through the mediation of Barani a letter to the Sultan to the following effect: 'The *Sadah-amirs* of Baroda and Deohvi are not of sufficient importance for the Sultan to march against them. They have rebelled on account of the bad ways and the punishments of Aziz Himar; if they hear that the Sultan is marching against them, they will take refuge in Hindu territories, but resentment against the Sultan will spread among the *sadah-amirs*'. Qutlugh Khan undertook to raise an army out of the *inams* he had received from the Sultan's generosity and to defeat the rebels of Gujarat in the same way as he had defeated the rebels of the Deccan. Barani read out the letter to the Sultan, but the Sultan did not like the suggestion of Qutlugh Khan and gave no reply.[21]

2. During his march against the Gujarat rebels, the Sultan stopped for four or five days at the town of Sultanpur on account of the Ramazan month. "Once towards the end of the night", Barani tells us[22], "I was summoned by the Sultan. 'You see how many rebellions are arising', the Sultan said to me, 'I am not afraid of these rebellions'. But people say that these rebellions are due to the excessive capital punishments of the Sultan. Well, I am not going to give up my punishments owing to what people say. You have read many histories. Have you read anywhere about the

crimes for which kings have inflicted capital punishments?" Barani quoted from one of his favourite bogus books, the *Tarikh-i Kisravi.* Punishments were necessary for the maintenance of the state. But Jamshed in reply to a question had said: 'The infliction of capital punishment by the king is justified in the case of seven offences; if the king goes beyond these limits, troubles for the kingdom will arise. Barani then proceeded to enumerate the seven offences for which alone Jamshed had prescribed capital punishment:— '(i) Apostasy—leaving the correct creed and insisting on that error; (ii) Murder—killing a subject of the king intentionally (and without justification); (iii) Adultery—the cohabitation of a married man with the wife of another; (iv) Conspiracy—planning rebellion against the king, provided the conspiracy is proved; (v) Rebellion—leading a rebellion against the king or helping a rebel leader; (vi) Aiding the king's enemies—if a subject helps the king's enemies, opponents or rivals by giving them information, arms, or assists them in other ways, and this fact is proved; (vii) Disobedience—disobedience to the king in a way that endangers the state but not disobedience of other kinds'.

To the Sultan's question about offences for which the Prophet had prescribed capital punishment, Barani replied—'Apostasy, murder and adultery'. Capital punishment for the other four offences are the responsibility of the king for the welfare of the state. He then quoted a supplementary remark of Jamshed: 'Kings have selected wazirs, raised them to a high status and put the affairs of the kingdom in their charge. In consequence of this, wazirs have been able to make laws (*zawabit*) for the state and to enforce them permanently; and owing to the enforcement of these laws, it has not been necessary for the king to sully his own hands with the blood of any creature'.[23]

The Sultan replied: "The punishments prescribed by Jamshed were for ancient times. In these days plenty of wicked and mischievous people have been born. I inflict capital punishments on the basis of suspicion and presumption of rebellion, disorder and conspiracy. I put people to death for every slight disobedience I see in them, and I will keep inflicting capital punishments in this way till either I perish or the people are set right and give up rebellion and disobedience. I have no wazir who can frame such laws for my kingdom that it may become unnecessary for me to smear my hands with blood. Also I inflict capital punishments because people have become my enemies all of a sudden. I have distributed so much treasure among the people, but no one has become my sincere well-wisher. The temper of the people has been clearly revealed to me; they are my enemies and opponents."

3. After Mohammad bin Tughlaq had crushed the rebellion of the Deccan *amirs* but before he could pacify the territory, he heard of the rebellion of Taghi in Gujarat and decided to march against him. Barani, who was then at Delhi, was sent by Firoz Shah, Malik Kabir and Ahmad Ayaz—the triumvirate to whom the duty of acting for the Sultan at Delhi had been assigned—with a letter congratulating the Sultan on his victory. The Sultan had crossed Ghati Satun (the Ford of Satan) and marched one or two stages when Barani presented himself.

"The Sultan", writes Barani, "received me with great cordiality. One day I was riding by the side of the Sultan's stirrups. The Sultan kept on talking till the question of the rebels cropped up and he said to me: 'You see what troubles the ungrateful *sadah-amirs* are raising. If I suppress their rebellion in one direction and pacify the country, they raise trouble in another direction. Had I at the very beginning ordered the extermination of all the *sadah amirs* of Deogir, Gujarat and Bharoach, I would not have had to face so many troubles on account of them now. And this ungrateful slave of mine, Taghi,—had I put him to death or sent him as a present (*yadgar*) to the king of Adan (Aden), he would not have been able to rebel today'. I had not the courage to say in the presence of the Sultan that the troubles and rebellions which arose in every direction—and the general detestation which was visible—were due to the excessive capital punishments of the Sultan; and that if these punishments were stopped for a time, may be, the people would be pacified and the general detestation in the hearts of the select and the commons would decrease. But from fear of a change in the Sultan's temper, I could not say this openly before him. Still I said to myself: 'What (Providential) wisdom is this that the very policy which is bringing about the ruin and destruction of the kingdom appears to the Sultan's mind as a means for its pacification; and rehabilitation.'"[25]

4. The fourth conversation recorded by Barani concerned the diseases of the kingdom. Taghi was still at large, but the Sultan had decided to see to the pacification of Gujarat. Then news came

about the second Deogir rebellion and the Sultan had to reconsider his programme. "In those days when the Sultan was undecided about going to Deogir, he summoned me and said, 'My kingdom is diseased and its illness cannot be cured by any medicine. If the physician treats it for lumbago, the fever increases; if he treats it for fever, there is an obstruction of the arteries. Different diseases have appeared in my kingdom simultaneously. If I put it right at one place, disorders appear at another place; if I put it right at the second place. Disorders appear at a third place. What have kings of the past said about these diseases of the kingdom?'

"I replied, 'Books of history have described the remedies prescribed by kings for the diseases of the kingdom in a variety of ways. Some Sultans, on seeing that the people have ceased to trust them and that a general resentment against them has appeared have abdicated from the kingdom and assigned it to one of their sons, whom they have considered deserving, in their own life-time. They have then retired to a corner of the kingdom, devoted themselves to engagements that keep away weariness and contented themselves with the cheerful company of a few courtiers. They have not (after their abdication) meddled with the affairs of the kingdom. Other Sultans, owing to that disease of the kingdom which is due to the hatred of the people, have given themselves up suddenly to hunting, music and wine, and have assigned all affairs of the state—both principles and details and the solution of every problem—to their wazirs, high officers and the supporters of the kingdom. They have not thereafter made any inquiry or investigation or given orders about any matter. Such a remedy, provided it is acceptable to the people and the king is not reputed for seeking vengeance, cures this disease of the kingdom. One of the most dangerous and fatal diseases of the kingdom is the detestation of the select and the commons and the lack of confidence among the generality of the *rai'yyat'*.

"The Sultan answered, 'If the affairs of the kingdom were settled according to my wishes, my desire was to go to the sacred Ka'ba and assign the affairs of the Delhi empire to these three persons—Firoz Shah, Malik Kabir and Ahmad Ayaz. But these days I am angry with the people and the people are angry with me. The people have discovered my mind and I have discovered the evil and rebellious designs of the people. Every remedy I try fails. My remedy for rebels, opponents, disobedient persons and evil-wishers is the sword. I will continue punishing and striking with my sword till it either cuts or misses. The more the people oppose me, the greater will be my punishments.'"

III

The rebel Taghi fled to the Jam of Thatta and the Sultan decided to pursue him. Trans-Oxiana was in those days nominally under a Khan, who had to be a descendant of Chengiz. But the real ruler of the territory was Amir Qazghan (the maternal grandfather of Tamerlane) and Qazghan sent an army of 4900 or 5000 Mongols under Altun Bahadur to help the Sultan. The Sultan marched against Thatta to defeat Taghi and the Jam with an army 'numerous as ants and locusts', but he developed fever on the 10th of Moharram, 752 A.H. and died on the 21st of the same month (March 2, 1351 A.D.).

The Mongols planned to plunder the leaderless army by attacking it from one side while the Sumeras of Sind were attacking it from the other. Under these circumstances all the leaders present (including Shaikh Nasiruddin Chiragh) elected Firoz Shah their Sultan and placed him on the throne on the 24th of Moharram. The election of the new Sultan restored order and discipline; the Mongols were induced to depart, and the march to Delhi began. On reaching Bhakkar the army heard that the Khwaja-i Jahan Ahmad Ayaz, whom Mohammad bin Tughlaq had sent as his Deputy (*Naib-i Ghibat*) to Delhi, had put a boy on the throne, declaring him to be the son of the late Sultan and, technically speaking, was guilty of rebellion. On the face of it his action seems inexplicable. Mohammad bin Tughlaq had no son. Though there has been some controversy on the point, the following caustic verse of Isami, written and published while the Sultan was alive definitely settles the matter: "If the king (*khusrau*) has no son, he wishes the whole world to be like himself."[27] Add to it, Ahmad Ayaz was eighty-four years old; he was a pure civilian and had never shot an arrow or mounted a troublesome horse. Barani quotes Firoz Shah as stating that Ahmad Ayaz used to get quite out of breath when mounting the stairs of the Hazar Sutun Palace and that there was a danger that his heart would be affected. Why should such a man embark on a hopeless rebellion when the *amirs* and the army had accepted Firoz Shah?

Shams Siraj Afif in his *Tarikh-i Firoz Shahi* admits that people in general believed that Ahmad Ayaz had rebelled *after* hearing of the election of Firoz Shah but affirms that this opinion was not correct. On the basis of his own investigations and of what he had heard from Kishwar Khan son of Bahram Aibah Kishlu Khan, the former governor of Multan, Afif gives the following account of what happened. On hearing of Mohammad bin Tughlaq's death, the Mongols attacked the chief market of the army-camp and the men were scattered. The Khwajah-i Jahan had a confidential slave, Malih Tuntun, whom he had sent to the Sultan. Tuntun left the army-camp while it was being plundered and gave the following report to the Khwaja-i Jahan at Delhi. "Sultan Mohammad is dead; the Mongols have attacked the main market and plundered it. The whereabouts of Firoz Shah and Tatar Khan are not known; it is not certain whether they have fallen into the hands of the Mongols or have been killed." Even to this day, Afif adds, the people of Delhi remember the name of Malih Tuntun.

The Khwaja-i Jahan wept both for Sultan Mohammad and Firoz, "There was a great affection between the Khwaja-i Jahan and Firoz Shah—such an affection that no third person could come between them; the wife of the Khwaja-i Jahan used to call Firoz Shah her son and did not observe *purdah* from him." But believing that Firoz Shah was dead, 'the Khwaja-i Jahan took an initiative (*ijtihad*) and placed the boy on the throne'. This initiative proved to be an error, but most of the officers at Delhi seem to have agreed with him at the time. When the Khwaja-i Jahan heard of the advance of Firoz Shah, he kept on collecting an army from political policy, though he had no intention of fighting. But the late Sultan's generosities had exhausted the treasury and he could only collect some twenty thousand soldiers.

When Firoz Shah's army approached Delhi, Qiwamul Mulk (later on, Khan-i Jahan Maqbul), the Naib Wazir and the second senior-most officer at Delhi fled to Firoz Shah. The Khwaja-i Jahan was greatly distressed, "With a cloak of single-fold, his rosary between his fingures, and both his hands folded behind his back, the Khwaja-i Jahan went up and down the Hazar Satun, wearing his shoes." But he refused to allow his officers to go in pursuit of Qiwamul Mulk. He reflected that his design had been an error; it would be best to submit to Firoz Shah and confess his mistake, So the next day, after Friday prayers, he marched with all the officers who had joined him out of the city of Delhi and encamped by the Alai Tank. To the questions of his officers about his future intentions, his reply was: "You should know that in this design of putting a son of Mohammad bin Tughlaq on the throne, I had no personal ambitions. The place of leadership (*imamat*) belongs to kings and of *wizarat* to wazirs. If kings set their heart, on doing the work of wazirs, or wazirs try to do the work of kings, the country will be ruined in due course. People on both sides invent stories, but I have nothing to do with the affair of king-making. Still, in the reign of Sultan Mohammad I used to address Firoz as my son; my wife used to appear before him; and he used to address me as his father. I do not know what is going to happen. But you should come with me; Sultan Firoz is a kind man; he will not ignore my words and will forgive you also." Afif tells us that the Khwaja-i Jahan was an old man of eighty-four years; his head was shaved; his beard was white; he was a disciple of Shaikh Nizamuddin and looked like a mystic *shaikh,* who has a mystic inheritance (*sajjadah*).

Some of his followers protested against this policy, but the Khwaja-i Jahan drew their attention to the futility of trying to defend the city of Delhi and the misfortunes it would bring to Muslim women. Some of his officers kept him company, while others preferred to fly away. Qiwamul Mulk met Firoz Shah at the stage of Fathabad; the Khwaja-i Jahan reached the royal camp at Dhansur near Akranda on the following day. When Firoz Shah was holding his Court after the *'asr* (afternoon) prayer, he appeared at the door of the Court with a chain round his neck, a mystic cap (*tagia*) on his head instead of a *pagri* (*pag*) and a naked sword tied to his neck. "At the time of the afternoon Court, there is the distance of an arrow-shot between the king and those who come to salaam him." When Firoz Shah's eyes fell on the Khwaja-i Jahan, he ordered his officers to dress him properly, to place him in the royal litter, to take him to a tent (*khurramgah*) and to tell him that he (Firoz Shah) would come to see him there.

Firoz Shah's intention was to forgive the Khwaja-i Jahan and restore him to the post of Wazir. But his officers discussed the matter and vetoed his design. They came to his palace and sent Imadul Mulk Bashir Sultani to ask for an audience. When Firoz Shah admitted them, they showed excessive reverence: 'The *Haj* was binding on every Muslim; they wanted his permission to go for the sacred pilgrimage. Small political offences, like revenue offences, could be forgiven but not treason. The Khwaja-i Jahan had put a boy on the throne, squandered the cash in the treasury and then stretched his hands to the gold and silver vessels of the state. He had only come when his cause was lost'.

"Firoz Shah", says Afif, "was intelligent enough to understand that unanimously and with one voice they were demanding the destruction of the Khwaja-i Jahan. He became pale with excessive thought and caution." Nothing like this could have happened in the reign of the late Sultan. The officers had not come to discuss but to dictate to a ruler, whom they had themselves made. Firoz's nerves failed him as they were going to go on many future occasions. So after some days of reflection, he summoned Imadul Mulk and asked him to inform the officers *confidentially* that they could deal with the Khwaja-i Jahan as they liked; he would not interfere in the matter. The officers informed the Khwaja-i Jahan on behalf of the Sultan that, owing to his old age, the *iqta'* (province) of Samana had been assigned to him. But while dispatching him to Samana, they also sent one of their senior-most officers, Sher Khan, who was even older than the Khwaja-i Jahan, in the same direction. Sher Khan pitched his tents at the same stages as the Khwaja-i Jahan, but did not come to see him. "He has been sent to destroy me", the Khwaja-i Jahan told his friends; and he made up his mind to anticipate the event.

"Next day the Khwaja-i Jahan sent a request to Sher Khan for some pieces of cloth for a tent and Sher Khan sent them to him. The Khwaja-i Jahan ordered his men to pitch the tent in an open plain and to make the ground clean and even. After this had been done, they carried him to the place. On reaching the tent with a troubled mind, the Khwaja-i Jahan asked for water, performed his ablutions and said two *rak'ats* of prayers like one of the elect. Then he put on the cap (*kulah*) he had received from Shaikh Nizamuddin and tied round it a *dastar* (*turban*) which also he had received from the great Shaikh. Then he turned towards the swordsman (*sayyaf*): 'Have you a sharp sword?' The man showed his sword. After that the Khwaja-i Jahan asked a friend of his to perform his ablution and offer two *rak'ats* of prayer. When his friend was ready the Khwaja-i Jahan placed his forehead on the ground and kept on reciting the Oath of Affirmation (*Kalima*). His friend (as directed) took the sword and severed the Khwaja-i Jahan's head from his body."[28]

A correct and impartial account of these events has been given in order to explain the circumstances of Barani's 'fall', concerning which he has preferred to remain silent. Two things seem clear. First, he was at Delhi at the time and must have been implicated in the so-called rebellion of the Khwaja-i Jahan, since all men who mattered had concurred in the plan. He was not the man to go against a general movement. This presumption is strengthened by the abusive manner in which he speaks of the Khwaja-i Jahan in order to ingratiate himself with the rulers of the day. He does not tell us that the Khwaja-i Jahan acted on wrong information, though he must have known that fact; he also tells us nothing about the ultimatum of the officers to Firoz Shah or of the manner in which the Khwaja-i Jahan met his death. Secondly, he had plenty of enemies in the new regime; both his words and circumstances prove this fact.

At the beginning of the new reign we find him interned (*shahr-band*) in the fort of Bhatnir. He may have fled to that place, like the officers who deserted the Khwaja-i Jahan at the Alai Tank, or he may have been sent there by the order of the government. In any case he passed five months in suspense awaiting the decision of the authorities. In the Introduction to his *Na't-i Mohammadi,* he writes[29]: "After praises of God and blessings on the Prophet and his Descendants and greetings to the Companion: Zia-i' Barani, the greatest sinner of the Prophet's community, states that when the age of this sinner had passed beyond seventy (lunar) years, my strength gave place to weakness, the senses grew dim, I became frail, and the fear of facing the last moment (of life), which is a fearful time, overpowered my breast and the thought of meeting the Angel of Death, which is a terrible meeting, took possession of my body and mind. I swear by Mohammad—and God himself has sworn by the head and life of Mohammad—that though I reflected a lot, I could not remember a good act or an acceptable deed during the last two *qarns* of my life, which had not been ruined and made worthless by the influence of sin and inequity. I could not find in all my life any devotion or virtue under the firm hold of which I could seek protection at the time of surrendering my life, or owing to the strength of which I could go from this world to the next, or by clinging to which I could pass through the trials and dangers of the next world. Hour after hour as I remembered the sins and errors of my past, I became more and more hopeless."

Such confessions are formal and traditional among Musalmans approaching the hour of death and no great significance attaches to them. But what Barani proceeds to tell us is more to the point. "During the five months I was interned (*shahr-band*) in Bhatnir, I lived in sorrow and gloom. *In this sorrow, if I saw the dawn, I did not, know whether I would live till the night: if night came, I was not hopeful of being alive till the morning.* And in this tortured condition it came to my mind that I should write it book in praise of the Prophet Mohammad, bring into the Persian language all I had seen and read in the books of traditions (*hadis*), and use this book as a firm handle for the moment of death. In truth, I considered this idea of mine a good inspiration and strength came into my heart. *In the condition in which I am—for my affairs have come to such a pass that all my friends and acquaintances have turned away from me and owing to my misfortunes my enemies and opponents have attained to their heart's desire*—owing to the composition of this book, which is the protection (*pusht wa panah*) of my religious and worldly affairs, I feel a new strength in myself from time to time."

Barani was apparently free to move about within the fort and he makes an incidental reference to his being there in the *Tarikh-i Firoz Shahi*[30]: "When I was in the fort of Bhatnir, some danger of disturbances arose during the winter. The people of the villages (*talaundis*) came round the fort-wall and the dust raised by their horses and cattle was so great that the bright day became dark as night and people could not see each other's faces. Hardly a thousandth part of the *ra'iyyat* could enter the Bhatnir fort with their horses. I counted the horses in the stable of Ikhtiaruddin Maddhu, the barber (*hajjam*); thirteen horses worth one thousand or two thousand *tankas* were tied there."

The new rulers wisely decided not to inaugurate their regime with bloodshed. Only some fifteen persons were put to death[31] among whom Barani mentions Ahmad Ayaz, Nathu Sodhal, Hasan, Hisam Adhang, and two slaves of Ahmed Ayaz. But the relatives of these rebels were not put to death. Ziauddin Barani's life was spared by Firoz Shah, probably on the recommendation of Malikal Umara Malik Shikar Bek Wamlan Sultani. "*After the death of the late Sultan* (*Mohammad bin Tughlaq*), *I, Zia-i Barani, author of the 'Tarikh-i Firoz Shahi', fell into a variety of mortal dangers. Ill-wishers against my life and powerful and strong enemies and rivals strove for my death. I was, so to say, driven to madness by the polo-sticks of their hatred. They attributed to me a thousand kinds of poisonous words before his Majesty.* If next to the kindness of God the mercy, modesty, affection, kindness, sincerity and regard for truth of the Sultan of the time and the age, Firoz Shah-us Sultan, had not come to my rescue, and if he had heard and accepted the poisoned words of the powerful and influential enemies of this weak creature, I would have been sleeping in the womb of mother earth. If the virtuous character of this king, the cherisher of the helpless, had not caught hold of my hands, how could I have been alive today? *I owe my life to the Sultan.*"[32]

IV

But if the government spared his life, it certainly confiscated his property. He may have had to share his father's house at Kailugarhi with other heirs, but he had himself built his house at Ghiaspur. Then the late Sultan had loaded him with gifts and presents. What happened to all his wealth and property? The only possible answer is—confiscation by the government. The late Sultan had been reckless in his gifts with scant regard for merit or service; a good deal of gold and silver had gone out of India and there was no possibility of getting it back. But what had been left intact—and at Delhi—could be recovered. The new government, as we have seen, was desperately in need of cash and commodities; very probably while Barani was awaiting the decision of his fate at Bhatnir, an inventory of his property was made; some income from it was left to him—something which Amir Khurd could in courtesy refer to as 'pension'—but the rest of it was confiscated. Firoz Shah might have been willing to let him go scot-free, but his hands were tied by his officers. The charge that Barani had been using 'poisonous words' was probably correct; his books are too full of abusive phrases of a type that do no credit to a man of his age, and he may, as a courtier, have too frequently used poisonous words to please the late Sultan.

So on his return to Delhi, Barani found 'nothing to live on except his regrets'. That he was in great want, specially in view of the standard of life to which he had been accustomed, is certain; it is equally certain that they did not leave him to starve to death. Barani from fear of the government and the hope that he may be forgiven, is silent both about the charges brought against him and about the confiscation of his property. But silence under such circumstances is a confession.

In his old age and poverty, Barani not only longed for the affluence that had left him but wrote as if he was still capable of sex-life. But what plagued him really was not desire but the desire for desire.

The following account of the Majlis of Sultan Jalaluddin Khilji, appertaining to a time when Barani was barely eleven or twelve, but written in the *Tarikh-i Firoz Shahi* when he was seventy-four, is significant.[33]

"The *Saqis* of the Majlis (of Sultan Jalaluddin Khilji) were Yilduz, the *Sar-saqi* (the chief cup-bearer), and the sons of Haibat Khan and Nizam Kharitadar. They were so lovely, handsome and graceful that a religious mendicant, if he happened to look at them, would have tied his rosary round his waist-band and fled from his cell to the tavern out of love for these breakers of religious vows.

"Among the musicians of the Majlis were Mohammad Shah, the *changi,* who played on the harp (*chang*) while Futuha and the daughter of Fiqai and Nusrat Khatun used to sing. The sweetness and melody of their voices induced birds to descend from the air, but the consciousness of their human hearers flew away, so that bereft of their senses their very life seemed to ebb and flow. Mahr Afroz and the accomplished daughter of Nusrat Bibi, whose excessive beauty and charms captivated whichever part of the audience they chose to glance at, danced to the music. Their motions were so graceful that the onlooker felt like sacrificing his life for them and never raised his eyes from the captivating movements of their feet.[34]

"In short the Majlis of the Sultan was such as can only be seen in dreams. Amir Khusrau, the chief courtier (*malikun nudama*) of the Sultan's Majlis, brought new *ghazals* every day in praise of moon-faced young boys and heart-enchanting beauties; and these *ghazals* were recited while the *saqis* invited the audience to drink amidst the music and blandishments of graceful beauties and the dancing of fair girls. In that company, the like of which cannot be seen on the face of the earth nor described in words, the disheartened and the weary were recalled to life, while pleasure-seekers found their paradise on earth and the sensitive felt like resigning the world and its toils. The man who did not feel intoxicated in such a majlis, where the *hurs* sat at the door and fairies (*paris*) swept their skirts along the ground, must have been entirely devoid of feeling, a strong man with a stony heart.[35]

"As for me, a misguided old man lost in the desert of failure, only a few breaths of life are left to me now. But when I write about the scenes of those Majlises, I wish, in memory of those young, life-giving and moon-like beauties, *whose charming and graceful dancing I have seen and whose songs I have heard,* to tie the Brahman's thread round my shoulders, to put the Brahman's *tika* on my accursed forehead, to blacken my face, and in that condition to wander through every market and every street, disgracing and humiliating myself in lamentations on the misfortunes of those queens of the world of beauty and moons of the sky of refinement. Though sixty years have passed since then, I feel like tearing my clothes, plucking off the hair of my head and beard, and giving up my ghost in sorrow at the foot of their graves. Regrets, a hundred thousand regrets for my past! *For I have neither attained to eminence in my religious affairs, nor have I obtained in my worldly life the prosperity that could satisfy a refined and cultured mind.* And now that I am old and blind and confined to my corner, helpless and poor, with nothing but my regrets to feed upon and nothing to carry away with me (to the other world) save my unfulfilled desires, I often repeat to myself these verses so applicable to my case:

"I am neither an infidel nor a Musalman; neither my heart nor my faith is in my hands; God alone can inform my heart about my real condition. I am neither strong in the hope (of Divine kindness) nor firm in my conviction of attaining to salvation, for the path of my hope has broken in a thousand places. Where am I to go? What am I to do? To whom can I explain the feelings of my heart? I have neither the power to walk, nor the will to remain sitting. The East and West of my world are contracted like the breast of an ant; my earth and sky have become small like the circle of a ring. May the Lord open the doors of His favour to me, for I have reached the limits of helplessness, weakness, anxiety and sorrow,"[36]

The following lament of Barani also deserves to be noted: "I have seen this munificent man (Malik Nusrat Sabbah). He was often a guest at my father's house. Although these days I am in great helplessness and distress and beggars (*khwahandgan*) go away disappointed from my door, nevertheless as I am the son of a generous man, and the descendant of munificent ancestors, I consider death a thousand times better than such a day. *I have nothing of my own and I can borrow nothing from others.* Day and night I pine in the desire of practising generosity and giving away *dirhams* and *dinars*.[37] If in the writing of this *History* no other advantage accrues to me, I have at least included in it an account of the munificence and generosity of the liberal people about whom I have heard from my father and grandfather and some of whom I have seen. Owing to the remembrance and the description of the munificent, I feel peace and satisfaction in my desolated heart. At their name I am brought from death to life."[38]

V

Under these circumstances the main attempt of the eleven chapters Barani has written on the first six years of Firoz Shah's reign was to flatter those in power and to praise the regime. He even praises the regime for certain things he has himself clearly condemned elsewhere.—(a) The army is not sent on any long campaigns.[39] (b) The shopkeepers are more prosperous than at any other time. "The shopkeeper is now the ruler of the market; he buys as he likes and sells as he likes".[40] (c) The property of shopkeepers, merchants, bankers and regraters has exceeded lacs and reached karors.[41] (d) "There is no space for anything in the houses of *khots* and *muqaddams* owing to their horses, cattle and corn."[42] (e) There are no intelligence officers of any sort to disturb the life of the people—neither secret spies (*mukhbir*) nor open reporters (*munhi*).[43] All these things have been condemned by Barani in the *Fatawa-i Jahandari* or the earlier part of the *Firoz Shahi*. But he adopts a different standpoint now.

Barani naturally praises the members of the royal family—the two sons of Firoz Shah, Shadi Khan (who was Vakildar) and Fath Khan, who were known to the public, while the other princes were still kept in the *harem*; and the Sultan's two brothers, Qutbuddin and Fakhruddin Ibrahim.[44] Among the high officers the following are selected for special praise: (1) Khan-i Jahan Maqbul, the *Wazir*. "The Sultan has given him full powers; and no king has shown such favour to his wazir as Firoz Shah has shown to the Khan-i Jahan." (2) Tatar Khan. (3) Malikush Sharq Imadul Mulk Bashir Sultani, the *Ariz-i Mumalik.* (4) Malikul Umara Shikar Bek Wamlan Sultani. "He has been very helpful to me, the author of the *Tarikh-i Firoz Shahi,* and a great man like him has spoken a few words in my favour before the throne." (5) Iftikharul Mulk, the governor of Gujarat. (6) Mahmud-Bek Sher Khan. Baram puts his age between 90 and 100. "In his long career, during which he has risen through the grades of *sipahsalar, amir* and *malik* to that of a *khan,* he has never taken part in any rebellion." (7) Zafar Khan, the *Naib Wazir.*

It is no secret that while the Khan-i Jahan showed the greatest respect for the Sultan, the decisions of the government were the decisions of the Khan-i Jahan Barani has (for good reasons from his own point of view) ignored the early career of the Khan-i Jahan, but Afif in his *Tarikh-i Firoz Shahi,* records it as follows:

"The Khan-i Jahan was from Tilang and his name before his conversion to Islam was Kunnu. He was a man of the greatest honour in his own community and had a position of distinction before the Rai of Telang. Mohammad bin Tughlaq captured the Rai and sent him to Delhi, but the Rai died on the way. The Khan-i Jahan came obediently to Mohammad bin Tughlaq and recited the Oath of Affirmation (*Kalima*). The Sultan gave him the name of Maqbul (Accepted) and treated him with favour. Later on, when the Sultan saw all the signs of intelligence and wisdom in the Khan-i Jahan, he appointed him *naib wazir* for the city of Delhi and opened the doors of promotion to him. When the Khan-i Jahan[46] sealed and signed a document, he wrote his name as follows—"Maqbul, slave of Mohammad Tughlaq." Though the distinguished *wazir* did not know how to read and write, still he was the wisest of men and through his wisdom he adorned the capital of the empire. The title of Qiwamul Mulk was given to him during his early career. The governorship of Multan was assigned to him and later on he was appointed *Naib Wazir.* The Khwaja-i Jahan was the *Wazir* of Sultan Mohammad.

"The Khan-i Jahan as *Naib Wazir* (Deputy Wazir) made laws and regulations and put the Department of Revenue in perfect order. The governors of the provinces had not much fear of the Khwaja-i Jahan but they stood in mortal dread of the Khan-i

Jahan. If the Khwaja-i Jahan wanted the governor of a territory to be severely treated, he handed him over to the Khan-i Jahan; and the latter treated him with excessive sternness in accordance with the regulations. Also when the Khwaja-i Jahan, a religious man, retired from the *Diwan* (for his devotions), the Khan-i Jahan sat in his place; he dealt severely with the governors and collected plenty of cash and commodities for the royal treasury. The Khwaja-i Jahan had nothing except the title of *Wazir*; all the work of the Diwan-i Wizarat (Revenue Department) was carried on through the experience and intelligence of the Khan-i Jahan."

The two colleagues became bitter enemies, as we have seen, and the primary reason why the officers demanded the destruction of the Khwaja-i Jahan was that the post of Wazir—and the direction of the policy of the government—had to be assigned to the Khan-i Jahan.

Afif gives us an idea of his methods of work. "In accordance with the traditions of the great Wazirs, the Khan-i Jahan sat before the pillow of his office every day; he carefully investigated the accounts of governors and other officers and realised the share of the treasury. The income and expenditure of the treasury were placed before him every day. He insisted and re-insisted that money beyond reckoning should be daily put into the treasury. If on any day the money received by the treasury was not sufficient, he would be extremely harsh towards all his officers and would often go without food owing to his thoughtfulness and anxiety: 'The stability of the government', he would say on such occasions, 'depends upon the treasury. If there is not enough money in the treasury, or if the money is improperly spent, the foundations of the government will be shaken. If, God forbid, the treasury of a farsighted king becomes empty owing to any cause, the maintenance of the government becomes impossible'. For this reason the Wazir was bent on collecting treasures night and day." [47]

Another aspect of the Khan-i Jahan's life should not be overlooked because it is relevant. He was very fond of women and utilised to the full the permission of the Muslim *shari'at* to keep any number of slave-girls. His agents searched for them in all countries. "It is said," Afif tells us, "that he had two thousand slave-girls of all countries from Rum (Byzantine) to China in his *harem*; every one of these girls adorned herself with fine dresses and ornaments; and the Khan-i Jahan in spite of pressure of work spent much of his time, specially the religious holidays, in his *harem.* He had plenty of children. Firoz Shah fixed an annual grant (*nan*) of eleven thousand *tankas* for every son of the Khan-i Jahan and of five thousand *tankas* for every daughter. Firoz Shah reconciled himself to his position. 'The real king of Delhi', he would say, 'is the Azam-i Humayun Khan-i Jahan'.[48]

To us, in retrospect, the Delhi Sultanate with a Turkish Sultan born of a converted Hindu mother on the throne and a converted Hindu with an international *harem* of females as his Wazir, may seem to be some slight rectification of those great defects, which were inevitable when the government was in the hands of a small Muslim governing class. Also, the position attained by the Khan-i Jahan was the result of a long series of efforts and many failures. The Abyssinian Yaqut was killed by the Turkish bureaucracy, though he was a good and pious man by all accounts. We know nothing of Raihan, but he was killed by the party of Ghiasuddin Balban on account of his Indian birth. The Khilji Revolution, within very narrow limits, opened the door to new men—to the Indian Musalmans whose ancestors had been converted to Islam and who were the bulk of the Musalmans in the country, to new converts from Hinduism and to unconverted Hindus. Malik Kafur is the first converted Hindu who carved out an excellent career in the administration; the degeneration of his policy in the later days of Alauddin Khilji was probably due to the fact that the mass of the officers were against him on account of his origin. Khusrau Khan, a royal favourite only, does not count. But in the time of Mohammad bin Tughlaq we have seen a number of Indians, Hindus as well as Musalmans, pushing their way up the administrative ladder through loyalty and efficiency. Of these officers the Khan-i Jahan was the most brilliant.

To Barani, a scion of the great free-born Turkish officers of the Balbani regime, all this seemed wicked and a violation of the eternal ordinances of Providence. He hated Hindus; he hated converted Hindus no less, for to him Islam was a matter of birth, not of choice. He hated new men in the administration, whose ancestors had been of no account. He hated efficiency and loyalty as the two criteria of service, for his only criteria for government posts was noble birth, compared with which no other qualification mattered. And good birth for him meant belonging to an immigrant family from Central Asia or Persia, which had held high office in India and was, preferably, free-born and not servile in its origin.

The Khan-i Jahan could not have read Barani's books, which had not been written by then, but everything Barani said in the Court of the late Sultan must have been brought to his notice. Words against converted Hindu, the low-born, etc. which seemed divinely inspired to Barani, naturally appeared 'poisonous to the members of these groups. So the Khan-i Jahan made up his mind. He spared Barani's life out of regard for Firoz Shah, but confiscated most of his property and ordered him to keep away from the Court. This order also implied a command to the men of the Court to keep away from Barani. It is to be wished that the Khan-i Jahan had been more liberal to Barani in the matter of expenditure, but substantially the order was correct. There could be no place for Barani in the new governing-class or in a Court dominated by the Khan-i Jahan. Barani has nowhere named his enemies. The reason is simple, for the only enemy he could have named was the great Wazir of the day!

REFERENCES

1. Pages 165–166.
2. I am inclined to interpret 'my majlis (*majlis-i man*)' to mean that Barani was himself at one time in a position to employ these dancing-girls, *bhans* (baffoons), etc., or at least to pay them for entertaining his friends at his parties.
3. I take this sentence to mean that *Qubbatut Tarikh* was the name Barani had given to a volume of his erotic ghazals.
4. The term 'masters of literature who were my friends and companions', obviously refers to Amir Khusrau and Amir Hasan. No one of their stature was left. Still there were literary persons of note, like Ainul Mulk (whose *Insha* has been edited by Professor S.A. Rashid of Aligarh); Tatar Khan, whose *Fatawa* (Legal Judgements), compiled by a group of scholars under his direction, was to be a monumental enterprise of which only parts have survived; Maulana Jalaluddin Rumi, head of the College of Firoz Shah by the side of the Alai Tank, and Saiyyid Najmuddin Samarqandhi, who was in charge of the College near the Siri Dam (*Imarat-i bala bar ab-i Siri*). Barani praises all

the four in his account of Firoz Shah's reign. But obviously he praised them from afar and was denied personal access as well as the privilege of correspondence (*Firoz Shahi*, pp. 562–565, 579–596).

5. *Firoz Shahi*, p. 354.
6. Ibid., p. 349.
7. *Tarikh-i Firoz Shahi*, pp. 359–360.
8. *Khusrau* means king.
9. Amir Khusrau started his five volumes or romantic verses, the *Panj Ganj*, with a challenge to the *Khumsa* (five poetical volumes) of Nizami Ganjvi. But in his last volume he admitted that Nizami was superior: Because he specialised in one art, he has remained unsurpassed—(*Chun yak fanah bud, shud yoganah*)."
10. That is by anticipation. Khwaja Sanai lived in the reign of Sultan Bahram, the last descendant of Sultan Mahmud to reign at Ghaznin.
11. In a verse quoted by Daulat Shah in his *Tazkiratush Shu'ara*, Amir Khusrau declares that his musical inventions, had it been possible to write them, would have filled three volumes in the same way as his *ghazals* filled three *Diwans*. His fourth *Diwan* was written later.
12. Not Sanjari as is often written by mistake. Sijzi means belonging to Sijistan, the ancient Shakistan (the land of the Shakas), now called Sistan.
13. This assertion seems strange in view or the fact that Amir Khusrau and Amir Hasan were both in the service of Sultan Mohammad (*Khan-i Shahid*) while Barani was still in his cradle. But may be, the relations between them became closer owing to the friendship of both of them with our author.
14. The *Fuwaidul Fuwad* was prepared in five thin volumes; printed together they make a book of about 250 lithographed pages.
15. The Persian text of the *Siyasat Nama* was edited by the late Prof. Scheffer. But that edition has been long out of print. I have used the excellent edition of Agha Abbas Iqbal, printed by the Majlis Press Tehran Urdi Bihisht, 1320. Prof. Scheffer translated the *Siyasat Nama* into French. There is no English translation.
16. A medieval game played with dice.

17. That is, the medieval polo.
18. *Tarikh-i Firoz Shahi*, pp. 465–466.
19. Ibid., p. 466.
20. 'Isami describes these rebellions in his *Futuhus Salarin*, pp. 456–480, in some detail.
21. *Firoz Shahi*, pp. 507–508.
22. Ibid., pp. 509–511. Since it was the fasting month, this conversation must have taken place at the time of *sahiri* or the pre-morning meal.
23. The author of the *Tarikh-i Kisravi* was obviously trying to define treason under medieval condition. He also wanted punishments for treason to be based on *permanent laws* as well as *evidence* and not on the personal discretion of the king. Barani has developed these ideas in his *Fatawa-i Jahandarl* (Advice VII).
24. *Tarikh-i Firoz Shahi,* pp. 510–511. By the term, 'people' we should understand officers and select men—and not the mass of the inhabitants.
25. Ibid., pp. 516–517.
26. Ibid., pp. 521–522.
27. 'Isami, *Futuhus Salatin,* p. 433 (Dr. Mehdi Husain's edition).
28. These facts about the Khwaja-i Jahan are related by Afif in his *Tarikh-i Firoz Shahi* (up to p. 78). Afif refers to Barani's work and says he is going to continue it; but, nevertheless, he gives a complete account of the Khwaja-i Jahan's 'rebellion' because Barani had grossly misrepresented the actions and motives of the dead Wazir.
29. The only known manuscript of the *Na't-i Mohammadi* is in the Rampur Library. Some extracts from its Introduction were made for Professor S.A. Rashid. This passage has been translated from these extracts.
30. p. 554.
31. *Tarikh-i Firoz Shahi*, p. 552.
32. Ibid., p. 557.
33. Ibid., pp. 199–201.
34. A careful examination of this paragraph will show that after the lapse of some sixty years Barani was unable to recollect the names of the following: the sons of Haibat Khan and Nizam

Kharitadar; the daughter of Fiqai; and 'the accomplished daughter of Nusrat Bibi'. But Barani seems to have had a very strong emotional memory, and he remembered what he had felt. Elsewhere in the *Firoz Shahi* also we find that Barani is unable to recollect the names of persons and refers to them indirectly—e.g. 'Aziz Himar and his brother'.

But what about Barani's visual memory? The reader of the *Firoz Shahi* will not find an account of the personality—the external forms and features—of any of the persons whose characters—he has delineated. What did Alauddin Khilji, Malik Karur, Khusrau Khan, etc., look like? Barani could have easily described them but he never does. Did Barani's *visual memory* fail him or is this unfortunate gap in the *Tarikh-i Firoz Shahi* due to historical tradition? I am inclined to the latter alternative, for the tradition of Persian history did not demand a description of the personality of its prominent figures.

35. *Hurs* are beautiful women who will console good Musalmans in Paradise; *paris* are beautiful women who inhabit the Caucasian mountains at present.
36. The translation of these verses has been taken from Professor S.A. Rashid's work. *Ziauddin Barani, a Study.*
37. *Dirhams* and *dinars* were copper and silver coins of the Roman empire adopted by the Musalmans. A gold coin was generally called *dinar-i surkh* (red dinar).
38. *Tarikh-i Firoz Shahi*, pp. 204–205.
39. Ibid., p. 553.
40. Ibid., p. 554.
41. Ibid., p. 554.
42. Ibid., p. 554.
43. Ibid., pp. 556–557.
44. Ibid., pp. 576–586 are devoted to the praise of the royal family and the high officers. Shahzada Faith Khan was only six years old, but Barani claims that the Shahzada was kind to him.
45. Ibid., pp. 394–398.
46. I have referred to him as the Khan-i Jahan, but this title was given to him by Firoz Shah after his accession.
47. Ibid., pp. 397–398.
48. Ibid., p. 400.

CHAPTER VII

Theory of Kingship

Barani talks as if monarchy has been a universal political phenomenon of human history and he has no suspicion that there have been different types of monarchies based on different principles. And he reduces the theory of monarchy to the utmost simplicity. From the time of Adam to the rise of Islam only a few royal families governed the globe. The Prophet and the Pious Caliphs were not 'kings' in the ordinary sense of the word. Their advent was due to divine intervention and it was not possible to continue their system. Barani is not a believer in the later Caliphates nor in the so-called 'theory of the Muslim state'. With the Umayyads the world returned to the old ways. Barani is convinced that there is a real difference between the monarchy of the Musalmans and the old pagan monarchies; no Muslim king, for example, could openly claim divinity like the Pharoahs of Egypt; still he has no clear conception of this difference, which he confines entirely to the religious sphere. But he believes that pre-Muslim precepts of government are still valid; and because Muslim kings adopted what was believed to be the Sasanian Court-procedure, Barani tends to overlook the basic differences between the Sasanian and the Muslim monarchies. Barani's knowledge of world history, and even of the history of Ajam, is not only superficial but grossly misleading. Since his *Fatawa-i Jahandari* is supposed to have been written in the time of Sultan Mahmud, he is debarred from referring to any ruler of Delhi. But he discusses the Indian social and political order in the *Jahandari,* and the real value of his political thought lies in the fact that it is based on an examination of the working of the institutions of Delhi Sultanate for over ninety-five years. But other elements of quite different origin had also taken possession of his mind and it is necessary to separate the two.

If Barani's postulates about monarchy are carefully examined, it will be seen that he has not one but two theories of monarchy or kingship. His first theory is based on tradition (or supposed tradition), the postulates of the cheaper *mullahs,* out of date canons of wisdom, and current proverbs of the most superficial type. This theory naturally lands Barani in a mass of contradictions. It is unnecessary to examine them in detail, and only the most important of them need be enumerated.

(a) The king is a great sinner by the very nature of his office, which the Quran and the Prophet have not sanctioned. Nevertheless if he acts according to the precepts of Barani, his place will be among the saints and prophets. It is like saying that a Muslim robber will be divinely blessed if he is a good robber—if he robs non-Muslims on an extensive scale for the good of the Faith, gives a fair percentage of his income in charities (including generous gifts to the *mullahs*) and is guided in his work by religious precepts.

(b) The king is the 'Deputy' and 'Representative' of God on earth; he is the 'Shadow of God' (*Zillallah*) and his mind and the minds of his advisers are divinely inspired. This postulate contradicts the preceding proposition; it is also contradicted by facts. In practice the Musalmans were not prepared to admit that the mind or the king was divinely inspired; most of the hereditary kings among the Musalmans have been hereditary asses, while the usurpers have been generally tyrants. The power of the king lasted only so long as he could maintain it by the excellence of his administration and the sharpness of his sword. If he failed, his opponents had no mercy for him. They would kill him like a dog and publicly display his carcass or his head on a spear. The majority of the Muslim kings have been murdered atrociously, and so were the majority of the Abbaside Caliphs after Mutawakkil. So long as a Muslim king was sovereign *de facto,* he was hedged by a sort of pseudo-divinity and people prostrated themselves before him. But when his power vanished, his divinity also vanished, Muslim political consciousness did not recognise any king as sovereign *de jure*. A deposed king was generally a severed head or a corpse publicly displayed.

(c) The king, according to Barani, governs the kingdom through his contradictory qualities—like God himself. In doing so the king has the insolence to claim partnership with God and this is *shirk,* the one unpardonable sin according to the Quran. Nevertheless it is necessary for the king to have these contradictory qualities for the conduct of the administration. But he should be thoroughly repentant of his actions in his heart, if he is to obtain divine forgiveness; otherwise his place will be with the Pharoahs. This doctrine of the contradictory qualities of God and of the king contains a dual error. It is true that the attributes given to God by the Quran, supposed to be ninety-nine in number, contradict each other in their dictionary meaning. But it is emphatically not true to say that thinking Muslims have conceived God as a bundle of contradictory attributes. Their basic conception of God has been a God of mercy *rahmat*). The fearful qualities of God are really due to His mercy, for they have mercy (or their object). Similarly the king (or the state) is not a bundle of irreconcilable contradictions; the object of the state (as Barani has himself made clear) is the public good through the enforcement of state-laws. Punishment and reward, employment and dismissal, taxation and expenditure may seem opposed things; but they are not really contradictory. If the powers of the state are properly exercised, the chief feature will be harmony and not contradiction. Of course, the complete elimination of contradictions is not possible; still harmonious action for the public good should be the main objective.

In fairness to Barani he should not be blamed for these stupid ideas, which he inherited from tradition and needlessly enlarged.

Barani's second theory, for which alone he is responsible, places the institution of monarchy on the needs of the social order, specially the enforcement of justice. The primary needs of man as a member of society demand the maintenance of a centralised executive authority. Barani was not aware of the existence of democracies or the slave-owning city-republics of Greece and the ancient world. This knowledge, in any case, would have been irrelevant to his purpose. Republican governments were only possible in small states. There could be no slave-owners' democracy in Islam; for while on the one hand the slave-merchants kept bringing slaves into the country, on the other hand the judicial procedure of the qazis kept setting free those slaves of the working-class groups who could satisfy the qazis that they would give one-third of their daily earnings to their masters. Slavery is a hideous institution. But whatever its defects, the basis of Indian society was wage-labour and not slave-labour, and in the sphere of contract the Muslim *shari'at* permits no discrimination on religious grounds. Further, Muslim political consciousness, for a variety of reasons, demanded large territorial states and these states could not be administered except by that centralisation of power which only the institution of monarchy made possible under medieval conditions.

Monarchy given, its other institutions are implied. The king should be able to appoint, promote and dismiss the officers of the state, both secular and religious, and Barani gives detailed advice as to how this should be done. He should also be able to appoint various types of spies, reporters and intelligence officers to tell him how his bureaucracy is working. One of the foundations of the king's authority is physical power; the king should, therefore, be careful about his army, and with reference to the army, Barani thought all talk of economy to be out of place. *But above all the king should have the power of making state-laws (zawabit), even if in extreme cases they had to override the 'shari'at'.* If these laws were properly made and enforced, the uniform working of the departments of the government over the vast area covered by it would be assured, and the subjects would also know where they stood. "A state-law in the technique of administration", he declares, "means pursuing (a line of) action which the king imposes as an obligatory duty on himself and from which he never deviates (Advice XIV)." This definition includes administrative orders, which concern only government employees, as well as laws, properly so-called, which impose obligations and confer rights on the subjects. But we must remember that in Barani's time the state was not expected to interfere, unless very necessary, in the personal laws of the various communities.

But if the laws were to be made by the king personally, everything would depend upon his intelligence and strength of character, upon his wisdom and his will power; a weak king may not have the strength to resist illegitimate pressure. In any case it would be useless making laws if they kept on changing with every new occupant of the throne. Secondly, the making of laws is a difficult and delicate task; it requires knowledge of existing laws and existing circumstances, wisdom, sanity and foresight. So keeping these and other considerations in view, and basing his argument on the Qranic injunction about consultation, Barani wanted to *institutionalise* the monarchy by giving the authority of framing laws and administrative regulations to the King's Council (Advice III). The members of the Council were to be selected by the king with care, presumably in accordance with the principles laid down by the Council itself. The king was to be present at the discussions and to propound the question. But the Council was to be left quite free to discuss every aspect of the matter without being informed of the king's opinion. If the members could reach unanimity, their advice was to be accepted by the king; if they disagreed, it was better, when possible, to discuss the matter once more. A mere majority of the Council had no meaning, for it was only an appointed body. But as the basic principle the Council's work Barani boldly lays down the precept—*"No opinion for Kings"*. The type of Council suggested by Barani was never tried. The Majlis-i Khas of the Delhi Sultans was a different institution. It could be ignored; it could also be overridden. Of course, kings, like other persons, resort to consultation when in difficulties; and the greatest achievements which Barani had witnessed—the land-revenue and other reforms of Alauddin Khilji as well as his economic regulations—were due to the Majlis-i Khas of the Sultan. But Alauddin later on gave up consulting the Majlis. Mohammad bin Tughlaq overpowered his opponents in discussion; he never consulted, Jalaluddin Khilji (if Barani is to be believed) consulted his Majlis quite often; but his great officers talked like courtiers; the Sultan interfered and overrode his nephew, Ahmad Chap; and consequently, the Majlis never came to a correct decision. The other rulers were either guided by their favourites or consulted their officers separately.

Believing in monarchy but distressed at the erratic character of the kings he had seen. Barani evolved the theory that the King's Council should, by custom or convention, be made a quasi-independent body, so that the policy of the administration may not vary with the occupants of the throne or their changing moods. The difficulties of the scheme are obvious. The king was responsible—responsible because his head had to answer for his misgovernment. Of the seventeen rulers of Delhi from 1206 to 1357, ten (including Khusrau Khan) were killed, poisoned or left to die in prison. If the responsibilities of kings were to be ensured by capital punishments, then this was certainly a reasonable percentage. But a Council discussing in secret and acting by unanimity of votes could not be held responsible either by the public or by government officers. Add to it, there was the danger that the Council would extinguish the royal authority and its members would inaugurate an era of anarchy like that of the Chahalgani Turks. Be this as it may, the Delhi Sultans saw to it that the Majlis-i Khas never developed any traditions of its own.

Another defect of monarchy, which Barani wished to correct, appertained to the sphere of political punishments. The Quran refers to persons, called *munafiqs* (hypocrites), who were either opposed to the Prophet or were slack in the performance of their duties. But the Quran does not name them and the Prophet did not punish them. No question of treason arose in the time of the first two Caliphs; in the later reign of the third Caliph anarchy prevailed and in the reign of the fourth Caliph there was civil war. The Pious Caliphate, as Barani correctly points out, was based on the agreement of the people and not on any injunction of the Quran or the Prophet. The crime of treason, properly so-called, could only be possible after the Umayyads had established their power on the principle of a hereditary monarchy and a governing-class drawn exclusively from the noble Arab clans. There is nothing in the Quran or the precepts of the Prophet ordering a Musalman to obey such a government or preventing him from opposing it. The Umayyads had they virtues, but they based their government on 'force and terror'; things unknown in the period of the Pious Caliphate. There were plenty of rebellions and all of them—except the last—were brutally suppressed. The ruthless punishment of opponents was the method by which the Umayyads sought to maintain their power. The Abbasides, when they overthrew the Umayyads, behaved in the same way.

The 'shari'at' of the Sunnis was organised during the period of the great Abbasides; it preferred to remain silent both about monarchy and treason.

During the ninety-five years of the Delhi Sultanate, which Barani surveys, all governments resorted to the ruthless punishment of their opponents, except during a few short reigns.

He records these punishments from the time of Balban till they reached their maximum during the reign of Sultan Mohammad bin Tughlaq. It is a tragic and heart-rending story, specially the murder of innocent women and children.

Barani is prepared to maintain the prestige of the government by a reasonable amount of punishments and his sympathies throughout are with the central government, never with its opponents. Even if he dislikes a king, he will never sympathise with rebels. He is well aware of the danger of a weak and overmild government like that of Jalaluddin Khilji. 'These mischievous Hindustanis', he affirms, 'cannot be controlled except by a stem and harsh-tempered king'. But he was horrified by the punishments and tortures he saw around him and repeatedly condemns them in his *Tarikh-i Firoz Shahi.* In the *Jahandari* (Advice XIII), he sets out to discover the principles of a law of treason, which while maintaining the stability of the government would not be unduly harsh to the subjects and would not be a complete negation of the principles of humanity. His recommendations certainly deserved the most careful consideration of those in authority in medieval India. It is to be regretted, therefore, that as the *Fatawa-i Jahandari* was never properly published, Barani's very sane views on the question of punishments for political offences could not get a hearing.

Though Barani believes in monarchy, he has no illusions concerning its shortcomings. He is not satisfied with the policy of any of the Sultans he examines except Ghiasuddin Tughlaq, who was called upon to continue the system of Alauddin Khilji without having to resort to those terroristic methods by which that system was established. It is obviously this conviction that monarchy as a system has its unavoidable shortcomings and that a king as king would never be up to his duties, which drives Barani in his last Advice to recommend that the heart of the king should be always full of supplication to the Almighty and that he should be always conscious of his need for Divine mercy and grace.

Though the *Fatawa-i Jahandari* was written after the *Tarikh-i Firoz Shahi,* all the ideas in it were present in the author's mind when the *Firoz Shahi* was composed. Thus, to take one example, Barani makes Balban give a long advice (covering some ten pages) to his son Sultan Mohammad (Khan-i Shahid). All the ideas in this advice are to be found in the *Jahandari.* The object of the *Fatawa-i Jahandari,* as Barani planned it, was to prescribe a norm for the working of the institutions of the Delhi Sultanate and to give the necessary directions to its officers. It has been already pointed out that a traditional theory full of contradictions and sheer nonsense, got mixed with a theory evolved by Barani himself in the light of experience and observation, which was fundamentally secular. If the first theory is completely ignored, then the second theory, which remains, can be accepted subject to the reservations already discussed. One danger for the historian of medieval India lies in the fact that he is tempted to judge medieval institutions by modern concepts and modern standards. The value of the *Jahandari* lies in the fact that it gives us the standards prescribed by a great medieval mind for the evaluation of medieval institutions.

It has been necessary in the course of this work to point out many things derogatory to our author—his failing memory, his hopeless vanity of birth which partly contributed to his ruin, his irrational prejudices against the Hindus, for which Islam supplies no justifications and which were not acceptable to those in authority, and his very superficial comprehension of the Muslim creed. It has also been necessary to quote much that Barani wrote to his own discredit. But after all these deductions have been made, the *Tarikh-i Firoz Shahi* remains the greatest book that has survived to us from the Sultanate period. Its eminence in this respect is unchallengeable. No single work of Amir Khusrau or Amir Hasan can be compared with it. They were more capable men with greater reputations, but their achievements are bound up with a particular system of thought and a specific language. The greatness, or perhaps the good luck, of the *Tarikh-i Firoz Shahi* lies in the fact that it is bound up integrally with the history of India; and so long as the history of India is studied, Barani cannot be ignored. The manuscripts of his work were not easily available in the middle ages; very often people came to know of it only through summaries or by hearsay. "Sher Khan", says Abul Fazl, "divided the whole of Hindustan, with the exception of Bengal, into forty-seven *iqtas.* He resorted to the branding of the trooper's horses. He also heard of the designs of Alauddin Khilji, which have been described by the *Tarikh-i Firoz Shahi,* and adopted some of them."[1] Today the graves of Balban and Alauddin Khilji are unknown; only two mounds in Siri indicate the place where the Hazar Sutun Palace once stood. But Barani, old, half-blind and in acute distress, brought the dead to life by a tremendous effort of memory and very deservedly he lives along with them. No historian under conditions so distressing and at an age so advanced has produced a work so great.

REFERENCES

1. *Akbar Namah,* Bib. Indica. Vol. I, p. 196.

Appendix A

Glossary of Persian Technical Terms
(The references are to pages)

Abdal—A grade of saints. The grades generally mentioned, in order of merit, are *ghaus* (*qutb* or *qutbul aqtab*), *ibdal*, *autad*, *akhyar*, etc. (3n.)

Alim—see *Ulama*.

Amir—Plural, *umara*; from *amr*, meaning 'order' or 'command'; an *amir* is, therefore, a person entitled to command. The Caliph Omar took the title of *Amirul Muminin* (Commander of the Faithful) and this designation since then has been considered equivalent to *Khalifa* or Caliph. The rulers of the minor dynasties of Persia, who were technically subordinate to the Caliph, took the title of *amirs*. During the Sultanate period the *amirs* were the third and the lowest grade of high officers (148). But throughout the middle ages the term *umara* was used to designate the higher officers of the state collectively. For the present-day use of *amir* to indicate 'a rich man' there is no authority except the popular parlance of northern India.

Amir-i dad—Judicial officer (4, 7).

Amir-i sadah—A commander of one hundred (148).

Ansar—Musalmans of Medina who helped the Prophet when he came there.

Ariz-i Mumalik, Ariz-i Asl—Minister of War (23, 23n, 24).

Arz—Muster of the soldiers, in which their horses, their weapons and their capacity to use them were examined prior to the payment of their salaries (25).

Aslub—Government orders, projects or enterprises.

Baitul Mal—House of treasure; the Public Treasury. According to the principles of the *shari'at* the Public Treasury belonged to all Musalmans and the Prophet and the Pious Caliphs were only its custodians. But with the rise of the Omayyad Caliphate, the Public Treasury became the personal affair of the ruler; he had to meet public expenditure from public revenues, but he could take from the Treasury what he liked and his custodianship became a mere fiction (141-143).

Barids—Intelligence officers (Advice VIII, 30-33).

Barsbakal—The Indian monsoon or *barsat*. Barani attributes it to countries where the monsoon is not known (43n).

Bast—See *Qabz*.

Bid'at—Novelty; doing what the Prophet and his Companions did not do (4, 4n).

Caliph—See *Khalifa*.

Chaudhary—Leader of a local group or headman of a village.

Chihalgani—Literally 'forty', reference is to the limited number, not necessarily forty, of the high officers who dominated India from the death of Iltutmish to the reign of Balban (ii, 146).

Dahriyat—Agnosticism (5n).

Dihqan—A feudal magnate; this is the earlier meaning of the term; in later literature it came to mean a peasant or villager.

Dirham and *Dinar*—Roman copper and silver coins adopted by the Musalmans (165n).

Diwan—A ministry, department or office. But unless a qualifying adjective is added, *Diwan* means the Ministry of Revenue.

Diwan-i Hashm—Ministry of War (26).

Fatawa-i Jahandari—A *fatwa* in the technique of the Muslim *shari'at* means an opinion given by *mufti* or jurist on a legal principle on which there has been some controversy. *Jahandari* means keeping the world (*jahan*) under control; it is to be distinguished from *jahandari* conquering the world. Barani, however, uses both words in a general sense in selecting them for the title of his book—i.e. Precepts or Advice on Government of the State. This is made clear by the fact that he divides his book into 24 parts, each headed as Advice (*Nasihat*).

Farz—Obligatory religious duties (4).

Fiqh—Muslim law.

Futuh—The unsolicited charity of neighbours. According to the Chishti mystic of the Sultanate period, the only livelihood permitted to the mystic was either *futuh* or *zamin-i ihya*, the produce of virgin soil brought under the plough.

Hadis—The Prophet's traditions, i.e. the Prophet's precepts and actions.

Hal—A mystic term indicating the state or spiritual condition of a mystic (ion).

Hudud—Crime for which punishments have been prescribed by the Quran (vii-viii; 42n).

Ibadat—Religious devotions.

Ibahati—People who permitted what religion has not permitted, in particular, incest. An abusive term for the Ismaili sect, against whom plenty of false and baseless charges were made (16, 16n).

Iddat—A period of four months and ten days prescribed for the Muslim widow as the time which must pass before she can marry again after her husband's death.

Ihtikar—Regarding, purchasing a commodity at a low price and selling it at a much higher price because the regrater is the sole owner of the commodity in the particular area. Barani is bitter against regrating and implies that it can only be practised by the Hindu merchant-princes of the country (Advice IX, Price Control; 35, 37n).

Ilabiyat—Speculations concerning things divine (17n).

Imam—The term is used in a variety of senses. (a) The ordinary Sunni usually means by this term the prayer-leader of a congregation. Sunni *shariat* books also refer to the head of the state as the *imam.* The Sunnis also recognise the twelve *Imams* of the Family of the Prophet from Hazrat Ali to Imam Mehdi on the ground of their birth, sanctity and piety. (b) The Shias believe that these twelve Imams were *de jure* heads of the state and had the power of interpreting the sacred law. (c) The Ismailis, who only believe in the Imams of the Shias up to Hszrat Jafar Sadiq, postulate that Ismail, and not Hazrat Musa Kazim, should have been his successor; they also believe that an Imam, whether hidden or revealed, is necessary for the guidance of mankind. The hidden Imam guides mankind through his agent or *da'i*; the revealed Imam has the power of amending the Quranic law to suit changing circumstances (112n).

Istibdad—Tyranny.

Istihsan—Principle of public welfare (vi).

Jahandari—Government (see *Fatawa-i jahandari*).

Jama'at Khana—A mystic house, generally consisting of one hall, in which all the disciples of the *Shaikh* lived (18n, 118n).

Jasus—Spy; he worked in secret and is to be distinguished from publicly appointed officials like *barids* (intelligence officers) and *waqia-nawises* (writers of official reports).

Jizya—In the terminology of the *Shariat books,* the *Jizya* means a poll-tax on a non-Muslim for remaining a non-Muslim. It was not difficult to levy the *Jizya* from the small minorities of Muslim lands. But no *Jizya* was imposed in medieval India. Also it was a retrogressive tax in the proportion of 12, 24 and 48 and hit the working classes most severely. But the term was not used in medieval India in the *shari'at* sense. Both Amir Khusrau and Amir Hasan refer to *Jizya* being levied from Musalmans. Barani seems to use *Jizya* to mean any tax, which is not a land-tax. He says that the pre-Muslim rulers of Persia collected the *Jizya,* and with reference to his own time he asserts that Hindu *rais* collect both taxes—*khiraj* and *Jizya*—from their Hindu subjects and that these taxes are a hundred times higher than in the Delhi Sultanate (46, 69n).

Kafir—See Kufr.

Kalima—Oath of affirmation: 'There is no god but Allah and Mohammad is His Prophet.'

Khalifa—(or Caliph)—Literally *Khalifa* means *successor* or *representative.* Both meanings are legitimate but the sense in which they are used must be clearly distinguished. (a) The Quran declares that God has sent man as His representative on the earth, because man alone of all living creatures has been made morally responsible. But there is nothing in the Quran to justify the contention of Barani that the king, as king, is the *deputy* or *representative* of God; this claim on the basis of the Quran, can only be made for mankind as a whole, because mankind is the expression of a divine cosmic purpose. (b) The Pious Caliphs called themselves *Khalifas,* because they were the *successors* of the Prophet as the head of the state; they certainly did not claim to be the exclusive representatives of God. In later days the title degenerated. Barani uses *khalifa* (caliph), *badshah* (king) and ruler as equivalent terms. I have not been able to find why in modern Urdu barbers are called *khalifas*.

Khan—A Turkish term meaning 'hero', 'brave warrior', 'ruler.' In Mongolian and Turkish lands (e.g. the empire of Chengiz Khan and his descendants and the Ottoman empire) the title of *Khan* was used only for the head of the state. We find Turkish rulers of small states calling themselves *Khans* in the ninth and tenth centuries. In India the title of *Khan* was given to the officers of the highest grade during the Sultanat period. During the Mughal period only persons to whom the title of *Khan* had been given by the Emperor as a personal distinction were entitled to use it. Later on in India everyone of alleged or real Afghan origin began to call himself *Khan*; in Afghanistan it is now a title for all citizens, like our term *Shri* (p. 148).

Khanqah—A somewhat large house for mystics (18, 81n).

Khawas—Notables; the leading people of a country. Barani uses the term to include the higher members of the official hierarchy and religious scholars, including historians, for whom he claims the same status as for priests.

Khiraj—Tribute; generally used either for the land-tax or for payments made by a subordinate prince to his superior.

Khot—It is generally interpreted as equivalent to the *muqaddam* or headman of a village. It may have been derived (by a certain violence to grammar) from the term *Khot* or deed he gave to the government for the collection of revenue.

Khusrau—Emperors of Byzantine or New Rome. In Persian literature the term, *Rum*, is generally used for the area of the Byzantine empire. Thus Alexander the Great is often referred to as *Sikandar-i Rumi*.

Kisras—Emperors of pre-Muslim Persia. (Arabic plural—*akasira*).

Kufr—Literally 'ingratitude'; a *Kafir* is one who, owing to his ingratitude, does not recognise his obligations to God.

Langar-Khana or Ziafat-Khana—A charitable kitchen, maintained by the king or by private individuals, from which food was supplied to the poor (46, 46n).

Lauh-i Mahfuz—The Preserved Tablet (9n).

Mahzar—A meeting, usually of religious leaders, summoned by the king for the decision of a controversial matter (106); also the decision of such a meeting.

Majlis—Literally a place where persons sit; a meeting. Barani uses the term for meetings summoned by the king. If public, they were called *Majlis-i khas, Majlis-i rai, Majlis-i mahram* or *Majlis-i khilwat* (11n, 103-104).

Maktum—A hidden saint.

Malik—*Malik* in Arabic means 'king' or 'ruler', and is used by the Quran in that sense. But the Persian kings began to give this designation to their high officers and during the Sultanate period the *maliks* were the second grade of the highest state officers. During the Mughal period the title *malik* was given by the emperors as a personal distinction. After the fall of the Mughal empire both Hindus and Musalmans, whose ancestors had been *maliks*, began to use the title as a hereditary privilege (148).

Mankulat—Ilm-i Mankulat—Knowledge based on tradition, i.e. the Quran, the *Hadises* and the precepts of the *mujtahids* (48).

Mansukh—An order that has been cancelled by a later Quranic verse (14, 15, 15n).

Ma'qulat or *Ilm-i Ma'qulat*—Knowledge based on reason and experience (48).

Mu'amilat—Human affairs; legal relations.

Muhajir—A Musalman who migrated from Mecca to Medina with the Prophet.

Muhtasib—Censor of morals (4, 6).

Mujtahids—(a) The Sunnis apply the term to the eminent founders of the *shari'at,* who flourished during the period of the great Abbasids (754-861 A.D.). After them the door of *ijtihad,* the formulation of new *shariat* principles, is believed to have been closed (141-2). (b) According to the Shias the *mujtahid* is a scholar who has a certificate traceable to one of the first eleven *Imams*. (see *Imam*).

Mukhbir—A secret reporter.

Mullah—A religious man or *alim*.

Munafiqin—Hypocrites; technically the residents of Medina, who professed to be Musalmans but were not sincere in their profession. The Quran threatens them, but it does not name them and does not prescribe any punishments. The Prophet, as Rousseau remarks, governed by persuasion and not by force. He did not, consequently, lay down any law of treason (1, 170-1).

Munhi—A public reporter concerning things forbidden.

Muqaddam—The headman of a village or a group of villages.

Muqam—A mystic term indicating the station or position of a mystic (ion).

Mushrik—See *Shirk*.

Nadim—Courtier (155-6).

Nasikh—A Quranic verse that cancels a previous order (14, 15, 15n).

Nirkh-baraward—Prices according to production-cost. In his *Tarikh-i Firoz Shahi*, Barani declares that Alauddin fixed the price of all commodities according to this principle. In his *Fatawa-i Jahandari*, he claims that all things should follow the same principle. When sufficient facilities for transport exist, the prices of commodities will be automatically determined by production-cost. But in the middle ages, roads were unsafe and a few merchants had a monopoly of the means of transport—carts and cattle. They were, consequently, in a position to fix the prices of commodities regardless of production-cost. Barani, therefore, insists that the prices of all commodities should be determined by the king personally (xi, Advice IX, Price Control, 34-34; 35n, 38n).

Qabz and *Bast*—Contraction and expansion in mystic terminology (85, 85n).

Qalandars—A curious semi-mystic group of the middle ages which has now almost completely vanished. Its chief features were—(a) living in groups, which were constantly on the move, (b) celibacy, (c) rejection of the principle of private property, which reduced them to begging or to demanding things they needed by force, (d) lack of education, (e) negligence of the devotions prescribed by Islam, (f) saffron clothes, an iron ring round the wrist and a begging bowl, (g) shaving of the beard, moustaches and a hair of the head. Muslim mystic writers, who generally accuse them of bad manners, were unable to discover their origin. They seem to have been the *bhikshus* of Buddhism, who were continued into Islam. They were found in most of the Muslim lands.

Qasd—Resolve; determination (Advice IV, 13-16).

Qazi—According to the *shari'at*, the *Qazi* is a judge and his duty as a *qazi* is confined to trying cases brought before him either by the government or private parties. He had no power to prosecute, which lay within the sphere of the *amir-i dad*. But often other duties were assigned to him. For example, he was often appointed *sadr* and put in executive charge of charitable endowments, state charity-grants, upkeep of mosques, etc. within his jurisdiction.

Qiyas—Extension of an acknowledged legal principle to similar cases (vi).

Qutb—Literally, 'axis'; also 'post-star'. The term is used by popular mysticism to indicate the highest grade of saints (3n).

Qutbal aqtab—Literally, 'axis of axes'; means in practice the same thing as *qutb* or the highest saint (3n).

Rawayat—Traditions; in the sphere of the *shari'at* it means knowledge of how things were done in the days of the Prophet and the Pious Caliphs (viii).

Saaah amirs—Commanders of one hundred (148).

Saffar—Copper-smith; the title of Saffarid is given by Muslim historians to the short-lived family founded by Yaqub bin Lais (2, 2n).

Satihash—Despotism.

Saudagar—Barani uses the term to indicate merchants of standing, whom he divides into transport-merchants (*saudagar-i karawani*), merchants who managed whole *karawans*, and market-merchants (*saudagar-i bazar*, apparently wholesale dealers). It seems from the context of Advice IX (Price Control) that both these groups belonged to Hindu communities (34-38). Mere shopkeepers are dismissed by Barani as *bazaris*, *bazar*-people.

Shaikh—*Shiakh* in Arabic means a man of note or a chief. Orthodox Muslim literature has no term equivalent to the Hindu *guru*. But in mystic terminology the term *shaikh* was used for this purpose. Accurately speaking, a *shaikh* was a mystic whom his spiritual teacher had given a written and properly witnessed document, called *khilafat-nama* (deed of succession) authorising him to enrol disciples to his *silsilah* (18n).

Shari'at—*Shari'at* literally means path, i.e. the Path of the Prophet. Owing to its insistence on externals, it has been contrasted with *tasawwuf* or the spiritual interpretation of religion (vi-viii, 136).

Shirk—Setting partners to God; a *mushrik*, consequently, is a person who believers that God has partners.

Silsilah—Mystic order. These *silsilahs* seem to have originated towards the end of eleventh or the beginning of the twelfth century, with the exception of the *Silsila-i Khawajgm* (later on known as the *Nakshbandi Silsilah*), which appeared in the tenth century or earlier in the Turkish lands beyond the Jaxartes, and the founder of which it has not been possible to discover. The basis of the *silsilah* for the mystic disciple was obedience to his *shaikh* or spiritual teacher. But since the authority of all *shaikhs* was final for their disciples, Muslim mystics never succeeded in establishing religious orders like those of the Roman Catholic church.

Sultan—Literally 'strength', 'power', etc. in its derivative sense it came to mean king or ruler. Minhajus Siraj Jauzjani says that Mahmud of Ghaznin was the first ruler to be given the title of *Sultan* by the Abbasid Caliph, though his coins only refers to him as 'Amir Mahmud'. The rulers of the Delhi empire used to call themselves *Shahus-Sultan*. Later on, the title degenerated and even rulers of very small territories began to call themselves sultans.

Sultani—A slave of the Sultan, this title was often assumed by slaves who had risen to high office.

Sunnah—Literally 'tradition'. Three grades of this *sunnah* are recognised—the *sunnah* of Allah, the *sunnah* of the Prophet and the *sunnah* of the community of the *millat* (3n, 58, 58n). The *sunnah* of Allah is hard to discover. In practice, partly owing to the strength of pre-Muslim customs and partly owing to new conditions of life, the *sunnah* of the community has often overriden the *sunnah* attributed to the Prophet.

Sura—Chapters into which the Quran is divided. For the purpose of convenience, the Quran is also divided into thirty equal parts, called paras.

Tafsir—Commentary on the Quran.

Tasawwuf—Muslim mysticism or the spiritual, as contrasted with the mechanistic, interpretation of the Faith. It has often been said that the Faith has four paths—*shari'at* (external law or mechanistic observances), *tariqat* (devotions), *haqiqat* (reality) and *ma'rifat* (gnosis). The mystics did not question the *shari'at* or external law, but declared that mechanistic religious observances were not by themselves sufficient. The gnosis of God (*ma'rifat-i Allah*), the aim of all mystics, is explained by Shaikh Shahabuddin Suhrwardi as follows. The *ma'rifat* of any particular topic, *e.g.* grammar, means the simultaneous apprehension of its principles with all their applications; the *ma'rifat* (gnosis) of God would thus mean the simultaneous apprehension of all the principles of existence (or at least of spiritual life) along with their applications. The mystic claimed that they were quite distinct from the *ulama-i zahiri*, whom they condemned. The best traditions of *tasawwuf* required that the *sufi* or mystic should have nothing to do with the government and its officers (iv, xi, 17n, 94, 94n).

Tawafuq-i ara—Unanimity of opinion (iii, II-12).

Ulama—Plural of *alim*. Alim means a scholar or a person who has *ilm* (knowledge). In practice the term *ulama* has been confined to scholars of religion; pure scientists, like al-Beruni, have not been generally included in this category. Tradition divided *ulama* into two groups—(a) Externalist scholars (*ulama-i zahiri* or *ulama-i dunyavi*) who sought the goods of the world in any shape on form, but generally in the service of the government as *qazis*, *sadrs*, teachers, etc. (b) *Ulama-i dinavi*, *ulama-i batini* or *sufis*, who refused to use their religious knowledge for worldly advancement and sought the Lord alone (xi, 17, 17n, 136-7).

Urf—Custom or customary law (viii).

Wali—General designation for a saint (3n).

Wasaya—Testament or will.

Zakat—Obligatory charity prescribed by the state but has been left to the choice of individuals, who have the prescribed amount of property. It works roughly at about 2½ per cent of income. But some non-productive commodities like female ornaments, are also liable to *zakat*. Confusion has sometimes been caused by the fact that the term *zakat* has also been used for customs and import duties; these duties according to the *shari'at* ought to be

2½ per cent for Muslims and 5 per cent for non-Muslims. But in practice this discrimination was not possible; it only meant that non-Muslim property would be passed under Muslim names. The Mughal emperors agreed to take a lump sum from the European mercantile companies, which was also a violation of the *shari'at-law*.

Zawabit—State-laws (Advice xiv, 64-71 and Chap. IV, 136-143).

Zillallah—Shadow of God. A title given to kings.

Appendix B

Books Referred to by Ziauddin Barani in the *Fatawa-i Jahandari*

(The character of these books has been discussed in the Introduction, pp. iii-iv. They have been listed in the order in which they are referred to by the *Jahandari*, except the *Tarikh-i Mahmudi* to which Barani refers in the Introduction of his *Tarikh-i Barmaki*. The references are to pages.

1. Maulana Qaffal: *Tarikh-i Mahmudi* (History of Sultan Mahmud); (Introduction, iii).
2. *Tarikh-i Samanian:* (History of the Samanid Dynasty, 837-999); author not mentioned, (2).
3. Imam Asma' i: *Tarikh-i Khulafa-i Abbasiah* (History of the Abbasid Caliphs) (6n).
4. *Wasaya-i Jamshed:* (Testament of Jamshed); author not mentioned (8, 8n).
5. *Ma-asir-i 'Umari* (Traditions of the Caliph Umar); author not mentioned (11).
6. Imam *Waqidi: Tarikh-i Mukhtasar* (Short History) (13).
7. *Tarikh-i Ma-asir-i Shabah* (History of the Good Deeds of the Companions). Author not mentioned (21).
8. Imam Saulabi: *Tarikh-i Abbasiah* (History of the Abbasides) (21).
9. *Tarikh-i Akasira* (History of the Iranian Kisras); author not mentioned (27).
10. *Ma-asiral Khulafa* (Good Deeds of the Caliphs); author not mentioned (49).

11. *Sharhus Sunnah* (Commentary on the Prophet's Traditions); author not mentioned (48).
12. Muin Asam: *Tarikh-i Sanjari* (History of Sultan Sanjar) (88).
13. *Ghadrus Siyar*: Probably a book on the revolt against the Caliph Usman; author not mentioned (97).
14. *Tarikh-i Khorasan* (History of Khorasan); author not mentioned (99).
15. *Tarikh-Nausherwan* (History of Nausherwan); author not mentioned (113).
16. *Tarikh-i Umamul Awwalin* (History of the First Communities); author not mentioned (114).
17. *Tarikh-i Sikandari* (History of Alexander); author not mentioned (115).